The Frenzied Dance of Art and Violence

The Frenzied Dance of Art and Violence

DAVID E. GUSSAK

OXFORD
UNIVERSITY PRESS

OXFORD
UNIVERSITY PRESS

Oxford University Press is a department of the University of Oxford. It furthers the University's objective of excellence in research, scholarship, and education by publishing worldwide. Oxford is a registered trade mark of Oxford University Press in the UK and certain other countries.

Published in the United States of America by Oxford University Press
198 Madison Avenue, New York, NY 10016, United States of America.

CIP data is on file at the Library of Congress
ISBN 978–0–19–006449–5

DOI: 10.1093/med-psych/9780190064495.001.0001

1 3 5 7 9 8 6 4 2

Printed by Sheridan Books, Inc., United States of America

Contents

List of Illustrations

Acknowledgments

This project has been a labor of love for over 8 years. In that time, there have been a great many people who have come in and out of its evolving trajectory, contributing greatly to its genesis, development, and—after many struggles—its eventual completion.

While developing and completing a previous publication that was released in 2013, I had the incredible fortune of working with Jennifer Perillo as my editor. One of our many discussions became derailed and diverted into a lengthy conversation on the art of violent artists. What particularly fascinated her was the work that came from many of the violent people I worked with, the drawings made by multiple murderers, and the potential interrelationship between art and violence. Despite my initial self-doubt, she knew there could be a book in this and that I could perhaps be the person who could do it. With her ongoing encouragement—even after stepping away from the publication house she had worked for, and thus she would no longer be my editor—Jennifer often served as an informal sounding board and champion for this project. I am infinitely grateful for her encouragement and confidence that I could actually do this and for providing the first steps of this long journey.

I am so lucky to have as my dear friend Michael Kathleen Svetlik, a school librarian who, as a deep and creative thinker, excels in writing, editing, and research. I have known Kat for almost 35 years. In fact, when I was an undergraduate and graduate student, she helped me a great deal with my writing, helping me conceptualize and edit papers for my undergraduate courses and then, later, was instrumental in my completing my master's thesis. We have enjoyed countless rich discussions and debates about many things including art, literature, research, and education. Even after all this time, I can always count on her erudition, curiosity, and slightly skewed way of looking at things for help in lifting my projects higher and further. This book was right up her alley. Volunteering her assistance, she once again proved invaluable in digging deep in the literature that helped inform this manuscript while carefully combing through these emerging pages to offer feedback and suggestions. It is a much stronger book because of her.

I had known my friend Doug Fitton for almost 20 years. For the past 5, Doug and I met almost weekly at a nearby coffee house. We spent many of these hours laughing at the inanities of what we experienced around us and pontificating with great passion about our respective interests. As this project became more consuming for me, he would often provide me the space to discuss sections I was wrestling with, and, as a brilliant and unusual thinker, he was invaluable in helping me figure out different ways to articulate some of the more knotty sections. Even in the age of COVID, we made it a point to meet for "virtual coffee" for a few special occasions.

Throughout these years, Doug had a long-term, debilitating, terminal illness. Despite this—or perhaps because of this—he maintained bottomless positivity, a grounding and calming presence and a wicked sense of humor. Sadly, shortly before this project went into production, he passed away. I will forever be immensely grateful for all that he offered. I will miss you horribly, Doug.

Over the life of this project, I got the chance to work with a number of graduate assistants who have contributed to its research and development. This included three, all now clinicians in their own right, who really helped me launch the project years ago: Ashley Beck, Jaimie Berkowitz, and Carla Lopez. They were with me during my initial struggles, helping me sort through the ambiguities and complications of this topic, and were valuable contributors in the development of the working blueprint for what this project would eventually become.

Two years ago, a new graduate art therapy student, Elizabeth Odom, was assigned as my new research assistant. She reached out to me the summer before she began to ask what projects I was working on and what I would expect from her so that she might prepare. This book was on the list of projects I sent her. Her calm, measured, matter-of-fact tone belied the enthusiastic investment she would soon exhibit for this project. She was all in. At the time, this project was still at a frustrating, nascent stage where I was not entirely sure that we would be successful in meeting the contractual deadline. It didn't matter—she was. Her contributions to this project and my reliance on her cannot be exaggerated.

Her willingness to review each page and offer comprehensive and creative suggestions on how to make a single sentence clear and concise and to then, again, hear each line read out loud—often several times—so that we could obsessively edit what was thrown into the shared Google Doc was inexhaustible and invaluable. Her ability to hunt down all of the copyright holders of every single art piece that required permission and negotiate with each so that we were provided consent to reproduce them—an experience new to both of us—required amazing organizational detail and administrative tenacity. As we dug down many a rabbit hole, looking for some of the most obscure references to support or refute a single thought or concept, she proved to be an innovative, confident, persistent, and conscientious researcher. Simply stated, this project would not have been successful without Elizabeth. I learned as much from her as I trust she learned from me, and I look forward to seeing all that she contributes to the field through her own creative endeavors. Thank you, Ms. Odom.

I also need to acknowledge with gratitude and relief the person who was willing to take a risk with this project. When my previous editor left her publishing company, she suggested that I reach out to Oxford University Press as a potential new home for this project. After looking online at their list of editors to determine who might be the best fit for the topic I was proposing, I cold-called Sarah Harrington. She answered while she was sitting at a table outside of a crowded New York café. After taking the call and listening to my ideas, she encouraged me to submit my proposal and potential sample chapters. From that point forward, her calm and quiet support, confidence, flexibility, and indefatigability provided necessary grounding and scaffolding—not only did she take a big chance on this unusual topic, but she also has been instrumental in helping turn this idea into a tangible product. Thank you so much Sarah, and all of the amazing team members at Oxford University Press.

I would also like to express my gratitude to those who contributed art from their respective collections and insights to several of the narratives: Dr. Tom Anderson, Ken Dickerson, Mirko K., Charles Salvador, and Jim Taranto. The following section, "A Note on Obtaining Permission to Include Selected Artworks," acknowledges all those who provided support in obtaining the rights to reproduce many of the pieces in this text.

I also would like to thank the Florida State University Small Grant Program for providing financial support for this project.

Of course, throughout these years, there have been so many more people who have provided incredible support and encouragement: this includes the faculty from the Florida State University art therapy program—Dr. Barbara Parker-Bell, Dr. Theresa Van Lith, and Dr. Nancy Gerber, and the College of Fine Art's Dean, James Frazier, Associate Dean, Scott Shamp, and Associate Dean and Art History Professor, Dr. Michael Carrasco.

In addition, there have been many friends and colleagues who I would not—nor did not—hesitate to pick up the phone, corner them in their office, and/or set up a coffee meeting/happy hour to pick their brains, even eliciting their help in obtaining permission for several images. They included Carrie Ann Baade, Paula Gasparini-Santos, Dr. Elizabeth Hlavek, Dr. Maxine Junge, Dr. Girija Kaimal, Juliet King, Bani Malhotra, Susan Messersmith, Dr. Stephen Pfeiffer, Justin Reddick, Dr. Marcia Rosal, Kris Salata, Craig Siegel, Anne Stagg, Dr. Matt Stanfill, Va Bophary, and Steven Webber; and, finally, my wonderful cousin Dr. Elena Hollender and mother-in-law, Nicoletta LoRe.

With so many people over so many years, I am sure I have forgotten others—please, accept this as a reflection of my failing memory and not your contribution to this project. Please know that I greatly appreciate all of you.

Last, I wish to acknowledge my deep love and appreciation for my wife Laurie LoRe Gussak. She would be the first to tell you that as I tend to get lost in my various intellectual and scholarly endeavors, particularly evident toward the end of this project, she almost becomes an academic widow (and for that I deeply apologize). Her patience, support, and belief in me and my work has been a secure comfort and balm throughout the various trials and challenges that this—and my other endeavors—have offered.

A Note on Obtaining Permission to Include Selected Artworks

Each figure provided in this text contains identifying information on each work. Specifically, if the information was available, each image includes the following label:

Figure number: Artist's Name [birth–death]
Name of the piece
Date piece was created
Materials used to complete the work

Where the piece can be found, if applicable [collection, museum or gallery, and city/country of location]

Permission granting entity, if applicable

Reproduction provided by, if applicable

In addition, I'd like to offer special acknowledgments to those who worked with us to obtain these copyrights and the representatives of the collections in which some of these pieces were held.

With gratitude for the representatives of the Artists Rights Society, who were instrumental in obtaining permission to reproduce the works of Dali (Figures 1.4–1.6), Pollock (Figures 1.9–1.12), Beckmann (Figures 2.4–2.6), Nussbaum (Figures 2.7–2.9), and Picasso (Figure 7.1). Thank you to Art Resource Inc. for providing the reproduction of one of Dali's images (Figure 1.4), one of Pollock's (Figure 1.12), the three Beckmanns, two of Nussbaum's work (Figures 2.8 and 2.9), the Picasso; and The Smart Museum of Chicago for providing the reproduction of Nussbaum's *Masquerade* (Figure 2.7). In addition, thanks to the Museum Boijmans Van Beuningen, Rotterdam/Studio Tromp for providing the reproduction of one of Dali's paintings (Figure 1.5). Bridgeman Images was instrumental in providing images for those works that were out of copyright; these included the works of Caravaggio (Figures 1.1 and 1.2), Cellini (Figure 1.3), Modigliani (Figures 1.6 and 1.7), Dadd (Figure 1.13), Goya (Figures 2.1–2.3), and Hitler (Figure 3.1). They were also able to provide one of the Pollock paintings (Figure 1.9). Thank you to the Anderson Collection at Stanford University for providing another one of Pollock's paintings (Figure 1.11) and to

Mike Mueller of The Norman Rockwell Family Agency c/o IMG Worldwide for help in obtaining the permission and reproduction of four of Norman Rockwell's images (Figures 2.18–2.21).

My heartfelt gratitude goes to Leslie Umberger of the Smithsonian American Art Museum who provided incredibly invaluable assistance in helping us connect with those who could provide permissions for the works by Bill Traylor. Thanks to Nettie Alford of the Bill Traylor Family Trust, and collectors Jan Petry and the representatives of the Kravis Collection for providing permission to include Traylor's drawings, and photographer John Faier, photographer William H. Bengtson, and the Smithsonian American Art Museum for providing the images (Figures 2.13–2.17).

Gratitude to Getty Images for providing two of Vann Nath's paintings (Figures 2.10 and 2.11) and the Bophana Center for providing one of them (Figure 2.12), and a very special thank you to the son of Vann Nath, Channarong Vann, for providing permission to include them.

Michal Feiner and Liat Deissy of the Yad Vashem Art Museum were valuable in obtaining Pavel Fantl's drawing (Figure 3.11), and, along with Jens Oertel and Stefan Hensel, in obtaining Yehuda Bacon's drawing (Figure 3.9). Lena Hartmann of Elektronisches Publizieren Rechte & Lizenzen was instrumental in providing permission for Helga Weissová's drawing (Figure 3.14). Thank you Tereza Maizels of the Beit Theresienstadt Archives for help in obtaining the works of Karel Fleischmann (Figure 3.12) and Leo Haas (Figure 3.13), Agnieszka Sieradzka of the Auschwitz-Birkenau State Museum for help in obtaining the works by Wincenty Gawron (Figure 3.4), and, along with Ewa Huczkowska and Pawel Huczkowski for the painting by Waldemar Nowakowski (Figure 3.5), for the work of Franciszek Jazwiecki (Figure 3.7) and, along with Katarzyna Nowak and Margaretta Haładyn, for the works by Mieczyslaw Koscielniak (Figures 3.3 and 3.6). And finally, thank you to the United States Holocaust Museum for providing the cover of the book, *The Poisonous Mushroom* (Figure 3.2).

I wish to thank the collectors and artists again for providing their works for this project; Mirko K. for providing the works of the multiple murderers (Figures 4.1–4.7), Ken Dickerson for providing the painting by Charles Manson (Figure 5.3), and Jim Taranto for allowing me to include the works of John Wayne Gacy (Figures 5.4–5.7); Charles Bronson, now Charles Salvador, for allowing me to include his drawings (Figures 6.1–6.8), and for Dr. Tom Anderson for providing me permission to include the two works by the Guernica Children's Peace Mural Project (Figures 7.2 and 7.3). In addition, thank you to Museum Syndicate for making the remaining two Manson images available (Figures 5.1 and 5.2).

And finally, I would also like to acknowledge all of the clients and participants in art therapy sessions over the years who allowed the inclusion of their products (Figures I.1–I.5 and Figures 8.1–8.7).

This book would be a great deal less without the art pieces that illustrate it. I appreciate all of you.

Prologue

Just What Is This Dance?

In an early publication (Gussak, 1997a), I suggested that art emerged from the same instincts that drive people to violence and could, in turn, be used to mitigate aggression and frustration in prison. This was drawn from the theoretical constructs of Dissanayake (1988, 1992), who suggested that the libidinal impulses that drive one to aggressive acts also compel one to create, and from Kramer's (1971/1993) assertion that art making can sublimate aggression and violence.

Shortly after, I was discussing this very thought with an artist colleague of mine during a lengthy car ride. She took issue with this notion. She believed that making art in fact induced aggression and violence. She said that often, when working on particular pieces, she would begin to feel angry, to feel a need to impulsively harm something, to strike out. I was initially taken aback as I had never heard this perspective—that art making could *induce* violent urges. I was also surprised because she was a fairly gentle and quiet person.

However, as I thought about this, I came to recognize that this supposition, rather than contradicting my assertions, did in fact support them; that what was really happening was that creating art provided a release of dormant aggressive feelings. I countered that painting gave vent to her true emotions, which she obviously did not realize were percolating below the surface.

She vehemently stood by her assertion that making art spontaneously made her hot-blooded. While our friendship never suffered from this diametrically opposing disagreement, this discussion was never resolved between us.

Over the past 20-plus years, there has been little change in my perspective. I have continued to assert that art making emerges from the same libidinal impulses that drive one to act out and that it, in turn, can help free contained and restrained aggression. However, I also realized that this question warranted further exploration, not just from the perspective of art therapy but also from historical, sociological, and criminological perspectives. Specifically, what is this intense relationship between art and violence?

I began reflecting in greater depth on the association between them. I thought about all of the different sites I had worked in and the clients I met whose work transpired from—and expressed—deep and strong violent tendencies.

My professional experiences provided an impetus, a springboard that forced me to really examine this relationship between art and violence; my career has offered me many chances to examine the complex connections between them. I spent years providing art therapy to prison inmates. I worked with adolescents in various psychiatric and juvenile justice programs who reveled in their aggressive artistic expressions; some relied on their visual imagery and drawings to mark their territory and assert a sense of belonging. I served as an art therapist testifying for the defense in a capital murder trial and provided support for two other murder trials in which the defendants had begun creating art once on Death Row. I provided lectures on the art of John Wayne Gacy, the notorious Chicago-based serial killer, with his original paintings serving as the backdrop.

Exploring Art and Violence: More Than an Impulse

Ideas for this book began to emerge following conversations with my editor of a previous book project. In the midst of discussing final details prior to its release, the topic turned to a series of lectures I gave on the paintings of John Wayne Gacy in Las Vegas several years before. She became fascinated, wondering how common it was for such a violent person to create art. She was surprised when I related that many multiple murderers created art. She suggested that I develop a book exploring the art of serial killers as a follow-up to my book *Art on Trial*. For various reasons (explored in Chapter 4) I felt that I could not focus solely on this topic. However, through ongoing dialogue, I began to consider the idea of exploring the interrelationship of art and violence by examining the work of serial killers as just one component.

Over the ensuing years, in fits and starts, I immersed myself deeply into examining this potential relationship. I revisited my notes on clients with whom I worked, some cases almost 30 years old. I began combing through biographies and psychohistories of artists who had exhibited violent and aggressive tendencies. I sifted through horrific and titillating articles and popular magazines that gleefully flaunted the primitive sketches and fully realized paintings of notorious murderers and serial killers. I wrestled with the definitions of violence and aggression, the many facets of these terms, and how they might be applied to certain artists. More so, I considered in depth not only the work of famous artists who had exhibited violence and aggression but the work that seemed to rely on the artists' experiences within violent environments. I spoke with clinicians, sociologists, and artists for their insights, as well as friends and acquaintances of notorious murderers. I spoke with a Berlin-based collector of the art of serial killers to better understand the phenomena of "murderabilia."

As this examination began, I held a vision of a frenetic dance; a constant, active interplay between two entities, one leading, the other following, and then switching directions. As the book evolved and other interactive dynamics became clear, I began recognizing it as a frenzied dance among several entities, perhaps changing partners, perhaps changing directions, perhaps all dancing together, frantically, with great energy. Hence, I call this the "frenzied dance of art and violence."

Initially, I focused on one fairly straightforward question: What is the relationship between art and violence? In other words, does art *rely* on aggressive impulses? Or does, as my car-ride companion believed, the art making itself induce aggression and violent impulses? Does art mitigate or channel violent tendencies, and, if so, how? Does the art reflect such violence and aggression? How does art ultimately provide an escape from or a means to cope with violent situations?

As the chapters developed, I began to see this relationship in a new light. While in some ways what I uncovered strengthened my already existing beliefs, in other ways new concepts replaced previously held assumptions and biases. My original vision began to shift, new ideas developed, and a different project than the one originally envisioned evolved.

In first exploring the relationship between art and violence, I had already assumed several interactions existed: that art naturally and necessarily emerges from the same aggressive drives as violent behavior. In turn, art mitigates, channels, and sublimates such tendencies. And that art has often provided a means to escape from violent situations. However, upon reflecting on some of the most violent offenders, I realized that there were some situations where these assumptions simply did not apply, particularly in the work of multiple murderers. In these cases, it became apparent that their art making neither mitigated nor sublimated their aggressive tendencies. The art neither turned aside their violence nor provided a reprieve or sanctuary. In fact, what seemed to emerge was that the art was used as a weapon to perpetuate their wantonly destructive patterns. Rather than halting it, their art seemed to preserve the narcissistic cycle from whence their violence originated. Once this realization materialized, other pieces fell into place.

Frankly, this book was a long, often overwhelming venture. Due to the nature of the topic, some of the information uncovered was quite overwhelming—particularly when exploring the psyche of sociopathic murderers. What materialized over the past 7 years is a series of theoretical, narrative, and anecdotal essays that explore the often parallel, sometimes intertwining pathways of destruction and creation. As it is written, each essay can stand on its own; taken together, they provide perhaps a compelling conversation—or even a conversation starter—on the surmised interrelationship. Ultimately, while far from exhaustive, this series of essays begins the exploration of the frenzied dance of art and violence.

The Dance's Ternary Structure: The Format

The Introduction, eight chapters, and one Interlogue are divided up into three distinct parts: Part I "The Dance Between Creation and Destruction," Part II "Art of Psychopathy," and Part III "Art for Change."

Part I comprises four distinct chapters that define and explore the dynamic interchange of art and violence. To first explore their relationship, the Introduction provides the scaffolding on which the book is built. The first section of the Introduction, "The Art of Violence," provides an essential summary of how the terms "violence" and "aggression" are defined. This is followed by various psychological and sociological perspectives on the etiology of violence. The second part, "The Violence of Art" begins to explore the relationship between art and violence; particularly, how creativity emerges from aggression and how "art making turns aside aggression," as explained through neurobiological, psychological, and sociological lenses.

Relying on psychobiographical narratives (Wilson, 2016b), the next two chapters present well-known historical artists to explore this interrelationship. Chapter 1, "Angelic Demons: The Capricious Creators," underscores the contention that "particularly sordid personalities often lurk behind captivating works of beauty." Six artists from different historical epochs with very different aesthetic styles were chosen because they all had one thing in common: each had his own underlying demons that were revealed through aggressive behaviors, demons that seemed to be simultaneously fed and controlled by creative endeavors. Michelangelo Mersi de Caravaggio, Benvenuto Cellini, Salvador Dali, Amadeo Modigliani, Jackson Pollock, and Richard Dadd each seemed to represent different prototypes—almost archetypes—of the violent artist. The chapter captures snapshots of their art and how it potentially reflected and mitigated their violent and impulsive inclinations.

Chapter 2, "Creating in Conflict: Art Amid Environmental and Societal Violence," explores how the creative endeavors of six additional artists, Francisco Goya, Max Beckmann, Felix Nussbaum, Vann Nath, Bill Traylor, and Norman Rockwell, materialized from their experiences of social and environmental upheaval. Divided among three categories of societal turmoil, each artist, in his own way, was impacted by far-reaching conflicts and used his work to maintain a semblance of control and resistance.

Chapter 3 explores what happens when you lay side by side the artistic endeavors of one of the world's most violent perpetrators and those who suffered under his regime. "Art of the Perpetrator and the Oppressed: Unveiling the Art of the Holocaust" juxtaposes the work of Adolf Hitler against those of whom he persecuted, artists whose work provided both evidence and resistance.

As this chapter took shape, many other contrasting notions occurred and are evident throughout the telling of these stories. The art underscored the contrasts between the emotionally connected and the disconnected, technical skill compared to passionate expression, violent explosion against courageous resistance, and inhumanity versus humanity. Finally, it lays bare the rationale for such art making: the narcissistic self-aggrandizement as seen with the serial killers in the following chapters, and the desire to be seen and made whole, as seen in works in Chapter 2. While Hitler's work and the work from the Holocaust have been explored in many forums, rarely have these works been explored together to examine these different facets.

Part II, "Art of Psychopathy," includes two distinct chapters. However, to best understand these chapters, "Wielding a New Weapon: Perpetuating the Multiple Murderer's Psychopathic Cycle Through Art" and "Extremes on the Same Continuum: Comparing the Art of Gacy and Manson," a working understanding of psychopathy and sociopathy is necessary. Therefore, the "Interlogue: Examining Psychopathy" has been provided as a comprehensive yet succinct overview of this enigmatic disorder. This informs Chapter 4, "Wielding a New Weapon," which first explores our culture's fascination with multiple murderers and "murderabilia." This is then followed by seven appalling profiles of multiple murderers: Tommy Lynn Sells, Richard Ramirez, Danny Rolling, Gary Ray Bowles, Glen Rogers, Charles Ng, and Gerard John Schaefer. These chosen representatives seemed to create works to reflect and further perpetuate their own narcissistic glorification, using their art to fortify their grandiose identities and continue their potential predatory dominance over their victims. However, two well-known multiple murderers were conspicuously excluded—Charles Manson and John Wayne Gacy. Instead, Chapter 5, "Extremes on the Same Continuum," rely on Manson's and Gacy's psychobiographies, criminal narratives, and artistic output to explore the extreme variations in psychopathic personalities and how such tendencies were reflected through their creative attempts.

The final three chapters comprise Part III, "Art for Change," and demonstrate how art has been used to mitigate and turn aside violent tendencies. Chapter 6, "Charles Bronson Becomes Charlie Salvador: The 'Most Violent Inmate' Liberated Through Art" focuses on the most notoriously violent inmate in England. Initially, Bronson seemed to revel in the original identity that labeled him as incorrigibly violent. However, through a single fortuitous interaction, Bronson eventually found art and began to redefine who he was. This chapter, drawing from various published accounts of Bronson's crimes and subsequent imprisonment, his autobiographical memoirs, direct communications with Bronson and his then-fiancée, and reproductions of his drawings, will reveal the power that art had in redirecting his aggression and relabeling his violent identity.

Chapter 7, "Guernica: Painted from Violence, a Palette for Peace," reflects on how Pablo Picasso's masterpiece captured his rage and fury in response to turbulent and violent events. As a container to the Spaniard's anger and frustration, this painting became the quintessential template for the art education program, The Guernica Children's Peace Mural Project. This chapter provides a succinct examination of Picasso and the painting that captured the destruction of a small peaceful Basque village during World War II. Following this, gleaned through literature and an in-depth conversation with one of the founders of the Children's Peace Mural Project, Dr. Tom Anderson, a comprehensive examination is presented. This chapter ultimately explores how a single painting provided the blueprint on how art can help children around the world develop connections and community and make sense of senseless violence. In turn, this arts-based program helped allay the powerlessness, fear, frustration, and anxiety that derived from their overwhelming circumstances.

Chapter 8, "Continuing the Dance: How Art Therapy Can Reveal and Mitigate Violent Tendencies," draws on my professional experiences as an art therapist, particularly as one who worked with violent and aggressive clients. This chapter provides a brief introduction to art therapy, case examples with violent clients, and a summation of why and how art therapy is effective in slowing, and, at times, halting the cycle of violence. In addition, it will summarize how art therapists, as peace-makers, may also provide a sense of safety and well-being within extremely volatile environments.

The book's Epilogue, "Bringing the Dance to a Close," examines more closely the issues raised in this Introduction; that while I intended to use the metaphor of the two-person tango to illustrate the dynamics, that notion was no longer adequate as the book developed.

Identifying—and Embracing—the Selective Lenses of This Book

To write an exhaustive account on this topic and include all of the artists with violent dispositions—historically and relationally—is nigh near impossible and quite frankly cumbersome. The ensuing result would become encyclopedic. This was not the intention of this text.

While I recognize that this book only serves as an hors d'oeuvre for a much larger buffet, these accounts and explorations are here because I was *compelled* to write about them, and they are, in their own right, *compelling*. In some fashion, each of these cases found me. As they were explored, it became clear that each provided a unique and different perspective on how art draws from—and turns aside—violence.

To be certain, this text focuses on the visual arts. While perhaps limiting, given the extent of literature and examples of the relationship between the other expressive arts and violence such as music, dance, and theater, as an art therapist, I am only drawing from what I am familiar with. As a result, I look forward to future endeavors and explorations conducted by my colleagues in the neighboring artistic fields on the relationships between *all* of the arts and violence.

I also recognize the limitation of providing the narratives of men and not women. In complete transparency, when I first provided a rationale and defense of why this was in the original book proposal, it was recommended by one reviewer that I remove it and simply acknowledge that the bulk of my own experiences have been with men. However, this still felt disingenuous and, given the current climate, unbalanced.

It is true—my own work has primarily been with violent and aggressive *men.* Yet further examination underscored that, at the risk of appearing biased, there is support (Raine, 2013) for the perception that men seem, on the whole, simply more physically aggressive and violent. While this is recognizably a stereotype, some such stereotypes are built on genuine characteristics and experiences. Citing a number of evolutionary and biological considerations, Raine argued that while women can be aggressive, men have *more* of a tendency to direct their violence outward. Archer (2009) argued that the sex of a perpetrator becomes more of a variable the more *physical* the aggressive act; Buss and Dedden (1990) recognized that while women could indeed be hostile and destructive, men tended to be more physically violent, particularly against others. This has borne out in my own experiences and research.

In a comparative study and review of male and female offenders, women did indeed demonstrate a more external locus of control prior to the study when compared with their male counterparts (Gussak, 2009a). What emerged was that their crimes and behaviors were more linked to dependence on others, whereas the men demonstrated more acting out and were independently aggressive. So, while I acknowledge there is a great deal of resources that reflect aggressive and violent acts perpetrated by women, given the limitations of my experiences and the available sociological reflections, the focus of this book remains the acts of men.

The vignettes and narratives throughout the text were provided to allow for a deeper understanding and examples of the relationship between art and violence. They are individual stories used to illustrate the very different ways that art reflects and interacts with violence. In some cases, many of these anecdotal narratives serve as brief *psychobiographies*; essentially examinations of an artist's history to inform the potential psychodynamic meaning of their artistic creations.

Wilson, who relied on this approach in examining the work of Alberto Giacometti (Wilson, 2003) and Louise Nevelson (Wilson, 2016a), believed that as an art therapist, focusing on "the biography of artists makes it somewhat easier to consider the artwork of our patients. By examining the life of one artist, we can begin to understand how the visual world affects all people" (Wilson, 2016b, pp. 17–18). By creating "two psychoanalytic/biographical studies of [Giacometti and Nevelson], [Wilson was] able to see startling connections between their early life experience and the sculpture, paintings, and drawings they made as adults" (p. 18). This then informed her understanding of the work that her clients did. Yet while Wilson relied on single, in-depth examinations, the chapters in this book provide numerous, brief historical and biographical summaries. While not nearly as extensive, to examine and understand the artists' relationships between art and violence, I briefly recounted the artists' lived experiences, personal developments, and their relationship to their times and environments. Only then was I able to appreciate and understand the work they produced and just how much it came to rely on the violence and aggression they embodied or experienced.

During this project, something interesting also occurred. I went into this project with several artists in mind that I knew I had to examine. However, when I discussed this project at conferences, research symposia, art showings, and around the dinner table with friends and colleagues, I would often be asked if I considered certain particular artists; other names would be bantered about, some I had heard of, some I had not. As a result, while I certainly included many of the artists with whom I have personally been intrigued, several were included only after such interchanges occurred. If I hadn't been open to this, artists like Vann Nath, Traylor, Modigliani, and Beckmann may never have been considered. For example, I never would have thought to include Rockwell in a book about violence. However, after Rockwell's drawings and paintings that were informed by civil unrest were exhibited at a local art museum, a lively discussion with its education director ensued, and I couldn't imagine *not* including him.

One Final Note Before the Dance Begins

While finishing up this text, major changes began to occur around the United States and the world. We were hit consecutively by violent and aggressive events that rocked the physical, social, and cultural fabrics of our nation: the advent of the COVID-19 pandemic followed by the Black Lives Matter movement. While neither have been directly addressed in these chapters, they both loomed large within my own psyche. Along with all of the fear, anxiety, helplessness, and anger that global citizens experienced was the creative responses that many of my colleagues and friends used to address these violent upheavals. The power of art became apparent, providing various mechanisms to address and adjust to the changes. Various forms of artistic expression were used to make sense of all that was happening, as an escape from immediate anxiety and fear, and as a weapon against injustice, ignorance, and anger while providing opportunities for burgeoning hope and gathering strength.

While this book presents historical accounts, these events reminded me that the frenzied dance never stops.

PART I

THE DANCE BETWEEN CREATION AND DESTRUCTION

Introduction

Art of Violence/Violence of Art

The Art of Violence

Clearly, this book is about the interrelationship between art and violence. To be able to successfully explore this, an understanding of what constitutes aggression and violence is necessary. Thus, this chapter provides an initial definition of "violence," followed by a series of theoretical ideas of where and how violence and aggressive behaviors emerge. While this chapter does its best to cast a wide net, it can only touch on a select number of perspectives given the amount of information available on this topic.

Violence: What Is It?

Mider (2013) recognized that "violence has invariably accompanied humanity; there has not yet been a period in our history in which it has not been present. It seems impossible to separate violence from human existence" (p. 702). In many publications and studies the terms "aggression" and "violence" were interchangeable, in others sequential—that is, it was assumed that violence emerged from aggression. For the sake of this book, as the notion of violence is teased apart, working definitions will draw from literature that examines violence *and* aggression.

Regardless of this simple interchange of terms, "we can't always be sure just what is meant when a person is described as 'aggressive' or an action is labeled 'violence' " (Berkowitz, 1990, p. 3). The definitions remain broad in scope and application. Pontara (1978) indicated that what editorials on violence and aggression usually miss is the necessity to "clarify the context in which or the purposes for which the sought definitions are expected to serve" (p. 19). Why define these terms, and in which context are we to apply them?

Mider provided a rather literal and simultaneously broad and reductionistic definition.

> The English language etymology of the term "violence" is normative; violence is derived from the Latin *violentia . . . vis* meaning force and *latus* an adjectival passive participle for "carry," "administer" or "pass onto." The Latin

> *violo* is strongly negative and means "to assault," "rape," "insult," "slander," "dishonor," "stain," or "insult" . . . The Polish word *przemoc* [indicates] the use of a stronger position or force against someone to force them to obey. . . . In some languages, the concept of violence does not have pejorative overtones. . . . There is a lively discussion ongoing between researchers on what type of the use of force, by whom and against whom or what, can be substantially described as violence. (p. 703)

In due course, Mider underscored that there is still some discrepancy on what might constitute violence, ultimately recognizing that such a definition is neither straightforward nor categorical.

Holmes (1971) indicated that violence, while in some cases physical—deliberate acts of force to cause damage or death to someone—can be also an undefined and ambiguous *violation* that in some manner diminishes and humiliates another; in other words, a psychological act. Whether physical or psychological, such acts may be conducted to create an intentional power shift. While violence is not directly correlated with power, and not all power relies on violence, a deliberately violent act does in fact result in power being wrenched from another. Building on this, Govier (2008) argued that psychological violence may be just as detrimental, forcing change through manipulation and coercion.

Interestingly, Govier also recognized that the term is often strategically applied to delegitimize an action through negative association—label something as violent and it becomes irrational and should be denounced regardless of its impetus. An act is patriotic if it is for *our* purpose; it is terrorism if done by an ideologically opposing team—for *their* purpose.

Separating violence from its intended or unintended outcomes, Walby (2012) recognized the need to examine violence as a singular phenomenon. While she claimed that historically violence has been studied within other categories and for many specific reasons, there have been times that violence is recognized as its own "form of practice, a set of social institutions, with its own rhythm, dynamics and practice" (p. 96). In other words, violence is conducted for its own sake.

Others attempted to approach in a more pragmatic way. One method I found particularly helpful was Krause's (2009) classifications. He claimed that the most common means to categorize violent acts was through three foci, sometimes distinct, sometimes overlapping: meaning and purpose of the act, level or scope of organization of the actors, and nature of the violence (pp. 338–339).

Meaning and purpose can be divided into four groups:

- Politically motivated (i.e., war, terrorism)
- Economically motivated (i.e., organized crime)

- Socially conditioned (i.e., riots, rituals)
- Interpersonally driven (i.e., pathological acts, domestic abuse, rape)

Scope of the organization refers to whom the violence is directed and how many actors are involved. This includes

- Self-directed
- Interpersonal
- Collective

Nature of the violence can range from

- Physical
- Psychological
- Gender-based
- Deprivation through neglect or omission
- Systemic or structural

Of course, Krause also stressed the obvious: while these classifications make it simpler to consider this phenomenon, violence is not nearly so categorical.

To take this further, while I also recognize that violence may not be so easily recognizable or reductionistic, I believe that, for focus and clarity, this book needs to rely on distinct parameters on what is meant by violence. Thus, I am relying on a very simple principle based on my own experiences and research: an act of violence is one which involves a deliberate attempt to physically harm another for the purpose of dominance and personal gain. In this sense, aggression, understood to be an instinctual drive (Horney, 1939), will only be considered when it results in a violent act. Thus, unchecked and misdirected aggression may become violence. In addition, this book will focus on violent and aggressive acts that are conducted by someone on a person or persons, usually in an illegal fashion.

The Cause of Violence: Theoretical Perspectives

There are various theoretical perspectives on the origins of violent tendencies, each of which has taken volumes to enumerate. Each position requires extensive examination, a consideration this book simply cannot accommodate. Therefore, the following sections contain preliminary understandings of the genesis of violence divided into several chosen theoretical categories: evolutionary/neurobiological, psychodynamic, cognitive and social psychology, and sociological/social interaction.

Evolutionary Roots of Violence: Neurological/Neurobiological Influences

The notion that violence and aggressive tendencies have biological and neurobiological predispositions has gone out of—and come back into—vogue over the decades. Lombroso, a nineteenth-century army medic working as a psychiatrist and prison doctor first proposed that there were neurological predispositions to aggressive acts (Wolfgang, 1961). He believed that the propensity for criminal activities could be traced back to the now debunked notion of "atavistic stigmata" (Raine, 2013, p. 12)—physical attributes associated with ethnic backgrounds resulting in inferior traits. Directly linked to the rise of Nazism and their belief in eugenics (Friedlander, 1995), such ideas have fallen into disrepute. As a result, the biological evolution of violent tendencies has given way to sociological considerations. Yet, despite its bad rap, there are convincing arguments for evolutionary influences.

Anthropologists have theorized that violence and aggression have evolved to instill survival of the fittest, a means to dominate sexually. This, in turn, ensures the continuation of the dominant bloodline, exerting power and control within their given culture (Harpending & Draper, 1988). Dawkins (2006), in his seminal work *The Selfish Gene*, argued that such success is passed down through the generations, instilling a desire and need to dominate through strength and fitness, thus ensuring survival. Such adaptations remain embedded in our neurological wiring.

There is a flip side to this coin. While some have argued that a "lack of conscience, superficial charm, high verbal skills, promiscuity, and lack of interpersonal bonds" (Raine, 2013, p. 20), may indeed ensure prosperity and success, such traits are often associated with psychopathy. While such characteristics might be initially advantageous, it might also push some people away, creating an opposite desire, a cessation of one's bloodline. Yet there is no denying that some are attracted to these characteristics, finding such people powerful. In this case, such genes might be carried to the next generation.

To take this even further, some have argued for and against the presence of what has been labeled the "killer gene" (Raine, 2013), the inherited predisposition toward crime and violence. One twin study conducted by Baker, Jacobson, Raine, Lozano, and Bezdjian (2007) revealed preliminary findings that suggested that twins, regardless of socioeconomic and ethnic backgrounds, had a fairly significant propensity for sharing antisocial tendencies. Ultimately, aggressive tendencies may be entrenched in genetic structure, and, while environment may influence end behavior (Bouchard & McGue, 2002), it is not nearly as instrumental as some perceive.

Brain chemistry, influenced by genetic structure, may also offer many clues in the genesis of violent tendencies. For example, a low serotonin level (a neurotransmitter that regulates, among other things, mood) combined with a high level of dopamine (a neurotransmitter that regulates the brain's pleasure center) may create what Raine described as an "explosive combination" (2013). On the other hand, Caspi et al. (2002) argued for restraint and moderation: ".genetic and biological factors *interact* with social factors in predisposing someone to later antisocial and violent behavior . . . genes are important—but in a specific social context" (Raine, 2013, p. 52).

So, was Lombroso completely off the mark? Let's put his ideas into context. He developed his theory of the genetic predisposition to violence after examining the brain of a notorious outlaw (Wolfgang, 1961). He recognized an abnormality "an unusual indentation at its base, which he interpreted as reflecting smaller cerebellum . . . seated under the two larger hemispheres of the brain" (Raine, 2013, p. 11). While contemporary theorists have discounted Lombroso's conclusions due to its eventual connection to eugenics, current neurological discoveries support the notion that brain aberrations may reflect a predisposition to violent tendencies. For example, there is evidence that damage to the *prefrontal cortex*, the home to executive functioning (i.e., decision-making and complex behavioral regulation) may result in violent tendencies (Brower & Price, 2001). As well, some have inferred that damage to the *angular gyrus* (the portion of the brain responsible for visual input and language comprehension) can also result in violent tendencies.

Raine (2013) argued that if this area is unable to develop well, then a child's ability to learn suffers, interfering with social and educational processing throughout his formative years. This may also result in less of a chance of "success" later in life. Such frustrations would be difficult to control, in turn creating a situation that may result in poor impulse control and explosive reactions. While this seemingly supports the interrelationship between genetics and social factors, it can also be argued that the physiological damage *causes* the social difficulties.

Damage to the *hippocampus*, where fear and emotional behavior are regulated, has also been correlated to psychopathic and antisocial behaviors (Kiehl, 2006; Soderstrom et al., 2002). Thus, if such an area is not functioning to its full potential, the ability to refrain from certain behaviors due to negative outcomes may be unlikely; if a person suffering from such damage becomes overtly angry, he would be less likely to modulate his rage. And finally, adults with psychopathic behavior and youth with conduct disorders have been found to have a poorly functioning *posterior cingulate cortex*, the area of the brain that aids in emotional memory retrieval and the ability for self-reflection (Ochsner et al., 2005).

However, to avoid perpetuating the pessimistic perspective that such injury is irreversible and that violence and aggression is inevitable, such damage does not close the door to intervention. Damage to the brain alone does not cause the undesirable outcome. Rather, it is a perfect storm of situations that involve environmental, social, and/or educational limitations that may cause such violence and aggression. Thus, while medication and surgery may be used to a certain extent to mitigate neurological damage, other therapeutic methods may be used to mediate and intercede to help assuage or reverse potential negative behaviors.

Psychodynamic

Aside from neurological predispositions, there are prevalent psychodynamic explanations about what might cause aggression and, in turn, violence. This perspective extends along a continuum that aggression is an innate, instinctual force that is hardwired into the psyche, as an unavoidable reaction to poor parenting/familial connections. Early on, Adler posited that there existed an "aggression drive," which kicks in when one feels that basic needs—such as nurturance—are not being met (Adler, Ansbacher, & Ansbacher, 1964). He also developed the notion of "compensatory" reactions to situations, which is when one strives to overcome one's limitations. He also believed in the "masculine protest," a desire for boys to assert their superiority and dominance, to be seen as strong and aggressive, reinforced by the culture to which these children belong.

Although Freud initially disregarded Adler's concepts of aggression, believing it detracted from the importance of the sexual, libidinal drive in human development, he later changed his mind and developed his own perspective. He believed that aggression was an "energy," a force or drive that resulted in the clash of the life force (Eros) and the death force (Thanatos) (Freud, 1990).

Jung believed that children are born with a striving for power over others, to ultimately create his or her own ego separate from others. In addition, violent and aggressive tendencies emerge when the *shadow*—the animalistic or libidinal part of us that we repress (think Dr. Jekyll's Mr. Hyde)—becomes the dominant archetype, or when the individual is not able to assimilate and integrate this archetype into his psyche. In some cases, the shadow might be projected onto members of an outside group, causing conflict. "[P]rojection of the shadow onto members of an out-group . . . perceived as menacing . . . [may emerge as] xenophobia, paranoid distrust, and violent hostility" (Stevens, 1995, p. 11).

Lorenz likened aggressive responses to those expressed by animals; energy from the fight instinct is spontaneously generated and aggression comes from the release of the accumulated energy. Known as the "hydraulic method," if this energy is not released gradually, then it may be released as an "explosion" (1967).

Fromm (1973/1992) disagreed with this simplistic explanation, arguing that there existed two forms of aggression that are solely unique to mankind—benign and malignant. *Benign aggression* is an instinctual, rational response "that seeks to preserve and enhance the lives of individuals and groups" (Swanson, 1975, p. 1243), engaged when self-defense and preservation are needed. This is considerably different from *malignant aggression*, which is an irrational striving for destruction, encompassing sadistic tendencies. While the former is a means of natural preservation, Fromm (1972) believed the latter emerged as a direct response to a society that has become bureaucratized and capitalistic. Rather than an innate characteristic, Fromm believed that it develops into a specific character trait that craves dominance and is thrill-seeking. "Man seeks for drama and excitement; when he cannot get satisfaction on a higher level, he creates for himself the drama of destruction" (Fromm, 1973/1992, p. 29).

For May, power is a natural drive, and aggression is just one way to achieve and succeed (1972). For all of these theoretical perspectives, aggression is not deemed a negative characteristic; in fact, such drives are necessary to succeed. However, it is when these drive energies cannot be integrated or there is no opportunity for productive or gradual release, that out-of-control behaviors may emerge.

Klein also saw the value of aggression as a drive, but unlike Freud and early psychoanalytic thinkers, her object relations perspective stressed that proper development emerges through an early, healthy relationship with the mother (Goldenberg, 1986). As such, she believed that "aggression is an innate instinct in every human baby . . . [and that] angry feelings caused anxiety because babies felt anger as a terrifying internal destructive force. (pp. 39–40). It is closely bound with love: neither are inherently good or bad, and while both can serve as driving forces, they can equally be potentially destructive (Riviere, 1964). "We can in fact say that both the self-preservative and 'love' instincts need a certain mixture of aggression if they are to attain satisfaction, that is, an aggressive element is an essential part of both of these instincts in actual functioning" (p. 5). Like love and security, certain fears, anxieties, and anger can inspire curiosity and exploration of the world around them and, eventually, a healthy separation and identity formation.

However, if children's responses are rejected and they are not provided a safe and secure arena in which to explore their anxiety and aggression, they may become reluctant to express such volatile feelings. In such situations, they may develop "the unconscious fear of being incapable of loving others sufficiently, and particularly of not being able to master their aggressive impulses toward others: they dread being in danger to the loved one" (Klein, 1964, p. 63) and soon learn to hide their true emotive responses. As a result, "he or she would be cut off from the outside world" (Greenberg, 1961/1989, p. 40) and self-doubt or even loathing may develop. Even still, unhealthy defense mechanisms emerge; for example, *projective identification*. This is when parts of the self that are identified as hateful, repulsive, and unlovable are placed on the external object, the mother figure, resulting in perpetuating the unhealthy connection and an aggressive and hostile object relationship (Klein, 1946; Waska, 2000). If unaddressed, this defense mechanism is solidified, maintained, and replicated in future relationships, perpetuating ongoing hostility and aggressive conflicts with others (Klein, 1964, 1975).

Bowlby also distinguished between functional and dysfunctional aggression: one is an appropriate reaction to a frustrating situation, whereas the latter is the result of an adverse parental relationship (Bacciagaluppi, 1989). Bowlby also believed that everything depended on either a healthy or poor attachment to the "mother figure." In this case, attachment is "an affectional tie with some other differentiated and preferred individual who is usually conceived as stronger and/or wiser" (Bowlby, 1977, p. 203). If this is disrupted at an early age, aggression—and eventually violent tendencies—will likely emerge. "Disruption of attachment during the crucial first 3 years of life can lead to 'affectionless psychopathy'; the inability to form meaningful emotional relationships, coupled with chronic anger, poor impulse control, and lack of remorse" (Levy & Orlans, 2000, p. 3).

Horney (1945/1992) indicated that aggression was a response to narcissistic injuries. Compensatory grandiosity and pathological rage come from the pain of not being loved and accepted by parental figures; this compels the individual to replace what Winnicott (1965, 1971) termed the "true self," one that is authentic and alive, with an emerging "false self," one that is idealized and self-aggrandizing yet vulnerable. Others tend to be turned off by this "false self," and, as a result, the person is rejected by others. This rejection causes further anger about not being loved or accepted. Seen as an additional betrayal, this develops into even further anger, eventually expressed through hostility or violence. Thus, an unchecked cycle will result in hostility and violence. In addition, Horney also recognized that aggression could result from a neurotic need for power, social recognition, personal admiration, and achievement—all attributes that a pathologically grandiose person would crave.

While the psychodynamic perspectives cover a wide range of theoretical and philosophical concepts on the antecedents of aggressive tendencies, all rely on the notion of an innate drive for power and identity, familial attachment, and preservation. Many use these perspectives to guide their clinical interventions; still others find them a bit too esoteric and have developed more concrete, cognitive models to understand how violence emerges.

Cognitive and Social Learning Perspectives

Deep in scope and wide in breadth, many theorists engaged a cognitive and social learning model to not only understand, but also to alleviate aggressive and violent behavior. The theorists who subscribed to the cognitive and social learning models were seeking explanations that were based on real-world, tangible interactions: how the environment influenced one's learning, in turn, altered how one thinks of the world, ultimately influencing one's behavior.

Early explanations for aggression included Dollard and his colleagues' "frustration-aggression hypothesis" (1939). In this simplistic premise, aggression occurs when one's goals are frustrated by a person or situation, and, in turn, the aggressor scapegoats and/or becomes aggressive toward whatever is blocking them or may redirect his aggression toward another person or party.

Bandura, one of the leading theorists of social cognitive perspectives, argued that simply observing aggressive behavior teaches children that such acts are not only acceptable but expected. In his well-known Bobo doll study, Bandura and his team (Bandura & Huston, 1961; Bandura, Ross, & Ross, 1961) were able to demonstrate that children mimicked aggressive behavior that they were exposed to. If the children saw someone punch the inflatable clown, they would do the same.

Building on Bandura's work, Perry, Perry, and Rasmussen (1986) discovered that what children know about their own capacities and what they can expect from the consequences of their actions contributed to the likelihood of engaging in an aggressive manner. In other words, those who were aggressive were more likely to believe it was easier to be aggressive than not and that such behavior could benefit them. They were that much more confident that engaging in such a manner would result in much more tangible and desired results. When this behavior is, in turn, reinforced through desirable outcomes, then it is more likely to be repeated.

While Huesmann (1988) recognized that there are a number of precipitating factors that contribute to aggressive tendencies, including neurological and physiological challenges, his belief was firmly rooted in the notion that

> the presence of environmental, familial, and cognitive characteristics that promote the learning and emission of aggressive behavior probably account for the greatest portion of the variation in aggression . . . conditions most conducive to the learning of aggression seem to be those in which the child has many opportunities to observe aggression. (p. 14)

Such observational learning relies on several "social-cognitive structures: schemas about a hostile world, scripts for social problem solving that focus on aggression and normative beliefs that aggression is acceptable" (Huesmann, Moise-Titus, Podolski, & Eron, 2003, p. 201). This even includes watching violence on television.

Some cognitive approaches challenge the original view that anger is an initial response to feeling wronged (Beck, 1999). A chain reaction of violence begins when a person is in distress. It is this feeling of distress that triggers the "I have been wronged" response, which then leads to violence and retaliation.

> We take the role of the protagonist and other players are our supporters and antagonists. . . . Our egocentrism also leads us to believe that other people interpret the situation as we do; they seem even more culpable because they "know" that they are hurting us but persist in their noxious behavior anyhow. In "hot" conflicts, the offender also has an egocentric perspective, and it sets the stage for a vicious cycle of hurt, anger and retaliation. (p. 27)

What these approaches share is that internal processes are influenced by external factors. Learning begets self-perceptions and skewed thinking patterns. When aggressive responses are rewarded and reinforced, this becomes one's internal script. Contrariwise, behavior can be changed when the negative input is interrupted and the cycle is disrupted. Only through a learned, mindful awareness of one's reactions, emotions, and responses to given situations can real change occur. A conscious decision to change can alter the outcome.

Many of these theories also share one particular component: social influence. Social interactions, and the interpretation of these interactions, contribute to and maintain aggressive propensities. So, while a psychological theory may be enough to explain the genesis of aggressive tendencies, acceptance of a sociological perspective can be used to further clarify aggressive actions, their perpetual existence, and how they can, in turn, be mitigated.

Sociological/Social Interaction Perspective

Aggression and violent tendencies emerge from social action. While a person may *feel* angry, he or she *acts* violently toward others or themselves. In order to make sense of social actions, social researchers focus on the *inter*action that occurs between individuals. Early social interactionist theorist James (1890/1918) believed that the social self is the result of the interaction between the individual and social groups. Cooley (1964) indicated that a mutual interdependence between the social environment and individuals exists. Mead (1964) understood that the self developed from the "process of social experience and activity . . . [which] develops in the given individual as a result of his relations to that process as a whole and to other individuals within that process" (p. 199).

Meaning emerges from the interaction between people. It is through the continual act of interpreting—redefining each other's acts—that a societal context is defined. "By making indications to himself and by interpreting what he indicates, the human being has to forge or piece together a line of action" (Blumer, 1969,

p. 64). Ultimately, people are defined through such an interface. Meanings and interpretations are social products. Aggression and violent responses can emerge from interpretations of unsatisfactory or misperceived interactions.

According to the theories just explored, an unacceptable interaction with someone can result in an aggressive response; aggression can also emerge from a desire to coerce someone to bring about a "desired social and self identit[y]" (Anderson & Bushman, 2002, p. 31). Similar to some of the psychodynamic and cognitive perspectives on aggression, social interactionism maintains that "aggression is often the result of threats to high self-esteem, especially to unwarranted self-esteem" (p. 31). Aggression may emerge through how a person sees him- or herself within a social context and how this perception is challenged.

Aggression is perpetuated through continual social interaction as well. Aggressive and violent acts are deemed unacceptable by society, and those who engage in such acts are labeled deviants (Becker, 1963/1991; Sagarin, 1975). Since aggression is created and defined through social interaction, a person becomes identified through this undesirable behavior. Once a person is labeled "aggressive" or "violent," this moniker is maintained through continual social interactions. Unless this characterization is lifted and this identity changed, aggression may continue. Bartusch and Matsueda (1996) believed that the mechanisms of role-taking and labeling were a major influence on delinquency in adolescent boys and girls. Labels provided by parents and teachers perpetuated the delinquent identity.

Zimbardo, Haney, Banks, and Jaffe (1973) recognized that people may develop aggressive and dominating characteristics after roles and labels are assigned and accepted. In his famous study, a Stanford University class was divided into two groups (one group role-played prison guards and one group played the inmates) to

> understand more about the process by which people called "prisoners" lose their liberty, civil rights, independence, and privacy, while those called "guards" gain social power by accepting the responsibility for controlling and managing the lives of their dependent charges. (p. 38)

The "guards" locked up the "inmates" in the basement of the psychology building. The study had to be terminated earlier than originally planned because both groups inhabited their roles more seriously than anticipated. The original identities of the students were quickly transformed. The "guards" became aggressive toward their "wards," and the "inmates" became docile and cunningly resistive. The authors soon realized that aggressive actions or reactions emerged from role-taking and labeled identities.

Not So Categorical

Each of the above theories seem to make a territorial proclamation that theirs is the predominant explanation that correctly defines and understands aggression and violence. However, what seemed to emerge fairly quickly is that all of the violent and aggressive reactions stem from a number of different causes and circumstances. While there might certainly be a predisposition toward aggression or poor impulse control because of neurological and physiological factors, poor social learning or a lack of parental support might have flipped the switch of these factors, thus creating an uncontrolled situation. As well, what many of these seem to underscore, either through subtle hints or blatant proclamations, is that while there may be a predisposition toward violence, a social situation or interaction might certainly have triggered the reaction. While any one factor could certainly be a triggering event to a violent outburst or reaction, I would argue that it may be any combination of them that could eventually result in an uncontrollable explosion.

The Violence of Art

Early in my days as a healthcare provider in a psychiatric facility in Los Angeles, I had an opportunity to work with—and learn from—"Rick." Despite his small stature, Rick, a 15-year-old boy, was tough and quite strong. Suspended from school for fighting and "acting out," he was often in trouble with the law for gang activities. In the facility he believed himself "tougher" than everyone there, including staff. Rarely did a day go by where he did not try to attack a peer or a staff member for what he perceived to be disrespect. This, in turn, required him to be restrained, thus reinforcing this perception.

He was proud that he belonged to a street gang and would often "tag" the name and symbols of his gang on the facility's walls. He became angry when the graffiti was erased and at times attacked those who were cleaning up the drawings. This was not unusual; often "taggers"—those who mark walls with colorful graffiti—will "turn to violence to protect their art" (Ayres, 1994, p. 20).

Tagging walls with gang markings is generally ego-driven and can make a name for someone out on the streets. Graffiti is a means of identity and discourse between and among the street gangs and provides a sense of identity: simply put, it's more than just indicating territory (Adams & Winter, 1997). This held true for Rick: because he received his identity and validation from his gang, by washing away the graffiti from the walls, he was essentially "told" that he was unacceptable—that all he was and all that he embraced should be erased. The perceived disrespect resulted in violence.

While there were rules stating absolutely no gang signs or evidence of graffiti within the facility, I was able to negotiate a compromise with Rick and the administration to avoid the ongoing cycle of violence. He could draw his gang tags on separate paper and keep them in his drawer, if he promised not to hang them on the walls. Reluctantly, and with obvious wariness, both sides agreed. He spent several afternoons drawing quietly with pencil on white paper. Each drawing was meticulously completed with more detail as time progressed.

After completing several drawings of his gang's name, he was instead asked to create a drawing of his nickname—a name given by his gang which most gang members have. Eventually, over time, Rick's drawing evolved into an embellishment of his real name. He was allowed to hang these on his walls, and he did so proudly. By the time he was released, he was decidedly less aggressive (Gussak, 2006, 2007, 2013).

While the previous section explored the various etiology of the terms "aggression" and "violence," this section will begin to explore the art that emerges from aggression and how, in turn, creating art can turn aside violence. To do so, it will present how art making can indeed turn aside aggression through neurobiological, psychological, and sociological lenses. However, first a working definition of creativity and its relationship to aggression needs to be delineated.

Creativity Emerges from Aggression

Creativity does not equate to artistic expression. While difficult to define, the National Endowment for the Arts reflected that, overall, "creativity combines 'novelty' with 'value' or 'utility' for some purpose or problem" (2015, p. 14). In and of itself, creativity is seen as the ability to make something tangible from an intangible idea or product that is innovative and new. Thus, creativity is neither positive nor negative; in fact, it may not even result in constructive and artistic results. "The distinction cannot be made by examining the product. The very essence of the creative is its novelty, and hence we have no standard by which to judge it" (Rogers, 1954, p. 252). Writing a symphony, inventing the light bulb, or writing the great American novel is just as creative as developing the atomic bomb or devising a Ponzi scheme that bilks millions out of investors: they all require abstract thinking and intricate problem-solving.

The mainspring of creativity appears to be the same tendency that we discover so deeply as the curative force in psychotherapy.

> [M]an's tendency to actualize himself, to become his potentialities. . . . the tendency to express and activate all the capacities of the organism, to the extent that such activation enhances the organism or the self. This tendency may become deeply buried under layer after layer of encrusted psychological defenses, it may be hidden behind elaborate facades, which deny its existence . . . and awaits only the proper conditions to be released and expressed. (Rogers, 1954, pp. 251–252)

Creativity bursts forth. Often, creative people are explosively driven to express themselves and may stop at nothing to make sure they succeed. When doing so, some may become hostile. In many regards, in order to promote their own ideas and novel perspectives, "creative people often respond aggressively" (p. 145).

However, while, again, creativity does not necessitate artistic expression or talent, it is understood that to produce—to "create"—artists engage their creativity. So, for the sake of this book, the notion of creative expression is reflected within the final, tangible creations as produced by the artist.

Creative Aggression

"Individual characteristics such as emotional susceptibility and irritability" contribute to creative expression and "[c]onsequently, aggressive behaviors may modulate creative performance by inducing an emotional state with negative valence or high level of arousal" (Lubart, Mouchiroud, Zenasni, & Averill, 2004, p. 148). To be creative one must have the aggressive will to break away from conformity, to take contraindicative, even destructive risks. Some who are constructively creative do so because of a burning need to express themselves; they are not looking for praise and criticism from others, but rather do so only to satisfy their own needs (Rogers, 1954). Yet such ego-driven tasks are still presented within a social context, at risk of being accepted or rejected. As an extension of the artist, this translates into acceptance or rejection of the person. So while creativity *relies* on the natural propensity toward aggression, it is countered by anxiety and emotional volatility emerging from vulnerability and fear of rejection. Paradoxically, such vulnerability may actually *help* someone perform better in artistically creative tasks (Akinola & Mendes, 2008, p. 8).

Art is what brings the implicit to the explicit through the process of creativity. It seems like these two systems integrate easily in the brain, but how do we translate this to understanding behavior and motivation? This query is particularly interesting when considering the role of creativity and aggression.

In his meta-analysis, Feist (1998) revealed that creative people, particularly artists, were more hostile and impulsive than non-creative people. Indeed, these artists were described as "aggressive, cold, impulsive, antisocial, creative and tough-minded" (p. 299). While seemingly negative traits, Feist understood that such characteristics were actually necessary for creative success. In general, those of the creative type were more likely to turn their energies "inward" and not only accept but revel in their own originality: if questioned or challenged, artists may vehemently defend their creation in what may be perceived as overly defensive ways, even striking out at the offender. Feist believed that, in many cases, "the observed level of hostility in creative people may be a defense of their creations against others who either inadvertently detract from time spent creating or who criticize or misinterpret their . . . novel solution or product [expression]" (p. 300).

MacKinnon echoed this in his 1962 address at Yale University

> Creative students [*note*: read people] will not always be to our liking. This will be due not only to their independence in situations in which nonconformity may be seriously disruptive . . . but because . . . more than most they will be experiencing large quantities of tension produced in them by the richness of their experience and the strong opposites of their nature . . . they will often show psychic turbulence. (p. 494)

Such turbulence is at risk of becoming a perpetual cycle: an aggressive drive emerges from vulnerability and fear of rejection, leading to creative expression which, when rejected or misunderstood, may lead to further aggression. The cycle begins anew.

It is for these reasons that creativity has long been linked to aggression and aggressive manifestations (Lubart et al., 2004) and why Dissanayake argued "the impulse that drives some people to violence are the same impulses that drive the artist to create" (1988, p. 140).

However, the converse is true as well. While aggression and violence may feed creativity, creative and artistic expression can assuage, contain, and redirect aggressive and violent impulses. The following section examines various theoretical constructs that argue how creative expression helps mitigate aggressive and violent energy.

Art Turns Aside Aggression: Various Theoretical Perspectives

Paralleling the theoretical orientations that help explain violent expression in Chapter 1, this section examines briefly how neurological/biological, psychodynamic, and cognitive-behavioral theories help explain how art helps turn aside violence. This will culminate with an overview of the social interaction theory that relies on—and stands alone among—these various theoretical perspectives.

Neurological and Neurobiological Considerations

Art and art making can be a reflection—a mirror—of brain operations.[1] As Lusebrink pointed out "the most elementary expressive forms may reflect

[1] Special appreciation for Juliet King, ATR-BC, an expert in the neurological considerations of art therapy, who spent a great deal of time with me in developing this section.

underlying brain structures" (2004, p. 133). This concept is essentially isomorphic in that what we create has similar properties to what is on the inside—it just looks differently. Zaidel (2010, 2014) relied on creativity and art making as a means to understand various neurological functioning. She eventually recognized that engaging in art making is much more complex than other forms of expression—such as through verbal language. As a result, it is mapped throughout the brain, relying on the interactions and simultaneous processing of many neurological regions. Dietrich (2017) supported this, stating that there is no cohesive entity of creativity in the brain, and it cannot be considered as one certain thing. Creativity is an interaction between explicit and implicit system processing, and there is a significant challenge to understanding the neural basis of cognitive processes because the concepts become too amorphous and unwieldy to measure.

Dietrich and Kanso (2010) indicated in their extensive meta-analysis that it is extremely difficult and complex to reveal creativity's effect on various neural functioning through brain imaging. Yet, clearly, "[i]mage-making . . . consists of many different types of brain processes" (Belkofer, Van Hecke, & Konopka, 2014, p. 62), and some art therapists have been able to specifically reveal the effects of creativity on various brain areas (Belkofer & Konopka, 2008; Bhattacharya & Petsche, 2002, 2005; Pike, 2013; Stallings, 2010).

The majority of studies that explore creativity and the brain are found in the literature on *neuroaesthetics*. The use of *quantitative electroencephalography* (qEEG) as a viable method of clarifying our understanding of creativity and correlated brain function holds great promise (King et al., 2017).

In particular, Belkofer, Van Hecke, and Konopka (2014), relying on a qEEG, discovered that drawing demonstrated a significant effect on alpha activity in various regions of the brain. In addition, "Kruk (submitted) utilized the EEG as a tool to study the impact of several art materials on various areas of the brain during the art-making process. Using healthy adult women as participants, the data indicated that the lateral frontal and parietal lobes, mostly in the right hemisphere, were activated during art-making" (King, 2016a, p. 83).

Konopka reminded us that the processes of the brain are not distinguished when taking into consideration scientific invention and artistic activity (King, 2016a, 2016b). Taking this to its logical conclusion, if we can map the areas and the biological/neurological functions affected by art and art making, art therapists can take advantage of this and instigate desirable neurological and biological change.

As King pointed out,

> Conscious and unconscious mental activity, mind–body connectedness, the use of mental and visual imagery, bilateral stimulation, and communication between the limbic system and cerebral cortex functioning underscore

> and illuminate the healing benefits of art therapy—none of which could take place without the flexibility of neuronal processes, otherwise known as neuroplasticity. (2016a, p. 78)

Haas-Cohen and Findlay (2015) stressed that art both expresses and relies on the interrelationships between emotional expression, cognitive processing, and active engagement; as such, art making can activate "integrated change across brain areas, contributing to a sense of hope, well-being, flexibility, stability and overall wellness" (p. 371). In capturing measurements of brain activities with an EEG during an art making process, Belkofer and Konopka (2008) discovered significant differences in neurobiological activities, particularly in the alpha waves, of those engaged in art making. Later expanded in Belkofer, Van Hecke, and Konopka's 2014 study, such a realization reinforces that altering alpha waves can improve wellness: an increase in alpha rhythm is often associated with improved self-regulation and relaxation, among other things. Yet, no surprise, this is also tricky: although increased alpha wave activity has been correlated with healing physiological responses, even the most evolved neurologist can only venture a guess as to why this is and where the alpha actually "comes from" (King, personal communication, March 2018).

Franklin (2010) recognized that the mirror neuron system best explained how certain art tasks assisted with emotional regulation and interpersonal relatedness. In so doing, he developed a rationale for the importance of responsive art making as a mentalizing process that establishes relational change through interaction. His clinical vignette illustrated how the art response as a method of communication can be used when words have been unavailable, particularly in conditions of high affect arousal and avoidant attachment patterns.

Using nodal sessions in the case of a profoundly traumatized woman as an illustrative foundation, Buk's paper on the mirror neuron system explored the mutative actions of art making (2009). The efficacy of art-based interventions, which range from subtle to active, is supported by current research in the fields of neurobiology, infant development, cognitive science, and psychoanalysis. Focus is given to the continuum of dissociation as a survival response to overwhelming trauma, the relationship of dissociative processes to implicit memory, the mirror neuron system, and embodied simulation. In this manner, sensitivity to the impact of trauma and dissociation on the survivor can be harnessed to promote the healing process.

Researchers (Gantt & Tripp, 2016; Haas Cohen & Findlay, 2015; Tripp, 2016), recognizing the natural synthesis of applying a neuroscientific framework with direct practice and research, have been able to demonstrate that those who rely on art making as an intervention have been able to (1) facilitate the organization and integration of traumatic memories, (2) reactivate positive emotions and serve as a vehicle for exposure and externalization of difficult content, (3) reduce heightened arousal responses, (4) enhance emotional self-efficacy and maintain a space for the exploration of self-perception and psychic integration, and (5) enhance the development of identity (King, 2016a, 2016b).

In other words, improving cognitive function by understanding and identifying the areas of the brain affected through the art process is a common goal of those who work with people with brain injuries. Incorporating a neuropsychological perspective of neurodegenerative illness provides a more in-depth understanding of what the client is experiencing and a context for behavioral and emotional changes. Art making can help address and exercise areas of the brain that are functioning well and increase quality of life through self-expression and sensory stimulation (Stewart, 2004). Taken to its logical conclusion, promoting art-making may provide neurological relief from anxiety, hypervigilance, and impulsivity, often precursors to violent and aggressive acting out.

Other biological markers signifying change in mood, control, and impulse have revealed the interventions that art making can have. Recent studies reveal the benefits art making has on reducing cortisol levels, biological markers that indicate dysfunctional stress levels (Kaimal, Ray, & Muniz, 2016), and helping to propagate positive affect (Cela-Conde et al., 2004). In addition, studies recognize art's influence on dopamine centers (Ishizu & Zeki, 2011): "dopamine functions seem intrinsic to many of the activities and outcomes in art therapy" (Carr, 2008, p. 82). Creating art is also thought to be instrumental in boosting one's serotonin level (Phillips, 2015). Both dopamine and serotonin contribute to regulating mood and social behavior, which, when effective, could in turn mitigate destructive and impulsive behavior.

While some have speculated that art making can help create new neurological pathways that may help alleviate aggressive and violent tendencies, some have relied on the psychodynamic understanding of art making as a means of sublimating violence.

Psychodynamically Transforming Aggression

Freud proposed that creativity relied on aggression as a force that has been sublimated into socially productive endeavors, including artistic expression. In this manner, destructive catharsis can be transformed into socially productive art forms (Gay, 1989).

Catharsis is a primitive release, a purging of undesirable emotions. Freud likened it to hydraulics, believing that repressed feelings and frustrations would ultimately burst, causing an angry explosion and offering a temporary relief (Bushman, Baumeister, & Stack, 1999; Wegman, 1985). Lorenz postulated that a more gradual, controlled release of the pent-up energy is much more effective—and healthy—than allowing it to build up until it explodes. At one time, venting such frustrations and anger through hitting a punching bag or yelling into a pillow may have been considered useful. However, it is now recognized that not only is such cathartic action merely a short-term solution, but it may in fact propagate future violent expression (Bushman et al., 1999).

Sublimation, on the other hand, is a more mature, secondary process. It transforms primitive urges into more complex acts that do not serve direct, instant gratification. This process requires the displacement of the volatile energy onto a new task and a way to symbolize this energy into a new expressive form. In doing so, it identifies and, in turn, neutralizes the driving energy—the aggression—by integrating it into an act that is socially productive. In this manner, art making can be used to sublimate this energy, acting as the mechanism that can gradually release the pressure from the ever-expanding balloon.

Providing an opportunity for art making, sublimation can be induced. In doing so, a threefold change can occur in the potential aggressor:

- A new object is identified on which the person's interest now centers; no longer is it a person or object, but instead all of the energy is focused onto the art making
- A new social and productive goal is recognized
- A focused, less-impulsive energy is used through which this goal is attained (Kramer, 1971/1993)

While one street gang member may destroy personal property or harm others, another, such as Rick, may choose to focus on creating colorful graffiti on walls, reinforcing his or her own identity and territory. While not altogether acceptable, some would argue that such a process is much more productive, requiring rechanneled, displaced, and integrated energy.

Jung also believed in art's ability to bring one's subconscious forward. Even more significant, he believed that art can simultaneously provide an opportunity for someone to symbolically identify the "shadow," providing a mechanism for controlling the uncontrolled. He also believed that art making served as a mechanism for focus, calm, and centering, concepts antithetical to aggression. The *mandala*, a circle that represents a symbol of self, has also been employed to contain volatility. Swan-Foster recognized that creating mandalas may allow for containment of "challenging psychic energy" (2016, p. 177). In one case, a series of aggressive male prison inmates were directed to complete mandalas for the direct purpose of holding their aggressive and anxious energy (Figure I.1).

As the previous section underscored, a slight to the false self that emerges from a poor object relationship is put forth for survival. If the compensating

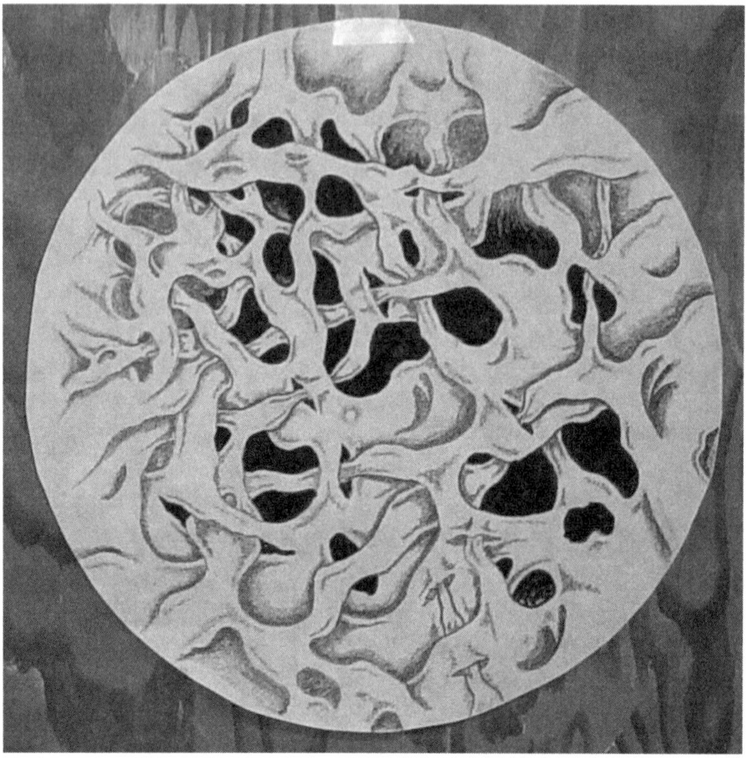

Figure I.1 *Mandala*. Pencil on paper.

narcissism is confronted or the false self is threatened by others' oppositions, a narcissistic injury may occur. This can lead to a potentially volatile and violent response, causing even further repulsion and rejection, thus perpetuating this cycle. Art making can help alleviate or even fully interrupt this. This is similar to MacKinnon's (1962) proposed cyclical relationship cited earlier, except that now acceptance and validation of the art can help halt the aggression cycle rather than propagate it.

While not likely to eliminate or even diminish narcissistic tendencies, creating art can redirect them. "Narcissistic investment in an art product, which in turn is then reinforced by others, can help the client to individuate, develop a true identity, to separate from the need to have his exhibitionistic yearnings confirmed in an archaic (infantile) fashion" (Chapin, 2016, p. 36). Eventually, external validation gives way to internal satisfaction. If the artwork produced is recognized as an extension of the person's self, and if received with care and respect, reparation of the fragile ego may begin. As the acceptance of the art becomes internalized, the person's identity relies less on external validation and more on internal strength, lessening the risk of a narcissistic injury or challenge to the constructed identity. This might eventually reduce the chance that the person will act out when challenged. In other words, accept the art, validate the person, and the ego becomes stronger and less reactive to challenges.

While the psychodynamic understanding of the benefits of art making on aggression might be seen as somewhat esoteric, cognitive-behavioral understanding of art on impulsive behaviors is seen as more pragmatic.

Cognitively and Behaviorally Redirecting Violence

As has already been made clear, there are many ways in which cognitive-behavioral interventions can interrupt the aggression/violence cycle. Rosal (2016, 2019) stressed that offering various art materials and encouraging certain forms of artistic expression can facilitate problem-solving (Packard, 1977), modeling (Roth, 1978; Rozum, 2001), relaxation techniques and mental imagery (Lusebrink, 1990; Rosal, 1986, 1993, 2019), stress reduction (Lusebrink, 1990), and systematic desensitization and/or flooding (De Francisco, 1983; Gerber, 1994; Matto, 1997; Reynolds, 1999). In each of these instances, art making substitutes or supplements the verbal processing used to intervene in each of these methods.

For example, De Francisco (1983) and Gerber (1994) relayed how they were successful in systematically desensitizing children to their fears by slowly exposing them to images related to that which they feared. Another method might include having people draw that which they fear, providing a sense of mastery and control. Recreating mental imagery through drawing and painting might also provide an opportunity for someone to rearrange their memories and alter the sequence of events by

> adding or eliminating aspects of the drawn image to make it less onerous or threatening. Creating images of tough events step by step can expose areas where the child can make changes to a cycle of aggression or offending behavior.
>
> For example, drawings of "before," "during," and "after" an argument can be enlightening. (Rosal, 2019, p. 98)

In essence, the art process provides a tangible reflection of the artist's thought processes. Once put down on paper or canvas, the artist might then have an opportunity to master, gain control over, or change the cognitive processes that are troubling or inducing aggressive and violent reactions.

Breiner, Tuomisto, Bouyea, Gussak, and Aufderheide (2011) demonstrated that certain art making tasks were instrumental in strengthening anger management skills and decreasing aggressive and violent expression in prison inmates. By visually mapping out problem-solving strategies and pictorially clarifying various emotional responses and dysfunctional thinking, participants eventually demonstrated less impulsive and emotional responses.

One art directive in particular was instrumental in illustrating the cognitive processes and dysfunctional thinking that resulted in aggressive reactions. A group of prison inmates was instructed to create a "vehicle that could move on land using [only] these two materials." These symbolized each inmate's thoughts and beliefs that led them to anger. After creating a vehicle that could travel on land, the inmates were instructed to make changes so it could float or fly, allowing it to take an alternate path. Making changes to the vehicle served as a metaphor for changing thoughts and beliefs in order to reach a better emotional consequence. That was their alternate path (Figure I.2).

Tuomisto (2014) recounted that

> I believed the inmates would struggle and become quite frustrated. While some of [them] did struggle, I was surprised to find several of them engaged. . . . The room became quiet; their intense focus was not anticipated as they made detailed and intricate vehicles. . . . Adding the art directives to correspond with the anger management curriculum helped make sense of the concepts, provided a visual metaphor and allowed the participants to experience and see the benefit

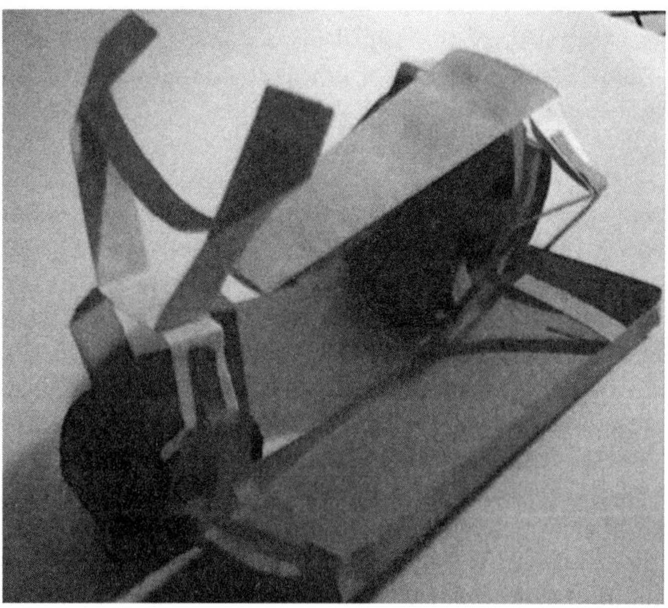

Figure I.2 *Motorcycle, with a Flotation Device.* Construction paper.

> of using the anger management techniques right there in session. Additionally, it created a space for the inmates to feel freer to express themselves and feel safer in connecting with one another. (para 15–16)

Clearly, this was not a directive that focused on making good art. This final piece is crude, primitive, and hard to identify, even after the viewer knows what it is. That is beside the point. It was the process of creative problem-solving in such a tangible manner that provided support for aggressive prison inmates to respond to various triggers in a much more productive and safe fashion.

Redirecting the Locus

Literature bears out that prison inmates are more likely to have an external—rather than an internal—locus of control (LOC; Griffith, Pennington-Averett & Bryan, 1981; Hunter, 1994; Love, 1991). LOC refers to the degree of control that someone feels they have over their environment; if one has a predominantly external LOC, one demonstrates more of a tendency to believe that outside forces control one's behavior; internal LOC indicates a stronger internal control (Bayse, Allgood, & van Wyk, 1992).

Österman, Björkqvist, Lagerspetz, Charpentier, Caprara, and Pastorelli (1999) examined the relationship between locus of control and three types of aggression: physical, verbal, and indirect, in both boys and girls. "In the case of boys, all three kinds of aggression correlated significantly with external locus of control. . . . When both sexes were aggregated in the analysis, external locus of control correlated significantly with all three types of aggression, but significantly higher with physical than with indirect aggression" (p. 61). Romi and Itzkowitz (1990) discovered that boys with a strong internal LOC demonstrated *positive* aggression (as a drive), while those with a strong external LOC demonstrated *negative* or *destructive* aggression. Storms and Spector (1987) found that individuals with a greater external LOC were more likely to engage in physically aggressive behaviors, such as property damage, than those with an internal LOC. Breet, Myburgh, and Poggenpoel, in their 2010, study further supported that "boys with an internal locus of control are significantly and substantially less aggressive than boys with an external locus of control with respect to physical, verbal, and indirect aggression" (p. 522). Such a correlation seems to emerge from common sense—those with an external LOC will feel that they have less control over their environment and take less responsibility for their actions.

Those with a greater internal LOC, although perhaps feeling angry and aggressive, would have greater control over their emotions, situation, and responses and be less impulsive in their reaction. Wallace, Barry, Zeigler-Hill, and Green

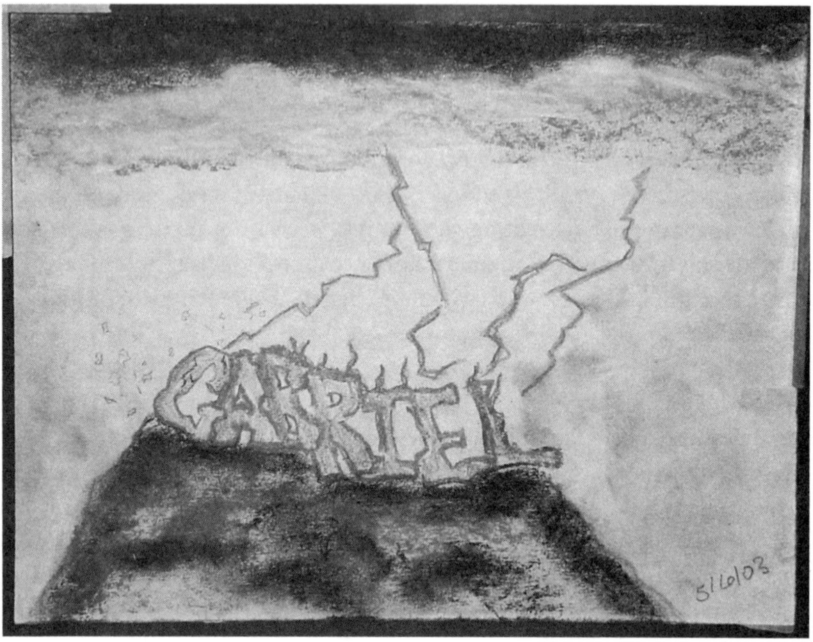

Figure I.3 *Name Embellishment.* Pastel on paper.

(2012) also recognized that "LOC moderated the association between self-esteem and aggression such that low self-esteem was associated with higher levels of aggression for individuals with an external LOC" (p. 213).

In studies conducted in prison to ascertain the effects that art making had on the LOC of male and female prisoners, the participants were encouraged to use a variety of art materials and were provided various directives for 15 meetings (Gussak, 2009a). These included simple directives such as name embellishments (Figure I.3), progressing into more deceptively complicated art tasks like white paper sculptures (Figure I.4). These culminated in large group projects that took several sessions to complete, such as creating a Dream Environment (Figure I.5). Pre and post psychological assessments were administered.

The results demonstrated a statistically significant change in score from external to internal LOC in both the men's and women's experimental groups as compared to the control groups. This led to the appropriate conclusion that the art making was indeed instrumental in the changes and ostensibly developed more control. It was speculated that as the participants learned to manipulate the provided art materials, learned more, and succeeded in accomplishing more intricate and complicated artistic processes, the success was internalized. In essence, the art making provided the participants an opportunity to learn to handle

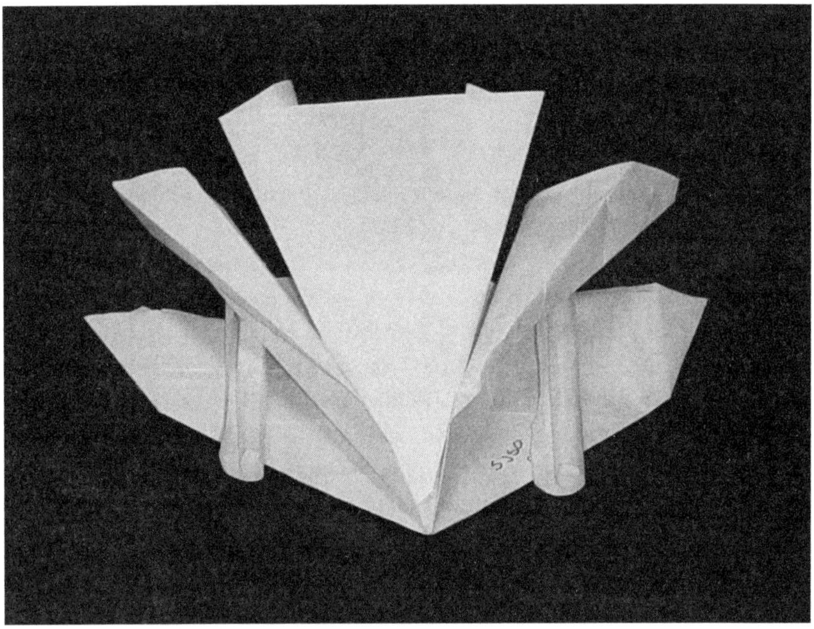

Figure I.4 Anonymous. *White Paper Sculpture*. White paper.

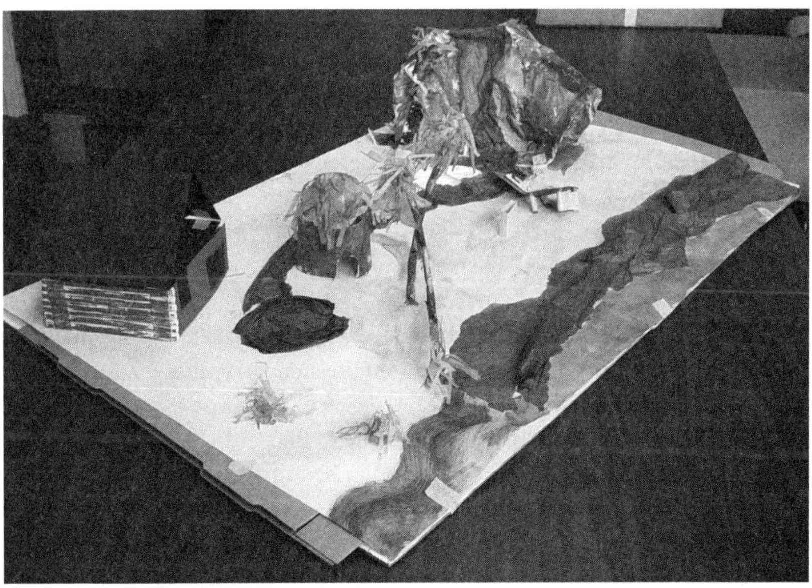

Figure I.5 Prison group art project. *Dream Environment*. Mixed media.

stressful situations while providing them an opportunity for open and accepted expression, decreasing the likelihood of aggressive reactions. Ultimately, "what they learned in the art room may in turn have been generalized to their everyday situations" (p. 10).

Regardless to which theoretical orientations of why art making might turn aside aggression one subscribes, all would agree that aggression and violence do not occur within a social vacuum.

The Art of Social Interaction

As the previous chapter stipulated, aggression is defined, propagated, and maintained through social interaction. Conversely, it is through social interaction that aggression can be redirected or alleviated.

It is through relabeling of people, validating new behaviors and identities, and redefining the actions of those seen as aggressive and violent that such tendencies can be halted and perhaps reversed. The art making process can aid in developing appropriate interactions and decreasing aggressive tendencies.

Interactions occur between people and objects as well as between people, in turn creating new—or reinforcing current—meanings. Meaning is "not intrinsic to the object but arises from how the person is initially prepared to act toward it . . . objects—all objects—are social products in that they are formed and transformed by the defining process that takes place in social interaction" (Blumer, 1969, pp. 68–69). It is through using, sharing, and interpreting the use of these artistic objects that action and interaction are defined. The introduction of art materials to an aggressive client creates a scenario whereby a new interactional pattern begins to occur. By interacting with the art materials and the art product, a person begins to redefine him- or herself. Such redefinitions become internalized and become the new mask in place when interacting with others.

A relationship is established between the artist and those around him or her, either as patrons, audience, or, dare I say it, therapist. They belong to the same "art world," constructed and maintained through the shared conventions of the media (Becker, 1982). Conventions are the shared symbolic meanings between members of a given subculture; they serve to define the parameters of what may very well be a large and diverse field. Becker believed these applied to artists; their subculture is not only comprised of the artists, but of the patrons and viewers as well (Becker, 1982; Gilmore, 1990). Such shared meanings are used to facilitate acceptance, communication, and interaction. Essentially, they link the members of the subculture together, providing an identity, a sense of belonging.

Assisting a person on how to use art materials for self-expression creates a new mode of interaction. Mastery of the materials promotes a new sense of self-worth apart from previously established hostile identities.

Through Rick's drawings, he was accepted and validated, and his concept of his true self was strengthened. He began to see himself as an individual within a productive societal context rather than dependent on an illicit one. His aggressive tendencies diminished. The art and the relationship and new interactions he created through the art making provided an avenue for him to feel valued, provided a means of acceptable expression, and paved a way for him to develop and maintain a new sense of identity. His cycle of violence was interrupted through his art.

Art processes provide a means to interrupt the cycles of violence and aggressive identity by strengthening a sense of self; providing an avenue to express negative emotions such as distress and sadness, which can result in anger and aggression; creating new meanings; and tapping into empathic responses (Gussak, 1997b, 2004a; Gussak, Chapman, Van Duinan, & Rosal, 2003). All those who create consider what the viewer may think of the result. "[I]t is crucial that, by and large, people act with the anticipated reactions of others in mind. This implies that artists create their work, at least in part, by anticipating how other people will respond, emotionally and cognitively, to what they do" (Becker, 1982, p. 200). Even when the artist creates an image with hostile content, he or she may be doing it as a means to "attack" the viewer. However, art is an acceptable way to express hostility. As art making continues, the creator comes to understand that these images, and by extension the self, are accepted. Once the artist feels validated, the images may begin to evolve into more complex and thought-inducing products.

Bringing It Together: The Frenzied Dance

This chapter revealed the interdependent relationship between art and violence. Lubart et al. (2004) underscored aggressive drives as a necessary component to successful creative expression. Feist's meta-analysis revealed the natural propensity for artists—particularly those considered critical successes—toward hostile and impulsive behavior. Far from undesirable, Feist stressed how valuable such characteristics were in their success. Overall, the creative impulse and its products rely on aggressive drives to propel the artist forward into reproducing what MacKinnon saw as "the richness of their experience and the strong opposites of their nature. . . [displaying their] psychic turbulence (1962, p. 494).

The frenzied dance emerges as the aggression feeds creative expression, while, simultaneously, creative and artistic expression mitigates, dissipates, and turns aside the aggression. Regardless of which biological, psychological, or sociological theory is applied, it becomes clear that art making can provide a safe container and an ultimate transformation for the aggressive energy that—if unchecked—may result in violence.

1
Angelic Demons
The Capricious Creators

Particularly sordid personalities often lurk behind captivating works of beauty: "Angels and demons lived side by side in man's soul, locked in a strangely captivating symbiotic relationship" (Lee, 2006, p. 4). The dawning Renaissance is considered to be the birth of unparalleled civility and cultural reawakening throughout Europe (Lee, 2006; Nethersole, 2018; Szalay, 2016). Yet behind the angelic facade of the work that emerged during this proclaimed age of beauty, there lurked decadence, corruption, and wickedness (Nethersole, 2018; Wittkower & Wittkower, 1963/2007).

> Although man did indeed have the capacity to ascend to the heights of heavenly beauty . . . he was also capable of plumbing the ugly depths of depravity. . . . [T]he achievements of the Renaissance coexisted with dark, dirty and even diabolical realities. (Lee, 2006, p. 4)

While Michelangelo was known for creating some of the most heavenly bodies known to the art world, he was just as likely to be "embroiled in fights," exhibiting fits of violent outbursts and explosive rages (Lee, p. 13). So was Torrogiano, a childhood comrade of Michelangelo's and a fine artist in his own right. In a fit of rage, Torrogiano punched Michelangelo so hard he knocked him senseless; this resulted in Michelangelo's signature crooked nose (Lee, 2006; Wittkower & Wittkower, 1963/2007).

Two of the most sublime artists, Botticelli and Donatello, expressed their frustration and anxiety through piques of violence and destruction. Lee (2006) indicated that Donatello, the famed sculptor of the delicate *David*, "smashed a bronze bust to smithereens in frustration" (pp. 75–76) when the bill over a commission was questioned by one of his patrons. When Sandro Botticelli, the artist of the transcendent painting *Birth of Venus*, was disturbed in his workshop by a weaver next door,

> anger took over. Rushing upstairs, [he] balanced a huge stone on the very top of the roof . . . and loudly proclaimed that it would fall unless the shaking stopped.

> Terrified of being crushed to death, the poor weaver had no option but to come to terms. (Lee, 2006, p. 78)

Their works were delicate, transcendent, and inspirational, hardly what one would expect from impulsive and volatile brutes. Yet these artists serve as early examples of the embodiment of the interrelationship between art and violence—the choreographed give and take that underscores how aggression feeds the creative impulse while simultaneously providing a means to mitigate, contain, or set aside violence. Where this drive comes from is not always consistent; they may emerge as responses to uncontrollable events or they may rise from the reduction of inhibitions through drugs or alcohol. It may stem from an artist's easily injurious narcissistic superiority and grandiosity. In rare cases, such impulsivity may be a by-product of a mental illness. Even still, their proclivities did not occur in a vacuum: in many cases, they were further informed, driven, and even encouraged by the social and political contexts of the times in which they lived and created. Regardless whence the aggression and violence derives, the artists' creativity seems to be fed from such libidinal and primitive impulses, which can, in turn, mitigate the destructive drives. Simultaneously, their art may have resulted from their need to cathart, sublimate, or contain their aggressive inclinations.

Indeed, the volatile and hot-tempered artist was certainly not a sole product of days long past. For example, contemporary minimalist Carl Andre was tried for the alleged brutal murder of fellow artist and girlfriend Ana Mendieta, in 1985. Although acquitted of these charges, he has since been skewered by many members of the court of public opinion, which includes members of the New York artist community; to them, it was not out of the realm of possibility that he had committed such an act. Andre apparently had a well-earned reputation for violence and an impulsive temper. As recently as 2020, actress Ellen Barkin publicly recounted the time Andre assaulted her more than 40 years before, shoving her against a wall and picking her up off the floor by her neck.

For this chapter, I have chosen several distinctive artists from various points in history, each embedded within his own social and political context and representing very different artistic eras. The works of Caravaggio, Cellini, Dali, Modigliani, Pollock, and Dadd are very different from each other. Nevertheless these artists are all recognized for their extraordinary and profound products. Yet each artist had his own underlying demons, and therefore all were chosen for this chapter to illustrate specific prototypes—almost archetypes—of the violent artist.

In addition, the six artists chosen could further be divided between two typologies. There are those whose violent energy and creative endeavors emerge from their narcissistic rage and aggressive grandiosity: this included Caravaggio, Cellini, and Dali. Then there are those whose locus of control was externalized and their violent and aggressive impulses emerged through the compromise of their cognitive and neurobiological abilities through drug use, alcohol abuse, or mental illness: this included Modigliani, Pollock, and Dadd.

The Violently Narcissistic Artist

The Introduction proposed that some violence emerged through pathological rage in response to a challenge to one's compensatory grandiosity and narcissism. An idealized, self-aggrandizing false self is developed when the true self is neither loved nor accepted—essentially, when this false self is rejected by others (Winnicott, 1965, 1971). Eventually a person is likely rejected by others for these narcissistic displays, causing further anger and resultant hostility which can often turn to violence. There may also develop a neurotic need for power, social recognition, admiration, and achievement to offset the rejection of the true self (Horney, 1945/1992). Such grasps for power and social dominance are often accompanied by strength and aggressive overreach. It bears repeating that while creating art may not likely eliminate nor even diminish narcissistic tendencies, it can redirect them and minimize violent reactions. In many cases, artists do not eliminate their narcissism; instead, they transform it into something productive for both the artist and, potentially, society (Kohut, 1971; Rangell, 1978).

The following three artists are examples of those who maintained grandiose and superior personas, turning to aggression and violence to dominate those whom they thought lesser. In some cases, the art provided a container for their grandiosity, a validation for their superiority, and it granted them their social recognition and admiration. Seemingly, these artists' creative endeavors emerged from the same narcissistic drives that fed their violent natures. Thus, while creating art did not necessarily diminish their self-aggrandizement, it did provide a focus for it.

Caravaggio: Putting the "Oscuro" into "Chiaroscuro"

The celebrated Italian Baroque artist Michelangelo Mersi de Caravaggio (1571–1610) was recognized as one of the "most important artistic innovator[s] of the seventeenth century" (Shoham, 1999, p. 81). Through his use of light and shadow, he created some of the world's most dramatic and powerful paintings. As Lambert stressed, Caravaggio "put the oscuro (shadows) into chiaroscuro" (Lambert, 2000, p. 8). Perhaps, upon closer examination, this quote may seem somewhat ominous because Caravaggio's dark side often overshadowed his light.

Born in 1571, in Milan, Caravaggio's parents moved him 5 years later to Caravaggio, Italy to escape the plague. A year later his father and grandfather died, followed by his mother in 1584. Orphaned at 12 years old, Caravaggio was apprenticed to the painter Peterzano, one of Titian's students. After wounding a police officer in 1592 during a melee, the artist fled to Rome. He continued to perfect his painting style while there, and, from 1600 to 1606, he became one of Rome's most famous and celebrated artists.

Well known by some was his predilection for violent and impulsive tendencies. A few early historians countered that his violent and aggressive tendencies may be somewhat exaggerated (Carrier, 1987; Wittkower & Wittkower, 1969/2007) and that his detailed and meticulous paintings belie such an impulsive streak (Hibbard, 1983). However, later sources confidently recount his explosive behavior, sexual promiscuity, and violent attacks without question (Drummond, 2006; Graham-Dixon, 2010; Shoham, 1999; Szajnberg, 2012), considering such behavior well beyond the norms of the time. Even within "the associations of the term 'Baroque' with high drama and darkness," Caravaggio's actions were still considered transcendentally violent and aggressive (Loughery, 2002, p. 294). "He had the psychopathic trait of ever looking for stimuli, be they creative or merely sensation-rousing. He would throw stones at his landlady, hurl artichokes at a waiter, and fight a notary . . . over the amorous attention of a woman" (Shoham, 1999, p. 67).

Graham-Dixon believed that his troublesome behavior was a direct consequence of the early loss of his parents. As a result, he would often fall out of favor with those who championed him: "It's almost like he cannot avoid transgressing. As soon as he's welcomed by authority, welcomed by the Pope, welcomed by the Knights of Malta, he has to do something to screw it up. It's almost like a fatal flaw" (Brown, 2011, para. 13).

Eventually, Caravaggio's impulses led him to murder. The exact details of this act had until recently remained vague "and the only known accounts of the murder were those given by [his] three principal biographers" (Graham-Dixon, 2010, p. 313). What they all agreed upon is that Caravaggio gravely wounded a gentleman named Tomassoni in a duel believed to have been arranged after Caravaggio was discovered sleeping with Tomassoni's wife.

While the duel initially progressed in a structured fashion, it deteriorated into a sword-driven brawl. Caravaggio was injured but still managed to elicit the death blow onto Tomassoni, thrusting the sword through his thigh, slicing the femoral artery. The surgeon was unable to stop the bleeding and Tomassoni eventually succumbed to his wound. In the confusing aftermath, Caravaggio fled.

Caravaggio was given a "capital sentence," with a bounty on his head. In 1610, he left Naples by boat to return to Rome, hoping to receive a papal pardon. Before getting there, however, he was detained by the local authorities. He resisted and was forcibly restrained and placed in a holding cell. The paintings that he had brought with him were left on the ship that returned to Naples. He eventually bought his way out of jail. However, because of the paintings' value, he needed to retrieve them. He knew where the ship that held these works would be docked next and set off in hot pursuit on horseback. Unfortunately, "the stress of his arrest, and the frantic ride . . . in the extreme heat of July, was more than a man in his condition could take" (Graham-Dixon, p. 432). He died a relatively young man, at the age of 39.

While perhaps hyperbolic, Shoham (1999) stressed that "[his] history of murder, assault and courting violence would shame many a violent psychopath in a contemporary maximum-security prison" (p. 68). Caravaggio's murder of Tomassoni did not occur as a singular incident in the vacuum of an uneventful existence. His entire life was punctuated by impulsive and explosive behavior. Despite the many people who knew about the duel, he failed to take responsibility for it. He believed he was not at fault. He returned to Rome, arrogant enough to believe he deserved a pardon, and this resulted in his own death.

Despite his callousness, murderous actions, and the potential parallels between his own persona and the figures in his works, Caravaggio remains a father and champion of the Baroque movement. "[O]f all the great sinners among artists, only . . . Caravaggio has never found an apologist. It is his conduct, and his conduct alone, that has always been singled out for special attention" (Wittkower & Wittkower, 1963/2007, p. 192). Quite frankly, Caravaggio broke away from what he perceived as the conventional studio training that he found stifling and forged his own artistic path. "It may seem natural enough that . . . a man who would not accept the word of authority but was determined to find out for himself—was the type most likely to find the keys of the future in his hands" (Mahon, 1953, pp. 41–42). He wasn't a product of his artistic time—he helped shape a new one. To do so required an aggressive, at times violent and narcissistic persona, to rise above the limitations of the art world that came before; his zeal and confidence knew no bounds.

His work is meticulously detailed, with an eye toward the profane and dramatic. While some artists chose to "minimize the effects of violence, Caravaggio's [volatility] drove him on . . . to produce some of the most *terrible* paintings in all European art" (Fried, 1997, p. 29). And why not? Caravaggio was simply projecting what he believed, that "when people are together, they are together intensely and often with murderousness enacted or in the air" (Szajnberg, 2012, p. 322). Yet, rather than disparage or demonize these passionate and horrid interactions between people through the proliferation of violent scenes enacted on his canvases, Caravaggio managed to elevate the seemingly antithetical mundaneness and profanity into an aesthetic—and at times, divine—loftiness.

Nevertheless, there still seems to remain a disconnect between the horrific drama in his works and the banal responses of the paintings' antagonistic subjects. Despite the violence and carnage depicted in many of his most celebrated pieces, the figures come across as aloof, as if the characters were simply going through the violent motions. There seems to exist an emotional gap between the characters in the paintings and the paintings and their viewers, seemingly reinforcing a sociopathic distance between Caravaggio and his patrons. There exists a "double or divided relationship between painter and painting—at once immersive and spectacular, continuous and discontinuous, prior to the act of viewing and thematizing that act with unprecedented violence—lies at the core of much of Caravaggio's art" (Fried, 1997, p. 22). This, then, reinforces the distance between the artist and the viewer.

The beheading of the giant Goliath by the soon-to-be King David was a favorite theme for Caravaggio. Figure 1.1, *David Victorious Over Goliath*, provides a glimpse of the aftermath, when David successfully slew the giant. Although we cannot see David's face, he is captured as a child-like, almost innocent figure. The dramatic and bloody carnage belies the almost calm and restrained David. Compare this to *Judith Beheading Holofernes*, where the women conducting this most egregious act seem minimally affected by their own violent action. Yet we are forced to bear witness to such horror. The figures are turned away, putting the viewer in the role of a voyeur happening upon a scene that we are compelled to watch. What both of these images capture are the horrific expressions of the victim as contrasted with the slick detachment of the perpetrators. Yet we, the viewer, are forced to watch.

> Caravaggio's bold representations of both negative and positive feelings, including ambivalence and moments of ambiguity about feelings, demands the viewer approach, feel moments of identity or uncertainty, and think harder about these works . . . David's somber look; the absence of wrath, disgust, or victory in Judith's moment of killing the evil Holofernes. (Szajnberg, 2012, p. 327)

The chiaroscuro underscore the drama; the almost *laissez faire* expressions of the executioners almost make it more profane.

In contrast, *Boy Bitten by a Lizard* (1594) (Figure 1.2) seems to depict a comparatively greater emotional range, particularly of horror and disgust. It captures "the fleeting moment in which sharp pain is reflected in the boy's expression" (Longhi, as trans. by Spear, 1985, p. 25) frozen in time (Fried, 1997). The tumultuous reaction is captured by a looser painting style; while the two previously discussed works are carefully rendered, as if he was sculpting with paint, *Boy* captures a great deal more energy, an instantaneously violent action in

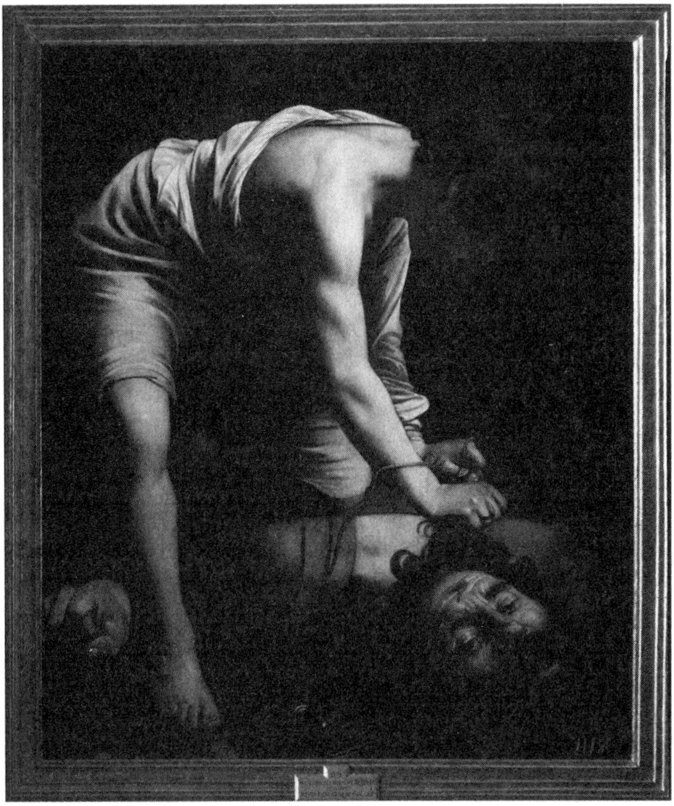

Figure 1.1 Michelangelo Mersi de Caravaggio (1571–1610). *David Victorious Over Goliath* (c. 1600). Oil on canvas.

Collection of Prado, Madrid, Spain. Reproduction provided by Prado, Madrid, Spain/Luisa Ricciarini/Bridgeman Images.

impression and in deed. Even still, it is an awkward depiction. The irony here is that a painting of a boy bitten by a lizard seems to be much more expressive than one capturing decapitation.

While less innocuous at first glance, even the whimsical painting *The Cardsharps* reflects a callous response to a dastardly, and likely punishable, act. The slick work depicts an innocent-faced boy about to dupe an opponent by sneaking in a winning card from his garment. Staged dramatically between three intimate figures, once again the viewers—or voyeurs—are happening upon an illicit act for which no intervention is possible—none of the figures engages the audience.

Throughout these images, Caravaggio seemed to rely on light and shadow to capture the severity of the scene—the darker the painting, the darker the act.

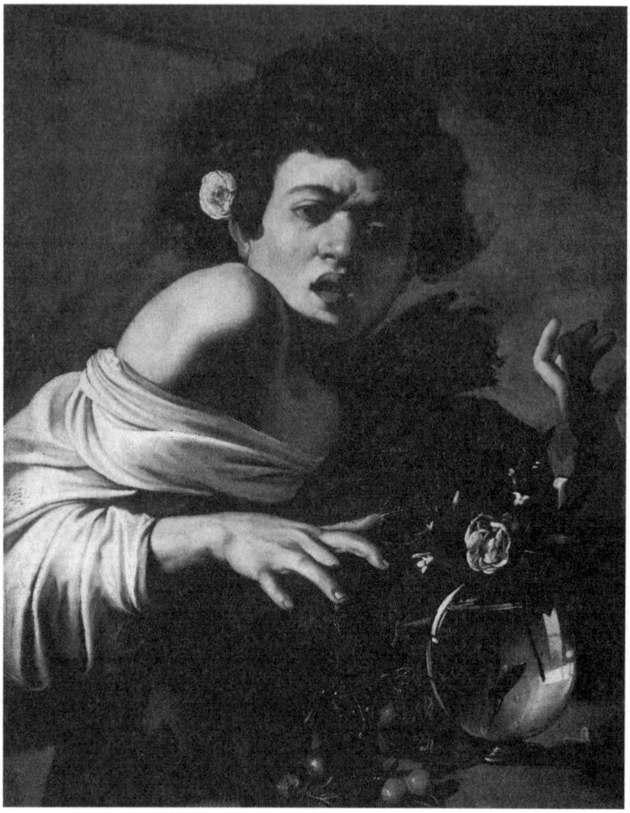

Figure 1.2 Michelangelo Mersi de Caravaggio (1571–1610). *Boy Bitten by a Lizard* (1596–1597). Oil on canvas.

Collection of Roberto Longhi Foundation, Florence, Italy. Reproduction provided by Roberto Longhi Foundation, Florence, Tuscany, Italy/Bridgeman Images.

Yet, even still, despite the excessive range of dramatic and violent depictions, his work embodies a certain detachment. Perhaps that accounts for the popularity of his works during his short life. His paintings reflected a complex combination of intense emotional representation and ambivalence, seemingly an indifference in the face of death and decay (Szajnberg, 2012). In a time when the Black Plague was still a recent memory, life was interwoven with horrific loss, and only in indifference, apathy and ambiguity can we reckon it; Caravaggio's esteem in his own time may have emerged from his ability to find and convey this fine balance. Furthermore, only someone as self-aggrandized as he would take the risk of capturing this abstruse dynamic (Mahon, 1953).

Indeed, it was his aggressive and narcissistic persona that, while his undoing, was also his salvation. For who else could rechannel this energy to break away from the conventional and forge a new direction—and, in doing so, capture the mundane and profane within a singular, sublime frame?

Caravaggio's depravities and narcissistic reactions to his narcissistic injuries have been documented by various historians and have become part of his myth. But his actions and narcissistic grandiosity paled in comparison to one other. A century before, there existed an artist whose grandiosity and narcissism led him to not only heightened wickedness, debauchery, and violence that far exceeded even the wicked environ for which the Renaissance was later recognized (Nethersole, 2018; Wittkower & Wittkower, 1963/2007) but also compelled him to boast about it in an autobiography. This autobiography provides

> [a] fascinating picture—this of the artist life in Rome and Florence amid the polished rudeness of an awakening people, full of enthusiasm, vivacity, and simple credulity, all seen through the eyes of a man in full sympathy with it, keenly alive and on the alert for everything life had to offer, a man of violent passions, hot-headed, sensual. . . . A man who breathes the spirit of the most fascinating of all periods in history, the Italian Renaissance. (Pyle, 1913, p. 235)

This was Benvenuto Cellini.

Cellini: *My [Sociopathic] Life*

Born in 1500, in Florence, Benvenuto Cellini, despite his parents' attempts to push him toward music, became one of the "greatest silver and goldsmiths the world had ever seen" (Collinson, 2010, para. 5). At 15 years of age, Cellini was apprenticed to the jeweler Marcone. Over the ensuing years, he traveled and lived throughout Italy and France before returning to Florence where he became the preeminent sculptor and jewelry maker of the sixteenth century. Consistent with Caravaggio, Cellini was known for his profane, deviant, and violent behavior as much as he was known for his art. Unlike Caravaggio, his transgressions were made known through his own admission, meticulously and painstakingly detailed in his autobiography *My Life*. This book was an unexpected juxtaposition of self-championship of his self-described genius and magnificent artistry with his wicked behavior. Cellini was certainly aware of how unusual it was to write about himself; he acknowledged this through his obviously insincere humility.

> All men of any condition who have done something of special worth or something that may truly resemble those things of special merit should, if they are truthful and good people, write in their own hands the story of their lives. (Cellini, 2009, p. 6)

His grandiosity becomes immediately apparent.

In recounting his many vices and foibles, the book's self-proclaimed honesty and greatness are likely exaggerated as some of his boasts seem amplified and self-serving, and his concept of what constitutes greatness is clearly skewed. This book, without reservation, embodies "his overwhelming egoism. To call him conceited is to offer him almost an insult" (Pyle, 1913, p. 235).

The book was dictated sometime between 1558 and 1566 to a teenage boy. As the book inferred, not only was this child his secretary, but also likely a personal sexual conquest. Cellini's depravity, pride, and sense of driven vengeance with little regard for others became notably apparent.

> Cellini regularly kept young women in his home to serve as models. Of one woman, Caterina, he writes: "I keep her in my house chiefly on account of my art—for I must have a model. But since I am a man, I have also kept her for my pleasure; and it may be she will bear me a child." One day, after returning home from "a party of pleasure in a garden" (he attends these frequently), Cellini discovers that Caterina has been sleeping with one of his assistants. He restrains himself, barely, from executing them on the spot, and instead devises a more intricate act of vengeance. First he forces the two traitors, at dagger-point, to marry each other. Then he rehires Caterina as a model for a fee she can't refuse. He makes her pose naked in uncomfortable positions for many hours on end; after this he beats her, and they have sex again. "I am wreaking a double vengeance," writes Cellini . . . . "For she is now a wife; and therefore I do him a more serious injury than he did me when she was a mere hussy in my house . . . not only have I the sweets of revenge, but I get both credit and profit out of her beauty as a model. And what more can I desire?" (Rich, 2010, para. 6)

Aside from these examples of his grandiosity and narcissistic self-promotion, he was quite impulsive and violent. Once he was arrested after harming two men during a brawl. He was also arrested for the murder of fellow goldsmith Capitaneis (Wittkower & Wittkower, 1963/2007).

Cellini retold the details of this murder with a sense of pride, impulsivity, and grandiose justification rather than remorse. As he recounted, while minding his own business, surrounded by those who "revered" him,

> Pompeo [Capitaneis—the jeweler] happened to pass by, accompanied by ten very well-armed men, and when he was standing directly in front of me, he stopped, as if he wished to pick a fight with me. The friends with me were brave young men and eager to fight, and they motioned for me to put my hand on my sword, which I had immediately thought of doing, except that if I put my hand

> on my sword there might have followed some serious injury to those who had committed no fault in the world. (p. 122)

Capitaneis walked off, mocking Cellini. Cellini insisted that his friends not go after him; after all, he was perfectly capable of fighting his own battles. His friends left in anger. This certainly was not the end of it, and, given Cellini's nature, he confronted Capitaneis again shortly after his friends left.

> Pompeo had gone into the apothecary shop at the corner . . . and stayed there . . . although I was told that he was boasting about the brave way in which he had confronted me. But in any case this turned out to be his bad luck, for just as I arrived at the corner he came out of the shop, and his hired cutthroats opened their ranks for him and then closed up around him. I grabbed a small sharp dagger, forced my way through the line formed by his escort, and grabbed him by the chest with such speed and courage that none could stop me. I aimed at his face, but the fear he felt made him turn it aside, causing me to stab him just under the ear; and after I struck him there only two more times, in an instant he fell down dead. (p. 123)

As the story unfolded, it became clear that he cold-bloodedly waited for the right moment to attack the man that slighted him, killing him without hesitation. Accordingly, the fault lay solely with the victim: it was his own "bad luck" as he turned his face that forced Cellini to deliver the fatal blow. Even after, his first thought following the murder was not of regret; it was coming up with a plan on how his friends could protect him.

Nevertheless, while recognized for his pathological traits (Elliott, 1983; Wittkower & Wittkower, 1963/2007), Cellini still maintained a singular reputation as a respected artist, a friend of popes and royalty, even of Michelangelo. In some respects, his violent and murderous tendencies were not only ignored, they were consciously accepted by some, considered appropriate behavior for the time in which he lived. As Molinier indicated (according to Pyle, 1913) "*au sixième siècle c'est le seul moyen de se faire respecter*" [trans: "In the sixth century it is the only way to be respected"]. Still others realized that even compared to the "lax standards of his time, his conduct was often reprehensible . . . and since he had as little caution as moral restraint his hasty passions got him into trouble" (Pyle, 1913, p. 236).

Along with outlining his depravity and self-aggrandizement, Cellini's *My Life* provided a valuable first-person account of what life was like in Renaissance Italy and detailed the processes he undertook to complete his sculptures and designs. Unfortunately, few of his pieces exist today. The exceptions, such as the cast bronze relief *The Nymph of Fontainebleau* (1542–1544), the bronze sculpture

Perseus with the Head of Medusa (1553), and the gold-cast, enameled *Salt Cellar* (1543) (Figure 1.3), demonstrated amazing skill and attention to detail. While there were marked flaws with his attempts at large-scale sculptures and reliefs, particularly with composition, lack of expression, and unnatural elongation—unacceptable in the time he was creating them—his smaller cast forms were highly lauded (Pyle, 1913).

The *Salt Cellar* is particularly intricate as this tiny piece captures male and female figures—the sea and the earth, respectively—facing each other in recumbent positions. In between sits the small vessel that holds the salt while next to the woman is a small temple in which the pepper sits. These sculptures are clearly labor-intensive; the act of casting bronze with intricate detail requires a great deal of focus, commitment, and precision, in stark contrast to his impulsive and passionate self-proclaimed actions. There is little to no reflection of his violent intensity within these cold metal pieces, yet they did seem to capture the meticulous calculation that underscored his sociopathic persona. These pieces may very

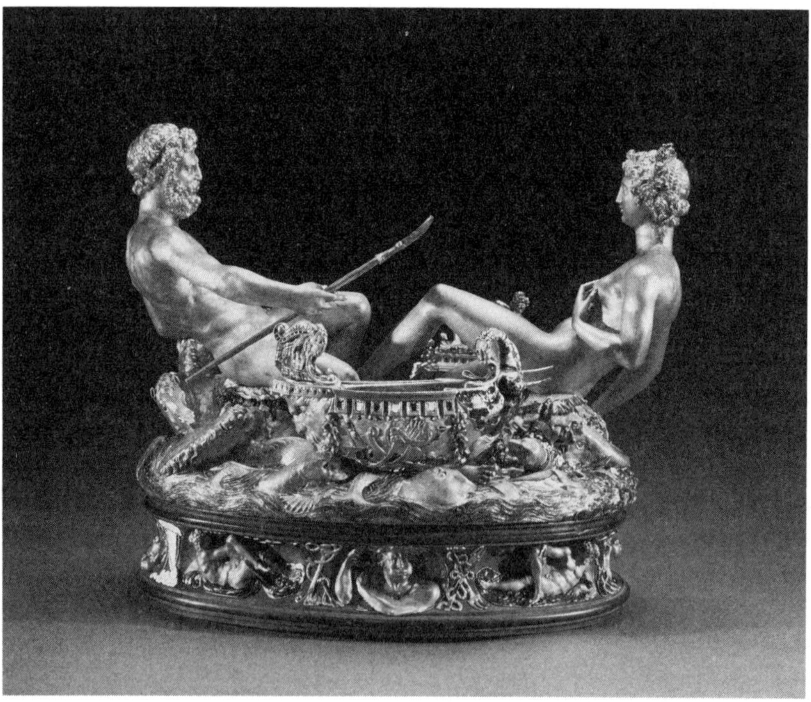

Figure 1.3 Benvenuto Cellini (1500–1671). *Salt Cellar* (1540–1543). Gold and enamel.

Collection of Kunsthistorisches Museum, Vienna, Austria. Reproduction provided by Kunsthistorisches Museum, Vienna, Austria/Bridgeman Images.

well have contained but not captured the fervor of his passions. Still, that could likely be due to the expectations of the medium and the time. Many of his cast forms were created for select patrons, and there would be an expected convention of form and utility (Pyle, 1913).

Little is really known about Cellini except for what he admitted in his own autobiography. As much a self-promotion as it is a confession, it is unclear whether his antics and antisocial tendencies are genuine or exaggerated; his violent and depraved persona may be a myth that was amplified for the sake of notoriety and publicity. Yet others stand by their assertion that Cellini was indeed "a man possessed by intense, absorbing egotism; violent, arrogant, self-assertive, passionate; conscious of great gifts for art, physical courage and physical address" (Symmonds, as cited by Macnab, 1888). Clearly, much can be—and has been—gleaned from his writings to determine the potential genesis and results of his hostility and depravity (Eng, 1956).

Similarly, Salvador Dali's autobiography, *The Secret Life of Salvador Dali*, filled with admissions of violence, depravity, and sexual deviance, was regarded by some as a relevant form of surrealism and rejected by others for its exaggeration and fabrication for self-promotion (Orwell, 1968/2019; Solomon, 1944). Regardless, by all accounts, it was remarkable.

Dali: "A Good Draughtsman But a Disgusting Human Being"

Born Salvador Felipe Jacinto Dalí y Domenech in 1904, in the small town of Figueras, Spain, Salvador Dali went on to become the world's preeminent Surrealist. The Surrealism movement emerged from the paradigm-shifting Dadaism, a decidedly disruptive and metaphorically violent shift away from rational thinking, blamed for the then perceived spiritual crisis that caused global destruction (Hoffman, 1948). Frey (1936) reiterated Bouvier's description of Dada as "a warlike weapon, the point of which was humor, or if you like, an instrument for the demolition of the Old World by means of a dynamite disguised as a simpleton's jest" (p. 12).

Surrealism embraced its predecessors' notions of creating works that served as a reaction against rules and standards associated with previous artistic movements (similar to how Caravaggio was able to forge *his* new path).

> In a series of successive steps, the Dadaists progressed from the simple effort to materialize the disturbing images of the dream-world, to the all-embracing philosophy of *surrealism* with its program of social revolution. Briefly, they passed from a scorn for the commonplace and real, to the exaltation of the unreal and the marvelous, to the belief that the illusory, the fantastic, the dream,

> have an importance and actuality as primary as "reality," to, finally, a desire to fuse the two seemingly contradictory states, dream and reality, into a sort of absolute reality, surreality, so to speak. (Frey, p. 14; emphasis added)

The poet Breton, credited for beginning this shift, wrote in his *Second Manifesto*, "[t]he simplest Surrealist act consists of dashing down into the street, pistol in hand, and firing blindly, as fast as he can pull the trigger, into the crowd" (Eburne, 2008, p. 6). To put an end to *rational* violence, *irrational* violent responses are necessary. From this emerged the art form that embraced the unconscious over the conscious, the absurd over the rational, the dream-like over the reality.

This further metamorphosed into aggressive and violent expressions, a means and opportunity to express what Knafo (2003) dubbed "male perversion" (p. 288). A movement sandwiched between two world wars in which masculine identity was reinforced by strength and anxiety, it was an artistic era punctuated by works depicting misogynistic sexualization and violent compartmentalization of the threatened man's projections. It was here that Dali found a home.

What may be unclear is whether the Surrealism movement was a haven for his already burgeoning violent and narcissistic nature or if it encouraged informed and instilled aggressive inclinations as an expectation for those embracing this group. Regardless, his extreme disposition seemed to exceed even their expected norms. "Dali's daring, exhibitionistic, taboo-breaking flaunting of his anal aggression, oral obsessions, and multiple fetishes 'tested the limits of even the surrealists' broadmindedness'" (Mundy, 2001; as quoted in Knafo, 2003, p. 289). His autobiography proudly flaunted an extremely aggressive and narcissistic persona, one that he thought could not—nor would not—be constrained by the conventions of society.

He had one sister who was 3 years younger; his parents also had another son who died 9 months before Salvador was born. In distress, his parents gave Salvador the same name as his deceased older brother. Dali recalled being taken to the grave of this brother by his parents and told that he was his reincarnation. While his father was a strong disciplinarian, Dali's mother would often temper this with overt permissiveness and generous allowances; by all accounts, he was considered a spoiled child.

Dali began life with great ambition, proclaiming that he desired greatness from the time he was a child. Ultimately, he believed the best way to achieve this was to become one of the world's preeminent artists. His parents encouraged Dali's creative endeavors and enrolled him in drawing classes; he began exploring modern painting by the time he was 12. He had his first public exhibition 2 years later.

At 16 years, Dali's beloved mother died; his widowed father later married his late wife's sister. Dali moved to Madrid 1 year later to continue his art studies. It was here where his fairly eccentric proclivities began to emerge. Simultaneously, his artistic persona began to solidify as he experimented with new and innovative expressions, including Cubism and Dadaism; he held his first solo exhibition in 1925. Shortly before completing his final exams, he left the Academy where he proclaimed to faculty,

> "I am very sorry, but I am infinitely more intelligent than these three professors, and I therefore refuse to be examined by them. I know this subject much too well." As a result of this I was brought before the disciplinary counsel and expelled from the school. (Dali, 1942/1993, p. 17)

Upon leaving, he became even more eccentric. His painting began taking on unusual themes; it was also around this time that Dali expanded into film-making as a form of creative expression.

In 1929, Dali met the woman who would later become his wife, Gala, a Russian immigrant 10 years older than himself. This provoked a strain in his relationship with his domineering and opinionated father, which came to a head after Dali displayed a piece entitled *Sometimes I Spit on My Mother's Portrait.* Threatened with disinheritance, Dali and his father eventually reconciled.

Dali's work began to evolve, and, in 1931, he completed his most famous work, *The Persistence of Memory*, which captured his transition into the Surrealist movement. He traveled the world, exhibited in multiple venues, and befriended many well-known people, including Coco Chanel and Sigmund Freud. When World War II ravaged Europe, Dali and Gala took off for the United States, where he continued to work in a variety of media; along with painting, Dali expressed himself by creating jewelry, furniture, stage settings, and store displays.

Dali and Gala moved back to Spain when the war ended. They lived in Port Lligat for the next 30 years, spending winters in Paris and New York. His work continued to evolve as did his behavior, both becoming more outrageous as he demanded the spotlight.

He bought a castle for Gala, from whom he needed written permission to visit; at this point, his relationship with Gala was tumultuous. He developed parkinsonian-like symptoms at 76 years; it was believed that they developed after his wife gave him unprescribed medication that wreaked havoc on his nervous system (Gibson, 1998).

Over his prolific lifetime, Dali completed thousands of creations, including more than 1,500 paintings, dozens of sculptures, countless drawings, book illustrations, lithographs, and even an animated short film for Disney. After Gala died in 1982, Dali slowly deteriorated, becoming more withdrawn and dispirited. He completed his last painting in 1983 and his last drawing in 1988. He eventually succumbed to heart failure in 1989 at the age of 84.

The public was exposed to his erratic and, at times, promiscuous and violent behavior upon the release of his autobiography in 1944 (Solomon, 1944). Shortly after its release, George Orwell indicated "Dali is a good draughtsman and a disgusting human being" (1968/2019, p. 161). The origin of Orwell's assessment becomes clear as Dali's narcissism and celebration of his own depravity unfolded throughout the book.

Dali provided numerous accounts of his burgeoning aggression, beginning at age 5 when he pushed a friend off a high bridge for no reason; he admitted no remorse. At 6, he deliberately kicked his 3-year-old sister in the head. It was unclear why, and even Dali acknowledged confusion over his ambivalent and ambiguous feelings he held for others. As an example, he indicated that he was overcome with wanting to protect the same sister when a doctor was sent to pierce his little sister's ears; this resulted in Dali whipping the doctor across the face. Simultaneously, he proclaimed he felt true love for this doctor and would deliberately feign illness in order to see him.

As he got older he remained demonstrably fearful and self-protective when attacked by children larger than he, yet he continued to demonstrate a cruel streak with those weaker. He deliberately attacked scrawnier peers when they intruded on his solitude. On one such occasion, not satisfied with merely knocking such a child down, Dali kicked him mercilessly and destroyed the boy's violin for no reason other than to exhibit dominance and sadistic tendencies. Justification for his aggression was underscored when such behavior went unanswered, and he began to revel in his cruel streak. "My unpunished success immediately caused such acts of aggression to assume this endemic character of a real vice which I could no longer forego" (Dali, 1942/1993, p. 120).

As an adolescent, he actively courted girls, showering them with passionate yet chaste attention, only to cruelly and deliberately abandon them when they showed signs of reciprocating. This would sometimes devolve into physical aggression. A young woman attracted to the then 29-year-old Dali

> kept remarking shrilly how beautiful my feet were. This was so true that I found her insistence on this matter stupid.... Suddenly she put her hand on one of my feet and ventured an almost imperceptible caress ... I jumped up, ... I pushed away my admirer, knocked her down and trampled on her with all my might, until they had to tear her, bleeding, out of my reach. (Dali, 1942/1993, p. 17)

His behavior continued to demonstrate a propensity for sexual dominance and brutality with intermittent acts of sadism and masochism—particularly in his self-proclaimed addiction to self-pleasuring. He recounted vivid fantasies of hurting and dominating women, such as the story he told of his relations with the imaginary figure Dullita, a character seemingly created to emphasize his sexual depravity (Murphy, 2009; Ungureanu, 2017).

> I threw myself at Dullita's body and I again squeezed her waist with all my might . . . she resisted my brutality feebly and all at once our struggle became slow, for I suddenly began to calculate everything . . . . I felt it would be easy for me to choke the least of her cries, crushing her little face against my chest . . . what I wanted to do was to turn her over on her other side, for it was just in the hollow of her back that I wanted to hurt her; I might for example have crushed her, just there, with the [gilded laurel] crown [lying nearby]; the leaves of those metallic laurels would have nailed themselves like blades into her smooth skin. I could have brought progressively heavier objects to keep her pinned there. And when I finally freed her from this torture I would kiss her on her mouth and on her bruised back, and we would weep together. (Dali, 1942/1993, p. 108)

Several passages recount violent actions toward others, reinforcing his uncontrollable rage and impulsivity that only his wife, Gala, could assuage. While she herself seemed to have become a convenient target for his fury, insecurity, and abusive dominance, he would forever describe her as his muse, his reason for living.

Questions remain whether or not his autobiography was accurate, or if it was simply hyperbolic self-promotion. He seemed to revel in his irreverent persona, bragging about his contrary ways to reinforce his dominance; as he admitted, "It was only necessary for someone to say 'black' to make me counter 'white'!" (Dali, 1942/1993, p. 116). It seemed his autobiography was yet another of his surrealist productions, exaggerating the profane to confront the status quo. Regardless, as Orwell stressed, it likely did not matter "which of the stories are true and which are imaginary . . . the point is that this is the kind of thing that Dali would have *liked* to do" (1968/2019, p. 165). As imaginative as some of these confessions might have been, they reveal at the very least a desire or tendency for such behaviors.

Surely Dali recognized the fascination society would have with his violent and sexual proclivities. Sex and violence sell. His book is a collection of self-ruminations that extol his own greatness—as an artist and as a predator. Whether or not this is accurate may be beside the point; by "confessing"—almost bragging—about these purported fits of rage, self-abuse, and brutality, Dali was assigning and reinforcing positive significance to violence. Such an emphasis of his own depravity and violent tendencies—wishful or otherwise—seemed to manifest itself in his work.

Aspects of some of his work have been tied directly to Freudian symbolism of sexuality, particularly those that reflect male dominance and aggression: "These symbols [in Dali's works] can be seen as elements with significant sexual connotations where the erotic lust . . . is manifested violently" (Dine, 2016, p. 60). Dali bragged of controlling his own excessive sexuality and libidinal aggression through an admitted preoccupation and obsession with masturbation. His art served the same function; much like onanism was for Dali, his paintings reflected his own self-aggrandizement, dominance, and indulgence. It seemed that Dali endeavored to capture and focus his animalistic and libidinal impulses through self-gratification *and* through his paintings.

With its clean lines, garish colors, and hyper-realistic imagery, Dali's images often portray fantastical sacrificial dominance. In some, an objectified or exaggerated form representing Dali's sexuality is overpowering a lithe, overly feminine nude. For example, his painting *Burning Giraffes and Telephones*, depicts a battle between a mechanical futuristic form made up of ill-fitted composites and a highly sexualized blonde woman. Behind this woman stand several giraffes engulfed in flames. While the seemingly sexual battle rages in the foreground, the burning, long-necked quadrupeds in the background hold no less importance. These giraffes, which have been featured in several of his works, symbolically depict his response to the chaos in his home country (Stanska, 2018; Williams, 2011) because they are

> considered by Dali as *"the masculine cosmic apocalyptic monster"* . . . . The viewer can understand that the actions of man towards stopping a war or any disastrous situations are nearly zero. . . . The Burning Giraffe . . . is like a warning to the world about the possibilities of war, apocalypse and disappearance of ethical values. (Classical Arts Universe, n.d., para. 7)

This painting seems to reveal a bizarre juxtaposition of Dali's sexual dominance and superiority against his anxiety and vulnerability. Depicting an image of overt and vulgar dominance and aggression, the background reflects his struggles with his own feelings of helplessness toward the excesses of war.

The following painting, *Dream Caused by the Flight of a Bee Around a Pomegranate a Second Before Awakening* (Figure 1.4), depicts at first blush two tigers ready to thrust themselves upon a woman, modeled from Gala, who is passively submitting herself to their imminent attack. Later, Dali indicated that the painting meant

> to express for the first time in images Freud's discovery of the typical dream with a lengthy narrative, the consequence of the instantaneousness of a chance event which causes the sleeper to wake up. Thus, as a bar might fall on the neck

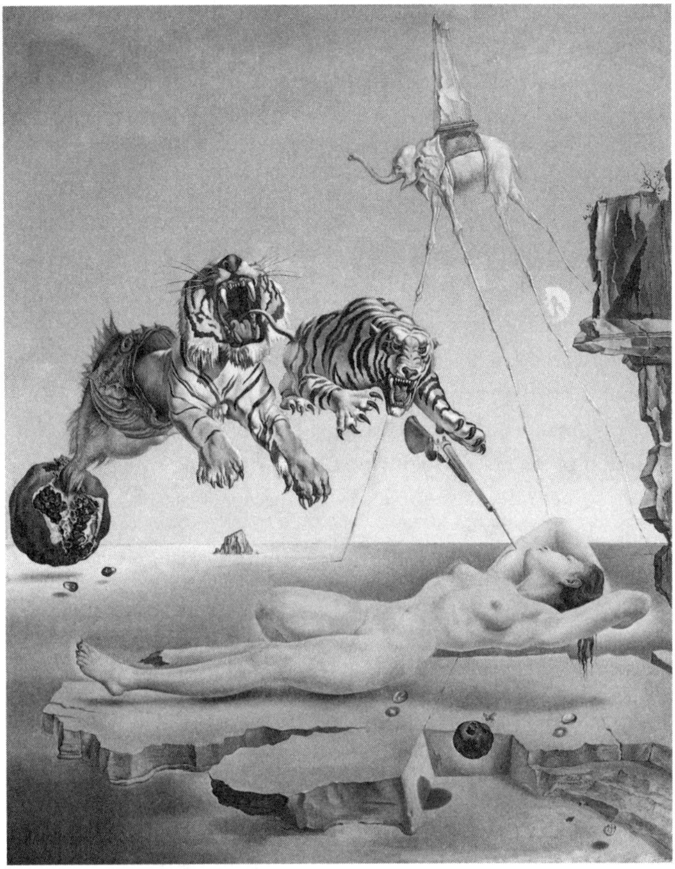

Figure 1.4 Salvador Dali (1904–1989). *Dream Caused by the Flight of a Bee Around a Pomegranate a Second Before Awakening* (1944). Oil on canvas.
Collection of Thyssen-Bornemisza Museum, Madrid, Spain. Permission provided by Salvador Dalí, Fundació Gala-Salvador Dalí, Artists Rights Society (ARS). Reproduction provided by Museo Nacional Thyssen-Bornemisza / Scala / Art Resource, New York.

of a sleeping person, causing them to wake up and for a long dream to end with the guillotine blade falling on them, the noise of the bee here provokes the sensation of the sting which will awaken Gala. (Alarco, 2008, para. 5)

While explained through the lens of a psychodynamic interpretation of symbolic dream-like imagery, there is clearly a blatant sexual and aggressive invasion.

The conclusions that I have made about the two pieces discussed here are merely inferential suppositions, yet it *seems* obvious that they rely on his sordid and perverse worldviews to communicate rather significant themes. Still, at other times, Dali's aggression and sexuality were not always sublimated into eye-grabbing imagery for the greater good. Indeed, he could and did wield his art as a blunt weapon, such as the drawing mentioned earlier that drove a deliberate wedge into his relationship with his father. Out of his disdain for the American child star Shirley Temple, Dali created *Shirley Temple the Youngest Most Sacred Monster of the Cinema in her Time* (Figure 1.5/see also color plate 1). Through this piece he brutally hypersexualized and humiliated the most iconic symbol of juvenile virginity of that era. Painting her as a Sphinx,

> [a] vampire bat sits on Temple's head, while around her lie the stripped bones from her latest kill. You don't have to look hard for phallic imagery in Dali and the fact that the skeleton of the predator's meal has conveniently broken down into single blunt, curved pieces clearly marks her as a maneater . . . .his erotic demonisation of an 11-year-old would be startling in any case, but becomes even more so because Salvador Dali's savage anger at the actress. (Lawson, 2007, para. 2)

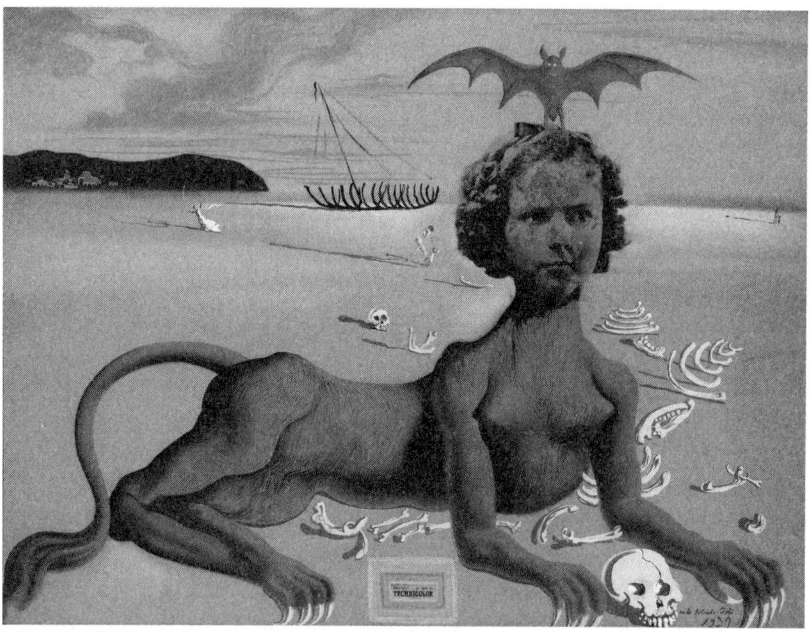

Figure 1.5 Salvador Dali (1904–1989). *Shirley Temple, le plus jeune monstre sacré du cinéma de son temps (Shirley Temple the Youngest Most Sacred Monster of the Cinema in Her Time)* (1939). Oil on canvas, collage.

Collection of Museum Boijmans Van Beuningen, Rotterdam. Permission provided by Salvador Dalí, Fundació Gala-Salvador Dalí/Artists Rights Society (ARS). Reproduction provided by Museum Boijmans Van Beuningen, Rotterdam. Photographer: Studio Tromp.

The last of Dali's images presented in this section may best embody the impetus of all of the works portrayed here. His painting *Ballerina in a Death's Head* (Figure 1.6) illustrates singularly the technique for which Dali became most known and to which the Surrealist movement is indebted. This slickly stylized yet grotesque composition further illustrates his emblematic *paranoiac-critic method*, a "spontaneous method of irrational knowledge based on the critical and systematic objectivity of the associations and interpretations of delirious phenomena" (Finklestein, 1975, p. 64). In this painting, Dali violated the laws of nature in his juxtaposition of two or more images to create a surreal and ambiguous composition that can be interpreted in multiple ways.

Rather than relying on passive reflection, he forced the viewer to engage actively with the piece as he deliberately fools the brain through the manipulation

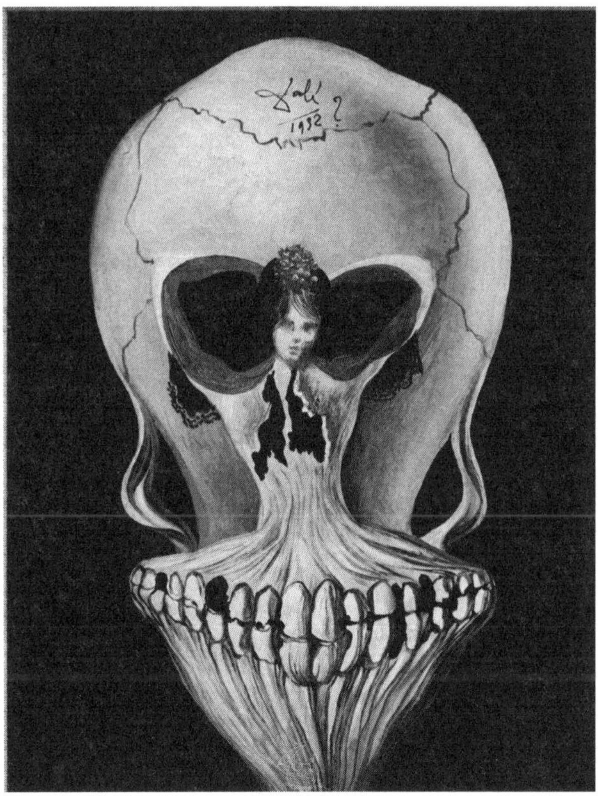

Figure 1.6 Salvador Dali (1904–1989). *Ballerina in a Death's Head* (1939). Oil on canvas.

Permission provided by Salvador Dalí, Fundació Gala-Salvador Dalí, Artists Rights Society (ARS).

of natural images. It took audacity and hubris to invent a method of art for which he himself set the rules. And what a set of rules they were: he wrestled with the viewer's perception of reality and made it bend and conform to his own wishes and desires. He was—and remains—in control.

Caravaggio, Cellini, and Dali relied on, relished, and even narcissistically promoted their aggressive, violent, and dominating natures. Some would argue that applying the neurotic and psychotic attributes of narcissism to artists from extremely disparate periods—even centuries apart—may be inappropriate, if not erroneous. Yet all have been described in the literature as narcissistic, self-aggrandizing, and egoistic, men who asserted their self-perceived dominance, and engaged in a "violent affirmation of [their] ego" (Fried, 1997, p. 30). In essence, a mastery of others through self. I would argue that it was not necessarily their narcissistic personas that differed depending on the epoch, but rather how their narcissism was fed, reinforced, and responded to. Still, their narcissistic drives and violent energies informed who they were and, in some cases, assured their success—two of them channeled their energy into forging and reinforcing new artistic directions, while one used it to compensate for his lack of artistic vigor and found other means of self-promotion. Still other artists, like Modigliani, Pollock, and Dadd, struggled with other demons that guided and were assuaged by their work.

The Impulsively Violent Artist

Although extremely complicated in its sociological and psychological influences and formations, with many social and political factors mitigating and influencing the resultant outcomes, research has demonstrated that there is certainly a lowering of inhibitions and an increase of impulsive, even aggressive acts in those who indulge in alcohol and substance use (Duke, Smith, Oberleitner, Westphal, & McKee, 2018; Savage & Wozniak, 2016). As substance usage impairs decision-making, stifles the ability to make rational and clear decisions, and essentially lowers defenses against impulsive and rash acts, those with a propensity toward reacting aggressively may more likely to act thusly after using such substances. In addition, recent studies bear out that those in creative and artistic fields are more prone to substance use than are those in other professions (Bush & Lipari, 2005). This is often attributed to a need to self-medicate to combat lack of confidence, self-doubt, performance/exhibition anxiety, and the disingenuous belief that such ingestion can increase creative output. In addition, while mental illness does not often result in aggressive and violent behavior, research demonstrates that, if unchecked, certain psychiatric illnesses may lower one's self-control and impulsiveness (Gussak, 2013; Stuart, 2003; Swartz et al., 1998). Delusions that are often attributed to severe psychosis may trigger, lead to, or even encourage violent reactions.

While extremely complicated in scope and deserving of a much more extensive review than this singular paragraph allows, art making has been demonstratively effective in controlling impulses and facilitating reality orientation, thus mitigating the aggressive effects brought about by substance use and delusional tendencies. Thus, while there are factors that can contribute to a lowering of inhibitions resulting in impulsively aggressive acts, art making can often feed off and mediate these reactions.

Modigliani: Self-Destruction, Unmasked

Amadeo Modigliani was born in 1884, in Livorno, Italy, a place that was considered a haven for the country's Jewish population. Once a vital cultural center, it had deteriorated by the time Modigliani was born and became "the ugliest place in the most beautiful province of Italy" (Meyers, 2006, p. 4). He grew up in a Sephardic Jewish family, the youngest of four children, with a domineering mother who held little respect for his relatively ineffectual father. Although at one time prosperous, it seems that the lack of success that Modigliani's father experienced led to dynamic tension within the household, which was

> divided into two: Flaminio [his father] alone on one side, everyone else on the other; they all depended on the formidable character of Eugenia [his mother]. It is not so much that she blamed her husband for their financial ruin, but for the fact he did not appear to have any redeeming intellectual qualities. (Mann, 1980, p. 8)

When Modigliani was 2 years old, his mother went to work to supplement her husband's meager earnings. By doing this, she simultaneously earned the condemnation of her husband's conservative family and her own self-righteous martyrdom (Mann, 1980). One of several endeavors, Modigliani's mother opened up an experimental, progressive school with her sister where Modigliani attended until he turned 10. It was here that he gained his intellectual curiosities and philosophical groundwork. Being a rather sickly child, stricken with pleurisy and quite possibly tuberculous, Modigliani was rather indulged, resulting in him becoming somewhat impulsive and unpredictable.

Although traditional Jewish beliefs forbade the practice of figurative art, Modigliani's desire to pursue such drawing lessons was supported by his parents, even while he neglected his other studies (Mann, 1980; Meyers, 2006). He began his formal training at 15 at the Livorna School of Fine Arts, learning how to draw and paint portraits, landscapes, still-lifes, and the nude figure—the latter more than a passing academic interest.

Despite the tumultuous circumstances in which his family found themselves, including a decline in their family fortune and Modigliani's older brother's arrest and subsequent conviction for political activities, the burgeoning artist remained indifferent, focusing entirely on his own artistic development. He eventually left Livorna to enroll in fine arts schools in both Florence and Venice. While his father remained detached from him and apathetic about his work, his mother encouraged it, supporting his move to Paris when he was 21 so that he might further pursue the life of the artist. He lived there until he died 14 years later.

Modigliani struggled to settle into his chosen artistic lifestyle in a city that should not have been entirely foreign to him—his mother's family had in fact lived in France since the early to mid-nineteenth century. Yet, because of the country's political climate, "Modigliani's position as an artist, a foreigner and a Jew in Paris was a precarious one" (Mann, 1980, p. 38). Such animosity was new to the spoiled and sheltered young artist. He was also impulsive and would often react violently toward any real or perceived slight. He once fiercely challenged a group of military officers for a perceived anti-Semitic slur (Klein, 2017). Regardless, he further embraced his Jewish identity. While he generally remained isolated and reclusive, he did gravitate toward other Jewish artists such as Chaim Soutine, Max Jacobs, and Jacques Lipschitz.

Despite his genteel upbringing, he slowly adopted a vagabond, vagrant-like persona. To offset the unexpected isolation and insecurities, and despite his new familiarity with poverty, Modigliani relied on absinthe and hashish to escape.

Paris became a center for new artistic expression and experimentation; it was not unusual to find artists sitting about in cafes discussing these new perspectives. Modigliani, bolstered by narcotic substances, would exuberantly engage fellow artists with passionate debates that would often deteriorate into violent arguments, particularly if the focus was on an artistic style with which he did not approve. It was not unusual for such interactions to come to blows.

His "aggressively theatrical manner" often sabotaged his chances to be accepted into the various artistic communities (Mann, 1980, p. 42) of which he so strongly desired to be a part. One of his first serious collectors, a young doctor named Paul Alexandre, introduced him to an artists' commune he had begun in the Rue du Delta. Modigliani, in a fit of generosity and so badly wanting to become part of this new brotherhood, gave each one of them a painting. However, like many of his relationships, this one soon deteriorated. His stay at the commune ended abruptly when, in an explosion of violence brought about by too much drink and fueled by his own insecurities, "he destroyed all of the works he could lay his hands on" (Mann, 1980, p. 49).

His remaining years vacillated between creative productivity and expressions of self-loathing, violence, and destruction, peppered with frequent love affairs and debauchery amplified through his substance abuse and unconventional excess. Despite his ongoing physical and spiritual deterioration, Modigliani developed a long-term relationship with Jeanne Håbuterne. However, rather than curb his wantonness, Jeanne enabled his erratic behaviors (Mann, 1980, p. 172; Stanska, 2018). Such devotion and care was often rewarded with impulsively violent reactions: Modigliani "often . . . respond[ed] to her entreaties with brutality, which he would alternate with tenderness" (Mann, p. 172). He would go off on drunken escapades for days on end, and she would end up looking for him to bring him home, often resulting in physical altercations when found. As one witness observed, "he was a madman, crazy with savage hatred" (Mann, 1980, p. 172).

Yet, through all this, his paintings belied his impulsive violence. While alcohol and drugs seemed to reveal the turmoil beneath his veneer, his mask-like imagery seemed to portray sought-after peace and serenity. Influenced by his teacher Brancusi and by tribal African sculptures (Klein, 2017), Modigliani's works revealed stylized figures with the "long faces" for which he was celebrated.

Broken down to their most elegant and simple shapes, Modigliani's portraits become masks themselves, hiding a true nature, seemingly to "remove himself from a full confrontation of identity" (Ferguson, 2018, para. 6). *The Jewess* (Figure 1.7) captures a caricature of an impassively simplistic coolness painted with bold, rich tones that still reveal a subtle nuance and mature technique. Yet there seems to be something hidden beneath the veneer.

Described by Updike as "serene limpidity," his faces seem shallow, as if he's avoiding true expression. "What makes many of his portraits linger in one's memory is the unease clouding his subject's face" (Stewart, 2005, para. 21). And, like many artists of his time, Modigliani "manipulate[d] the forms of nature to create an illusion, for themselves and others, [so] that they can control it" (Rangell, 1978, p. 37). Quoting the Russian novelist Ehrenberg, Stewart (2005) reiterated that "[a]ll [of the portraits] are like hurt children, albeit some of these children have beards or gray hair . . . the world seemed to Modigliani like an enormous kindergarten by very unkind adults" (para. 21).

Even through his nudes (Figure 1.8/see also color plate 2), portraying languid and heightened libidinal desires, Modigliani successfully distances himself—and in turn, us. The mask-like expressions continue to hide remnants of humanness, providing a sealed container of real passion. "It seems in equal measure he simultaneously viewed women in an 'objectivized' manner" (Parsons, 2005) while displaying their vulnerability.

While the final results often exhibited hidden serenity and subdued passion, how he painted them revealed his violent impulsivity. These paintings could not

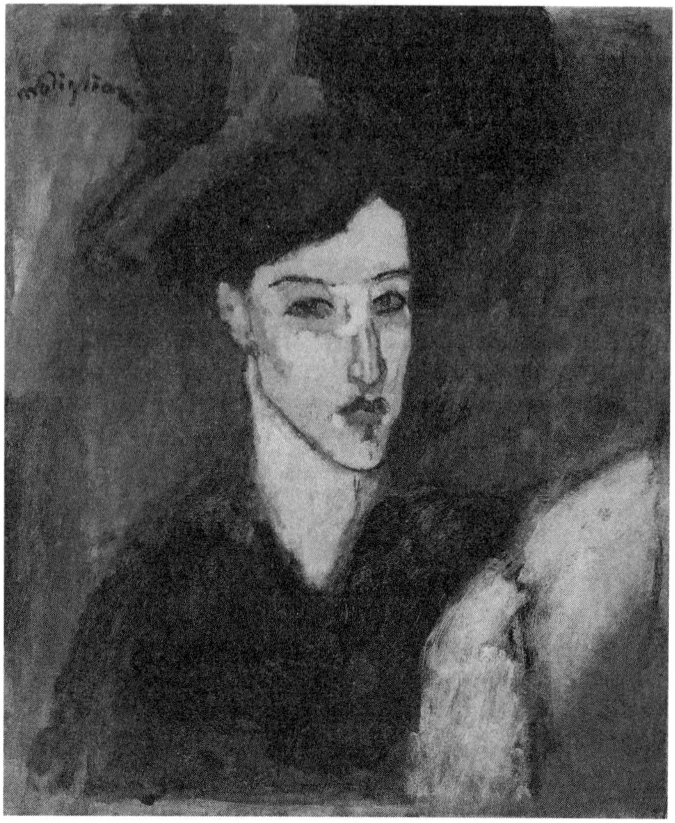

Figure 1.7 Amadeo Modigliani (1884–1920). *The Jewess* (c. 1907–1908). Oil on canvas.
Private collection. Reproduction provided by Christie's Images / Bridgeman Images.

hide his true nature. The stillness that his portraits attempted to convey paradoxically revealed through "erratic brush strokes and provocative compositions, coupled with [an] aggressive confrontation . . . [a] garish and powerful palette [whose portraits] often [held] confrontational gazes." As one model later recalled, "[h]e painted with such violence that the painting fell on his head when he leaned in . . . I was terrified" (Mann, 1980, p. 164).

Modigliani's excessive lifestyle and disregard for his health and well-being in favor of careless gluttony caught up with him. He died from tubercular meningitis when he was just 35. Yet he left behind a body of work that seemed to contain his explosive impulsivity behind a sturdy mask that successfully hid his true, vulnerable, anxious, passionate, and, at times, uncontrollable self.

Jackson Pollock's creative endeavors and violent and tempestuous outbursts were also fueled by substances and alcohol that seemed to lower his mask and

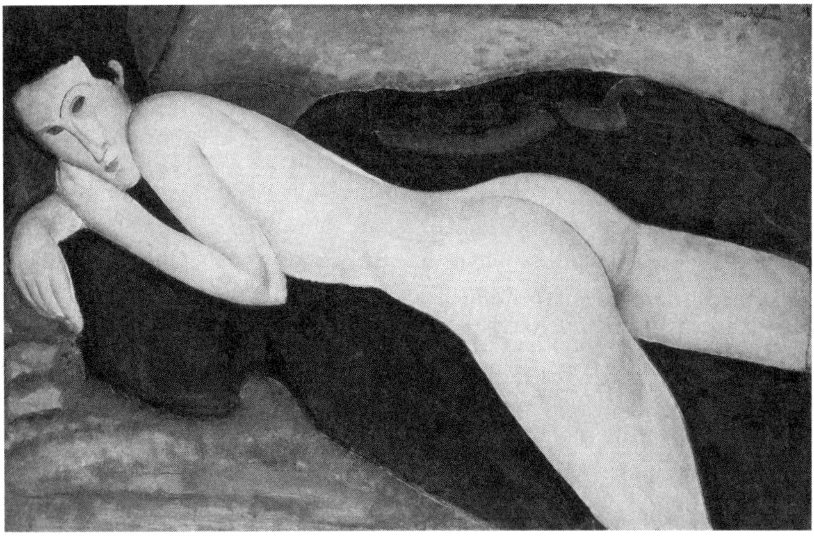

Figure 1.8 Amadeo Modigliani (1884–1920). *Reclining Nude from the Back* (c. 1917). Oil on canvas.

Collection of The Barnes Foundation, Philadelphia. Reproduction provided by Barnes Foundation / Bridgeman Images.

remove his filter. Yet, unlike Modigliani, Pollock's paintings did not contain nor subdue his aggressive impulses; rather, Pollock's explosive persona was clearly depicted splattered all over his canvases.

Jackson Pollock: "No Chaos, Dammit!"

Jackson Pollock is considered one of the foremost torchbearers of the Abstract Expressionist movement (Naifeh & Smith, 1998). Similar to the earlier Surrealists who were reacting to the impotence of societal conflict and modern warfare, the artists of Abstract Expressionism—described as a "tense, explosive movement" (Fleming, 1970, p. 531)—shunned what they perceived as overly contrived and constrained expression for one that embraced spontaneity, impulse, and improvisation (Fleming, 1970; Golub, 1955; Kleiner, Mamiya, & Tansey, 2001). As a reaction to the technologically driven horrors of World War II, its followers produced process-oriented works that were abstract in form and movement and emotional in content in an attempt to "express the artist's state of mind" (Kleiner et al., 2001, p. 1077). "The Abstract Expressionists relied more on the artistic medium as the bearer of their ideas than did the Surrealists . . . [and] attempted to suspend thought and work in a medium in the hope that the medium itself would evoke feelings, spiritual intimations, and understandings" (Hobbs, 1985, p. 301).

They sought what Golub referred to as "pre-logical, pre-cognitive, and a-moral" expression (1955, p. 143). To do so, many relied on "improvisatory techniques" that would begin with "scribbling and doodling to coax the mind to release its sub-, pre-, or unconscious elements, reflecting on these improvisations . . . and ordering all the elements into a composition" (Hobbs, 1985, p. 299)—in other words, they strove to bring order out of chaos. They fervently sought to express what Jung labeled the "collective unconscious." It was believed that Pollock himself embraced Jungian philosophy as his work evolved so that he could connect directly with his audience (Bowditch, 2008).

Born in 1912, in Cody, Wyoming, Pollock and his family would move nine times over his first 16 years; they eventually settled in Los Angeles. He studied art in high school, and, under his influential instructor, Frederick John de St. Vrain Schwankovsky, he was not only exposed to modern art, but also was encouraged to explore theosophy through literature. This later opened him to adopt various metaphysical and Jungian views and tenets. He left for New York when he was 18 and continued to study painting under the tutelage of Thomas Hart Benton at the Art Students League.

Living first with one brother and then another during the Great Depression, his early years were marked by abject poverty. In 1935, however, he was employed as a painter for the Works Progress Administration (WPA) Federal Art Project (Naifeh & Smith, 1998). However, these years took an emotional and spiritual toll on him. Two years later, Pollock sought treatment for alcoholism and was hospitalized the following year after suffering a nervous breakdown. Described by many to be a gentle soul, he became extremely volatile and quite violent when drinking.

His intense persona began at an early age. Learning by observing his father and older brothers, as a teenager Pollock used alcohol to escape his pain and confusion. There were times when Pollock's alcoholic binges were so intense that he became violent, so much so that his older, bigger brothers needed to intervene. This would then be followed by intense social withdrawal and remorse.

This seemingly self-destructive cycle followed him into adulthood. As a man of intense feelings and social anxiety, he developed the incompatible disposition of wanting to be liked by others yet also contemptuous of them. His emotional disposition swung widely and wildly between gentle and truculent to abrasive and callous. He lived his life veering unsteadily between pent-up frustration and fits of anger, venting them in marathon drinking binges that usually ended with explosions of verbal, emotional, or physical violence (see ineedartandcoffee.com).

However, he also relied on another way to express and release his internal strife and angst—his art. Shortly after his first hospitalization, where he was being treated for a bipolar disorder (Rothenberg, 2017), his art evolved from landscape paintings to semi-abstract works that contained layers of symbolic import for

Pollock. Following the dissolution of the WPA Federal Art Project in the early 1940s, Pollock was represented by the owner of one of the most renowned galleries in New York. Even still, he continued to struggle with his own artistic identity; often, he would express his increasing frustrations through his impulsive temper.

His early work was more representational than his later-known drip paintings. Stylistically, they seem to represent someone still coming to terms with his frenetic drives, unsure of how to express them.

His self-portrait (Figure 1.9) of "a rather brooding troubled figure . . . suggests a reflection of Pollock's inner turmoil" (Feldmann, 1989, p. 204). The bold colors, primitive yet compelling compositions, and almost fearful expression seem

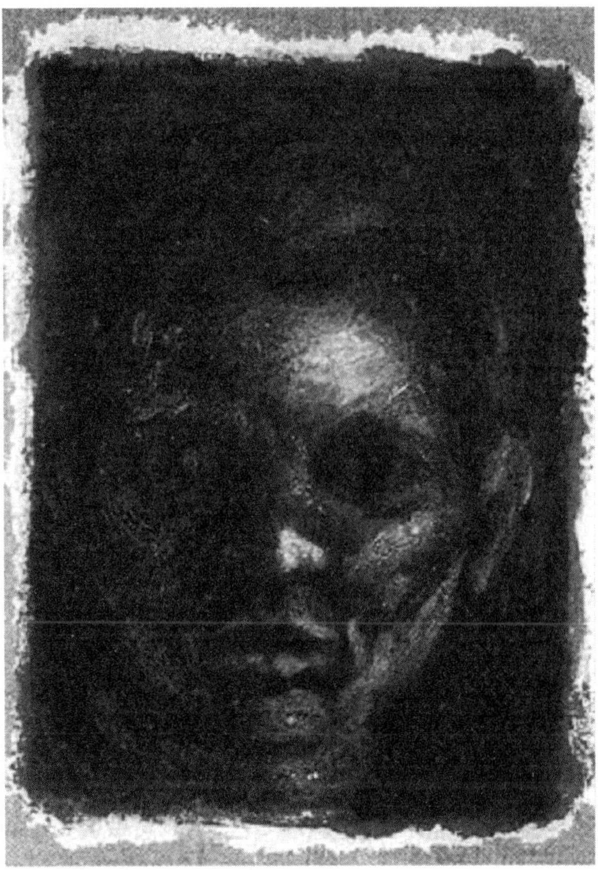

Figure 1.9 Jackson Pollock (1912–1956). *Untitled (Self-Portrait-Age 20)* (c. 1931–1935). Oil on canvas.

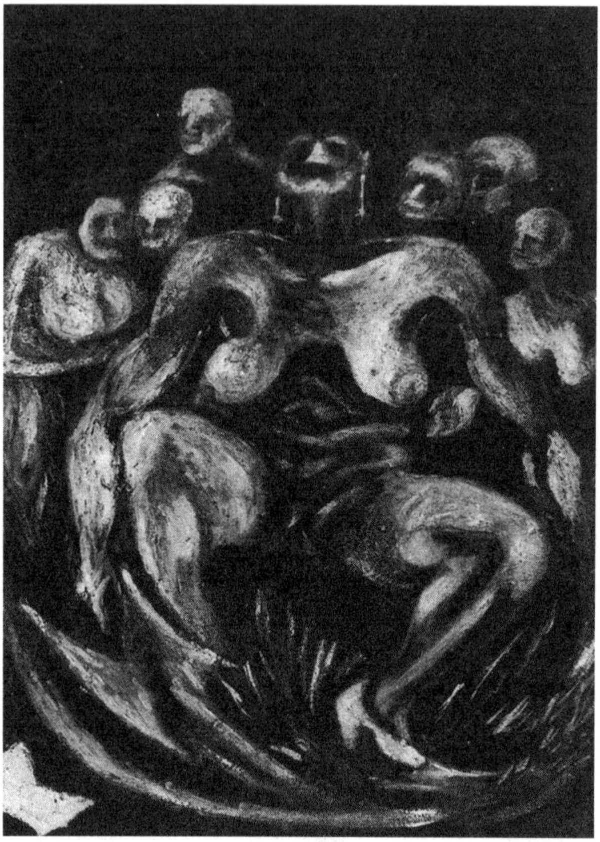

Figure 1.10 Jackson Pollock (1912–1956). *Woman* (c. 1930–1933). Oil on canvas.

reflective of an artist at odds with himself; his ambitious and aggressive drives conflict with his self- doubt, revealed through this audacious, tumultuous, and insecure depiction.

The powerful and dramatic painting *Woman* (Figure 1.10/see also color plate 3) seems to have emerged from someone perhaps still learning to express his burgeoning conflictual feelings toward women. The painting includes a faceless, monstrous, sexualized woman around which six ethereal figures stand. While entitled *Woman*, it seems to depict much more than that: "it has been speculated that this painting represents Pollock's view of his family" (Feldmann, 1989, p. 205), the female form likely symbolizing his strong mother dwarfing the remaining, somewhat diminutive family members.

In 1942, Pollock met the well-known and respected artist Lee Krasner at a gallery during a shared exhibition; she proved to be the one person who could provide the closest thing to stability for him. Shortly after, encouraged by the patron Peggy Guggenheim, Pollock began the poured works and drip paintings that seemed to most closely reflect his volatility. The style for which he would be most associated was a true sublimation of his aggression—known as "drip," "all-over," or "action" painting—that freed him up as he moved his canvases from the easel to the floor (Greenberg, 1961/1989).

> The "all-over" painter weaves his work into a tight mesh whose scheme of unity is recapitulated . . . . [T]he very notion of uniformity is anti aesthetic. . . . [T]he dissolution of the pictorial into sheer texture, into apparently sheer sensation, into an accumulation of repetitions, seems to speak for an answer something profound in contemporary sensibility . . . all hierarchical distinctions have been, literally exhausted and invalidated; that no area or order of experience is intrinsically superior . . . to any other area or order of experience. (p. 157)

As the figures in his paintings disappeared and his style became more process-focused and seemingly chaotic (Taylor, 2002), the more in control he became of his impulsive temper.

The rhythmically compelling and powerful painting *Lucifer* (Figure 1.11), completed in 1947, was one of the first compositions where his figurative representations disappeared entirely; it is truly "evidence of high, innovative creativity" (Fishmann, p. 206).

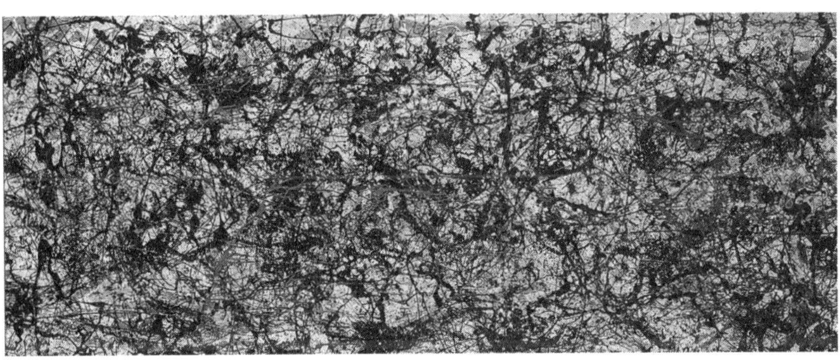

Figure 1.11 Jackson Pollock (1912–1956). *Lucifer* (1947). Oil and enamel on canvas.
Collection of Anderson Collection at Stanford University, Gift of Harry W. and Mary Margaret Anderson, and Mary Patricia Anderson Pence.

Reproduction provided by Anderson Collection at Stanford University. Photographer: M. Lee Fatherree.

As Pollock insisted, however, he did not control his painting, but rather, it controlled him, and he would give himself up to the process without equivocation (Fisher, 2010). "I have no fears about making changes, destroying the image, etc.," said Pollock, "because the painting has a life of its own. I try to let it come through. It is only when I lose contact with the painting that the result is a mess" (para. 17).

As his artistic identity solidified, his relationship with the art establishment deteriorated, and he found a target at which to direct his frustrations. It was inevitable; while his reputation as an artist grew, the responses to his work varied greatly from supportive criticism to outright derision. He developed a new movement, one he called "negation," the "absence of artistic definition[;] that art should not directly support a particular set of policies, but indirectly criticize existing ones" (Fisher, 2010, para. 21). By having such a focus to direct his rage and frustration, he found a reason for his sublimated expressions, one that was not readily understood by the establishment. "Despite occasional attempts in the art press to understand his work seriously, his name became synonymous with extreme artistic caprice" (O'Connor, n.d., para. 12). Pollock disagreed: for him, the apparent loss of control, the intended messiness of the compositions, his rhythmic painting exemplified the apex of control. Contrary to how they appeared, Pollock passionately insisted that his paintings exposed "No chaos, dammit!" (Jones, 2015). Yet, clearly "[h]is 'tormented' psychic and physical energies found their way onto canvas" (Court, 1990).

Such disrespect would eventually take its toll, and he became even more unstable. "He viciously attacked anyone who questioned his work and dismissed criticism as unimportant. These reactions were expressions of narcissistic rage and devaluation" (Feldmann, 1989, p. 206). Krasner's alleviating presence was no longer effective; he continued his excessive bouts of drinking followed by alcohol-fueled fits of rage. This lack of control did indeed eventually find its way onto the canvas, as his later paintings openly revealed his raw and monochromatic frenzy.

The formidable, provocative, and audacious painting, simply entitled *Number 14* (Figure 1.12)—completed in 1951—seems to stand in stark contrast to his rhythmic paintings: "[t]he chaos takes over, and he watches himself lose" (Jones, 2015, para. 7).

> Out of the morass emerge fragments of imagery. Distorted faces, floating breasts, an anguished confrontation of male and female bodies—these paintings tell of a terrible crisis in his life. (para. 5)

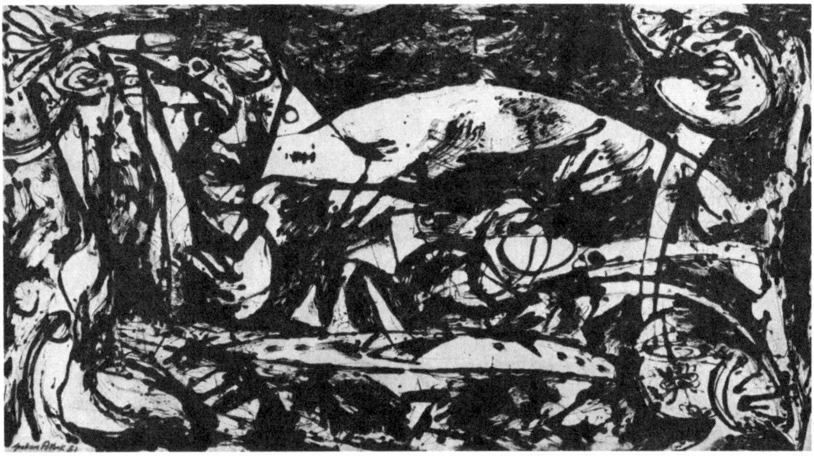

Figure 1.12 Jackson Pollock (1912–1956). *Painting Number 14* (1951). Enamel on gesso-covered paper.

Greenberg recognized Pollock's starkly black and white linear series of 1951—to which *Number 14* belonged—as contradicting his earlier colorful and light-infused works, "as if in violent repentance" (1961/1989, p. 228) of all he had done before.

For a time, Pollock was able to harness his demons to create his revolutionary works. With the mitigating influences of Krasner, his brothers, and colleagues, Pollock was able to channel his rage and quite simply, become great. But the energy was too much, even with so much support and his intensely creative outlet. His self-destruction and fury eventually and mercilessly caught up with him. Jackson Pollock died when he lost control of his car one drunken night in 1956 and slammed into a tree. He severely injured one passenger who was thrown from the wreck; he and another passenger were killed instantly.

It was believed that, throughout all of this, Pollock suffered from a bipolar disorder (Mueller, 2018; Rothenberg, 2017). He became more productive during those periods in which he was meeting with his therapist on a regular basis, and his work was much more effective in containing his demons. However, his alcoholic self-medication fueled his violent tantrums and soon he could not control his aggression.

Certain mental disorders, when gone unchecked and unrecognized, may—and not often—result in impulsive, violent, sometimes deadly actions. Like

Pollock, Richard Dadd suffered from a mental illness. An artist in his own right, Dadd found that he could use his art to organize his thoughts, express his confusion, provide him focus, and control his impulses.

Richard Dadd: "Tell the Great God Osiris, I Have Done the Deed"

A Victorian English painter in the 1800s, Richard Dadd was known for his meticulously detailed renderings of fantastical beings and enigmatic compositions. The Victorian era is a decidedly specific span during the Romantic period, occurring in Great Britain during the reign of Queen Victoria. The artists evolved during the 60 years of her reign to create works to offset growing industrialization and its corresponding societal deterioration, and the art's thematic foci transitioned from realistic scenery with subtle moralistic undertones to fantastical and mythological imagery as despair deepened. To offset the drabness of their modernized and dour surroundings, the paintings were generally colorful and bright, often depicting nude women and fairies (Benson, 1998). Richard Dadd's work evolved in parallel with this period, even during the last 40 years when he was locked up in psychiatric institutions after murdering his father in a fit of delusional hysteria.

Much has been explored about Dadd's impetuous crime, some arguing that his deterioration was indicative of British society's corrosion.

> Contemporary fascination with Dadd's case depended not only on his promise as an artist, the sensationalism of his crime, or the exoticism of his delusions, but also on the perception that his mental and moral collapse was symptomatic of the larger malaise then causing national concern. (Lippincott, 1988, p. 75)

Dadd was already recognized as a fine artist when he traveled throughout Europe and the Middle East in the early 1840s. Dadd accompanied a local politician to act as his draughtsman, visually recording the images they saw around them. As the trip progressed he began exhibiting erratic, unpredictable excitability, bordering on unaccountable aggression (Greysmith, 1973; Tromans, 2011).

After some grueling days in the Middle Eastern desert and wilderness, he became quite ill on a return boat ride on the Nile. He began exhibiting severe delusional symptoms and became increasingly violent; his patron and traveling companion, Sir Thomas Philips, began to grow concerned. At one point Dadd indicated a "strong inclination to attack the Pope," but thinking he would be easily overmatched by his security, "overcame his desire" (Greysmith, 1973,

p. 51). The others with whom he traveled became more concerned for his "deranged" paranoid exhibitions; they encouraged him to seek medical attention once they arrived in Paris. Believing this to be unjustified, Dadd immediately fled back to London. However, his symptoms did not abate.

His father persisted in his belief that Dadd's erratic behavior, which he himself had not really witnessed, was attributed to severe sunstroke suffered during his lengthy treks. Dadd's physician implored his father to watch him carefully in case his behavior was due to more insidious reasons. Although the doctor recommended that he be hospitalized, Dadd convinced his father to travel with him back to the countryside whence his family came. Later that evening, Dadd urged his father to take a stroll with him in a nearby park.

> In the dark, suddenly [Dadd's father], so long worried and concerned, was forced to face the truth he had tried to avoid. [Dadd] attacked him with a terrible violence, using the knife and razor that he brought. They fought fiercely and desperately . . . [L]eaving the body of his dead, or dying father, [Dadd] . . . fled. (Greysmith, 1973, p. 57)

To escape, Dadd took a train to Paris, where the desire to kill rose in him again. Dadd struggled

> against the voices which had bid him to slay his fellow traveler. At last, weary with the contention, he resolved to leave the question to kill or not to kill to the stars . . . one of which . . . he knew to be Osiris. If Osiris moved nearer to a neighboring star, he would take it as an unmistakable mandate to destroy. (p. 60)

In Dadd's tortuous imagination, the stars had indeed grown closer, and "his mission . . . was to kill" (p. 60). Despite his attempts to escape, Dadd was eventually arrested. He was immediately taken before the justice of the peace in the nearby town where he subsequently confessed to the murder of his father.

In his confession, his paranoid delusions became abundantly clear. He explained that "he was 'the son and envoy of God, sent to exterminate the men most possessed with the demon,' that in killing [his father] he had done a good thing by destroying an enemy of God, and that he intended to continue his campaign" (Tromans, 2011, p. 66). Shortly after, he began his long life of imprisonment in various asylums and psychiatric institutions.

Dadd immediately stabilized upon hospitalization. The doctors, recognizing the calming and focusing effects art had on Dadd, offered him supplies and encouraged him to continue painting. While he initially refused, Dadd eventually accepted them and began painting the fantastical and enigmatic scenes for which he was most known while interned at the Bethlem and Broadmoor asylums (Lippincott, 1988). In particular, most emblematic of his style was *The Fairy Feller's Master-Stroke* (1855–1864; see Figure 1.13/see also color plate 4).

Impressed with Dadd's fairy paintings and wishing to support his work, the head steward at Bethlem requested a painting of his own. After working on the painting for 9 years, the painting, *The Fairy Feller's Master-Stroke,* remains unfinished.

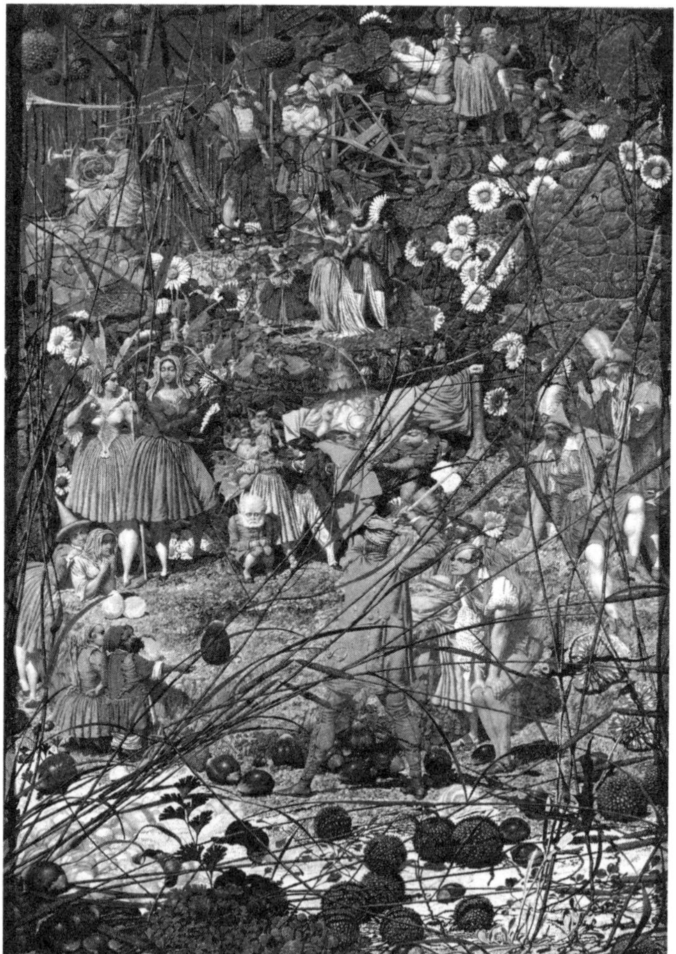

Figure 1.13 Richard Dadd (1817–1886). *The Fairy Feller's Master-Stroke* (1855–1864). Oil on canvas.

Collection of the Tate Museum, London. Reproduction provided by Derek Bayes (photographer)/ Bridgeman Images.

For a painting that is intricately detailed and required such a lengthy amount of time, it is relatively small, measuring only 21 by 15 inches. Prior to even applying paint to canvas, Dadd drew a fully detailed sketch. To transfer the sketch onto the canvas, Dadd relied on a magnifying glass to render the intricate and painstaking details. He applied the paint in thickly layered blobs, giving the work a rough and uneven surface and an almost three-dimensional quality in some areas. Focusing on singular figures or objects, he made sure that each was completed to his full and critical satisfaction before preceding to the next figure or object. The result is such a complicated and convoluted composition—even by Victorian-era standards (Benson, 1998)—that Dadd later wrote a guidebook explaining each of the more than 100 major and minor characters that make up the tale of the fairy feller (Tate.org.uk, n.d.).

The painting's focus centers around the Fairy Feller, raising an axe to split a large chestnut, from which he will build the queen's carriage. A white-bearded figure, seemingly the patriarch, raises his hand to signal the woodsman when to strike his blow. The other fairies look on, anticipating whether or not the fairy feller will successfully split the nut. The patriarchal figure wears a crown, reminiscent apparently of the Pope whom Dadd had contemplated attacking. Included in the top right of the composition is a tiny apothecary, brandishing a mortar and pestle, modeled after Dadd's murdered father. Particularly and unusually salacious, Dadd included two distorted but voluptuous fairy women ogled by a satyr to the left of the martyr. The central figures in the top half of the painting depict the king of the fairies, Oberon, and his wife, Titiana, from Shakespeare's *Midsummer Night's Dream*. In addition, the remaining composition is made up of an assortment of unusual and mythological creatures including a large dragonfly playing a trumpet. In the foreground Dadd painted grass, creating almost a barrier between the viewer and the fantastical scene (Greysmith, 1973; Tromans, 2011).

Unfortunately, he was unable to finish the painting before he was transferred to Broadmoor asylum and forced to leave it behind; it has since been recovered and is currently part of the Tate Britain collection. He later completed a more finished, watercolor copy of this painting housed at the Fitzwilliam Museum in Cambridge. He lived for 20 more years, housed in Broadmoor in relative peace when he eventually succumbed to lung disease when he was 69 years old.

Not Such Simple Categories

While by no means an exhaustive compilation of violent artists, the six chosen for this chapter epitomize the potential categorical typologies provided. Recognizably, the proposed dividing line created between the etiologies of violence for these artists is overly simple, superficial, and limiting; the traits and situations from which violence may emerge is much messier than what is outlined here, and often the lines are blurred between and among such categories—even with these six artists. For example, some of those recognized as impulsive were equally grandiose and potentially narcissistic, such as Pollock and Modigliani; those recognized as narcissistic often had their inhibitions suppressed by alcohol and drug use, such as Caravaggio, Cellini, and Dali. The two categories were applied merely as a device by which to moderate and explore these violent and aggressive artists. Quite frankly, to be creative and to succeed in the art world, I would argue one must maintain plentiful doses of self-promoting narcissism and audacious and impulsive risk-taking.

Of course, as has been made clear throughout, there are many more mitigating circumstances that determine and shape the behavior of such men. Thus, I would be remiss if I did not once again emphasize that some of the behaviors exhibited by these artists were likely a reflection of—or had been influenced by—their times. While by no means dismissing or excusing their boorish and hurtful behaviors—given the social, political, and cultural periods in which these artists created—their actions may have been ignored, excused, or even accepted as their masculine rights (Bowditch, 2008). It seemed that many turned a blind eye from their alcohol- and drug-fueled dominance and abuse toward models, mistresses, and burdened spouses. On the contrary, it seemed their work was celebrated (and still is) *despite* their audacious behaviors. In many of these cases, it appears that a number of art history texts deliberately leave out their poisonous behaviors, instead focusing on their artistic contributions. However, taken through a contemporary lens, because of the earned backlash against masculine toxicity and the long overdue #metoo movement, there is dawning recognition that certain behaviors can no longer be excused or even celebrated as remnants of the unleashed creative mind. Nevertheless, these examples underscore the interplay between their violent and aggressive natures, their sociopolitical contexts, and their sublime creations.

2
Creating in Conflict
Art amid Environmental and Societal Violence

In the film noir classic, *The Third Man,* Orson Welles's Harry Lime famously reminded Joseph Cotton's Holly Martin, "in Italy, for 30 years under the Borgias, they had warfare, terror, murder, and bloodshed, but they produced Michelangelo, Leonardo da Vinci, and the Renaissance. In Switzerland they had brotherly love—they had 500 years of democracy and peace, and what did that produce? The cuckoo clock" (Welles, et al., 1949). In this romantic, embellished, and incisive fashion, Lime/Welles intimated that creative works are often born from discord.

Making art is often used as a means to react to, respond to, and regain a sense of power within an environment that foments powerlessness and victimization. Art provides a mechanism to transform darkness and pain into resilience, empowerment that allows a shift from victimization (McNiff, 2005). While art does not always deter violence, it may provide an oasis of safety.

Noted philosopher Theodor Adorno disagreed that such expressions were valuable; indeed, Adorno asserted that creating art during or after times of horrendous violence and destruction is barbaric and obscene (Adorno, 1982; Alfers, 2010). In reflecting on poetry from those who were in Auschwitz, Adorno believed that "casting a glow of happiness and harmony over an unhappy real world [is] loathsome" (Gablik, 1993, p. 31). He insisted that by representing or embodying acts of barbarism in such a manner, their impacts are lessened.

Perhaps there might have been something to this if the art was simply a means to make pretty the ugly, to sweep the atrocities under the rug, to cast a dishonest and amnesiac glow of happiness on all that occurred. Yet the art was not created to disguise the horror; it was and is created to lay it bare and to control it (Gussak, 2009c; Kalmanowitz & Lloyd, 2005a). Simultaneously, the art making provides an escape while confronting vulnerable mortality, primitive instincts, and natural barbarism.

Creative reactions to oppressive and destructive governments have historically emerged through works that reveal the dark underbelly of "civilization." "A way to deal with our fearful fascination with power and cruelty and death is to act it out vicariously, in art [revealing] something of what lies beneath the varnish of what we call civilized behavior" (Buruma, 2014, p. xi). The residence of the *Paradise Ghetto* in Theresienstadt [Terezín] were artists, poets, dramatists, and musicians tasked to provide the veneer of civility, culture, and normalcy in the face of destruction (see Chapter 3 for further details). Yet these empowered artists were able to use their talent as weapons to fight against their murderous oppressors. They painted and drew what was going on around them, wrote poems and stories that revealed the depth of their despair, and performed plays that allegorically captured the horror inside. These works were completed in secrecy, for knowledge of such works would result in torture and death—as it did for those involved in the *Artists' Incident*. They risked their lives to give evidence of what really occurred behind the razor wires, and, in completing their works, they regained a sense of value, empowerment, control, and an identity that the Nazi regime had tried hard to eradicate.

There are many examples of those who create during tumultuous times; we wonder with fascination what drives them. Kalmanowitz and Lloyd (2005b) responded in astonishment to the art students they met in war-torn Sarajevo,

> who daily risked their lives to get to their studio across the river and what was known as "snipers' alley." Once there, in the bombed and near-derelict art school, they would paint, often over old canvases, using the scant resources they could get hold of. (p. 22)

They wondered "why some individuals risk their lives or persist in making or participating in art despite the dangers associated with this" (p. 22). For Hazut (2005), the answer was obvious. She recognized that creating provided an opportunity to make sense of the senseless; by reacting actively, it prevents passively accepting such volatile circumstances: "facing fear directly reduces the threat of its existence, the intensity and the resulting empowerment of the individual lead to a capacity to contain and control the memory of the event" (p. 93).

Of course, we—and by "we" I mean humankind—seem to be fascinated by the ugliness of violence and persecution. Yet, what is it that draws us—and the artist—to such themes? Umberto Eco believed that art that has portrayed ugliness throughout history is a result of not just fascination but is created because artists are surrounded by it; the art gives voice to the sadness in the world.

> In everyday life we are surrounded by horrifying sights. We see images of children dying of hunger, reduced to skeletons with swollen bellies; we see countries where women are raped by invading troops, and others where people are tortured, just as we are continually exposed to images from the not too distant past of other living skeletons doomed to the gas chambers. We see bodies torn apart by the explosion of a skyscraper or an aeroplane in flight, and we live in terror that tomorrow it may be our turn. We all know perfectly well that such

> things are *ugly*, not only in the moral but in the physical sense, and we know this because they arouse our disgust, fear, and repulsion—-independently of the fact that they can also arouse our compassion, indignation, instinct of rebellion and solidarity, even if we accept them with the fatalism of those who believe that life is none other than a tale told by an idiot, full of sound and fury. No knowledge of the relativity of aesthetic values can eliminate the fact that in such cases we unhesitatingly recognize ugliness and we cannot transform it into an object of pleasure. So we can understand why art in various centuries insistently portrayed ugliness. Marginal as the voice of art may be, it attempted to remind us that, despite the optimism of certain metaphysicians, there is something implacably and sadly maligned about this world. (Eco, 2007, p. 436)

While not wished for, tension, strife, and conflict seem to be necessary ingredients for innovation and creativity. Or, it may be as Sontag stressed, "uglifying, showing something at its worst . . . [is] didactic, it invites an active response" (2003, p. 81). Beauty is passively accepted as an unattainable Kantian ideal while ugly requires reflection, interaction, identification, and even instruction.

Once again, as we did in the previous chapter, let us visit the unexpectedly violent and conflict-laden Renaissance. In his book, *Art and Violence in Early Renaissance Florence*, Nethersole (2018) stressed that it was common for the creative citizens of this most inspiring epoch to be exposed to the "quotidian brutality" of society.

During "the second half of the fifteenth century, an average of eight people a year were executed [in Florence] in a highly visible and cruel spectacle . . . 'the communal texture of everyday life was conducive to chronic violence' " (Nethersole, 2018, p. 22). It wasn't just physical cruelty that was endured, "but an emotional response to life that was violent in . . . tone" (Nethersole, 2018, p. 22). Witnesses to such brutality included such sublime artists as Fra Angelico (1395–1455), Leonardo da Vinci (1452–1519), and Sandro Botticelli (1445–1510), whose works—respectively—*Decapitation of Saints Cosmos and Damian from the San Marco High Altarpiece*, *Studies for the Battle of Anghiari*, and *The Discovery of the Body of Holofernes* speak truth to the times in which they were created.

Later still, Jusepe de Ribera, a follower of Caravaggio and seen as his potential successor, mirrored the violence he witnessed around him in Naples, Italy, in his own work. This Spanish-born artist, nicknamed "Lo Spagnoletto" (the Little Spaniard), moved to Naples in the early 1600s to paint during a most wretchedly violent period.

Although certainly capable of painting religious compositions such as the baby Jesus with Mother Mary, his exceptional technique in painting the imperfect man—the old, the decrepit, the remarkably ugly, and the poor—was widely recognized and revered. Some of his most known works capture extreme suffering, pain, and violence, so much so that Ribera was long thought violent in his own right. However, this is quite possibly an unearned label (Bray & Payne, 2018), and it was likely that he painted these violent compositions not necessarily to celebrate them, but merely to document them.

> Naples was inescapably violent, as well as populous, cosmopolitan and exciting. Horrific punishments such as the *strappado*—where a person was suspended by their wrists tied behind their back—were matters of public spectacle. He would have seen a lot of these punishments being enacted at, for example, the tribunal of the Vicaria in Naples. . . . One of his drawings depicts a man undergoing the *strappado* while functionaries from the Inquisition—paper and quill in hand—question him. The tortured man's shoulders are dislocated and he is defecating. . . . Ribera was recording the reality of these sombre acts . . . not reveling in them. (Higgins, 2018, para. 6–7)

Perhaps it is needless to say that history is replete with examples of artists who have emerged from violent surroundings. Yet this is what drives this chapter, the awareness that the sublime emerges from such ugliness. It's recognizing that art may *reflect* violence because artists *experience* violence—they create to tell their story in the only language available to them. As well, art emerges from the horrifying awareness that the world is sadly aggressive—they create to bear witness. Maybe such art is the natural by-product of catharsis and sublimation, the need for an emotional container or outlet of the horrors experienced. And finally, perhaps—independent of these three factors, or in conjunction with all three—art is created to provide control and empowerment when the horrors of what surrounds the creator threatens to alter or destroy them.

This chapter explores all of this by focusing on six artists who emerged from specific types of global and societal conflict, from within and outside their given society, through war and civil unrest. They created in an attempt to control the uncontrollable, escape from the inescapable, and document the unrecordable.

In this manner, I have divided the following into two major sections: *artists reacting to war-torn environments* and *artists impacted by societal conflict*. The first section is further divided into two subsections: those who illustrated what they witnessed and those who captured what they experienced as victims. Clearly, while recognizing a blurring of these distinctions, there is a symmetry in the manner in which these topics are presented.

As a result, the six artists have been divided neatly into the three categories: Francisco Goya and Max Beckmann represent those who bore witness to the global conflict around them; Felix Nussbaum and Vann Nath captured the responses and reactions to their roles as victims to the atrocities to which they were unwilling pawns; and Bill Traylor and Norman Rockwell serve as counterparts to the civil exploitation and volatility that plagued the United States throughout the nineteenth and twentieth centuries. Six men who, although geographically, temporally, and stylistically diverse, nonetheless together capture what a potent muse violence can be.

The Art *Out* of War: Creativity Emerging from the Rubble of Destruction

Bearing Witness

Almost as ubiquitous as the wartime correspondent is the artist or photographer who pictorially captures the brutality of the military conflict. Formalization of this genre—for perhaps lack of a better word—goes as far back as Da Vinci, who provided sound advice to artists painting war battles to sufficiently capture the horror and brutality of those suffering (Hewitson, 2017; Sontag, 2003). His concern was not whether it was a great work of art, but to be certain that the images were "sufficiently upsetting" to make it so fearful, that it "swamps pity. . . . The image should appall, and in that *terribilita* lies a challenging kind of beauty" (Sontag, p. 75). In this manner, the art serves a unique purpose, to convey the extent of what "human beings are capable of doing—may volunteer to do, enthusiastically, self-righteously" (p. 115).

Yet while the artists captured the scenes of conflict, they were undeniably transformed by what they witnessed. Goya was considered a technically adept yet uninspiring court painter; that is, until he saw the unremitting horror of battle and its remnants.

Francisco Goya: Transformation from Light to Black

Francisco José de Goya y Lucientes is considered one of the most important Spanish artists of the late eighteenth and early nineteenth centuries. As a court painter during the Age of Enlightenment., Goya was known for his traditional portraits His later works were dramatically influenced by what he witnessed during the Napoleonic Wars, his own medical ailments, and, later, political exile. He became an artist whose paintings, drawings, and etchings communicated through a new style the pain he experienced and the atrocities that surrounded him. Yet "there was a . . . common denominator of all his work . . . the human being. Man's joys and humiliations, his dreams and follies, his hopes and hallucinations, his vileness, his inhumanity, his saintliness—these were Goya's sole preoccupation" (Gassier, 1955, p. 13).

Born in 1746, in Aragon, Spain, into a lower-middle class family, Goya was the fourth of six children. Because his father was a reputable master gilder, Goya was surrounded by artisans and artists. He began a 4-year apprenticeship under a well-known local Spanish Baroque painter, Jose Luzan. He later moved to Madrid to study under another, Anton Meng, a popular royal portraitist. He competed twice for scholarships in the Academy of San Fernando in Madrid, first in 1763 and again in 1766, coming up empty-handed both times. While Goya did not demonstrate remarkable talents, he nevertheless persevered in his chosen vocation. He moved to Italy to further his own artistic education and eventually learned enough to win second prize for his work from the Royal Academy of Fine Arts in Parma. Returning to Spain shortly after, Goya had little difficulty obtaining commissions. However, conforming to the stilted conventions of the academic circles of those days (Gassier, 1955, p. 19), many of these early works were fairly uninspiring. However, as his confidence grew, his work began to break away from the expected, displaying a much more deft and carefree brush stroke and composition.

His work was soon noticed by the establishment, resulting in an appointment to the Royal Academy of Fine Art. Throughout the 1780s, various members and relatives of the established royalty commissioned him for portraits and light-hearted scenes. As a result, he was ultimately chosen to be Charles IV's court painter. However, his carefree days—and thus, his style—would change drastically following two life-altering events.

Goya's later dark works were anticipated by the series of 80 compositions, *Caprichos,* begun in 1792 shortly after becoming deaf from a prolonged illness. As a result, he became increasingly withdrawn and isolated, which couldn't help but be reflected in his work.

Seen as a condemnation of the follies of Spanish culture, *Los Caprichos* began as an experiment. The 80 prints embodied, as he described, "the innumerable foibles and follies to be found in any civilized society, and from the common prejudices and deceitful practices which custom, ignorance or self-interest have made usual" (PDR, n.d., para. 1). For example, one of his etchings, *The Sleep of Reason Produces Monsters* serves as a sample of Goya's ability to combine caricature-ish realism with surrealistic fantasy.

No one was safe from his acidic criticism; he threw shade at the clergy and ruling class, anything that he believed reflected the decline of rational thought and civility. The shift from carefree compositions to images loaded with symbolic and iconic meaning did not go unrecognized by those around him, and, consequently, his reputation suffered. When the series was originally released for publication in 1799, it was withdrawn from the public after only 27 were sold. "They were probably recognized as references to well-known persons," and they were withdrawn from sale after a few days. As the images fell further into disfavor with

Charles and the clergy alike, Goya admitted that it was prudent to pull them from circulation because of the impending Inquisition, and "in 1803 he presented the plates of Los Caprichos to the king in return for a pension for his son" (Harris-Frankfort, 2014/2020, para. 5), presumably to be destroyed (Georgievska, 2016).

Not long after, a second event occurred that would change Goya's palette, tone, and message—Napoleon's invasion of Spain and the 6-year conflict, the Peninsula War, that raged on after. Because he worked for Napoleon's brother, Joseph I, he kept his head low, fulfilling contracts for his new French patrons and sympathizers (Vega, 1994). Yet he was also asked by the Spanish military to record through his distinct imagery the conflict going on around him. Despite his apparent neutrality, what emerged was a disturbing, at times macabre series: *Disasters of War.*

Similar to *Los Caprichos,* this series consists of 82 aquatints and etchings completed from 1810 to 1820, and it is considered "the preeminent concentration on the horrors of war" (Sontag, 2003, p. 44). Within the series' broad themes historians recognized three subthemes: the horrors of war (Figure 2.1), ensuing and resulting famine, and political and cultural allegories about his disappointment with the restored monarchy and, with it, "a new standard for responsiveness

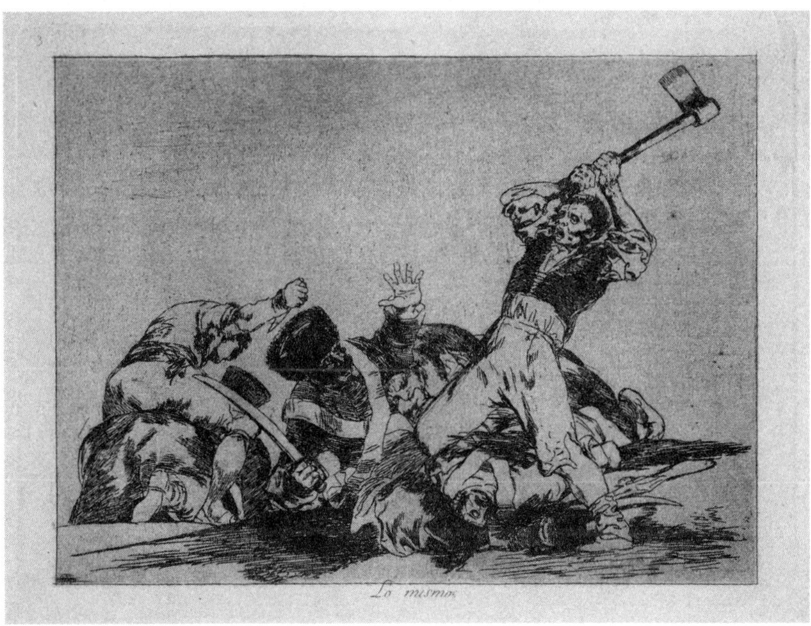

Figure 2.1 Francisco José de Goya y Lucientes (Goya) (1746–1828). *Lo Mismo (The Same) (from the Disasters of War series)* (1863). Etching and aquatint on paper. Collection of Manchester Art Gallery, UK. Reproduction provided by Manchester Art Gallery / Bridgeman Images.

in suffering enters art" (Sontag, p. 45). It was more than simply documenting the atrocities; this series has since been recognized as the "prodigious flowering [of Goya's] rage" (Viladegut, n.d., para. 17), and was "meant to awaken, shock, wound the viewer. . . . The account of war's cruelties is fashioned as an assault on the sensibility . . . " (Sontag, pp. 44–45).

The series was completed in 1820. However, given their sensitive nature and the controversy they would likely elicit, the series was not released for public consumption until 1863—almost 45 years later.

In the midst of completing this series, Goya finished two of his most iconic paintings: *The Second of May, 1808,* and *Execution of the Defenders of Madrid, 3rd May, 1808* (Figure 2.2) for a commission granted by the provisional Spanish government in 1814. These canvases depict the failed insurrection against the French occupation.

The frenzied, tumultuous composition of the painting, *The Second of May*, also known as *The Charge of the Mamelukes*, depicts the bloody battle in which Spanish Loyalists attempted to rebel against the French occupation. This painting captures the confusing fury of battle like few others.

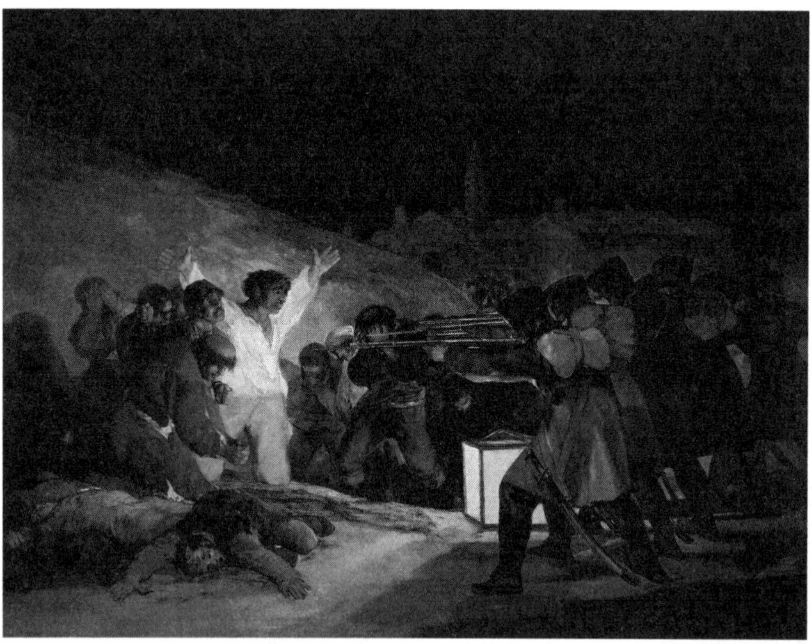

Figure 2.2 Francisco José de Goya y Lucientes (Goya) (1746–1828). *Execution of the Defenders of Madrid, 3rd May, 1808* (1814). Oil on canvas.

Collection of Museo National del Prado, Madrid. Reproduction provided by Museo National del Prado / Bridgeman Images.

> No classical composition here, no carefully plotted lines of force, no axes, center points, etc. A wild tangle of men and horses swirls across the canvas, the horses panic-stricken, rearing this way and that, the men cutting each other down in blind savagery. There are no heroes in this murderous confusion. (Gassier, 1955, p. 89)

With no place for the eye to rest, the furious brushstrokes capture the senseless frenzy of the battle. However, if *The Second of May* is all action, *Execution of the Defenders of Madrid, 3rd May, 1808,* captures the still moment just before an irrevocable and awful event.

Clearly *Execution of the Defenders of Madrid, 3rd May, 1808*, or *The Third of May, 1808*, was certainly not what they expected when the commission was offered to Goya (Arn, 2019). "Throughout his career, Goya was a master at convincing his patrons to sign off on one thing, and then delivering something else. . . whether [he] intended this event to appear glorious or heroic is, to put it mildly, questionable" (para. 3) The scene depicts the actions of the following day in which the French soldiers line the captured rebels against the wall to be executed. This "overwhelming revelation of barbarity" (Gassier, 1955, p. 94) captures a snapshot of the early morning following the battle in which 43 Spanish patriots were lined up and shot. The faceless executioners are displayed on the right with thick, black parallel strokes that capture the rigidity and impenetrable wall of soldiers. They are firing mechanically and with little sentiment upon those about to die on the left; these men are depicted in a convoluted and tumultuous composition, the figures an amalgamation of clenched fists, covered faces, and bulging eyes. In the middle of this convoluted group stands a single, helpless figure throwing his hands up in a final, futile gesture. His bright white shirt and light-colored pants assures that he is the focus of the composition. The overall tone of the image and the jarring juxtaposition of the extreme and varied compositions within the same scene captures the intensity and savagery of the experience. It seems now, in hindsight, that there could not be a more profound manner in which to capture this most terrible moment. Considered by some to be the greatest anti-war painting (Arn, 2019), "this is the most scathing indictment of man's cruelty to man that an artist has ever produced" (Gassier, 1955, p. 92).

Due to progressively increasing ill health and physiological isolation, Goya further withdrew from those around him. His later works, often completed in private, reflected his ever-darkening state. After a failed attempt at establishing a liberal government in 1824, he was driven to self-exile in France. Yet, before leaving, Goya completed his darkest series, the 14 *Black Paintings*.

With no intention for public display, these compositions were painted directly onto the walls of his house. One of his most famous paintings, *Saturn Devouring*

One of His Sons (Figure 2.3) was later carefully removed from the wall and transferred to canvas after his death.

This haunting image was completed when the artist was in his mid-70s. It captured the moment in which the Titan Saturn swallowed his children to prevent them from overthrowing him. His wife, Ops, managed to substitute their son, Jupiter, with a stone, which Saturn unwittingly swallowed. Jupiter managed to rescue his siblings from Saturn's gut and together they overthrew their father, to rule the heavens forevermore.

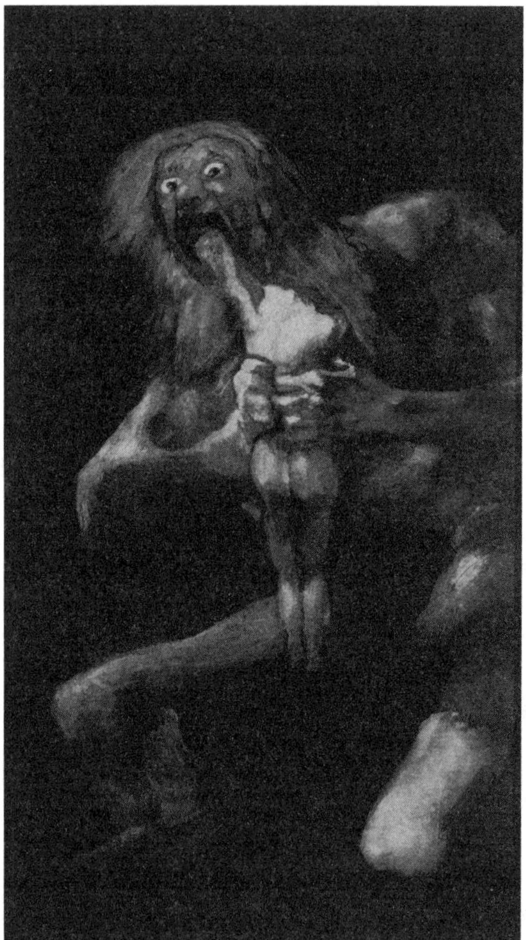

Figure 2.3 Francisco José de Goya y Lucientes (Goya) (1746–1828). *Saturn Devouring One of His Sons* (1821–1823). Oil on mural, transferred to canvas. Collection of Museo National del Prado, Madrid. Reproduction provided by Bridgeman Images.

To capture this brutal story, Goya painted a composition that was particularly grotesque. The less than subtle horrors are conveyed through the contrast of vividly garish colors against the dark tones; this is further enhanced through the bright red paint representing the blood pouring from the decapitated neck. This was certainly not meant to be a subtle composition. And yet the potentially powerful message of this image is belied by Saturn's comically exaggerated features, almost robbing the character of his power, counteracting the anticipated fear and terror. There is no way to ascertain if this was deliberately rendered to capture his own emotional disconnection, or whether it was an exaggeration in the features resulting simply from his own lack of commitment and continuing struggles to convey the depth and breadth due to his mediocre talent. Still, it is clear that this depicts a horrendous act perpetrated by a crazed being, and he took formidable artistic risks not often encountered in his previous works.

Goya's intention for this painting is unknown. The Black Paintings were for his own consumption, painted on the walls with no intention for public display. He left no written description of these works; he didn't even name the paintings, leaving that up to others after his death. It is fair to say that these violent and disturbing paintings reflect his growing depression and paranoia fomented by his isolation and impending death. Goya died in 1928, following a debilitating stroke.

Goya began his chosen career as an adept yet uninspiring painter. Yet it seems that he needed to experience horror, isolation, and anxiety to become all that he is known for—one of the most iconic, era-defining artists of his time.

Francisco Goya was not the only artist to be affected deeply by the horrors of war around him. Yet, while Goya's work seems to reflect a lack of emotional investment at times, conveying heightened violence and horror through technical and comical contrivances, Max Beckmann seemed fully invested in capturing his emotional reaction to the violence that surrounded him (Hewitson, 2017).

Max Beckmann: Expressing a World Gone Mad

One of Germany's most prominent artists at the beginning of the twentieth century, Max Beckmann was a German Expressionist who originally embraced New Objectivity, the subgenre that disregarded overt emotionalism (Dominiczak, 2017). However, while his early works were fairly representational and "objective," his style —like many artists who embraced German Expressionism—would change dramatically in response to the oppressive, politically charged, and often brutal German political climate throughout the first half of the 1900s.

Beckmann was born in 1884 into a comfortable, middle-class family in Leipzig, Saxony. His father, a grain merchant, died when Beckmann was 10 years old; his mother moved Beckmann and his brother to Braunschweig, where he lived for the next several years. He attended a few private schools, but, despite his family's objections, Beckmann decided early to pursue his love of the arts. He demonstrated marked talent early on: his first notable work was completed when he was 14 years old. His early work was fairly traditional, influenced by his education at the conservative Weimar Academy, from which he graduated in 1903. His works, such as *Young Men by the Sea* (1905) and *Small Death Scene* (1906), would further be informed by the Impressionists with whom he interacted during his many trips to Paris after leaving the Academy.

He continued to promote German Impressionism over the next several years through the arts movement, Berlin Secession, and was a founding member of the group Free Secessions several years later. However, World War I would have a profound and irreversible impact on Beckmann's style.

In 1914, Beckmann volunteered as a paramedic for the army's medical corps. At first, he, along with his compatriots, held a certain enthusiasm for the war: "[t]he clamor of battle became for him a sublime musical experience; the desolate landscape, lit up intermittently by the flashes of bombs and grenades, was an apocalyptic spectacle" (Haxthausen, 1984, pp. 71–72). He also saw it as fodder for his creative expression: "this 'terrible destiny' offered Beckmann incomparable raw material for his art. As he noted pithily: 'My art can gorge here' " (Haxthausen, p. 72).

However, as time went on, it slowly dawned on him all that was befalling around him; his correspondence with his wife, Minna, took on a depressive heaviness. Beckmann "was gradually devastated by these experiences" (Hauxtausen, p. 76). He eventually suffered a severe breakdown, resulting in deep despair, horrific nightmares, even debilitating hallucinations (Southgate, 2002). As Beckmann wrote to Minna, "Eventually, the dead come to visit me" (Haxthausen, p. 77). He was discharged shortly thereafter.

As his mood and temperament changed, so did his work. Whereas his earlier paintings were more light and bright, his later works became more distorted, dark, and limited in color range. He often inserted complex, sometimes cryptic symbols. Beckmann was no longer an observer; he was part of the horror, from the inside looking out, perhaps wanting the viewer to experience it as he did.

The canvases completed following his discharge from the war, including *Christ and the Sinner* (1917), *The Descent from the Cross* (1917), *Adam and Eve* (1917), and *The Night* (1918–1919) are crowded with distorted figures, heavily reinforced with black lines and drab tones with grating primary colors used sparingly on otherwise bleak compositions. Perspective disappears; Beckmann, instead, emphasized the jarring relationships between these exaggerated, almost grotesque figures (Southgate, 2002) that appear inhuman, almost mechanical.

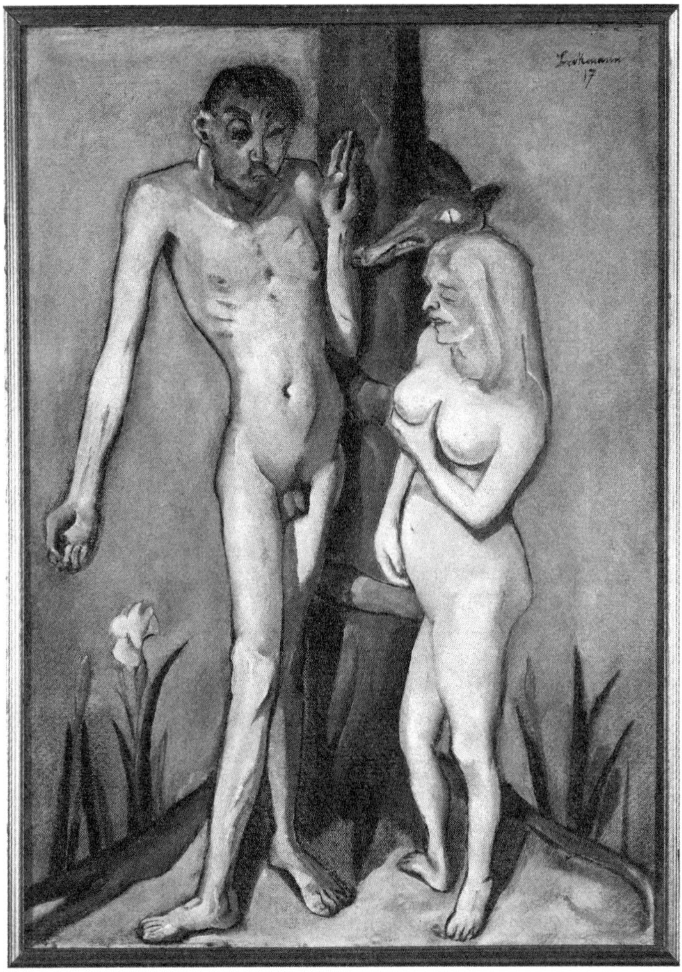

Figure 2.4 Max Beckmann (1884–1950). *Adam and Eve* (1917). Oil on canvas. Collection of Nationalgalerie, Staatliche Museen, Berlin. Reproduction provided by bpk Bildagentur / Nationalgalerie, Staatliche Museen/Photographer: Jörg P. Anders/Art Resource, New York.

They seem almost reminiscent of the destructive machinery Beckmann experienced in the war.

Adam and Eve's gaunt and tired figures are placed in a bleak landscape, painted in dreary gray and brown tones; the only exception is the bright yellow lily and the red eyes of the serpent (Figure 2.4). Perhaps like Adam, who earned a newfound awareness after eating the apple, Beckmann's understanding of the horrors of the world around him became more profound following his wartime experience. Simultaneously, Eve, grabbing her breast, demonstrates a dawning

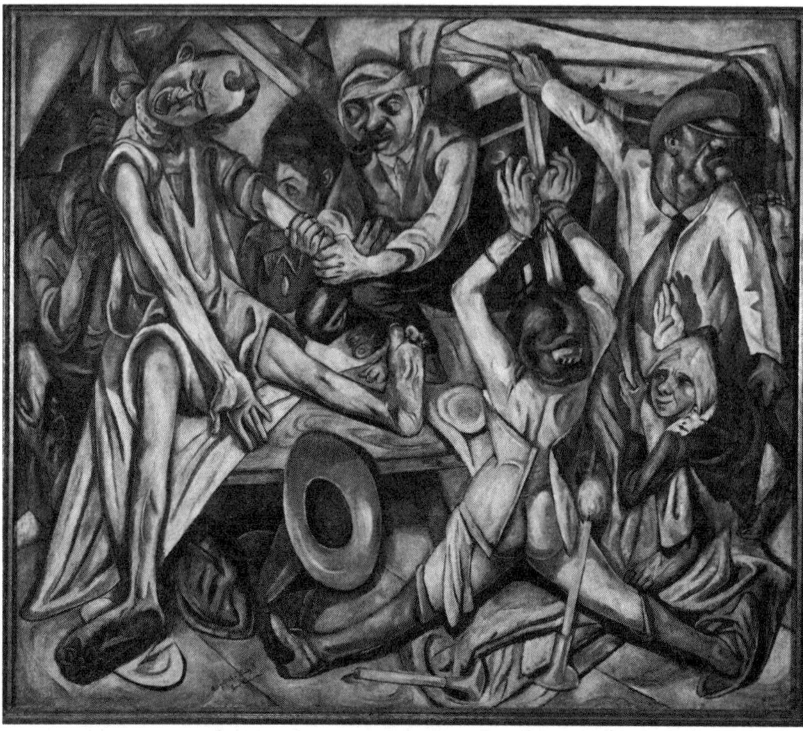

Figure 2.5 Max Beckmann (1884–1950). *The Night* (1919). Oil on canvas.
Collection of Kunstsammlung Nordrhein-Westfalen, Dusseldorf, Germany. Reproduction provided by Erich Lessing / Art Resource, New York.

awareness of her own sexuality and vulnerability. While some of his earlier nude figures are more sensual and romantic, these figures are gaudy, awkward, and *naked*—in short, they are uncomfortable and painful to look at.

In the painting, *The Night* (Figure 2.5/see also color plate 5), "the transformation of [his] art and the realisation of his wartime presentiments are complete" (Storr, 2003, p. 30). Considered to be one of the most gruesome paintings (Lackner, 1977), its composition is crowded with surreal, bizarre, and inharmonious beings. They include one man hanging by a bandana in the upper left corner and a woman whose wrists are bound together, completing what appears to be an involuntary split. The irrational violence all around reflects the horror of war with no glory or justice, "only senseless pain, and cruelty for its own sake . . . there is no exit" (Lackner, p. 82).

> Clearly, the experiences from the first War had a profound effect on his work.
>
> Beckmann probably had to become a victim of the War, had first to be slowly but profoundly shattered by the cumulative horror of such slaughter, suffering

and dying beyond measure in order to grow beyond this narrow, narcissistic view of his art. (Haxthausen, 1984, p. 80)

However, Germany was not yet done with its horrific destruction, nor was it done with Beckmann.

He continued to paint, seemingly exorcising the demons that were brought about by the World War I. Despite the burgeoning political chaos that would soon boil over in postwar Germany, as time progressed his "portraits, still lifes, and landscapes that he undertook in the 1920s [became] more conciliatory in mood" (Britannica, 2002, para. 3). While famously proclaiming himself as apolitical (Rainbird, 2003), Beckmann became engaged with "ideas about the relationship between the artist and the state" (Rainbird, p. 158). His work eventually reflected a "cautious optimism for the future" (Cole, 2009, p. 2403). In 1924, he met Mathilde von Kaulbach and married her a year later. He captured his affection for her in a painting in which "he is almost smiling. . . . Perhaps he felt the worst experience of his life was in the past, and the best was yet to come"(Cole, 2009, p. 2403).

However, the storm clouds of Fascism, as embodied by the burgeoning National Socialist Party, began to darken the cultural landscape. Soon after the Nazi party came to power, Beckmann was dismissed from his teaching post in Frankfurt and labeled a "degenerate" artist (Rainbird, 2003).

Following his dismissal and self-banishment (Rainbird, 2003), his work began to once again reflect Beckmann's reactions to the violence that surrounded him. One of his most famous pieces, the triptych *Departure* (Figure 2.6/see also color plate 6), was completed over a span of 3 years in the midst of and in response to these unsettling and uncertain times.

Triptychs had long been associated with the sacred form of medieval altarpieces (Kruszynski, 2003; Sassen, 2000). Beckmann, who recognized its traditional use, relied on the form as a profane, "secular subversion" (Sassen, 2000).

The first of three triptychs that Beckmann completed as Nazism began its rise, *Departure* embodied "physical violence and human enslavement [as its] central motifs." Through its brazenly garish and simple colors the monumental figures convey an interlocking of "blunt physical violence, slavery and psychological blindness . . . with contemplative peace and openness" (Schulz-Hoffmann, 1984, p. 38). Considered a prediction of the impending war, the work captures his rising anxiety as the noose tightens, through "people being tortured, dismembered and bound in a world gone mad" (Sassen, 2000, p. 25).

In a letter written about this piece, Beckmann indicated that

> Life is what you see right and left. Life is torture, pain of every kind—physical and mental—men and women are subjected to it equally. On the right

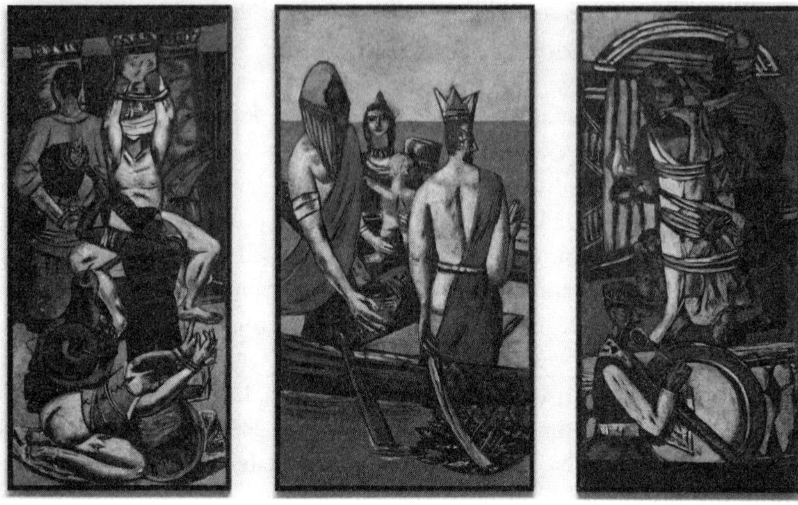

Figure 2.6 Max Beckmann (1884–1950). *Departure* (1932–1935). Oil on canvas, three panels.
Collection of The Museum of Modern Art New York, New York. Reproduction provided by The Museum of Modern Art/Licensed by SCALA / Art Resource, New York.

> wing you can see yourself trying to find your way in the darkness, lighting the hall and staircase with a miserable lamp, dragging along tied to you, as part of yourself, the corpse of your memories, of the wrongs and failures, the murder everyone commits at some time of his life—you can never free yourself of your past, you have to carry that corpse while Life plays the drum. And in the center? The King and Queen, Man and Woman, are taken to another shire by a boatsman whom they do not know, he wears a mask, it is the mysterious figure taking us to a mysterious land . . . [they] have freed themselves of the tortures of life. . . . The Queen carries the greatest treasure—Freedom as a child in her lap. Freedom is the one thing that matters—it is the departure, the new start. (Lackner, 1977, p. 116)

Similar to Goya's prudence, that pulled his prints from circulation before the impending Inquisition, Beckmann "was well aware of the political message that could be inferred from the side panels . . . and the impact such interpretations could have on his safety" (Rainbird, 2003, p. 172). As a result, he exercised restraint in showing the complete triptych. Despite the potential repercussions that he could have incurred through these works, many of his future pieces—his sculptures, landscape, portraits and mythological allegories—continued to rely on many of these leitmotifs.

As the Nazi regime continued its campaign, his work took on tones of loneliness and isolation (Lackner, 1977, 1984), Regardless—or perhaps because of—what was occurring around him, his production became even more prolific. In a letter to his friend and collector, author Stephen Lackner, Beckmann recounted "[m]ay I report about myself that I have had a truly grotesque time, full of the brim of work, Nazi persecutions, bombs, hunger and always again—work—in spite of everything. . . . My nerves and capacity for work are stronger than ever, and I hope to go on producing things " (pp. 155–156). And produce he did, completing 280 paintings and 5 large triptychs during his years of exile, from 1937 and 1947.

Beckmann painted many revealing self-portraits and complicated scenes that often reflected the violence of the Nazis and the torment caused by both world wars. His compositions also portrayed massive faith and incredible redemption. Within all of his works, he revealed his true self with little restraint as he wrestled with the conflicts surrounding him. In 1948, he left Amsterdam for New York, where he lived his few remaining years. In late 1950, Beckmann suffered a heart attack and died several blocks away from his apartment, on his way to see one of his paintings on exhibition at the Metropolitan Museum of Art (Bieber, 2003).

Victims of War

Some bore witness to the destruction around them and strove to communicate through their work the horrors they observed. Others were victims of their war-torn environments singled out, targeted as scapegoats. Despite this, they created works that lifted them above their destructive, dehumanizing victimization.

Felix Nussbaum: Defiance of a Degenerate Artist

The work of Nussbaum was anything but subtle: he painted to deliberately and clearly convey the fear, isolation, and heartache he experienced while hiding from the Nazis.

Felix Nussbaum was born in Osnabruck, Germany, in 1904, into a Jewish middle-class family. Encouraged to pursue painting by his father, who was himself an amateur artist, Nussbaum formerly studied in Hamburg in 1922, where he met fellow artist Felka Platek; she later became his wife. He subsequently relocated to Berlin, living there from 1924 to 1929. After painting in a shared studio for the next several years, Nussbaum received a scholarship in 1932 to study in the German Academy's Villa Massimo in Rome, Italy. That same year, as Jewish persecution began to intensify, a fire "of dubious origin" in his Berlin studio destroyed a majority of his paintings (Felstiner, 2000, p. 496). Shortly after, Joseph Goebbels, Hitler's Minister of Propaganda, closed the Academy, forcing Nussbaum and Felka to leave. After wandering around the Italian Riviera, Switzerland, and France until 1935, they eventually settled in Belgium (Kaster, 1997).

He and Felka set up a studio where Nussbaum continued to paint, unabated by the developing political turmoil around him. In 1937, he and Felka married and settled in Brussels. That same year the Nazi propaganda machine began its traveling exhibition, Degenerate Art (see Chapter 3). Concerned about "cultural disintegration," Adolf Hitler labeled works *degenerate* that he deemed were an "insult to German feeling, . . . destroy[ed] or confuse[d] natural form or simply reveal[ed] an absence of adequate manual and artistic skill" (Spotts, 2002, p. 163).

To promote and champion what Hitler deemed to be the racial purity of classical work, the Nazi Party developed the German Art Exhibition. Simultaneously, Goebbels developed the exhibition Die Ausstellung "Entartete Kunst" (Degenerate Art Exhibition) to hold up as a stark contrast to their German ideal. This show displayed modernist works by "Jewish-Bolshevists" that the Nazis claimed promoted the destruction of German decency; never mind that only six of more than 100 artists were Jewish. In 1938, artists in Paris responded by creating the Free German Art exhibition (Chametsky, 2010). Nussbaum contributed two paintings to this show. Kristallnacht, or the "Night of Broken Glass," began days later.

Under the pretext that a German diplomat was murdered by a 17-year-old Jewish boy in Paris, paramilitary forces and German citizens targeted the innocent Jewish people with no intervention from the authorities. The subsequent looting and rioting all over Germany, Austria, and Sudetenland destroyed more than 7,000 Jewish businesses and 250 synagogues; more than 30,000 Jewish people were arrested and deported to camps and more than 100 were killed outright (Gilbert, 2012). Nussbaum continued to paint dark, surreal, and at times grotesque works reflecting the horrible instability around him. Shortly after *Kristallnacht*, Nussbaum painted *Masquerade* (Figure 2.7), in which he depicted a collection of mask-like, distorted figures painted in garish colors. Each one borrows characteristics from previous self-portraits—the pearls, the green cap, their apparel, even some of the faces. The group, presumably revelers, hardly seemed to be celebrating; "Nussbaum was identifying his personal situation with the situation of the Jews in Germany after the Crystal Night" (Kaster, 1997, p. 278).

The hostility and despair is enhanced by the dead tree on a barren landscape to the left, silhouetted before a cloud-covered moon. The people are further hemmed in by the buildings on the right. It seems that there is no escape for these party-goers, and this knowledge has dawned on them a little too late.

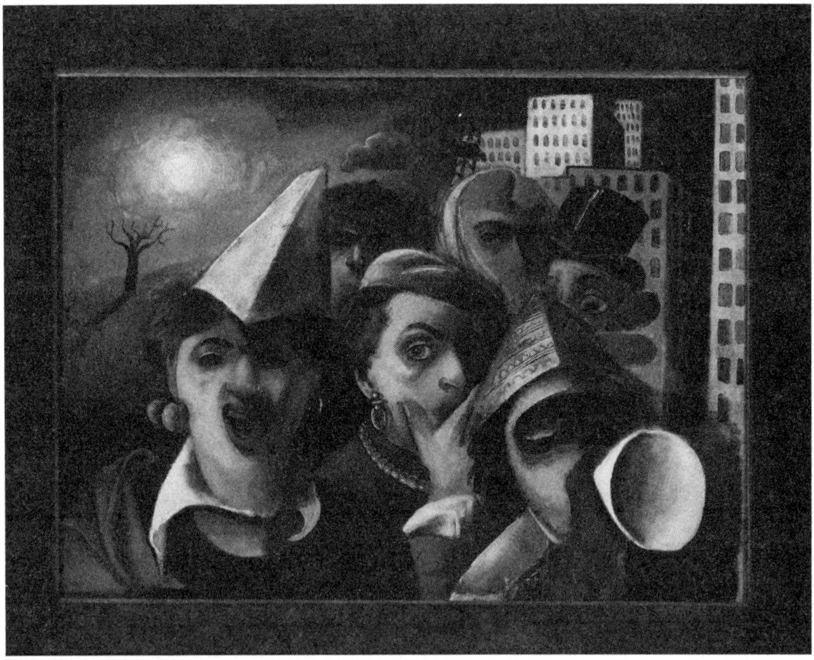

Figure 2.7 Felix Nussbaum (1904–1945). *Masquerade* (1927). Tempera and oil on canvas.

Collection of Smart Museum of Art, Chicago. Reproduction provided by Smart Museum of Art, Chicago.

When the Germans invaded Belgium in 1940, Nussbaum was arrested in Brussels as a "hostile alien" and was deported to a detention camp in St. Cyprien, France. After living in harsh and unforgiving conditions in the camp for several months, Nussbaum managed to escape. He was able to find his way back to Belgium, where Platek was waiting. Nussbaum and Platek hid "underground" for the next several years. However, by 1942, things really began to heat up in Belgium as the Nazi's Final Solution began. More than half of the Jews in that small country were transported in its initial deportation to the extermination camps; the Jewish population was decimated over the next 2 years. Of the 25,000 deported only 1,200 survived (Gilbert, 2012).

During these years, Nussbaum's drive to paint would not abate; he often left the relative safety of his attic hideout to venture into his studio. It was then that he painted some of his most renowned and impactful works, including the haunting *Self Portrait with an Identity Card* (Figure 2.8) and the overwhelming *Death Triumphant (The Skeletons Playing for the Dance)* (Figure 2.9/see also color plate 7).

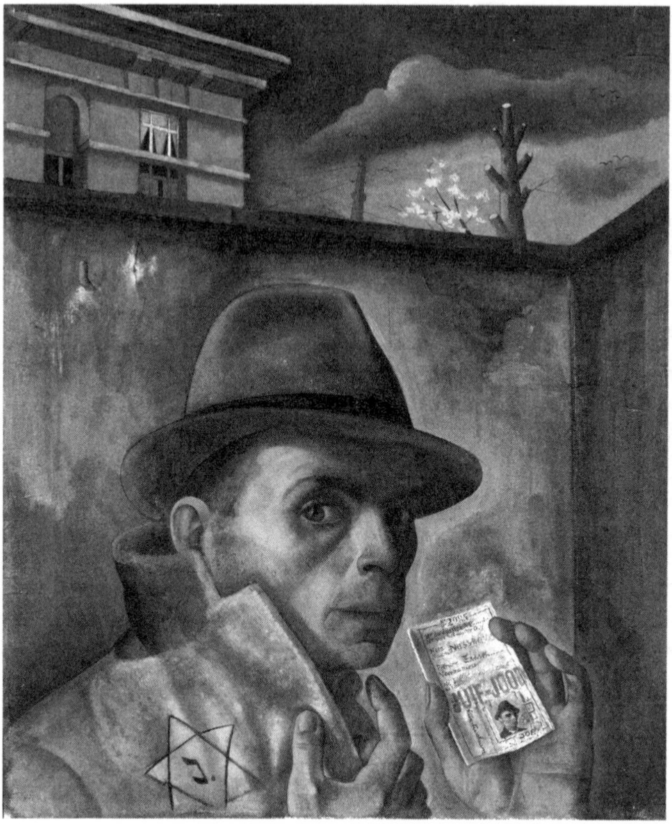

Figure 2.8 Felix Nussbaum (1904–1945). *Self Portrait with an Identity Card* (c. 1943). Oil on canvas.

Collection of Kulturgeschichtliches Museum, Osnabrueck, Germany. Reproduction provided by bpk Bildagentur / Kulturgeschichtliches Museum / Art Resource, New York.

This particular *Self Portrait* was painted a year before he died. Nussbaum appears before a filthy white wall, displaying his identity card in his left hand. He is lifting up the lapel of his coat to show the yellow *Juden* star that all Jews were required to wear so they could be immediately identified. Both the identity card and the patch, confirming his Jewish identity, were required by the Nazis as a means to degrade and humiliate. The emaciated expression seems simultaneously frightened and defiant. The decaying white wall, painted in muted yellows and browns, is a common symbol of menace that appears in many of Nussbaum's paintings (Elsby, n.d.). The wall is tall, either encapsulating or protecting Nussbaum; it could even appear that he is standing within a tomb. Storm clouds gather high in the sky behind a dead tree, similar to that displayed in *Masquerade*. The building in the upper right may provide some protection,

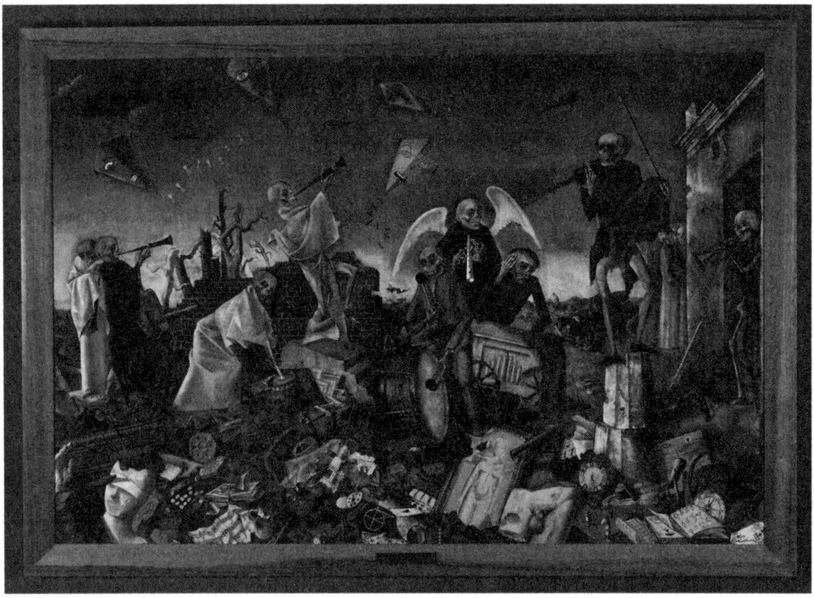

Figure 2.9 Felix Nussbaum (1904–1945). *Death Triumphant (The Skeletons Playing for the Dance)* (1944). Oil on canvas.

Collection of Lower Saxony Sparkasse Foundation, Germany. Reproduction provided by bpk Bildagentur / Lower Saxony Sparkasse Foundation / Art Resource, New York.

but, quite frankly, seems well out of reach. Unlike some of his earlier paintings the tone is more muted; the only real brightness emanates from the star and the identity card.

What is not clear to the viewer is who Nussbaum is gazing at. Someone who has cornered him, forcing him to show his identity card or a conspiratorial signal to an ally with whom he is conforming his identity? Or perhaps, as viewers, we are meant to be voyeuristic bystanders, giving witness to the horrors these people are going through, while we do nothing. In showing his card "he puts the viewer, to whom he has to legitimate himself, in the position of the scoundrel, the informer" (Kaster, 1997, p. 410). However, in showing his identity with such defiance, he seems to be taking back the power, his identity: "he is reversing the stigmatization. It is not Nussbaum who is driven into a corner in this picture and stands accused, but the viewer . . . the work is an act of resistance" (p. 410). The painting conveys an intensity, a sense of furtive insolence, the subject doing everything he can to maintain his humanity and his identity. Unfortunately, it is already too late.

He completed his final painting, *Death Triumphant (The Skeletons Playing for the Dance)*, shortly before he was arrested and deported. This grim and muted painting depicts many skeletons playing and dancing to music among the ruins.

The figures seem to be at various stages of decay, some with skin hanging from their bodies. In a manner of speaking, this, too, is autobiographical. The central rotting figure sitting by the organ looks a great deal like Nussbaum, and the motif of that figure is reminiscent of an earlier painting, *The Organ Grinder.* The figures are surrounded by debris such as a film roll, microscope, and musical scores, as well as by objects from his own life, like Felka's tailor dummy and his father's automobile (Arts in Exile, n.d.). Included in the rubble are two paintings, a portrait of a man and a woman. In destruction nothing is sacred; all will eventually disappear.

Yet, in the rubble lies a crumpled up page containing a musical score, the first few bars of a popular song from a well-known musical *Me and My Girl.* The words that go with these notes in the song, "The Lambeth Walk" are "Ev'rythin' free and easy / Do as you darn well please" (Kaster, 1997). It signals hope, defiance, or longing, feelings that belie the fate that awaited him and his wife.

Two weeks after D-Day, Platek and Nussbaum were denounced by an informer and arrested by the Wehrmacht. Shortly before his deportation, Nussbaum entrusted his paintings to a dentist in Brussels. He implored him "If I perish, don't let my paintings die, show them to people" (Felstiner, 2000, p. 495). He and his wife were sent to Belgium's collection camp, Malines. Shortly before this camp was liberated by the Allies, one last transport was sent to Auschwitz on July 31, 1944; Platek and Nussbaum were on this train. They were gassed 1 week later.

Similar to Felix Nussbaum, Vann Nath used his paintings to document the horrors he experienced in his war-torn country; unlike Nussbaum, Vann Nath survived, giving an added voice to these autobiographical images.

Vann Nath: Escaping the Ghost List

Vann Nath was a Cambodian artist and writer who later became a human rights activist following his release from the prison where he was kept and tortured by the Khmer Rouge. Of the thousands of Cambodians imprisoned in S-21, he was one of only seven adults to survive the fall of the Khmer Rouge at the hands of the Vietnamese army (Nath, 1998). His art bears witness to the terror that surrounded him.

The Khmer Rouge was a succession of repressive political parties in Cambodia. It first emerged during the conflicts of the 1960s and was initially supported by the Viet Cong. Embodying a number of different communist parties in the region, it rose to dominate Cambodia in the mid-1970s, under the repressive and paranoid leadership of Pol Pot. Throughout the early 1970s, factions warred with each other to gain dominance in the region, including the Maoist-focused Khmer. In 1975, the Khmer Rouge gained the upper hand and took over the region. In power for a little over 3 and a half years, the Khmer Rouge detained and executed more than 200,000 "enemies of the state," and hastened the death of hundreds of thousands more through starvation and overwork; it is believed that more than 1 million died (Clayton, 1998; Dunlop, 2005). Vann Nath was one of 14,000 arrested and detained at the former high school in Phnom Penh, since designated S-21. It was here, for exactly 1 year, that Vann Nath was tortured by this brutal regime until his escape in January 1979 (Nath, 1998).

Born around 1946 into a poor, rural family, Vann Nath became fascinated with painting early during his brief education. However, rather than pursue it, Vann Nath entered the monkhood, leaving it when he was 21 years old to help support his family. Eventually, he underwent formal training to become an artist and soon began painting portraits and billboards on commission. Vann Nath struggled to survive among the chaos and terror that accompanied the regime change in the mid-1970s. With friends and neighbors taken away, many to be executed with seemingly little provocation, Vann Nath feared for his own safety and for that of his wife and children. Over the next several years, his life was filled with dread and hardship. Along with many of his neighbors, he was forced into labor by the governing body, which slowly and severely limited their food rations, causing mass starvation (Nath, 1998).

In late 1977, Vann Nath was forced to leave his wife and children to join others to harvest rice. He was ordered from the field several days later to accompany one of the commune chiefs; during this transport, he was forcibly restrained with rope and shackles and detained with no explanation. Thus began his year-long nightmare (Nath, 1998).

Many died under these conditions, through starvation or illness, or they were simply shot. Nath was shackled to hundreds of other detainees and barely survived on mouthfuls of rice a day. However, he could paint, seen as a redeemable and exploitable talent. Several weeks after his arrest, Nath was taken out and interrogated by Duch, the chief of the prison (Dunlop, 2006). He was asked to render a portrait of Pol Pot from a photograph. This was a means to determine his skills. Despite the lightened conditions allowed while he painted the portrait, he was filled with trepidation, knowing he would be tortured if the sadistic guards were not satisfied with his painting. As Nath recalled "My destiny was hanging on this last picture!" (Nath, 1998, p. 63).

The result did indeed meet the Chief's approval. As a result, Nath was tasked with painting more portraits of the Khmer's supreme leader. In addition, some of the guards had him "paint some colorful pictures of villagers, people planting rice, and people harvesting. When I had free time I painted [these] pictures with approval from the room guard" (Nath, p. 66). Nath began to sculpt as well. He soon made himself indispensable.

As the political and military situation outside began to shift, life within the detention institution changed, simultaneously and paradoxically becoming more negligent yet more deadly; while there was less for the prisoners to do and fewer guards to watch over them, many prisoners simply "disappeared." They were eventually forced to march and carry rice for the local soldiers during attacks by the Vietnamese Army. With erratic gunfire overhead and despite a swollen foot, Nath escaped.

After wandering around for several weeks, Nath volunteered for the new Cambodian Army. He served with them for several months. He eventually received permission to go back to his hometown and search for his family. It was then he learned of the death of his children. However, he was able to find his brother, who had believed him dead. After their joyful reunion, he helped Nath find his wife, and they celebrated their reconnection while mourning all that they had lost.

Vann Nath continued his work in the new military. Several months in, he was asked to work alongside other survivors to help transform S-21 into a museum depicting the genocide. He was asked to paint scenes depicting the horrific existence of life within the converted school, "what he had seen or heard or what other former prisoners related to him" (Hinton, 2014, p. 9). While tasked to provide narrative and objective depictions, the illustrations (Figures 2.10 and 2.11) emotionally and viscerally captured the callousness and inhumanity rained upon the innocent; they are "among the most powerful and iconic images at the

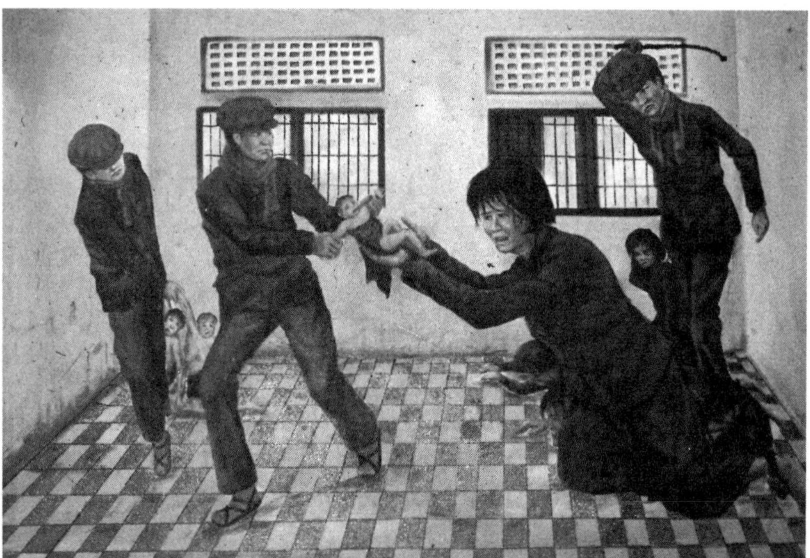

Figure 2.10 Vann Nath (1946–2011). *Imprisonment of Civilians by the Khmers* (1991). Oil on canvas.

Permission and reproduction provided by Francoise De Mulder (Photographer) / Roger Viollet (Collector) via Getty Images.

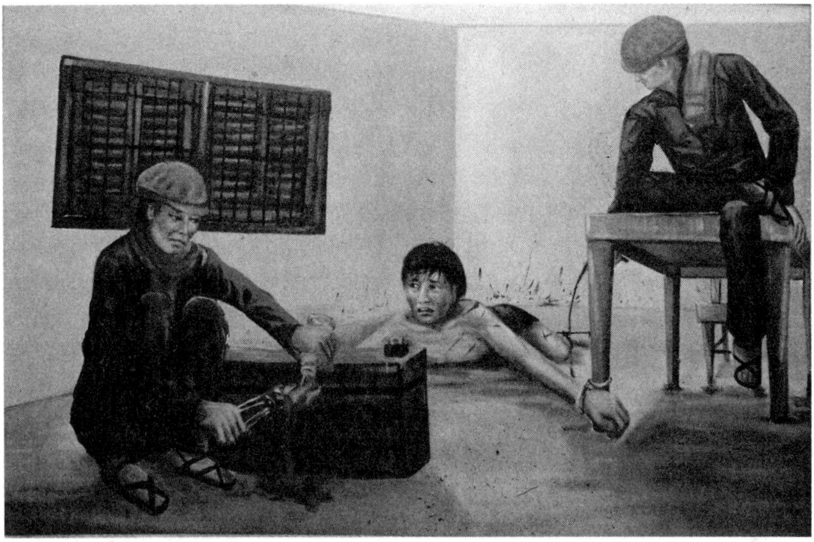

Figure 2.11 Vann Nath (1946–2011). *Torture of Civilians by the Khmers Rouge* (1991). Oil on canvas.
Permission and reproduction provided by Francoise De Mulder (Photographer) / Roger Viollet (Collector) via Getty Images.

museum" (Hinton, p. 9). While his paintings served as an autobiographical narrative, the "[a]rt also seemed to provide Vann Nath with a way of grappling with the past" (Hinton, p. 14).

Nath's final painting depicts Duch, the former commander of S-2, seated among piles of skulls and bones that stretch back toward the horizon within a desolate landscape (Figure 2.12/see also color plate 8). Such a backdrop was common in his paintings, perhaps an allusion to his desire to escape the confines of his cell and disappear into the vast and open terrain. Vultures, which are "a Buddhist symbol of the attachment and craving that drive people to sin" (Hinton, 2018, p. 140), fly overhead surveying the scene. The figure, far removed from the arrogant oppressor who terrorized the imprisoned, appears crestfallen, maintaining the same slumped posture and expression he used for his own self-portrait as a prisoner. A copy of the verdict sentencing Duch to life imprisonment by the Khmer Rouge Tribunal sits before him.

This painting amplifies the freedom that Vann Nath now had; he was once forced to paint the leaders of the Khmer Rouge when imprisoned. He is doing so again, but depicting him in the way he truly saw him and without fear. He has taken back control and, with it, his integrity, dignity, and autonomy.

At first blush, it appears that many of his paintings were devoid of emotion. Vann Nath set out to objectively reconstruct and document the inmates' experiences.

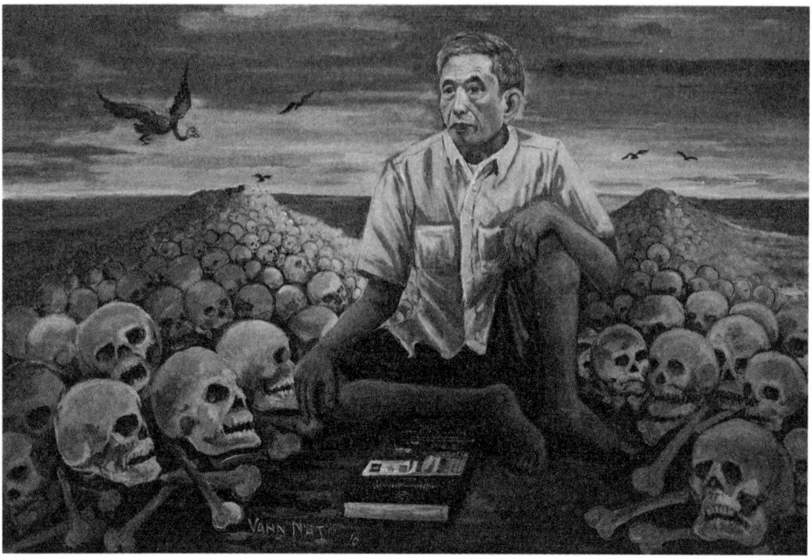

Figure 2.12 Vann Nath (1946–2011). *Duch's Verdict.* Oil on canvas.
Permission provided by Channarong Vann. Reproduction provided by Bophana Center.

Many of his compositions, filled with both literal narration and symbolic imagery, are crowded and dense. It almost feels that Nath is trying to convey as much as possible within limited time and resources. It seems, however, that Nath is controlling his rage, impotence, and overwhelming loss through exaggerated objectivity and unemotional depiction; while the imagery is overly controlling in style, his narrative is not. He doesn't or cannot hold back. Even still, there must have been some residual anxiety, a fear of reprisal, remaining from the time he was forced to paint for the regime. His paintings eventually became more expressive, perhaps as he began to feel secure and safe, that he could express himself freely without reprisals. When he was imprisoned, his paintings depicted flattering portraits of the supreme leader, pastoral landscapes. and working peasants. Once free and called upon to reflect and depict his experiences, he could recapture his humanity and sense of self. He could, at last, come to terms with all that he experienced.

Vann Nath far outlived the architect of his terror; Pol Pot, died in 1998. Vann Nath made it his life work to bring attention to the senseless genocide perpetrated on his people through his writings and paintings. From 2001 to 2002, he collaborated with Cambodian filmmaker Rithy Panh on the documentary T*he Khmer Rouge Killing Machine* (Boyle, 2009); in it he confronted and interrogated his former torturers. After suffering a heart attack and slipping into a coma, Vann Nath died in September 2011, in his hometown of Phnom Penh, Cambodia.

A year after Vann Nath began working at the museum,

> a staff person who was researching the prison documents called me over . . . he handed a piece of paper to me.
>
> "Have a look, Brother!"
>
> After I looked at the paper, my hands and feet became cold. It was an execution list. My name was there, but underlined in red ink with brackets at the end saying "keep." . . . Virtually all the people who were arrested with me . . . were included on that list. . . . Oh God! I didn't know my name had been put on the "ghost" list. . . . That meant that all my friends who shared the same shackles with me were killed that day. It was only at this moment that I knew clearly that none of my fellow prisoners survived. (Nath, 1998, p. 107)

Two Artists Experiencing the Same Civil Unrest: From Outside and From Within

The previous artists created art during wartime, when their countries were in armed conflict with another for various geopolitical reasons. In some cases, conflict and violence had been inflicted by their own countrymen; they were victimized by the very society in which they resided. In such situations, the sense of helplessness and overwhelming anxiety is immeasurable; people are unclear just who they are supposed to turn to, to protect them from those who establish the laws that suppress them. As such, people may have their identity stripped away and made subservient to the state.

The United States went through—and, some would argue, still is—going through such a time, originating with slavery up through civil unrest, and, at the time of this writing, with Black Lives Matter. Some are victims and some are witnesses. Yet it is up to the witnesses to determine if they will do something about what they are seeing or remain complicit through silence. In such cases, art may be the only weapon they have to stand up, fight back, and maintain their own identity and integrity.

The following two artists documented their own experiences during the time of slavery and civil upheaval in the United States, from the late nineteenth century through the late twentieth century. Bill Traylor used his art to reclaim his identity and give voice to what he dared not say out loud while slavery, Jim Crow, and civil unrest worked so hard to cancel him. Norman Rockwell, long tasked with documenting middle-class White America, finally decided that he could no longer bear witness to the unjust society he saw around him and took it upon himself to illustrate the horror.

Bill Traylor: An Outside[r] Artist Never Allowed In

Bill Traylor's life spanned the full experience of the violence and degradation faced by the African American person in the United States; as a Black man in the Deep South, he was born into slavery, had a front seat to the Civil War, was "freed" through Emancipation, survived Reconstruction, was oppressed through Jim Crow Segregation, and was swept up into the tide of the Great Migration. Although he did not live long enough to see the Civil Rights movement take root, he was one who helped plant the seeds (Umberger, 2018). In his late 80s, illiterate and homeless, living on the streets of Montgomery, Alabama, Traylor told his story and those of his people in the only way he knew how—through his art. In this way, Traylor wrest back control, perhaps calmed the demons inside himself, and struck out at his oppressors.

There have been many versions, some inaccurate, of Traylor's life story—perhaps not uncommon for a person clearly remanded to the outskirts of society. For example, Kurzmeyer (1999) relied on a single census document indicating that Traylor was born in 1856, while Sobel designated two different years for Traylor's birth date—1853 and 1854—in two separate publications (1996, 2009). Traylor himself said he was born in 1854 (Kurzmeyer, 1999; Umberger, 2018). However, after meticulous examination of numerous records, Umberger determined that he was likely born in 1853 (Umberger, 2018).

He was one of six children of Sally and Bill Calloway-Traylor who were purchased and enslaved by John Getson Traylor from Benjamin Calloway's plantation to work his lands near Benton, Alabama. Once he became of age, Traylor was forced to work on J. G. Traylor's land until the South surrendered to the North in 1865. He was 13 when his father died a year later (Umberger, 2018).

Even after Emancipation, Traylor continued to work at the plantation, entrapped and exploited by the constraining Jim Crow laws. During the last couple of decades of the nineteenth century, as racial segregation became the norm, violence against Black people increased and economic opportunities decreased. Traylor continued to live in Benton, Alabama, working for the White Traylors throughout Reconstruction and well into the beginning of the twentieth century to support his large family (Sobel, 2009; Umberger, 2018).

In 1880, Traylor married his first wife, Elsy Dunklin, with whom it was believed he had three children. Elsy "either died or was otherwise severed from the family shortly after she gave birth to Sarah in 1887" (Umberger, p. 61). Several years later, Traylor married Laurine Dunklin. Nellie Williams was born to Laura Williams, who some believed was Traylor's illegitimate daughter (Sobel, 2009), However, her death certificate recorded that she was the child of Laura and Burrell Williams (Umberger, 2018). Still, it has not been completely ruled out that Traylor was Nellie's illegitimate father (Umberger, 2018), and, by 1900,

Nellie was in the care of Laurine and Traylor, identified on the 1910 census as Traylor's step-daughter.

Bill and Laurine had five more children in the 1890s. He married his third wife, Laura Williams, in 1909, and, by 1914, Traylor had a total of 14 children, including Nellie. Various historians have underscored that Traylor was involved with both Laurine and Laura simultaneously, likely contributing to the claim that Nellie was his illegitimate child. However, it was just as likely that inconsistent, inaccurate, and incomplete records—marred by "illiteracy and racism" (Umberger, p. 74)—resulted in the propagation of misinformation. For example rather than Traylor being involved with both women simultaneously, it was just as likely the names Laurine and Laura were applied interchangeably to his second wife on birth certificates and family documentations. Such ambiguities may have contributed to Traylor's complicated and sometimes salacious folklore, which has been used to prolong the racial stereotypes assigned to him without putting him in the proper historical context and system of White supremacy.

By 1910, Traylor moved closer to Montgomery, Alabama, right outside the city limits. Sobel (2009) claimed he did so after apparently murdering a man for sleeping with Laurine. However, there is no evidence that Traylor did so; it seems just as likely Sobel was simply recounting an unsupported idea put forward by a previous author. While this charge has since been refuted, it has been accepted and disseminated perhaps by those who fail to question stereotypically racial narratives. Yet, even while there is no way to substantiate this claim, "the possibility that Traylor experienced some regrettable violence . . . that had a perceivably bad outcome is entirely possible—plausible even—in an era when violence was pervasive" (Umberger, p. 142). Such violence, whether he committed or witnessed it, would indeed weigh heavily on him and would certainly permeate his artwork later.

Traylor began to gain some independence and, by 1910, moved just outside of Montgomery, where he and his family worked "rented land, [where] Bill is called the 'employer' with his wife and children working for wages under him" (Umberger, p. 69). By 1920, Traylor and his family worked and lived on the old Seller Plantation. Laura soon disappeared from the records in the late 1920s; it is likely she died as Traylor was recorded as a widower in 1930. His family began to leave in the 1920s, moving all over the South and into the East Coast. Traylor settled alone in downtown Montgomery, making some money by working as a laborer and then as a shoemaker.

Tragedy struck in 1929, when his son Will was killed. While the official report indicated that he was shot by a police officer after he broke into a house with a gun, Traylor's great grandchild told Sobel (2009) that Traylor believed that his son had actually been lynched for "peeping in the window of a white woman" (p. 73). While this, too, has not been substantiated, it is possible given a time when "law enforcement in Alabama was unquestionably on the side of white society" (Umberger, 2018, p. 82) and where "without provocation police shoot Negroes so frequently there, it is no longer news" (Bagnall, 1929, as cited by Umberger, 2018, p. 82). Given how dangerous it was for Black people in the South to speak against those in power, the possible manner in which Will was killed was never reported or recorded. This devastated Traylor.

Shortly after his son's death, work became impossible for Traylor because of crippling rheumatism. He lost his job as a shoemaker around the beginning of the Great Depression (Shannon, 1999). Unable to pay rent, Traylor slept in the showroom of a local funeral home with permission from the owner. Around the late 1930s, Traylor began camping out on the sidewalk on Monroe Street during the day; "he selected a good spot to work, one in which he could see an amazingly full life, and yet would be protected by supportive people around him" (Sobel, 2009, p. 93). It was there he began to draw and paint.

An unexpected event occurred around 1939. While there is some disagreement on who may have seen Traylor drawing on the sidewalk first, Charles Shannon, a young White artist has historically been given credit for "discovering" Traylor (Maizels, 1996).[1] Shannon took an earnest if not paternalistic interest in Traylor's work (Umberger, 2018). He began providing Traylor with art supplies, mostly poster paints, which the artist used on torn, dirty cardboard.

In 1939, Traylor moved his sleeping accommodations to a nearby shoe repair shop and began painting next to "Isaac Varon's fruit store" (Sobel, 2009, p. 95), a space that was much better protected from the elements. It also had the additional advantage of being near the Varons, people who were quite helpful to Traylor, making sure that he ate regularly and was taken care of. Shannon soon sought out various markets for Traylor's drawings (Helfenstein, 1999).

While never clearly indicated, it seemed that the genesis of Traylor's artistic endeavors emerged from the turmoil he experienced, particularly Will's violent death. As Sobel (2009) asserted, like Goya,

> Bill Traylor's art similarly reflects his courageous imagination and his access to his inner turmoil, as well as his personal stake in the violence of his lifeworld. Unlike Goya, during most of his life, Traylor did not have any cultural, social or economic support to become an artist, but when it became critical for him after Will Traylor was killed, he made his own way to such a role. Bill Traylor's suffering after his son's death stands behind his life-altering decision to devote all his time to painting. (p. 92)

[1] This has since been contested; Jay Leavell of the New South Collective—a collection of White progressive artists who adopted what may now be called a social justice perspective—was considered the first person to see Traylor drawing and called Shannon's attention to it.

Unable to read or write, likely filled with unexpressed rage and sorrow for what he experienced his entire life, it seemed Traylor could no longer remain silent—he needed to express himself and regain control in his impotent world. He turned to painting, works that could be considered "both autobiographical . . . and clear and coded statements of his rage" (Sobel, 2009, p. 2).

Traylor's designs embodied an artistic style that has been described as *Outsider Art* (Petullo, 2001; Stokes Sims, 1999), a genre that Roger Cardinal (1972) described as work created by those on the margins of society, *outside* the mainstream art world. He considered the art of these self-taught artists as honest yet naïve, simultaneously pure and crude (Maizels, 1996); this category often includes the art of those with mental illnesses as well (Prinzhorn, 1922/1995).

Some have associated outsider art with *folk art* and even *Primitivism*, works that emulate art made by those who belonged to non-Western cultures, tribal civilizations, and even prehistoric societies. While some champion the term, acknowledging and bringing attention to those who have been consigned to the fringes and even disenfranchised (see intuit.org), for some, being called an "Outsider artist" is considered a pejorative and limiting label with prejudicial overtones, keeping such identified artists at a distance (Kempf, 2002; Krug & Parker, 2009).

> These artists are "outside" of what? Their own social contexts? Sometimes. The mainstream? Usually. In fact, these people, like some of the best artists who function within the art world, are really insiders. They are outcasts only because those who live in their head tend to be ignored in a society that primarily decorates the pocket and the outer self. Their isolation is actually a perceived but unacknowledged class difference. (Lippard, 1994, pp. 5–6)

In this very real sense, Traylor, as an artist, remained an outsider, marginalized and shunned by society, relegated to a life of subservience, dependent on the support of others. To underscore this, it seems that his story is told in such a way that it promotes the racial mythos that he needed a White man—a *savior*—to validate him and see value in what he created.

Certainly Shannon's support was life-changing and frankly unusual for a Black man to receive in the late 1930s: although it was unlikely that "Shannon was probably the first white person to see a large body of [Traylor's] paintings . . . his reaction was an affirmation of their worth" (Sobel, p. 94). However, even this relationship was uneven; it seemed that it never occurred to "Shannon to ask Traylor what his work was about, what his motivations were, what he was chronicling in his thousands of drawings. Now, decades later, academics more or less try to guess what the work was about" (Turl, 2019, para. 8). Several scholars have assigned various meanings and rationale for his works, intertwined with his complicated history and his context (Morrin, 1999; Sobel, 2009; Stokes Sims, 1999; Umberger, 2018).

> It is obvious that the Traylor images in [his] portfolio are deeply felt, self-sufficient works that can be read simply as triumphant celebrations of the human faculty for invention, quite independently of their author's biography. But Traylor's history also makes him part of a larger phenomenon: the vital culture of African-Americans [*sic*] in the rural South, a font of creativity and disguised protest. (Wilkin, 2015, p. 34)

At the risk of unfairly presuming that I know what is inside Traylor's mind, I, too, enumerate how Traylor's work may have reflected his impotence, rage, and sorrow concerning the violence around him while countering his own invisibility and giving power and dignity to the people in his drawings who may otherwise have had them stripped away.

Traylor's simple yet bold and colorful symbols revealed his lack of formal training, yet he found a style and process that became his own (Yau, 1989). "Traylor's drawing technique was quite deliberate; using a block of wood as a straight edge, he rendered a basic geometric form and built the rest of the image around that shape" (Petullo, 2001, p. 162). This is evident in *Untitled (Radio)* (Figure 2.13).

Traylor relied on straight lines to create a house-like structure containing a seated, top-hatted figure silhouetted in black surrounded by a blue haze. The man is pointing through the roof at a bird flying above the building. Outside is another male figure, also seemingly well-to-do in his hat and fine shoes, pointing a gun in the air at the bird, which is successfully evading the intended hunter. Behind the man stands a brown dog. Along the side of the house, deliberately incorporated into the structure is the boldly stamped word *radio*—the remaining evidence that this piece of cardboard on which Traylor painted was originally an advertisement for a wireless receiver (Umberger, 2018). While we don't know for sure, his seemingly innocuous depictions of animals and men became the vehicles to express his frustrations, fears, and sorrow while regaining a sense of potency and spiritual control.

One of his compositions, *Leg Construction with Five Figures*, depicts a vicious dog baring its teeth at five men, one wielding a hatchet trying to chop down a structure made out of a pair of legs. Traylor employed the disembodied legs in several of his pieces; Umberger (2018) indicated that these seemed reminiscent of the cobbler's anvil that Bill used when he worked in a shoe repair shop, a simple structure that "transform[ed] the shape of a human foot into something threatening, hammer-like and potentially cruel" (p. 141). This contributed to a more "violent and chaotic image"(p. 141) than some of his earlier works, perhaps

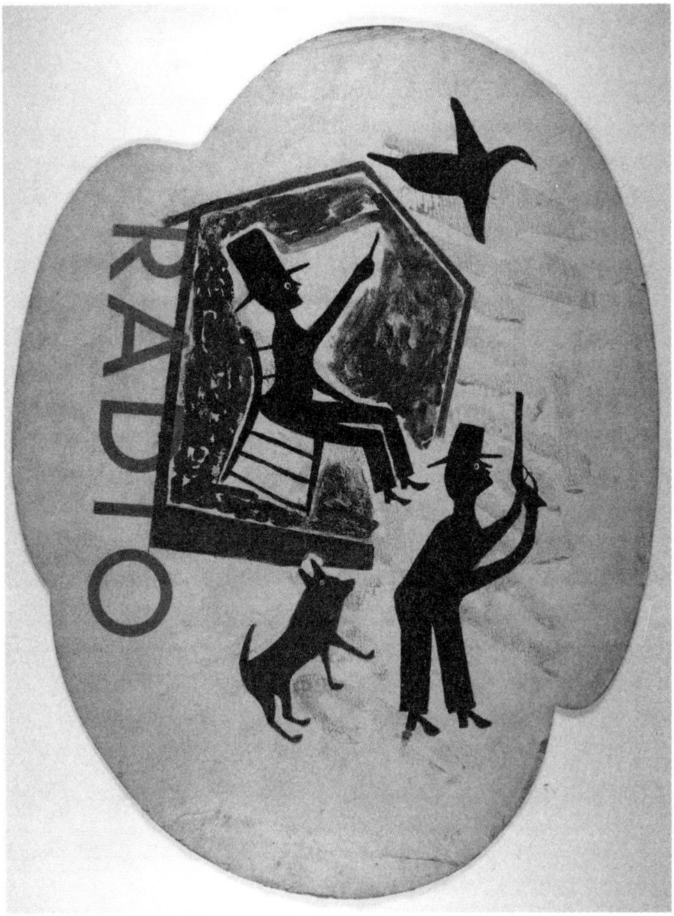

Figure 2.13 Bill Traylor (1854–1949). *Untitled (Radio)* (c. 1940–1942). Opaque watercolor and pencil on printed advertising paperboard.

Permission and reproduction provided by Smithsonian American Art Museum.

Museum purchase through the Luisita L. and Franz H. Denghausen Endowment, copyright 1994, Bill Traylor Family Trust.

suggesting a symbolic battle between good and evil within himself. Sobel (2009) believed that this particular composition depicted male sexuality dominating the female form. For her, the powerful legs with a protruding penile shape in the middle seems to represent a man prodding a form that is reminiscent of a woman's buttocks. (Sobel often believed that many of Traylor's pieces conveyed crude and blatant sexuality, what she thought underscored Traylor's potential power struggles with women.) Comparably, *Untitled (Construction with Yawping Woman)* (Figure 2.14), may also contain similarly implicit symbols.

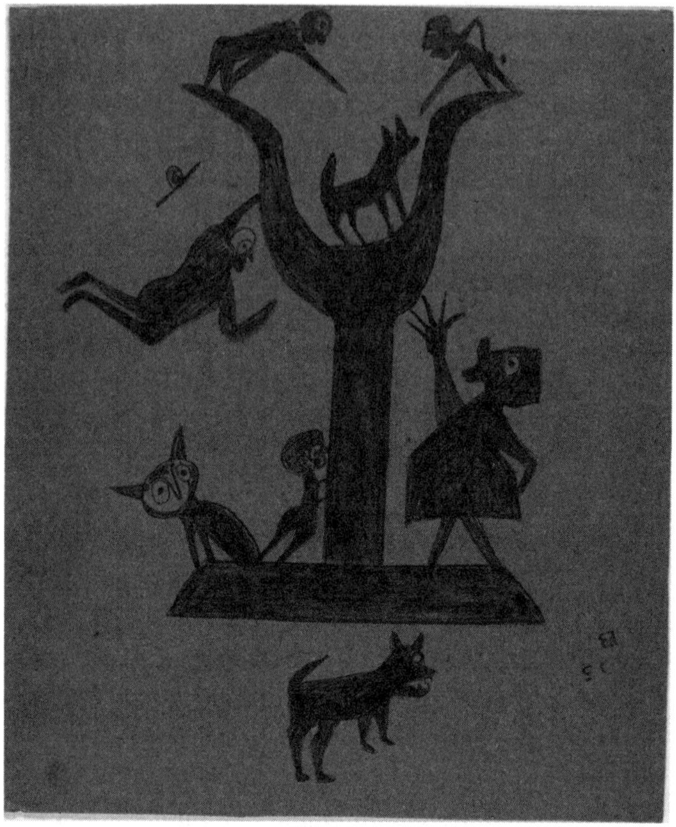

Figure 2.14 Bill Traylor (1854–1949). *Untitled (Construction with Yawping Woman)* (c. 1939–1942). Opaque watercolor and pencil on paperboard.

Atop the titled construction stands two men with rifles pointing at a dog in the bowl-like shape. There is a man hanging from the side by one hand with his hat flying off while a child stands on the base underneath him with a cat perched nearby. Standing on the other side of the base is a woman "yawping," or screeching up at the two men and dog. Beneath the base is another dog baring its teeth. Umberger (2018) saw this image as somewhat humorous and seemingly benign, a composition in which a "family probably, point, yell and panic to find a dog in the elevated bowl" (p. 245). For her, this represented a type of composition in which Traylor "comingled frolic with mayhem" (p. 244), juxtaposing playful "cavorting and fighting" (p. 245). This was perhaps a way to gain control through levity by "emphasiz[ing] waggishness and wildness over the clearly complex, often heavy memories" (p. 244); such humor, which Shannon and others focused on at the expense of the serious undertones of his work, was likely used as a "foil," to mask the real underlying darkness (Umberger, personal communication).[2] Predictably, Sobel (2009) believed that this image represented "coded sexual relations in which the penis appears as a powerful shafting rod" (p. 65). Regardless of which assessment is accepted, there seems to be a consensus that there is power hidden in these coded and sometimes humorous compositions.

Living in an era where voicing disapproval against the unjust horrors experienced by the Black community would be punished, such expressions were best displayed through covert and latent symbols. For Traylor—as for all Black people of his era—secrecy was protection and power, and certain artistic forms and symbols emerged from conventions within their culture that allowed for shared meanings that could be kept hidden from those outside. Much like the *Radio* (see Figure 2.13) that relies on invisible waves to convey messages, Traylor's forms, seemingly innocuous on the surface, transmitted notions that were best concealed for his own safety. "Art, while clearly visible, was meant to mask much of what it was created to communicate" (Sobel, 2009, p. 106). Traylor may very well have been drawing from his vast visual symbolic vocabulary to create hidden messages that conveyed the brutality and degradation he experienced and witnessed while re-empowering the members of his own community. Many of his seemingly simple renditions and compositions seemed to express impotent rage and provided a way to strike back.

> Violence—in the forms of people wielding hatchets and clubs or falling from dizzying heights or implied through the latent pressure that imbues Traylor's scenes populated by dogs or mounted overseers—is ubiquitous in Traylor's work but possible to underestimate or even read as humor or general mayhem. (Umberger, 2018, p. 249)

Two Men, Dog and Owl depicts a dog and two men assaulting an owl with sticks. This was a commonplace event in farm country. Yet its simplistic and innocent portrayal is reminiscent of a horrible and also common occurrence: the black-faced owl, a potential symbol of death for Traylor (Umberger, 2018), seems to suggest the many beatings received by those with black faces.

A more sanguine composition, Traylor's *Untitled (Legs Construction with Blue Man)* (Figure 2.15) implements yet another of his ubiquitous images—the blue man. Traylor's blue figures "seem to be in a category unto themselves"

[2] The power of humor in art as a way to gain control over powerlessness and violent circumstances is emphasized in the following chapter, while humor as a weapon is explored in Chapter 6.

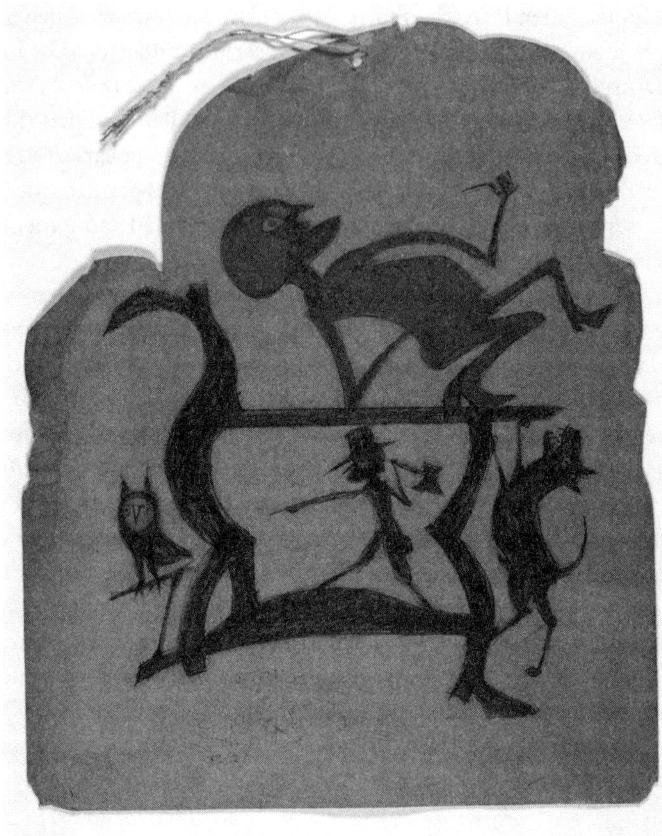

Figure 2.15 Bill Traylor (1854–1949). *Untitled (Legs Construction with Blue Man)* (c. 1940–1942). Opaque watercolor, pencil, and charcoal on paperboard.
Permission and reproduction provided by Smithsonian American Art Museum. Museum purchase through the Luisita L. and Franz H. Denghausen Endowment, copyright 1994, Bill Traylor Family Trust.

(Umberger, p. 241). While often appearing elderly in stature and bearing, they seem to adroitly overcome the challenges facing them in a spry and agile manner.

> [T]he kicking black feet create a parallelogram that is at once a container and a platform. The blue man, balding and bony, more clearly bears the feature of an old man; nevertheless, smoking his pipe all the while, he seems to defy gravity in a jig-like jump. Contained within the stage-like structure, a smaller man with an axe takes aim; his hat and gesture connote peril and power. The owl portends death, and the hellhound nips at the blue man's heels—yet somehow the blue

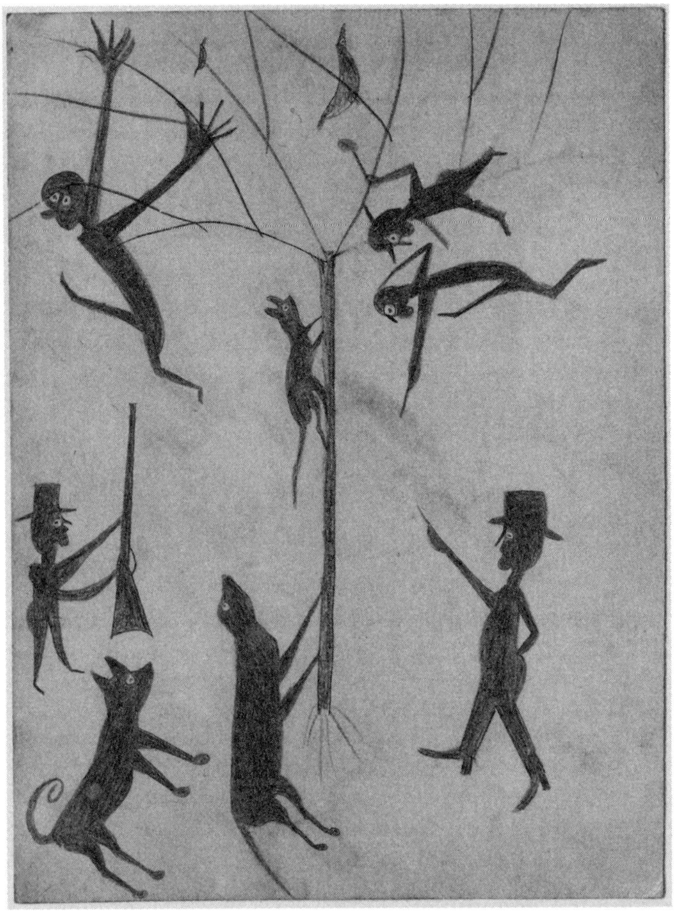

Figure 2.16 Bill Traylor (1854–1949). *Untitled (Chase)* (c. 1939–1942). Colored pencil on cardboard.
Collection of Jan Petry. Permission and reproduction provided by Jan Petry and John Faier, photographer.

> man rises above it all. He escapes unscathed. He is the ultimate trickster, just beyond reach. (Umberger, p. 242)

While this image seemed to hide guarded optimism and humor in the face of insurmountable oppression and danger, many of his drawings did not.

Untitled [Chase] (Figure 2.16) seems to illustrate a simple possum hunt. Two dogs and three men are sent up a tree to corner an animal that the two men on the ground are clearly hunting. However, at closer examination, the possum does not necessarily seem to be the focus of the hunt. The two men in hats appear to be the White overseers of the three vulnerable Black men in the tree; one of them is pointing to the man in the far upper left who is hanging by his fingers from a branch, seemingly signifying that it is he who is the target.

It is likely that this animal hunt may be a lynching in disguise (Umberger, 2018). Similar to the two men depicted in Figure 2.13 and the man wielding an axe in Figure 2.15, the armed men on the ground hunting the naked men in the tree are wearing hats and shoes. Such details seem to underscore the disparities of wealth and the vulnerability of the targets in the tree. Someone without clothes is seen as more vulnerable, submissive, and almost animal-like. Wearing a hat and shoes is a mark of civilization; to be hatless and shoeless is to be nakedly primitive and barbaric.

One of Traylor's more abstract compositions was considered by Sobel to be his "most dangerous" (2009, p. 86). *Figures and Trees* (ca. 1939–1942) includes five simple trees emerging from a crudely drawn shape at haphazard angles painted on a ragged, oddly shaped piece of cardboard (Figure 2.17). "He employed a minimum of detail and abstraction to his advantage, and at a glance the scene may not seem bleak. . . . The abiding feeling . . . is not playful but solemn and haunting. It imparts a heavy sense of ongoing fear and the inability to erase indelible memories" (Umberger, 2018, p. 251). The figure to the left seems poised to jump from a branch, but the armless figure on the right seems to be hanging from his neck.

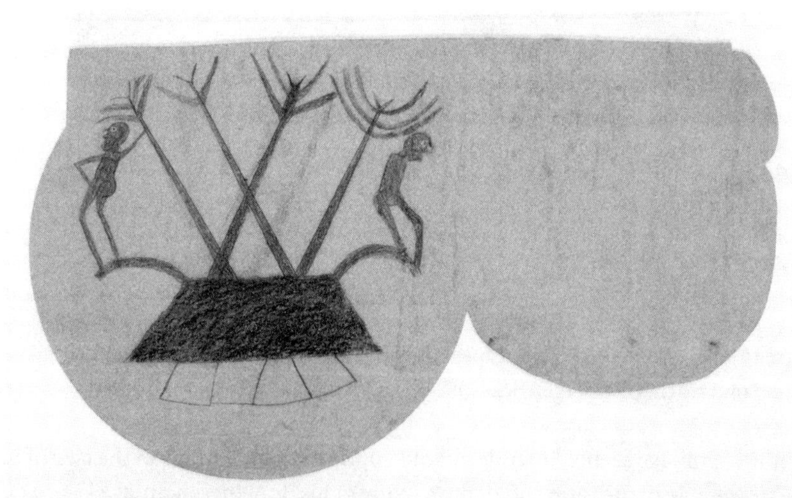

Figure 2.17 Bill Traylor (1854–1949). *Figures and Trees* (c. 1939–1942). Colored pencil on cardboard.

Permission provided by the Kravis Collection. Photo credit and reproduction provided by William H. Bengtson/Chicago, and the Smithsonian American Art Museum.

While the minimal composition almost seems to mask its meaning, of all of his works this painting seems most blatantly illustrative of a lynching.

Shannon took it upon himself to see to it that Traylor received the support that he needed to continue painting and that his work was exhibited. However, this was suspended for a time when Shannon was inducted into the army in 1942. For some time after, Traylor wandered up North, where his children lived. However, unable to find a suitable place to settle, he soon returned to Montgomery. Traylor was not a well man, and, shortly after his return, first his toes and then later his leg had to be amputated after they became gangrenous. While recovering, Traylor resumed painting on the sidewalk.

In the mid-1940s Traylor's welfare payments were suspended, and, as a result, he had to live with one of his daughters in Montgomery. For him, leaving his spot on the sidewalk where he was known and respected likely marked a spiritual death, particularly because no one would know where he went. He lost the identity, sense of belonging, and semblance of control that he cultivated through his art making. He became increasingly sick: "his immobility and lack of contact with the outside world no doubt further hastened his decline" (Sobel, p. 121). He eventually succumbed to his illness in a rat-infested, filthy hospital in the autumn of 1949.

The next artist is markedly different from the others included in this chapter and may even draw some controversy for his inclusion. Known for his illustrations for the *Saturday Evening Post*, Norman Rockwell embodies the privileged White Man who painted images that seemed to champion wholesome, suburban American values. Yet, it is just this paradox that seems to bring weight to the issues outlined in this chapter. Norman Rockwell was not chosen because he was the most responsive to the plights around him; on the contrary, Rockwell is rarely associated with social justice, particularly by those not familiar with his later works. Rockwell has been chosen to demonstrate that protection, isolation, and privilege cannot separate one from pain or suffering when surrounded by an environment of civil violence, *should he choose to see it.* His work underwent a profound and dramatic change in its content and style as he embraced a willingness, a drive, to depict his perspectives on the violence and aggression of his time. He serves as an example of how even the most defended and protected may eventually be affected by violence and aggression; although it may not have touched him, it did indeed reach him.

Norman Rockwell: America's Wholesome Painter Illustrating Its Darkness

Norman Rockwell, the second child of religious parents, was born in New York City in 1894. He aspired to become an artist early on (Walton, 1978). When he was 14 years old, Rockwell began taking Saturday classes at the Chase School of Art (now Parsons School of Design), and, when expelled from high school at 16, he enrolled in the National Academy of Design. He eventually graduated from the Art Students League of New York and became a staff illustrator for *Boy's Life* magazine (Claridge, 2001). It was here that his wholesome image began to take form.

Shortly after marrying his first wife, Rockwell visited the offices of the *Saturday Evening Post* in Philadelphia to persuade its art editor that he should be illustrating their covers. He must have been convincing because his samples were shown to the *Post*'s editor, George Horace Lorimer, who bought two of his completed paintings and several of his sketches. This began a relationship that lasted for 47 years. This success soon led to him doing covers for other well-known magazines. Rockwell's meticulously rendered realism with just a hint of humorous caricature was perfect for these slick and glossy periodicals (Claridge, 2001).

Several months after the United States became involved in World War I, Rockwell joined the US Navy. He was eventually assigned to illustrate and provide layout for the Charleston Navy Yard's newspaper. He served only a few months before Armistice was declared, and he managed to maneuver for a discharge based on being "inapt" (Claridge, 2001, p. 149)—but an honorable discharge nonetheless.

Rockwell returned to his studio and continued illustrating for the magazines; his illustration services were soon in high demand by well-established national companies. He was also commissioned to complete a painting for the calendar distributed by the Boy Scouts of America; he would continue to do so for the next 50 years (Claridge, 2001).

His income and social standing began to soar; after he and his first wife divorced, he met and married Mary Barstow, a school teacher. They had three sons together. After relocating to Vermont, Rockwell continued to paint, focusing on wholesome and charming—almost too perfect—small-town Americana (Walton, 1978). He admitted that "Maybe as I grew up and found the world wasn't the perfect place I had thought it to be, I unconsciously decided that if it wasn't an ideal world, it should be, and so painted only the ideal aspects of it" (Halpern, 2006, p. 3).

Rockwell had long been dismissed by critics for painting light and insignificantly trifling subjects. However, when World War II erupted, Rockwell's work began to take on deeper social meaning. In 1942, Rockwell listened to Roosevelt deliver his speech to Congress. In it, the President described the importance of the four freedoms: freedom of speech, freedom of worship, freedom from want, and freedom from fear. Rockwell was particularly moved by this passionate address and completed his celebrated series of the same name. Taking 6 months to complete, the paintings were eventually published in four consecutive weekly issues between February 20 and March 13, 1943. The series was so popular that the government sponsored a tour of the paintings to support the war efforts, events that successfully sold more than $100 million war bonds and raised even more money through the sales of the millions of posters that the government printed (Hennessey, 1999).

While Rockwell retained his hyperrealistic, illustrative style for these paintings, his compositions became increasingly complex. Still somewhat staged, the narrative of these images maintained a simplistic naïvete. *Freedom of Fear* depicts a mother carefully tucking the blanket under the chin of her two sleeping sons while the father proudly looks on. *Freedom of Want,* however, does something a little different; it places the viewer in the scene. The painting depicts a long table positioned perpendicular from the viewer; perspective exaggerates just how large the table is. Around it sit the family laughing and talking while grandma sets a large turkey down with grandpa proudly standing behind her. The scene is so expansive and crowded that the size of the canvas can barely contain it; many of the family members seemed to be pushed partly out of the frame by all that is on and around the table. Of course, a product of their time, while Rockwell is trying to portray a democratic vision of all that Americans can have when freedom triumphs, the paintings are patently lacking in diversity. However, Rockwell is slowly awakening.

In 1943, Rockwell's studio burned down, a devastation that claimed many of his paintings, drawings, and the costumes he used to stage his compositions. Despite this tragic setback, his professional career continued to expand because his work remained in high demand. Along with his responsibilities to create covers for the *Post* and advertisements for national brands, Rockwell also illustrated special issue stamps for the Post Office and created posters for the Treasury Department, the military, and Hollywood studio releases; he even designed cards for Hallmark. As well, he illustrated popular books, such as *The Adventures of Tom Sawyer.* However, several years after moving to Massachusetts, tragedy struck again. In 1959, his wife of 29 years died of a heart attack.

While taking time off from his work to grieve this loss, he and his son Thomas wrote and published his autobiography in 1960. Excerpts from this book, *My Adventures as an Illustrator*, were released in an eight-part series published by the *Post.* He illustrated the first part with his iconic *Triple Self Portrait* (Figure 2.18). This iconic painting depicts the seated artist facing the canvas, away from the viewer. He is clearly visible in the larger mirror in which he gazes to capture his likeness on the canvas, on which is sketched in black and white another detailed portrait. He seems to be capturing a moment, before he begins to add color. Although the background is white, he is surrounded by the detritus of an artist, with sketches and reproductions of other well-known

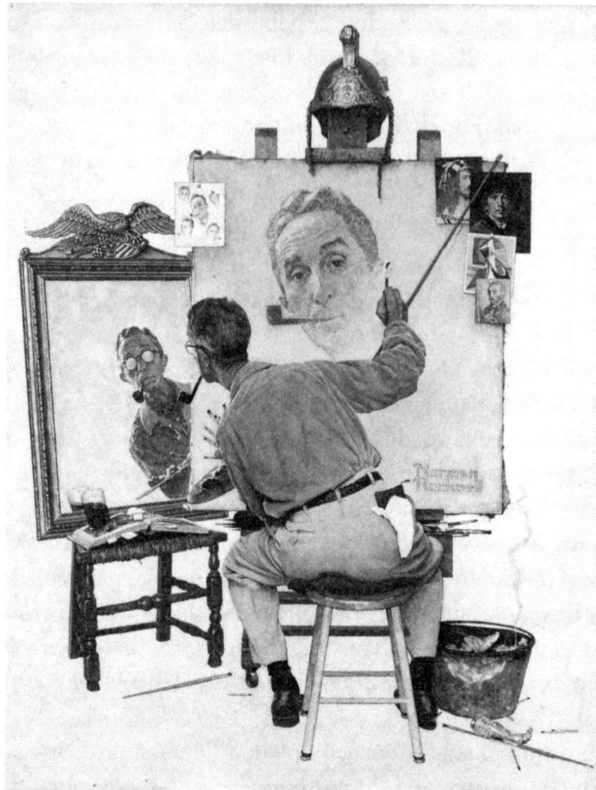

Figure 2.18 Norman Rockwell (1894–1978). *Triple Self-Portrait* (1960). Illustration for *The Saturday Evening Post.*

Collection of the Norman Rockwell Museum. Permission and reproduction provided by the Norman Rockwell Family Agency.

portraits. Capturing an artist at a crossroads, a person questioning his own identity, this piece is emblematic of the question of who he was and where he was going (Claridge, 2001).

Humorous and somewhat self-deprecating, the portrait is at once a self-portrait and a "treatise on the art of composing a self-portrait" (Rockwell, 1999, p. 76). The sketches tacked to the upper left of the canvas gives us an insight to the meticulous and detailed preparations his compositions underwent. On the upper right of the canvas are the self-portraits of four artists who have influenced his work: Durer, Rembrandt, Van Gogh, and Picasso. The inside joke is that each one of these artists was known for producing dozens of self-portraits while Rockwell had really only completed a few.

While it is a self-portrait, he remains somewhat obscured. The subject of the paintings has his back to the viewer; we only know what he looks like through the sketches, the painting he has begun, and the mirror image. Still, even the reflection is somewhat obscured behind fogged glasses. Although this is supposed to be a self-portrait, we never get a true glimpse of who he is. For his son, Peter,

> *Triple Self-Portrait* is both the most complete and the most complex statement. . . . [W]e are given a variety of images, and told, in effect to construct the meaning for ourselves. There is, however, another side to this. The artist has not told us who he believes he is. He has given us the material to construct an image and by doing so has avoided committing to any one image of himself. By leaving it up to us, has the artist opted out of the implied purpose of a self-portrait—to tell us who really is? We may not know the painter as well as we think we do. (Rockwell, 1999, p. 78)

I would argue that Rockwell may not have yet known himself either.

A year later, he married his third wife, retired school teacher Molly Punderson. She encouraged him to end his long-standing relationship with the *Saturday Evening Post*, and, in 1963, he painted his final cover for it. Breaking from the *Post* offered him the new opportunity to begin showing things as they really were, allowing him to create works that embraced his vision of social justice.

Rockwell once proclaimed "The view of life I communicated in my pictures excludes the sordid and ugly" and "I paint life as I would like it to be" (McNatt, 2000, para. 1). As he grew older, Rockwell began to recognize the violent and turbulent times that were happening around him—and his work began to capture it. The 1960s was a difficult time in the United States; Rockwell represented the turbulence with an uncharacteristic willingness to confront the country's political and social challenges. His 1968 piece *The Right to Know* represented his demand for more government transparency in the wake of Robert Kennedy and Martin Luther King Jr.'s assassinations, the controversial election of President Nixon, and our deepening involvement in the Vietnam War. His paintings of the Peace Corps celebrated action over inaction by working with developing nations in overcoming their struggles.

For the bulk of his professional career, Rockwell focused on a wholesome, pristine, and innocent America, an image that its African American citizens could only gaze upon from a distance. It wasn't until much later that Rockwell captured these inequities so readily, particularly in two of his more profound works, *The Problem We All Live With* and *Southern Justice*.

Inspired by an article about 6-year-old Ruby Bridges's escort by the National Guard into the newly desegregated William Frantz Elementary School in New

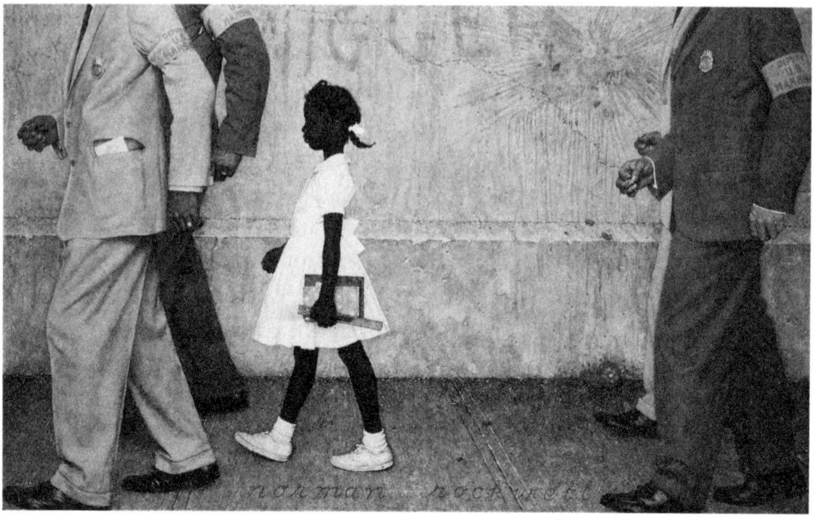

Figure 2.19 Norman Rockwell (1894–1978). *The Problem We All Live With* (1964). Oil on canvas.

Collection of the Norman Rockwell Museum. Permission and reproduction provided the Norman Rockwell Family Agency.

Orleans, Rockwell painted *The Problem We All Live With* (Figure 2.19). In the painting, Bridges is flanked by four, white, headless "giants." There is a racial slur painted on the wall behind her, with tomatoes dripping to the ground that ostensibly missed their target. This composition is a dramatic break-away from the images he painted for the *Post* (Cole, 1999).

The characteristics that made Rockwell's illustrations adaptable to the *Post* covers are also characteristics that drop away as he underscores the reality of the stories he began to tell in his later work. For example, he included a background in these later works, whereas many of the *Post* covers were left white. The background substantiates the story, alluding to a realistic environmental presence. He abandons the circular composition he relied on in his earlier illustrations, which allowed for an easier adaptation to magazine covers. His later paintings become more rectangular, suggesting a stronger narrative. The darker palette and tone seem to reflect a much harsher reality than the bright, positive caricatures he painted earlier; here he is painting real people. The stark scene and muted tones dramatically and vividly capture the bravery and resolve of this child.

While *The Problem* captured a more progressive, optimistic change, he also depicted one of America's most tragic events. In 1964, three young civil rights activists, a 21-year-old Black man from Mississippi, James Chaney, and two

White men from New York, Andrew Goodman and Michael Schwerner, were kidnapped and savagely murdered in Neshoba County, Mississippi. Working for the Freedom Summer campaign to register African American voters in the South, the three young men were arrested on a fake traffic violation. After paying a fine they were released, but were pulled over once again by the police just before they crossed the county line. Rather than return them to jail, the police handed them off to Deputy Chase and the Ku Klux Klan. They shot and killed the two White men outright; they savagely beat Chaney before shooting him three times. Their decomposing bodies were found in a shallow grave more than a month later. Rockwell was commissioned to illustrate the short essay "Southern Justice" in *Look* magazine, written by civil rights activist, Charles Morgan Jr., about this horrific event.

Rockwell gave this project his undivided attention, furiously completing *Southern Justice (Murder in Mississippi)* in 5 weeks. Reminiscent of Goya's *Third of May*, the original charcoal sketch reveals that this was conceived as a horizontal piece, with the three young men on the left and the Deputy and the Klan on the right wielding clubs. As Rockwell worked on it, the perpetrators on the right dropped out, until all that was left on the vertical composition were the ends of their clubs and their menacing shadows (Norman Rockwell Museum, 2020).

He sent a preliminary oil sketch to *Look* for its approval (Figure 2.20). The sketch depicted one of the White men, already murdered, lying on the ground. The second White man is standing, holding up a collapsing Chaney, who already had blood on his shirt. They are set off from the center of the composition, amid a barren and rock strewn landscape. Both are looking toward their now unseen perpetrators. The faces are barely detailed, giving the impression that they can be anyone. The sketch, painted in brown hues, is much looser than his previous paintings, giving it an energy and frenzy not seen in his previous works. There is minimal movement in the forms; the static images are broken up slightly with the hunched, falling Chaney, his elbows akimbo as he tries to hold on to the man supporting him. The art director liked the result so much he attempted to convince Rockwell to use it for the final publication.

Rockwell did not agree and was able to convince him to let him complete the painting as he intended. The finished version is certainly more polished and controlled; there is much more attention to detail (Figure 2.21). Yet while the first piece is somewhat more limiting in its color palette and muted, it exudes a warmth, almost a heat, reminiscent of fire or hot blood; it is an emotional reaction to what is happening in the moment—in the act of dying. It places us as witnesses to the action. The second piece, while a bit more varied in color, is colder in tone, evoking the sensation that death has already occurred and there is

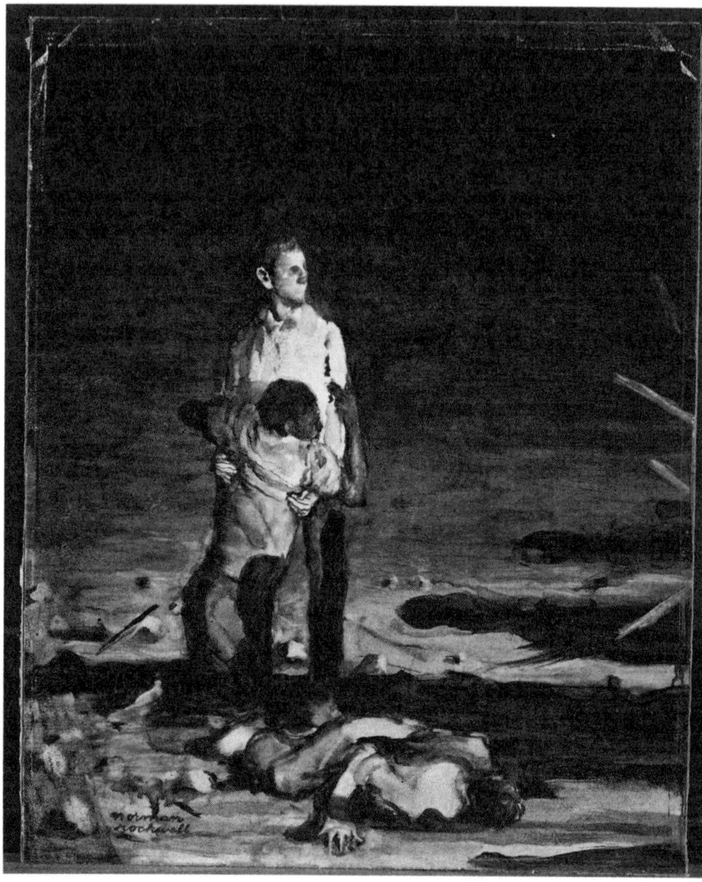

Figure 2.20 Norman Rockwell (1894–1978). *Southern Justice (Murder in Mississippi)* (preliminary oil sketch) (1965). Oil sketch on board.
Collection of the Norman Rockwell Museum. Permission and reproduction provided by the Norman Rockwell Family Agency.

nothing we can do; we are witness to the aftermath and looking at a snapshot of the event. The viewer is helpless.

The face of the one man who can be seen clearly is much better defined, with a great deal more detail. Yet Rockwell deliberately refrained from making them an exact likeness of the victims, perhaps reinforcing that the victims could be anybody. Even still, the weapons are removed so that all that remains are the shadows. Just as the men can be anyone, so can the perpetrators. The structure of the pieces seem to barely control their emotional impact of the scene.

While the art director certainly admired the finished piece, he was able to convince the artist "that the earlier oil sketch, with its loose brushwork, delivered

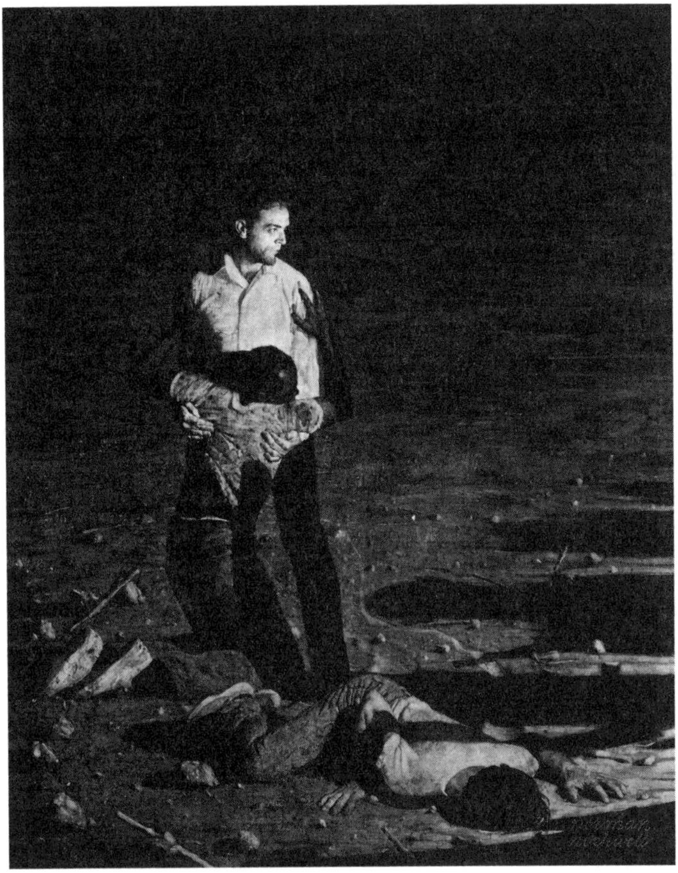

Figure 2.21 Norman Rockwell (1894–1978). *Southern Justice (Murder in Mississippi)* (1965). Oil on canvas.
Collection of the Norman Rockwell Museum. Permission and reproduction provided by the Norman Rockwell Family Agency.

more impact than the finished oil" (Claridge, 2001, p. 455). Certainly, once Rockwell polished up the image, although it remained impactful, it did lose some of its true reflection of the artist's angst over, frustration with, and impotence engendered by the violence. Rockwell admitted 3 years later "that by the time he had finished the final painting, 'all the anger that was in the sketch had gone out of it' " (Norman Rockwell Museum, 2020, para. 14).

He continued to paint during his final decade, focusing on the issues of the day (Walton, 1978). He also contributed a great deal to the culture of society, establishing trusts for artists. In 1977, a year before he died, Rockwell was awarded the Presidential Medal of Freedom by President Gerald Ford.

By the time of his death, Rockwell had created more than 4,000 original works and illustrated more than 40 books. Still, Rockwell couldn't escape from the negative views of his critics; Robert Hughes summed up the prevailing attitude in an obituary for *Time* magazine: "He never made an impression on the history of art and never will. But on the history of illustration and mass communication his mark was deep and will remain indelible" (McNatt, 2000, para. 21). Yet perspectives have been changing, particularly on the impact that his images for *Look* had of bringing to the forefront the tragedies that were occurring around him, events that were easy for some to ignore. As art historian Thomas Hoving (1999) wrote in the catalogue for a retrospective of his work in Washington,

> In American art there has rarely been a creator of such influence as Norman Rockwell. These days, now that the obsession for abstraction has cooled, his achievements are being discovered by scholars. Rockwell is more and more identified—correctly—as a cultural phenomenon, one who made a sea change in the perception of art in this nation. (p. 31)

Still, one cannot help but reflect that while Rockwell, a White artist, received recognition and accolades for his depictions of the horror he saw at a distance, Traylor received a pauper's burial after courageously depicting the horrors he experienced first-hand.

The six artists chosen for this chapter represent those who struggled to capture their experiences, turn their fear and horror into depictions of evidence, and express their defiance. Yet, while all were different from one another in style and abilities, their stories, experiences, and artistic expressions overlap in a number of ways. As noted, Rockwell's *Murder in Mississippi* is reminiscent of Goya's *Third of May.* Coincidentally, both artists began their artistic careers depicting lighthearted themes. As time went on, exposed to the violence around them, their focus and their styles changed. Their images confront the viewer with depictions of extreme violence without the buffer of allusion, metaphor, structural elements, or narrative—there is no filter. It is almost as if they are simply reporting what is there, allowing viewers to develop their own conclusions.

Similarly, Vann Nath does the same; yet, like Traylor, he seems to try to take back some power and agency by using his art to regain control and identity. Nussbaum relied on his paintings to simultaneously provide evidence of his experiences while reaffirming his own sense of self, his humanity—impotent defiance in the face of oppression and death. He, Goya, and Beckmann dared not reveal their work, withholding some of their visual commentaries from display, fearing reprisals from the powers that be. All of them took risks in creating these pieces; this included professional and personal rejection, the potential of becoming social pariahs, or even early demise. Yet still they were compelled to create.

In some manner, these narratives underscore the continuing and widening disparities that exist in cultures that contribute to the aggression and violence that surrounds us today. Yet they also remind us of the power of art to draw from the surrounding struggles and aggression and provide an opportunity to regain strength and identity.

3

Art of the Perpetrator and the Oppressed

Unveiling the Art of the Holocaust

For many summers, my university held an Institute for Holocaust Studies for Educators. Select K–12 schoolteachers throughout Florida visited campus each summer to learn from various experts on a number of topics relating to the Holocaust or *Shoah*. While learning about the Shoah, they also learned various ways that they could further educate their own students, "lest we never forget." For 10 of those summers, I provided a course on the art of the Holocaust.

While my work in prison was my professional focus, this topic was a passion. My course, entitled "Drawing Strength," explored the emergence of art as evidence and escape for the victims of the Nazi regime, focusing primarily on a select dozen or so artists out of the myriad of those whose work has emerged over time. After several years of presenting the work of the victims, I began to show the paintings of Adolf Hitler as a comparison.

Many who attended the presentations heard mention that Hitler was a "painter" before he was dictator; however, rarely had they seen any of his works. His paintings brought into sharp relief the work of a heartless psychopath, devoid of any emotion and passion when compared to the heartfelt, heart-rending, passionate imagery of the sufferers.

As this book was developing, and as various chapters solidified that focused on the art of violent artists, artists in violent environments, and serial killer art, I kept returning to the presentations I gave over those summers: this was a chance to explore the dance within a single, horrifying context. What emerged was this chapter, essentially a review of how various artists embodied and responded to violence along a particular continuum: an artist demonstrating extremely violent, even psychopathic tendencies on one end and, on the opposing end, the very victims of these atrocities.

As this chapter took shape, many other contrasting notions occurred and are evident throughout the telling of these stories. The art emotionally and humanistically underscores the connected versus the disconnected. It highlights passionate expression versus technical skill and humanity versus inhumanity. Finally, it lays bare the stark differences in the rationale for such art making—the narcissistic self-aggrandizement seen with the serial killers in Chapter 4 and the desire to be seen and made whole, as with the artists presented in Chapter 2.

The Art of a Monster: Hitler as Painter

I must confess, while I intended to include Hitler in this book, I couldn't quite figure out where to put him. At first, he was in among the serial killers because he was what one could only describe as a perpetrator of mass murder. However, this didn't quite feel right. Perhaps because the serial killers committed their own crimes, with blood literally on their hands and Hitler did not: he used politics, ideology, the country's already inherent anti-Semitism, and the Gestapo as his motivation and his weapon.

I considered including him in the chapter on violent artists, but I strongly felt it unjustified to include him among the ranks of Caravaggio, Cellini, and Modigliani. Thus, for the longest time, I could never determine where Hitler was going to land.

I must admit, I had one other reason that I hesitated with including him altogether. I was afraid: once someone engaged with examining Hitler as an artist, there was a tendency for others to respond vituperatively, accusing the examiner, the author, of championing the work of—and, by extension, excusing—the acts of the dictator. For example, when Werckmeister (1997) wrote about Hitler's work, he stated that "a small but vocal minority of the audience [where this paper was first presented, who] accused me of promoting the memory of Hitler and thus objectively, if not intentionally, contributing to the current resurgence of neo-Nazi sentiment" (p. 270). Schjeldahl (2002) was aware of such possibilities; he stressed that his meta-analysis of Hitler's paintings "won't alter our moral and political judgments of Hitler, whose crimes remain immeasurable, but it sure shakes up conventional accounts of modern art" (para. 1). Still, I felt it important to include him.

I recognized that, regardless of the perversity of a person's violent acts, it is certainly possible that elements of humanity may be revealed and validation offered through his creative endeavors. This, in turn, may contradict any assertion that such an individual is irredeemably monstrous and inhumane. However, let me be perfectly clear: while I historically and philosophically have championed the notion that creating can be humanizing, I offer this case as an exception. Thus, in this chapter, Hitler's work is offered as acidic substantiation alongside his monstrous deeds to demonstrate that, similar to the serial killers in the following chapter, his art—and his motivation for creating it—is used to emphasize that not only does the work not offset his atrocities, but they may in fact also reinforce Hitler's own lack of humanity. I recount Hitler's work not to civilize him but to further condemn him.

Adolf Hitler was born in 1889, in what is now Austria, the fourth of six children, to Alois Hitler and his third wife, Klara. Three of his siblings died as infants; he also had two step-siblings from his father's previous marriage. Hitler was often at odds with his father, who beat him regularly, while his mother tried to protect him, usually unsuccessfully. Historical accounts agree on one point: Hitler had no initial intention of becoming a statesman, a politician; he wanted to be an artist. This led to conflict with his father, who wanted young Adolf to become a bureaucrat. Hitler's father forced him to attend a technical high school, in which he performed rather poorly. In 1903, his father died, allowing Hitler to drop out of technical school and enroll in another institution that focused on the liberal arts. He graduated in 1905, with little focus or direction.

With his mother's blessing, Hitler moved in 1907 to Vienna, to finally pursue his dreams of becoming an artist. At the time, artists in Vienna were appreciated and highly regarded contributors to culture. Although the title of artist brought power and prestige, Hitler was unable to claim all that art could offer. Quite frankly, Hitler didn't have what it took to succeed. His emotionless art pieces, while technically adroit, never really connected with their viewers. He applied to, but was rejected twice by the Vienna Academy of Fine Arts that indicated that he was "unqualified"; however, the committee did suggest that he might have enough talent to become an architect. However, while Hitler changed his focus from fine art to architecture, he never formally changed his course of study and, as a result, never earned the appropriate academic credentials that would allow him to pursue architecture. Without such tutelage, he "embarked on autodidactic studies of architectural drawing" (Werckmeister, 1997, p. 277) claiming it was enough. It wasn't.

Hitler made ends meet by creating and selling small watercolor paintings and ink postcards of Venetian scenes, focusing primarily on architectural landscapes. He made—and sold—thousands. Still, his previous failures resulted in ambivalence toward his artistic identity.

> Several testimonies, both contemporary and later, leave no doubt that Hitler rated his paintings as mere subsistence work, below architecture, which he did not practice but which he rated as his true calling. In the registration forms . . . he could never bring himself to stick with an unequivocal professional self-designation, vacillating instead between "artist," "student," "writer," "artist-painter," and "architectural painter." (Werckmeister, p. 277)

Figure 3.1 is a typical example of Hitler's paintings. While it reveals some technical skills, it is cold in tone, with overwrought attention to detail. The scene is placed back a fair distance from the viewer, with very little occurring in the foreground. More significantly, there are no human elements within the work, resulting in no emotional connections. His architectural subject matter seems to demonstrate a potential preoccupation toward perfectionistic detachment; in addition, there is a marked lack of humanity. When he did include people in his

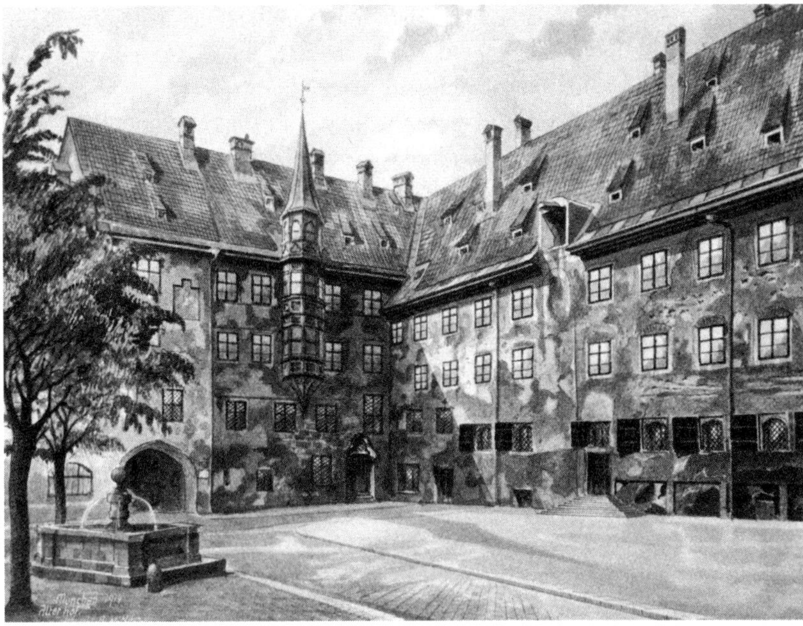

Figure 3.1 Adolf Hitler (1889–1945). *The Courtyard of the Old Residency in Munich* (1914). Watercolor on paper.
Universal History Archive/UIG/Bridgeman Images. Reproduction provided by Bridgeman Images.

land and cityscapes, they were far removed, only as ancillary figures that provided a scale for the overwhelming architecture. His relatively few experiments with portraiture and nudes continued to reflect a combination of timidity and academic stiltedness.

Still, while his emphasis was on architectural landscapes, he occasionally sketched dogs or made copies of Disney characters, popular at the time. While these additional images reflected a looser style and even a softness in his approach, there remains an unsophisticated, sophomoric quality to them. Similar to John Wayne Gacy, who would also appropriate Disney images 30 years later (see Chapter 4), such reliance on popular imagery may have further demonstrated Hitler's lack of his own artistic voice. Still, he found a few patrons.

Ironically, many of his earlier works were commissioned by a Jewish gallery owner, Samuel Morgenstern, whose shop was later "Aryanized" and taken over by the German Socialists in 1938 (Hamann, 1999). This relationship was sensationalized in the film, *Max* (Meyjes, 2002), starring John Cusack and Noah Taylor. Taking cinematic license, this film portrays a young yet ambitious Hitler who crosses paths with the fictional Jewish art dealer Max Rothman in 1918, while working on becoming an artist. On the way to the meeting with Hitler,

Rothman is attacked and beaten to death by anti-Semitic thugs. Hitler never understood why Max missed the meeting and, feeling betrayed, turned away from his artistic pursuits. This plot is outlined to highlight the argument that had Hitler succeeded in becoming an artist, he may not have continued in his violent and racist pursuits. The film assumes simplistically that if such a meeting had occurred, Hitler might have been content as an artist and not have sought revenge against bourgeois Jewish art collectors. Clearly, it is much more complicated than that (Junge, 2019). Hitler *relied* on his artistic and creative abilities to secure the political and dictatorial pedestal on which he stood, and from which he wrought devastation and abuse.

It is likely that, regardless of who his patron was or whom he felt slighted him, he was simply never going to succeed. His work was bland, and, while technically adequate, there was a complete emotional disconnection. This differs from the violent artists featured in Chapter 1 simply because there is no "him" in the work—his identity does not emerge. Caravaggio, Cellini, Pollock, and Modigliani succeeded because they relied on their work to contain, exhibit, and redirect their aggression, putting themselves wholeheartedly and without restraint into their work. Regardless of how violent and volatile they were, there was still a connection between who they were and what they produced. Hitler's endeavors and his relationship with his work seemed to correspond more closely with the serial killers featured in the following chapter. He portrayed what he thought an artist was supposed to be but without the emotional essence and connection. His desire was to feed his own narcissistic, self-aggrandizing persona and gain power and recognition in an environment where creating art was akin to superiority. However, as he could not succeed, was not—in his perception—*allowed* to succeed, a narcissistic injury occurred that has rivaled no other.

Art as a Tool of Oppression

Hitler possibly condemned and targeted certain artistic styles and their artists as a response to their involvement in the Munich Revolution which he helped quell. This condemnation/response transitioned into a political stance and an ultimate edict against "degenerate art" (Petropoulos, 2000).

As explained in the previous chapter, under the guise of concern about "cultural disintegration," Hitler considered any works that insulted "German feeling, . . . that destroy[ed] or confuse[d] natural form" to be *degenerate* (Spotts, 2002, p. 163). Accordingly, appropriate art underscored the ideal German, the *ubermensch*, with an aim to celebrate and reinforce racial purity as reflected in the classical ideal. These included works like Arno Breker's sculptures, a particular favorite of Hitler's which embraced the ideal and stylized masculine form. In this way, Hitler attempted to control the cultural and artistic identity of the Third Reich.

Simultaneously, Hitler and his regime recognized the power of the image. They relied on visual propaganda to shape the message of purity and racist inferiority and prejudice using powerful and frightening imagery to reinforce anti-Semitic hatred. One widely disseminated poster in German-occupied Poland in 1941 displayed a large outlined drawing of a louse advancing and overlapping a large skull that clearly had exaggerated Semitic features. The caption read "Jews are lice; they cause typhus." It's simplistic but quite horrifying. Posters like this were created to instill fear and dehumanize the Jewish people, making it easier for the Nazis to fulfill their drive for control, domination, and annihilation with support from the local populations.

Ernst Heimer's 1938 children's book *Der Giftpilz* (*The Poisonous Mushroom*) (Figure 3.2), illustrated by Philipp Rupprecht, underscored rabid anti-Semitic teachings. The title is derived from the metaphor that the difficulty in recognizing a Jewish person from the Gentile is akin to the challenge of recognizing a poisonous mushroom from an edible one. The book is promoted as a series of educational modules on various exaggerated characteristics and fallacies of Jewish culture and religious practices. Its intent is to blatantly warn of the underhanded danger of a Jewish person and protect the innocent and naïve German citizen from falling victim to these conniving and dangerous figures. Successful in its intent, it relied on juxtaposed illustrations of the ideal Aryan against the caricatures of Satanic-featured Jews to emphasize the inferiority of the "Jewish race" while striving to inure the citizen against the retribution against the Jews that must follow.

Like everything else they had in their arsenal, the Nazi regime used art in calculating, systematic, and manipulative ways to establish and maintain power and aggressive control. In some respects, Hitler merely exchanged the paintbrush for rhetoric; he recognized politics for what it was—an art not a science. "[W]hen he became a politician, Hitler maintained a profound artistic vision. His artistic skills in speaking, spectacle and design and his ability to move people through these methods manifested an aesthetic sensibility" (Junge, 2019, p. 48).

It was then, in this role as a politician, that his hatred and aggression could flourish toward those he viewed as inferior. In his autobiography, *Mein Kampf*, written while imprisoned in the Landsburg fortress, his identity as a politician and artist melded: "If I had become early on a political revolutionary, I become no less an artistic one" (trans. by Wermeister, p. 280). Art is both the metaphor and literal example of all that he defined as good or degenerative

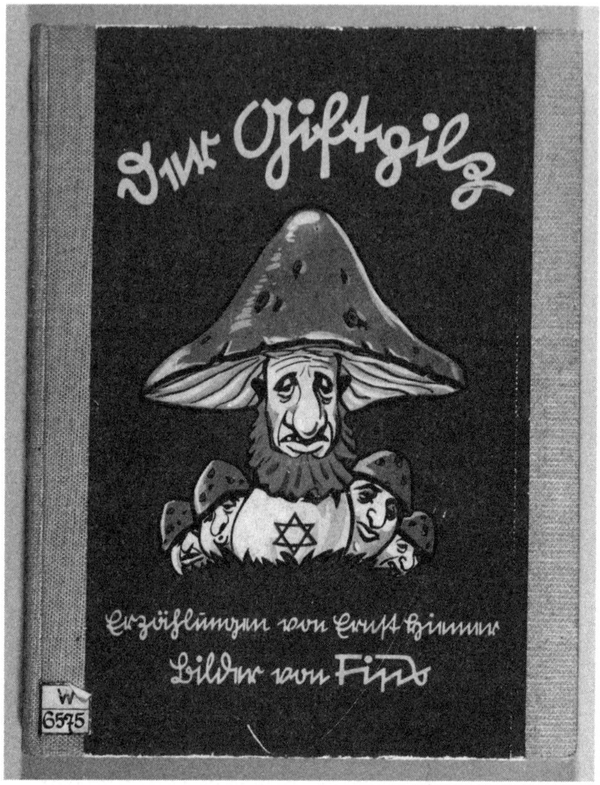

Figure 3.2 Philipp Rupprecht (Illustrator) (1900–1975). Cover of the anti-Semitic children's book "The Poisonous Mushroom" (1938).

Published by Der Stuermer-Verlag. Photograph by Arnold Kramer. Permission and reproduction provided by the United States Holocaust Museum, Washington, DC.

in the political climate he created. He controlled his new empire and oversaw attempts to destroy the old ones through bombastic oration and grand visions. And, through all this, Hitler rose to unprecedented power and unleashed unbridled violence and force against the innocent, culminating in an almost successful Final Solution.

Evidence and Escape: The Artists of the Holocaust

Despite Hitler's attempts to control the artistic ideals of the nation and define cultural righteousness, there are remarkable works of art created by those targeted; created not only *despite* the horrors, but—I would argue—*because* of them. These are the brave souls who were compelled to give voice and identity to the persecuted. Despite not knowing if in any given hour they would draw their last breath, they used their art to blatantly defy the Nazi regime by creating in the ashes of destruction.

In previous publications (Gussak, 2009b, 2016a, 2019), I have stressed that prisons succeed in controlling their populations through objectification and dehumanization; uniforms and numbers are thrust upon their charges because it is easier to control that which is less than human. Art is as successful and as powerful as it is in prison because it provides an opportunity to re-establish an identity above that of inmate, making possible an opportunity for success and well-being (Gussak, 2019). Nowhere is this more apparent than in what occurred in Nazi Germany. The previous examples demonstrate how art was used to further dehumanize and objectify—even vilify—the Jews in order to maintain control and undertake eventual extermination. Yet the very tool that the Nazis used to control and dehumanize, the Jews used to rediscover humanity, dignity, and self-value.

However, as I was writing this section, I became aware of an overbearing and weighty irony, one that I felt required disclosure and perhaps even forgiveness. Previous chapters presented biographical vignettes of individual artists as examples for each particular theme offered, including Felix Nussbaum (see Chapter 2), a victim of these atrocities. While the art that emerged from Holocaust victims was invaluable in reinforcing their humanity and identity in an environment that sought to strip it from them, a paradox exists within this chapter because it does not focus on nor provide distinct biographical narratives of many of the individual artists. Instead, the following paragraphs focus on the art, reinforcing what these artists already knew: that the images they produced were greater than any one person. These artists risked death so that their art might live on to tell the story. While this section briefly introduces various artists by name, the power and essence of their creations is reinforced—the art for resistance and evidence.

The following paragraphs furthermore underscore several ways in which the artists used their products to wrest back their humanity. Some of their images documented what was occurring around them so the world could know the truth. Some created portraits of others that established their existence and reinforced their humanity. Some engaged in humorous imagery, remarkable in a decidedly humorless environment. In doing so, they regained mastery, control, and power. And, through it all, these images provide, paradoxically and simultaneously, emotional containment and escape. Examples from the ghettos and camps are provided to emphasize these points. And finally, this chapter will retell not only the tales of the heroes of the "artists' affair of Terezín" but the children within those walls who were compelled to draw.

The Art Inside

Creating art inside these camps and ghettos was initially encouraged and promoted by the warders, provided the artists followed very strict guidelines and met their expectations. Within appointed studios, specially designated artists were expected to create *useful* images that could serve as information and propaganda in a style acceptable by the Regime.

During the light of day, under the constant eye of their "patrons," artists completed the images that were expected. These artists held relatively desirable positions. While others were forced outside to slave under grueling conditions or were responsible for feeding the crematorium with their compatriots' bodies, these artists worked in spacious, well-lit rooms protecting them from the elements. Some even received extra rations for "commissions."

Some of the work was to further the message of the Reich, reinforcing the falsehoods the Nazis were putting forth. In some cases, the artists were given tasks to create posters that promoted sanitation and good health. Figure 3.3 is similar to the one described earlier; instead of likening the Jews to lice, this one is a warning about how important it was to keep clean, as "one louse makes you dead." I am sure the irony was not totally lost on the Kommandants of the camps, promoting such care in an environment where it was simply impossible to achieve.

Often artists would be called on to complete pieces under commission, such as idealized and grandiose portraits of their captors and subjugators to be sent home. Some illustrated the camp manuals that established the regulations and policies of the facilities, such as Auschwitz's *Falsch-Richtig* (Guard's Manual).

Certainly, some of them accepted these assignments without complaint, accepting that their talents made their lives a bit more bearable, if even for a short time. Yet, by night, some of these artists relied on their positions to surreptitiously complete compositions that they knew would surely result in their torture and murder if discovered. "Not knowing whether witnesses other than themselves would ever see their work, these brave souls felt a need to capture the truth of what they saw and what they experienced" (Gussak, 2009c).[1]

[1] Artists in the ghettos did not incur the same level of brutality as those in the camps if caught making art. Yet, as time went on, creative endeavors that "were at first allowed became prohibited. . . . Any artwork depicting the realities of ghetto life was viewed as a defiance to the Nazis, and eventually, any artwork not commissioned by Nazis was forbidden" (Hlavek, in press).

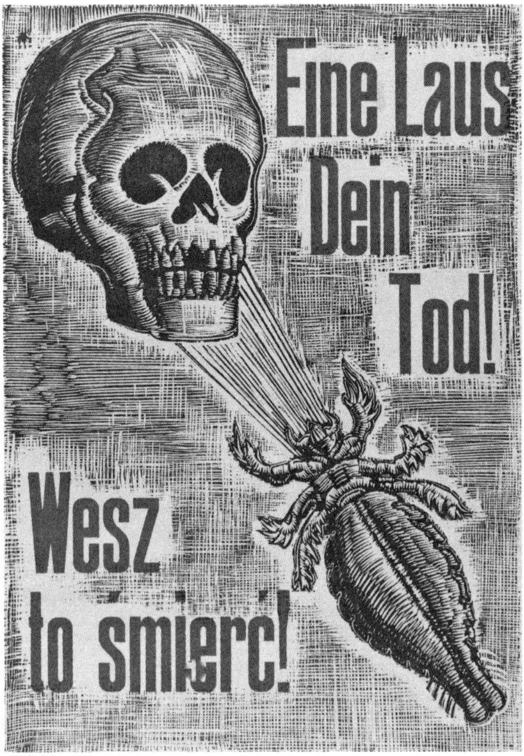

Figure 3.3 Mieczyslaw Koscielniak (1912–1993). *One Louse Makes You Dead* (1942). Color linoleum cut.

Collection of Auschwitz-Birkenau Memorial and Museum. Permission provided by Katarzyna Nowak and Margaretta Haładyn. Reproduction provided by Auschwitz-Birkenau Memorial and Museum.

Documented Evidence

While the architects of the Nazi regime proclaimed their right to assert their might by ridding all the land of Jews, there must have been some part of them that recognized the atrocities they were party to. Why else would they be so frightened that drawings and paintings documenting life inside the barbed wire might escape to show the world the truth?

Despite knowing the repercussions if discovered, many created evidentiary images throughout the camps of Dachau, Auschwitz, Buchenwald, and Ravensbruck and the ghettos of Warsaw, Lodz, and Riga. To them, it was worth the risk. While some of the artists survived, some did not, and all that was left behind were their images that told the truth.

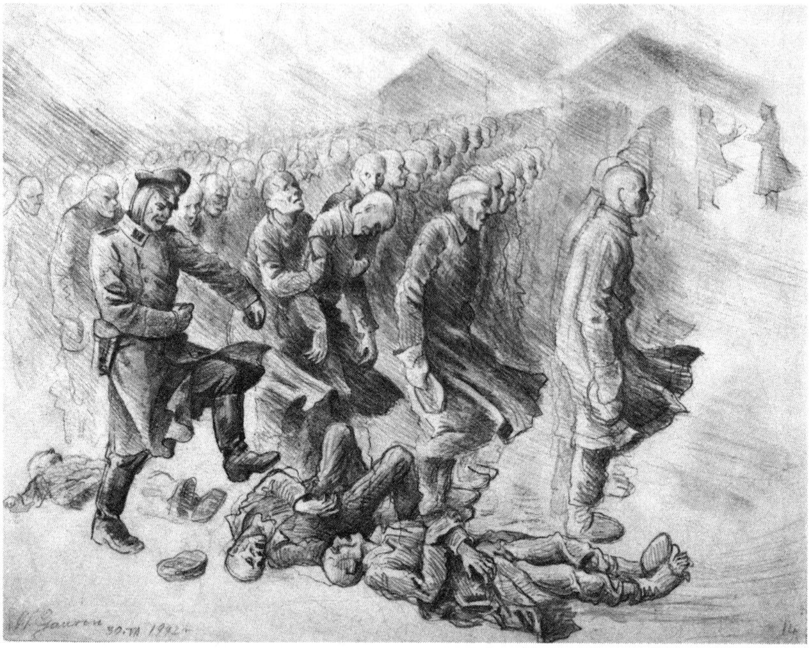

Figure 3.4 Wincenty Gawron (1908–1991). *Roll Call* (1941/1942). Charcoal on paper.

Collection of Auschwitz-Birkenau Memorial and Museum. Permission and reproduction provided by Auschwitz-Birkenau Memorial and Museum.

Upon his escape from Harmense, a subcamp of Auschwitz, Wincenty Gawron made it a point to carry with him not only his diary and drawings, such as *Roll Call* (Figure 3.4), but the works of two other artists in the camp with him: Leon Turalski who was liberated in 1945 from the Auschwitz infirmary, and Stanislaw Gutkiewicz, who was forced against a wall and shot (Blatter & Milton, 1981; Milton, 2003).

Although assigned to the stables, Waldemar Nowakowski created art throughout his time in Auschwitz; while he did *approved* work, such as constructing a puppet theater and organizing skits and readings, he also painted more than 300 simple, postcard-sized watercolors that captured the daily brutal existence of Auschwitz, including *Sport* (Figure 3.5). The bright colors and vivid lines belie the cruel scene in which three men are forced to squat for an inordinate amount of time; as their legs go numb and they can no longer hold the pose, they ultimately fall forward and receive beatings by the Kapo—the last person squatting "wins."

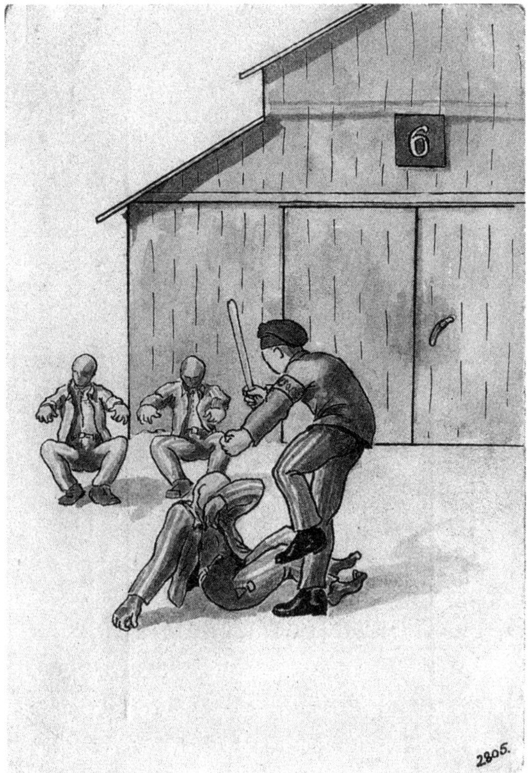

Figure 3.5 Waldemar Nowakowski (1917–1984). *Sport* (1940–1944). Watercolor on cardboard.

Collection of Auschwitz-Birkenau Memorial and Museum. Permission provided by Ewa Huczkowska and Pawel Huczkowski. Reproduction provided by Auschwitz-Birkenau Memorial and Museum.

While a favored artist of the SS, Mieczyslaw Koscielniak was encouraged by the resistance to "draw as his duty" (Blatter & Milton, 1981, p. 254) the reality of what he saw around him. One such piece, *A Friendly Favor*, captured in his rapidly scribbled crayon strokes, revealed how the inmates of Auschwitz were often reduced to weak, skeletal *muselmen* (Figure 3.6). Lives were risked to smuggle out 300 of these pieces to bear witness to these harsh conditions.

Helmut Bachrach-Baree chronicled in a dozen images his final days before liberation, when he was forced—like so many all over Europe—to take part in a senseless, horrifying Death March (Sujo, 2003). Forced from Buchenwald to Dachau by the SS ahead of the approaching Allied army, Bachrach-Baree's beautifully rendered sketches chronicled the struggles the prisoners experienced;

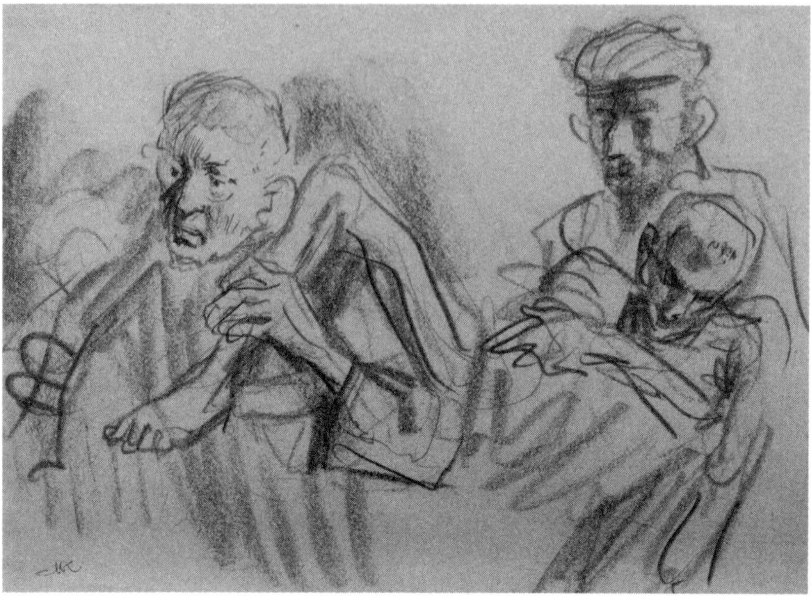

Figure 3.6 Mieczyslaw Koscielniak (1912–1993). *A Friendly Favor* (1942). Crayon on paper.

Permission provided by Katarzyna Nowak and Margaretta Haładyn. Reproduction provided by Auschwitz-Birkenau Memorial and Museum.

completed over several sessions, these images, taken together, tell a complicated and difficult narrative (Sujo, 2003). While the images are dated late Spring 1945, around the time he was forced on the march, it is not clear if he did them on the run, when he arrived at Dachau, or after liberation. "Did he work on the drawings in the full light of day as the events unfolded around him, or in clandestine circumstances at night?" (p. 57).

Regardless, the very act of creating these images provided a clear documentation of the events and provided him a semblance of control and mastery. By taking time to render these images, "time generally denied the artists, he might exert some control over his subject, and, by freeing the imagination, ultimately liberate himself and others" (p. 57).

Like Bachrach-Baree, some artists took the time to develop their well-rendered images. Others seemed to rapidly sketch their compositions, as if they were in fear of who may happen upon them while they were drawing. Some pieces were clearly completed by talented and practiced artists; other simplistic and unsophisticated images reflect the artist who had little skill and talent but more than made up for it with a desire to document their experiences. These pieces lay hidden under mattresses, in door jambs and in rafters, wrapped in protective cloth and buried in tin cans, not to be discovered until years later.

Some of the artists created their images after liberation to illustrate and give weight to the horrors of their existence. After her liberation, Zofia Rozenstrauch completed a series of 19 watercolor and ink drawings called *Death Camp Auschwitz* that detailed her daily experiences. A distorted parody of the Nazi regime's manuals on how to run the camps many were forced to illustrate, Rozenstrauch's mock manual

> documented harsh and cruel scenes . . . the elements of refinement, embellishment, and idealization in her oeuvre augment the horror, yet attest to the humanistic approach of the artist. . . . *Death Camp Auschwitz* is a direct testimony to crimes in the death camp. (Rosenberg, 2003, p. 93)

While she could not be located after the war to testify, her collected drawings were used as evidence in Adolf Eichmann's 1961 trial; they did as much to condemn Eichmann as the words of those who were able to testify in person.

> The surviving art reveals the fragility of human life. . . . The art made at Auschwitz [and elsewhere] whether produced on command, tolerated, or clandestine also reflects the indomitable will of inmate artists to document their horrific surroundings. Today, this art functions as a common language, providing visual evidence. (Milton, 2003, p. 67)

Portraiture

The statistics and numbers of the victims—the 6 million Jews, the Roma, the political and homosexual prisoners—-become overwhelming, desensitizing the world to the enormity of these atrocities. Such numbers force distance from rather than a connection to the people who were victimized. However, while the Nazi regime did its best to destroy all vestiges of its targets, artists inside worked hard to capture individual spirits and humanity through their portraits.

Franciszek Jazwiecki drew likenesses of those imprisoned alongside him during his days spent in Auschwitz, Gross Rosen, Sachsenhausen, Buchenwald, and Halberstadt. According to Agnieszka Sieradzka, an art historian at the Auschwitz-Birkenau State Museum, despite their varied characteristics and national affiliations, "'they shared the same haunting quality.' . . . The most interesting in these portraits are eyes—a very strange helplessness," she says (Boyett,

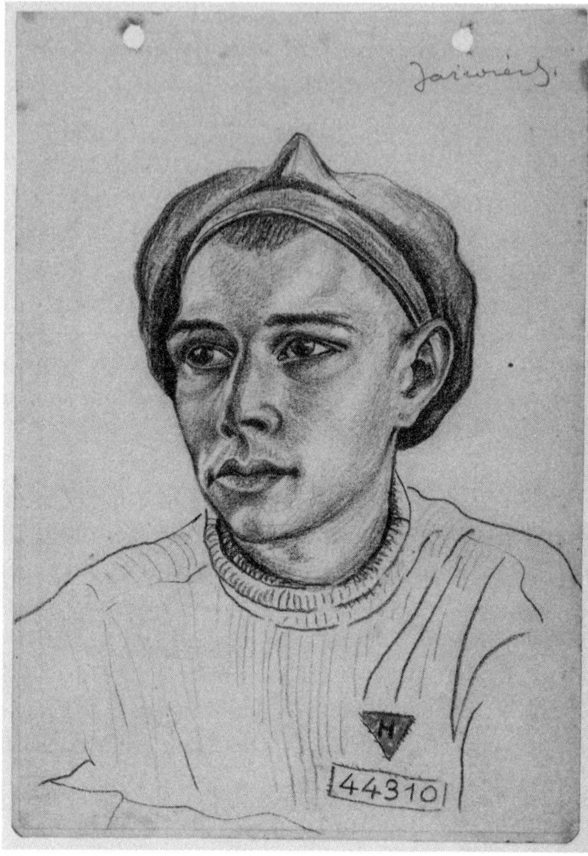

Figure 3.7 Franciszek Jazwiecki (died 1946). *Portrait of Landendum* (Date unknown). Pencil and crayon on cardboard.

Collection of Auschwitz-Birkenau Memorial and Museum. Permission and reproduction provided by Auschwitz-Birkenau Memorial and Museum.

2015, para. 4). His *Portrait of Landendum* (Figure 3.7/see also color plate 9) is drawn with pencil and crayon. We know who he is as much from the countenance as from the number and pink triangle on his breast.

Dutch artist Max Van Dam quickly sketched *A Jewish Woman in Hiding* while he was sequestered in Holland (Figure 3.8). He was later captured and sent to Sobibor extermination camp, where he served as an artist, painting portraits for the SS. Although unclear how he died, it was believed he was killed shortly after completing his final, commissioned piece.

Yehuda Bacon, a survivor and artist now residing in Israel, captured his haunting experiences through a portrait of his father (Figure 3.9), completed

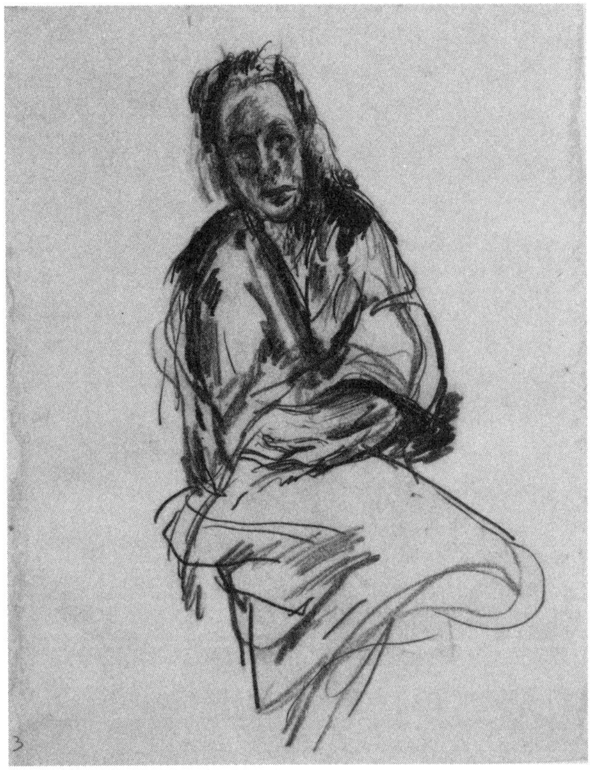

Figure 3.8 Max Van Dam (1910–1943). *A Jewish Woman in Hiding* (Date unknown). Charcoal on paper.

Collection of Ghetto Fighters House Archives/The Art Collection. Permission and reproduction provided by The Ghetto Fighters' House Museum, Israel/The Art Collection.

after his liberation from Auschwitz. It "depicts the moment in that night and that hour I realized that my father was gone. It was a commemoration for my father" (https://www.yadvashem.org/articles/interviews/yehuda-bacon.html).

Gela Sekstajn's self-portrait (Figure 3.10) was completed while she was inside the Warsaw Ghetto; this haunting, soulful charcoal sketch is all that remains of her: she was deported to Treblinka and she and her 2-year-old daughter were subsequently killed in 1942.

These images convey all that Hitler's work lacked: true humanity. These sketches are rendered as much through the heart as through the mind. Where Hitler's imagery was devoid of human attachment, conveying imagery from a great distance, these images provide a relationship with the viewer, allowing us to peer right into the soul of the artists' subjects. We can't help but recognize these were real, living people.

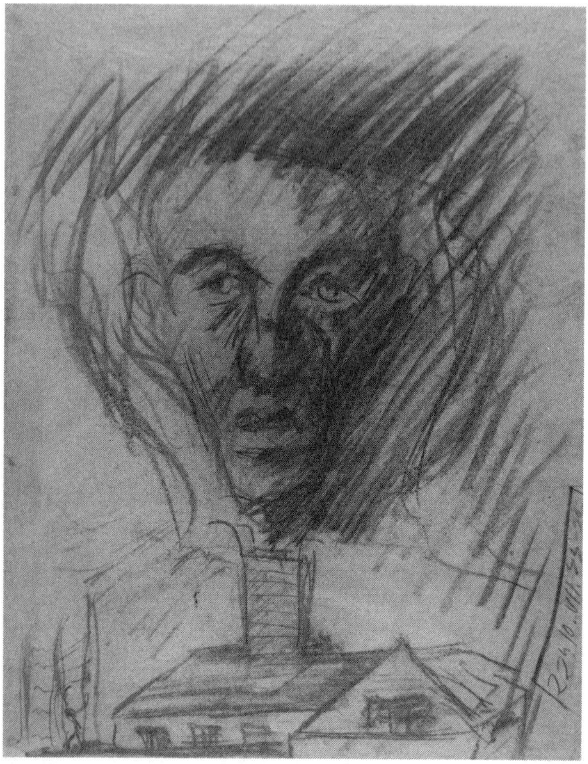

Figure 3.9 Yehuda Bacon (b. 1929). *In Memory of the Czech Transport to the Gas Chambers (Portrait of the Artist's Father)* (1946). Charcoal on paper.
Permission provided by the artist. Collection of the Yad Veshem Art Museum, Jerusalem. Reproduction provided by Yad Vashem Art Museum.

Humor

In *Man's Search for Meaning,* Viktor Frankl, a philosopher and a survivor himself, stressed that "the attempt to develop a sense of humor and to see things in a humorous light is some kind of a trick learned while mastering the art of living" (1959/2006, p. 44). In Chapter 6, "Charles Bronson Becomes Charlie Salvador," humor in art is closely examined and aligned both as an aggressive weapon and a mitigator of violence. Like Bronson/Salvador, some relied on humor in their drawings as a form of aggressive communication, to attack when no other weapons were available. It also redirected and sublimated their hostility.

However, there is another benefit to using humor in decidedly unfunny situations. It can provide at least the chance for a person to take back control from

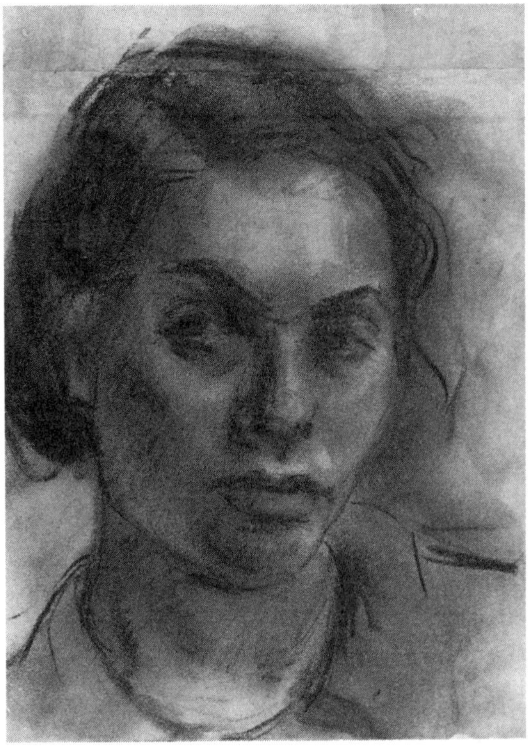

Figure 3.10 Gela Sekstajn (1907–1943). *Self-Portrait* (c. before 1939). Charcoal on paper.
Collection of Warsaw Ghetto Museum. Reproduction provided through Wikimedia Commons.

those considered hierarchically superior (Kotthoff, 2006). It effectively serves as a potent yet decidedly hidden way of rebellion (Meyer, 2000). Through humor "[c]ommunicators imply that others' actions . . . are . . . unacceptable, and hence worthy of opposition in the form of discipline by laughter" (p. 326). Using humor in a horrific situation, the powerless gain strength and the powerful are made impotent.

To be certain, there is no intention of disregarding or minimizing the serious and profound topic in pointing out the humor; it is not meant as disrespect.

> It is a difficult concept to understand because it goes against common rules of etiquette and violates the notion of a proper response to tragedy. I believe laughter provides relief from tragedy while still maintaining the intensity of the situation. Laughter does not change a situation, but it changes the way the victim internalizes the situation. (Carpenter, 2010, p. 13)

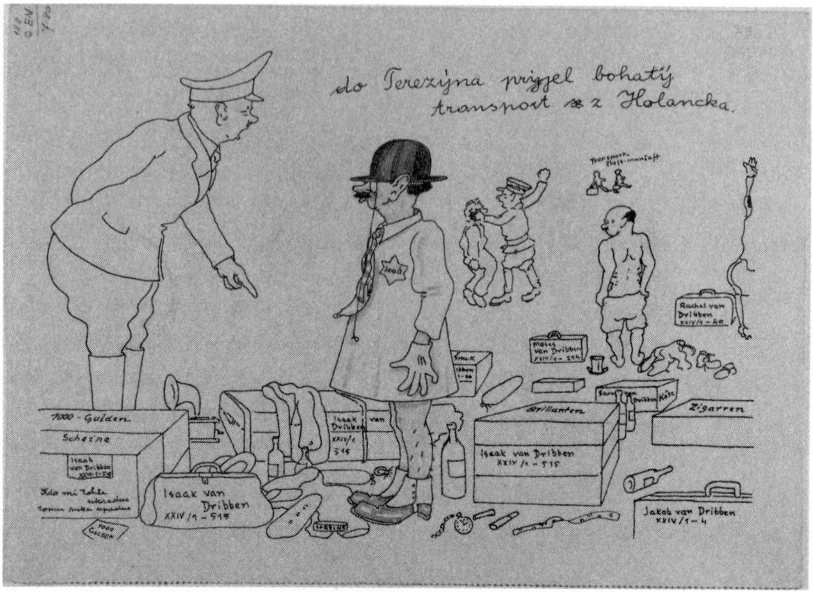

Figure 3.11 Pavel Fantl (1903–1945). *A Rich Transport from Holland Arrived at Terezín* (1942–1944). Ink and watercolor on paper.

Collection of the Yad Veshem Art Museum, Jerusalem. Gift of Ida Fantlova, the artist's mother, courtesy of Ze'ev and Alisa Shek, Caesarea. Permission and reproduction provided by Yad Veshem Art Museum.

Some humorous sketches robbed the subjects of their dignity, such as Jacques Ochs's unflattering caricatures of SS guards. Some images and cartoons tried to find the humorous side of very serious situations. Figure 3.11 is one of Pavel Fantl's numerous watercolor cartoons, *A Rich Transport from Holland Arrived at Terezín*. It captures the moment when a proper gentleman loses all of his possessions and his dignity—upon his arrival to the camp. Fantl was later transported and died in Auschwitz.

In the ghetto and concentration camp Terezín, there was a systematic attempt to create a body of work that would let the world know of what happened inside. While successful, it cost many of these artists their lives.

The "Artists' Incident": The Artists of Terezín

Theresienstadt, or Terezín, was a former military fortress and garrison in North Bohemia, now in the Czech Republic, about 40 miles North of Prague. Turned into a ghetto and concentration camp, it initially served as a way station for Jews from the surrounding areas. However, it was soon transformed into the *Paradise Ghetto*, a professed gift from Hitler to the Jews, where the privileged and the talented would be sent. An artist's studio was established, and elaborate musical and theatrical productions were performed. It became the Nazi's showpiece, a stage set to show the world that the Germans were, in fact, humane to their charges. Representatives of the Red Cross were provided scheduled visits during which the occupants were expected to act as if they resided in a healthy and happy environment.

The art studio was occupied by some of the most talented artists in all of Europe, completing and displaying pieces that reflected their ersatz pastoral surroundings. In addition, these men and women were often commissioned by the occupying Nazis to complete their portraits or other compositions to their desire. The reality, of course, was that the paradise ghetto was a sham. The ill and "ill behaved" were sent to the concentration camps to die, whereas those who cooperated and were healthy were detained long enough to satisfy visitors' expectations. Once used—or used up—these occupants would also be sent away (Dutlinger, 2002; Green, 1978).

It was in Terezín where the "Artists' Incident" occurred (Green, 1978; Troller, 1991; Vojtech et al., 2002). Some of the artists who worked in the studio, including Karel Fleischmann, Petr Kein, Felix Bloch, Otto Ungar, Bedrich Tausig "Fritta," and Leo Haas, fought back by documenting the truth through their imagery (Milton, 2002). These included Fleischmann's *L-306 Living Quarters* (1942) (Figure 3.12) and Haas's *The Safe Journey* (1944) (Figure 3.13). Such works, if discovered, would surely get them killed.

The elderly Czech merchant Frantisek Strass, imprisoned alongside them, had a penchant for collecting art and did not let his imprisonment damp down his passions. Using cigarettes, food, and money he smuggled in from his Christian relatives outside the ghetto, Strass purchased a number of pieces from these artists. These included incendiary, revelatory images by Haas, Ungar, Bloch, Fleischmann, and Fritta. While he kept a few of these under his mattress, many of them were smuggled out. Several of them had been sent out of Czechoslovakia, with a few finding their way to Switzerland.

The Nazi regime soon learned of their existence. After waiting for the latest Red Cross visit to end, Kommandant Rahm called into his office Strass, the artists Haas, Ungar, Bloch, and Fritta, and artist and architect Norbert Troller. Along with three other national officers stood Adolf Eichmann, head of the Jewish Office of the Gestapo's Internal Security Bureau, waiting to interrogate them. The artists were locked in the cellar for the next several days and brought up periodically to be "questioned" further.

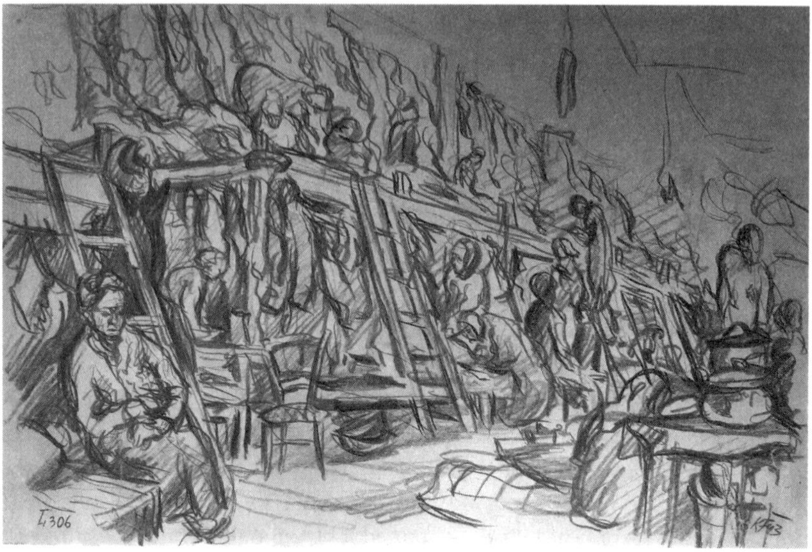

Figure 3.12 Karel Fleischmann (1897–1944). *L-306 Living Quarters* (1943). Pencil on paper.

Collection of the Beit Theresienstadt Archives. Permission and reproduction provided by Beit Theresienstadt Archives.

When their inquisitors realized that they would not receive satisfactory responses, the artists and the businessman were locked up with their families in the *Kleine Festung* (Little Fortress), the adjacent penal barracks. The four artists were brutally tortured, "beaten daily, methodically, with constant demands of information about the communist apparatus that has been disseminating their horror propaganda" (Green, 1978, p. 118). The artists never told them what they wanted to know.

Eventually, Troller was released as he was seen as an architect and thus not a true threat, and he was deported. He was eventually liberated from Auschwitz. Ungar, seen as the most sensitive and weakest of the group, and therefore most likely to break, was tortured mercilessly; all the bones in his hands were broken to prevent him from ever drawing again. He was also deported to Auschwitz. Bloch died while in the Festung, succumbing to the daily beatings.

Fritta and Haas were considered "ringleaders" of the group. They were kept longer, cruelly brutalized daily until they signed a confession for their "crimes." They were deported with their families to Auschwitz the next day. Because Fritta was in a great deal worse shape, Haas took care of him through the long, grueling cattle car ride. When they arrived at Auschwitz, Fritta was taken directly to the infirmary where he, too, succumbed to his injuries. His wife also perished in the camp. Haas and his wife survived. So did Tommy, Fritta's son. Following the war, The Haas's adopted the boy and raised him as their own.

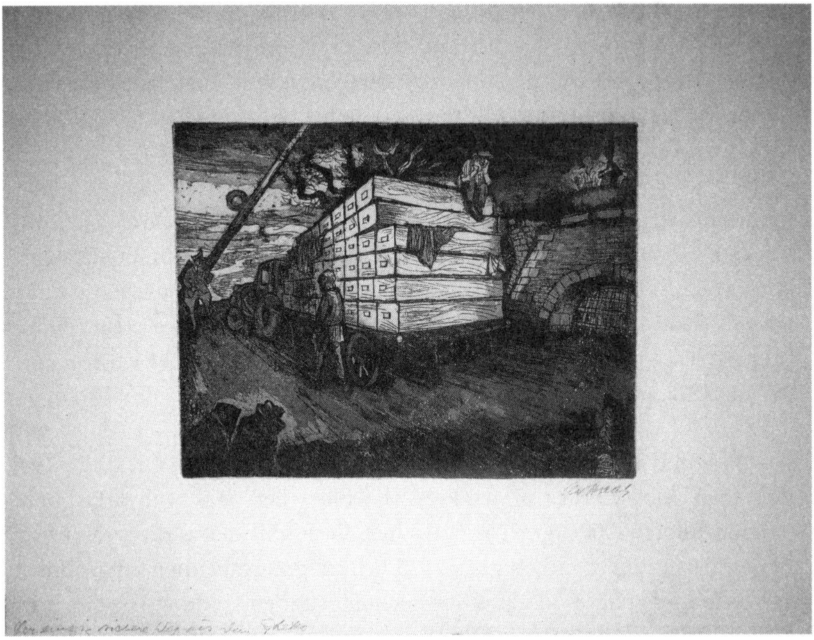

Figure 3.13 Leo Haas (1901–1983). *The Safe Journey* (c.1944). Wash and ink on paper.

Collection of the Beit Theresienstadt Archives. Permission and reproduction provided by Beit Theresienstadt Archives.

As the war was ending and the Allies neared Auschwitz, Ungar, a broken skeleton of a man, was forced to participate "in one of the worst of the winter death marches" to Buchenwald. He was eventually liberated but died of his illnesses in a sanatorium 3 months later (Blatter & Milton, 1981). Yet, courageously, even with his mutilated hands, his body wracked with debilitating illness, he continued to draw until his final day. It is told that he died with a piece of coal clutched in his hand, "scratching away the murky inferno into which he and millions of others had been plunged, still trying to force the truth upon a disbelieving world . . . a frail man he may have been; a man prone to weep; a worrier and pessimist. But he was still trying to draw" (Green, p. 125).

Friedl Dicker-Brandeis and the Art of the Children

Along with the artists were the children. Approximately 15,000 children found their way through Terezín; fewer than 150 survived. Yet many of their drawings—documenting their wishes, their hopes, and what they saw around them—lived on (Volavkova, 1993).

One person who made a difference in how the children responded to their environment was an artist and designer from Prague, Friedl Dicker-Brandeis (Dutlinger, 2002; Goldman-Rubin, 2000; Wix, 2010. She believed in the impact art can have for children. In a letter to a friend in 1940, Dicker-Brandeis wrote,

> I remember thinking in school how I would grow up and would protect my students from unpleasant impressions, from uncertainty, from scrappy learning. . . . Today only one thing seems important—to rouse the desire towards creative work, to make it a habit, and to teach how to overcome difficulties that are insignificant in comparison with the goal to which you are striving. (Salamon, 2004, para. 1)

Dicker-Brandeis was transported, along with her husband, to Terezín in 1942. Rather than pack clothes or trinkets, she filled her bags with art supplies (Goldman-Rubin, 2000; Wix, 2010). To help these children address their fears, anxieties, frustrations, and confusion, to help them escape their environment, and to keep them out of mischief, she encouraged them to draw. For her, it was important for the students to sign their work and complete self-portraits, emphasizing their sense of identity and value.

Upon her deportation 2 years later, she gave a fellow educator a briefcase filled with more than 4,500 drawings to hide. These drawings survived; Dicker-Brandeis did not. She was murdered in Birkenau in 1944.

Draw What You See

One child artist, Helga Weissová (Hoskova), upon separation from her father, was encouraged to "draw what you see" while in the camp (Weissová, 1998).

These images provide us a visual history of this child's experiences in Terezín (Figure 3.14) and of her time in Auschwitz—the drawings about her experiences in Auschwitz were completed after her liberation from the death camp. The transformation from her early, more colorful and spirited drawings compared to these later images brings home the changes these children underwent through their painful experiences.

I experienced my own visceral reaction when looking at a series of children's drawings during a visit to Terezín.

> They were small. I could see the stray crayon and pencil lines; cursory, unplanned marks; bold, assertive strokes; the tears; curled and wrinkled corners; the misplaced areas of paste. This art was done by children with found

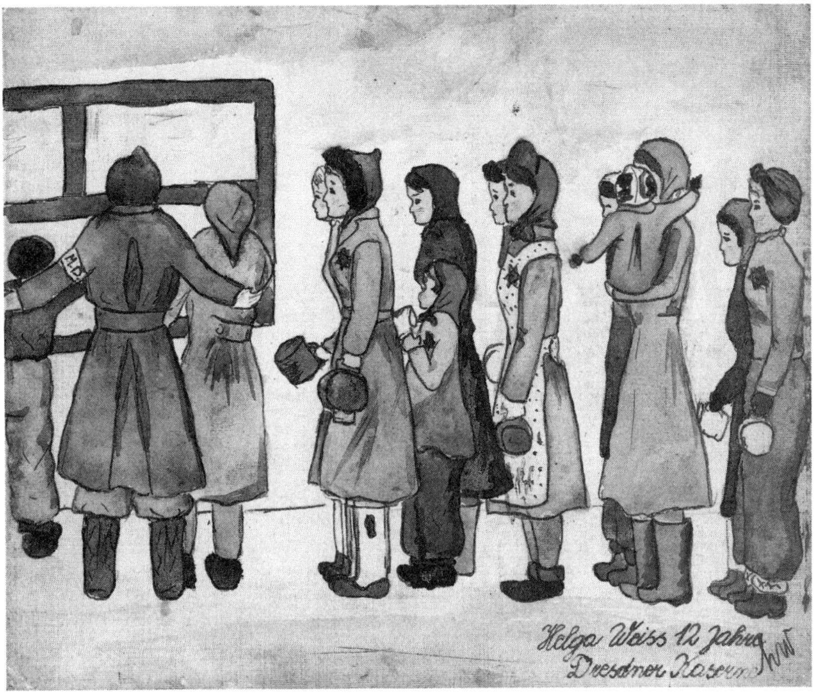

Figure 3.14 Helga Weissová (b.1929). *Standing in the Queue in Front of the Kitchen from Zeichne. Was Du siehst/Draw What You See: Zeichnungen eines Kindes aus Theresienstadt/Terezín*. Watercolor and ink on paper.

Hg. von Niedersächsischer Verein zur Förderung von Theresienstadt/Terezín e.V. Copyright Wallstein Verlag, Göttingen. Permission and reproduction provided by the publisher.

> materials. . . . Through their creative markings they gave soul to what was a soulless place . . . collectively they frame at least the children's experience of Terezín better than any of the talking heads on the video [elsewhere in the museum]. . . . [T]he work helped finalize the reality of the Holocaust for me. (Gussak, 2004b, p. 160)

The subtitle for this chapter is "Unveiling the Holocaust." An unveiling is a Jewish burial ritual in which, 1 year after the death of a loved one, the mourners return to the grave to witness the rabbi removing a cloth to unveil the memorial headstone. This act serves as much to celebrate the living as remember the dead.

PART II
ART OF PSYCHOPATHY

Interlogue

Examining Psychopathy

The previous section included chapters that introduced theoretical foundations of the interrelationship between violence and art. They also provided examples of well-established artists to explore the narcissistically aggressive artists; artists who were violently impulsive when restraint is compromised because of alcohol, substance use, or neurological impairments; and those who relied on their craft for evidence and resistance in violent circumstances. It even included a chapter that juxtaposed the paintings of the architect of the Holocaust against the work done by some of its victims. The following two chapters address the art created by those who have committed some of the most heinous crimes and embody the truest essence of systematic and cold-blooded violence: multiple murderers.

In some sense, these people defy any true understanding. However, as I researched them, I came across references often made that those who committed such crimes were called *psychopaths* and *sociopaths*. In my own work with violent criminals within various forensic contexts, many people used these terms interchangeably, with little distinction or nuance. In many cases, they were used as insulting slurs or as labels against those the staff did not understand. Certainly, in many of these situations, the terms were applied incorrectly. As I began to dig deeper into the realm of the serial killer, it became increasingly important for me to fully understand these designations as potential disorders and personality characterizations. Therefore, prior to exploring the work of multiple murderers, this interlogue is offered to clarify the similarities and distinctions of psychopathy and sociopathy.

Who Is "the Psychopath"?

The term "psychopath" has been used often in popular culture to describe anyone who is manipulative, selfish, or self-involved, with little to no emotional investment in others. The term itself has become "Hollywoodized"—Kevin Spacey seems to have become the poster child of the functioning psychopath in the numerous roles he has played in television and film, such as *House of Cards* and *Se7en*. However, it is a very real personality disorder.

Although often been used interchangeably, in fact, the *Diagnostic Statistical Manual of Mental Disorders* (DSM-V) (American Psychiatric Association,

2013) indicates that both terms—"sociopathy" and "psychopathy"—along with dissocial personality disorder, have been used to label patterns most associated with antisocial personality disorder (ICD code 301.7[F60.2]). In particular, this criteria indicates that the person being diagnosed as such must be more than 18 years old and exhibit a "pervasive pattern of disregard for and violation of the rights of others . . . since age 15 years" (p. 659). The diagnosis of such a person must include at least three of the following:

- Does not conform to social norms, particularly lawful behavior
- Deceitful, including pervasive lying and aliases
- Impulsive or does not plan ahead
- Irritable and aggressive, including fighting and assaults
- Disregard for safety of others
- Consistently irresponsible
- Lack of remorse, and commonly justifies hurting others

While the DSM-V is useful in establishing a base on which to build, it tends to paint with broad strokes. This makes it difficult to clarify just who is the psychopath.

Criminology professor Scott Bonn recognized the common similarities and differences between sociopathy and psychopathy (2014). Those labeled as sociopaths may be emotional, easily agitated, and have little to no regard for society. They appear disturbed, are generally uneducated, and their crimes—in particular murder—are generally executed in a disorganized and spontaneous fashion.

Those considered psychopaths, on the other hand,

> are unable to form emotional attachments or feel real empathy with others, although they often have disarming or even charming personalities. Psychopaths are very manipulative and can easily gain people's trust. They learn to mimic emotions, despite their inability to actually feel them, and will appear normal to unsuspecting people. Psychopaths are often well educated and hold steady jobs. Some are so good at manipulation and mimicry that they have families and other long-term relationships without those around them ever suspecting their true nature. When committing crimes, psychopaths carefully plan out every detail in advance and often have contingency plans in place [and] are cool, calm, and meticulous. (para. 4–5)

Regardless, many continue to use the terms "sociopathy" and "psychopathy" indiscriminately and consider the differences minute enough to be disregarded. In their article "Negotiating with Psychopaths" Cooper and Penn (2010) acknowledged the separation of these two terms and proceeded to essentially negate these differences, coming down firmly in the camp that such terms are one and the same. While "psychopathy" has been used since the early 1800s, the term "sociopathy" was introduced in 1930 to create a more precise label distinct from its predecessor; however, this created even greater confusion. Invariably, Cooper and Penn argued that, "the dual usage requires a now obligatory apologetic explanation that the two terms refer, without distinction, to one and the same thing" (p. 2). For some, the distinction between the two was necessary for proper characterization; for others, it has been merely semantic.

For a long time, there was little consensus on what constituted psychopathic traits. The description was in fact, fairly basic. "The 1959 Mental Health Act for England and Wales defined 'psychopaths' as those having 'a persistent disorder or disability of mind (whether or not including subnormality of intelligence)" (Ronson, 2011, p. 65). Those who subscribed to this description believed that such patients would exhibit unexpected aggressive or irresponsible behavior. The definition has since become more refined.

Based on his extensive work with people with psychopathic traits, psychologist Robert Hare (1993) developed the Hare Psychopathy Checklist (PCL) in 1991, later updated and revised (PCL-R). While it was initially designed to evaluate convicted criminals, it has since been applied for general use.

The process executed in determining if someone indeed has a level of psychopathy is fairly extensive. The participant's history and records are reviewed, and the information is supplemented by data obtained through a semi-structured interview to evaluate whether the participant reveals the following traits:

- Glib and superficial charm
- Grandiose (exaggeratedly high) estimation of self
- Need for stimulation
- Pathological lying
- Cunning and manipulative
- Lack of remorse or guilt
- Shallow affect (superficial emotional responsiveness)
- Callousness and lack of empathy
- Parasitic lifestyle
- Poor behavioral controls
- Sexual promiscuity
- Early behavior problems
- Lack of realistic long-term goals
- Impulsivity
- Irresponsibility
- Failure to accept responsibility for own actions

- Many short-term marital relationships
- Juvenile delinquency
- Revocation of conditional release
- Criminal versatility

This list was obtained from the online Encyclopedia of Mental Disorders at http://www.minddisorders.com/Flu-Inv/Hare-Psychopathy-Checklist.html.

Some of these categories mirror the characteristics outlined in the DSM directly; others reflect the participants' relationships, emotionality, responses to social situations, and personal lifestyle. Ultimately, those who are generally selfish, callous, unstable, and think nothing of victimizing someone else receive a high score. The higher the number, the more likely that psychopathy is present. Recognizing that this checklist is not completely free of subjective interpretation, it is used more to screen for potential indicators that such a characterization and additional assessments may be warranted.

Rather than being free of feelings or lacking emotional depth, Cooper and Penn (2010) stressed that those with such traits are in fact "motivated by the strongest of feelings" (p. 5)—feelings driven by self-interest. Indeed, they are quite capable of "experiencing anger, fear, lust and loathing" (p. 8–9), emotions that drive their behaviors and actions.

While their emotional range is still somewhat limited, people deemed as psychopaths may be excellent mimics; they learn by observing others and act in what may be perceived as an appropriate manner given proper social cues. They can feign guilt or compassion if necessary, even though true empathic responses are not actually in their repertoire.

Such thespian skills also provide the gift of gab, as it were—the designated psychopath knows how to talk himself out of a tight spot; in fact, such a person is often described as quite charming (Cooper & Penn, 2010). Still, regardless of how sweet and intelligent the identified psychopath appears, it would be safe to remember that such a person is "governed by a code of his or her own" (p. 11), one counterindicative to societal expectations. The concept of *right* and *wrong* is judged through their own lens, and often the person with psychopathy perceives his own perspective as superior to others.

Word of warning: such people will be charming and sweet until it no longer serves them. Their arrogance, superiority, and narcissism dictate that they are always in the right, and everyone else is wrong. However, unlike those with a severe mental illness and psychotic tendencies, such people are capable of self-awareness. This does not necessarily mean that they will change. Such knowledge is irrelevant and does not fit within their schema: they refuse to acknowledge responsibilities for the actions that emerge as a result from their beliefs and behaviors.

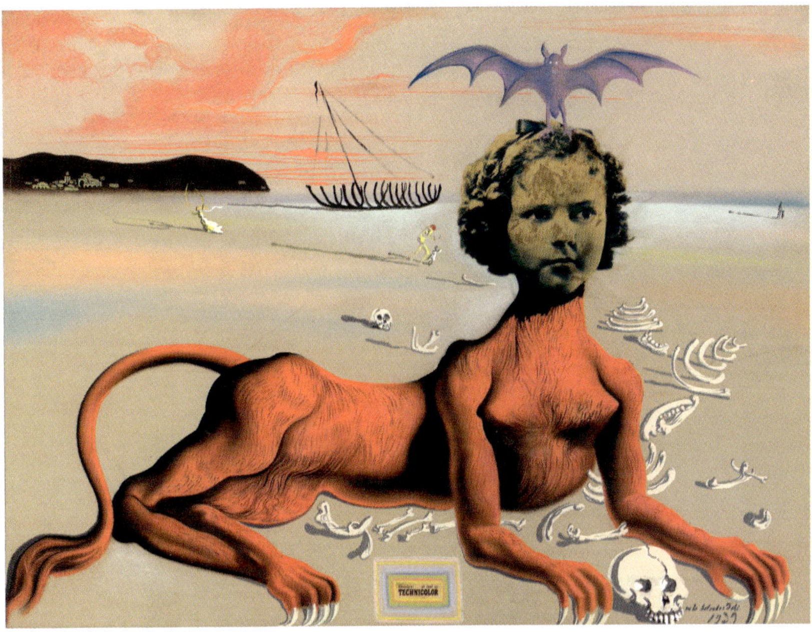

Figure 1.5 Salvador Dali (1904–1989). *Shirley Temple, le plus jeune monstre sacré du cinéma de son temps (Shirley Temple the Youngest Most Sacred Monster of the Cinema in Her Time)* (1939). Oil on canvas, collage.

Collection of Museum Boijmans Van Beuningen, Rotterdam. Permission provided by Salvador Dalí, Fundació Gala-Salvador Dalí/Artists Rights Society (ARS). Reproduction provided by Museum Boijmans Van Beuningen, Rotterdam. Photographer: Studio Tromp.

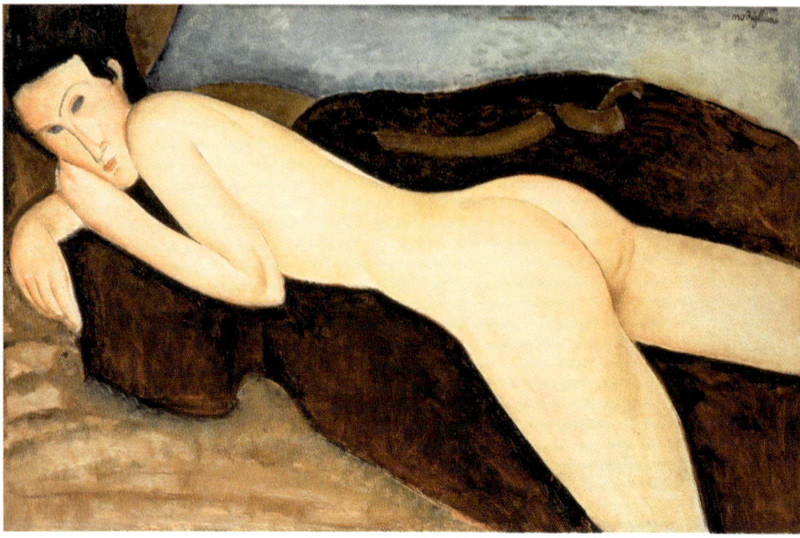

Figure 1.8 Amadeo Modigliani (1884–1920). *Reclining Nude from the Back* (c. 1917). Oil on canvas.

Collection of The Barnes Foundation, Philadelphia. Reproduction provided by Barnes Foundation / Bridgeman Images.

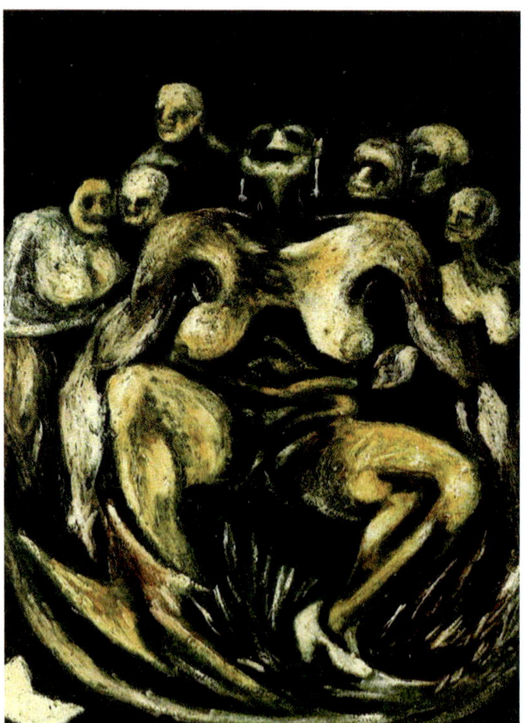

Figure 1.10 Jackson Pollock (1912–1956). *Woman* (c. 1930–1933). Oil on canvas.

Copyright 2021, The Pollock-Krasner Foundation / Artists Rights Society (ARS), New York.

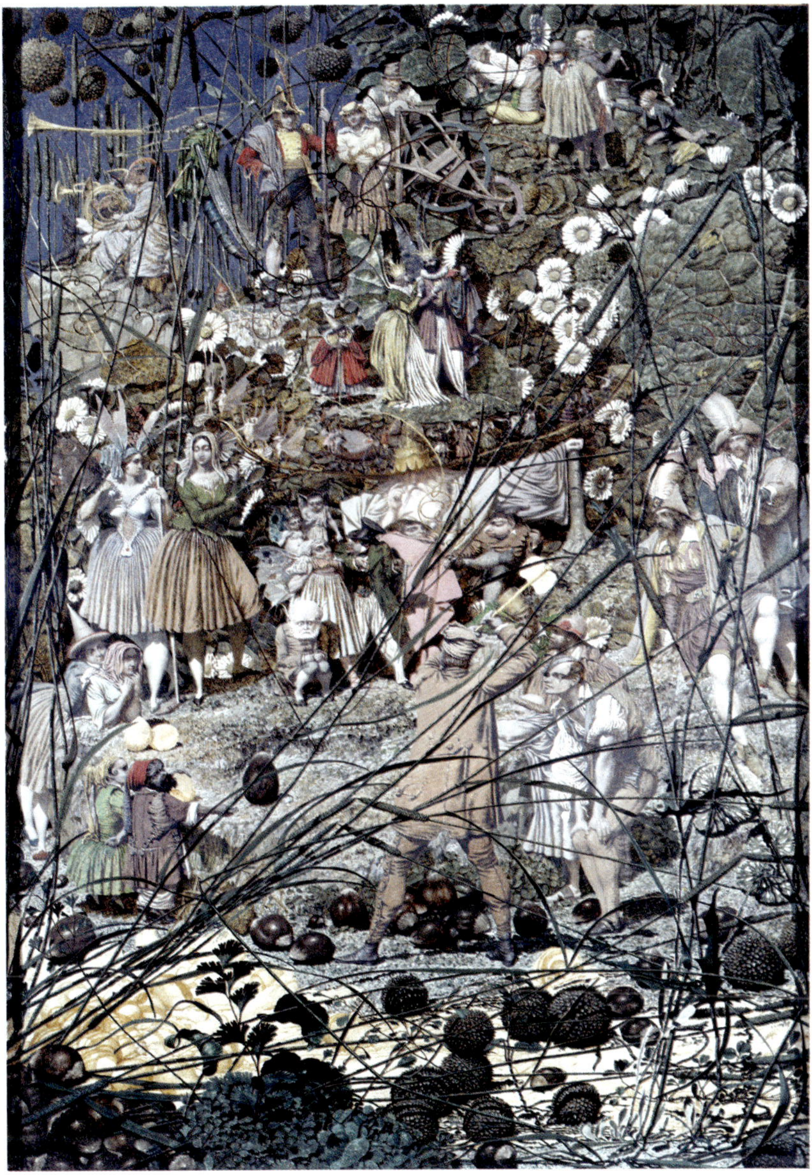

Figure 1.13 Richard Dadd (1817–1886). *The Fairy Feller's Master-Stroke* (1855–1864). Oil on canvas.

Collection of the Tate Museum, London. Reproduction provided by Derek Bayes (photographer)/Bridgeman Images.

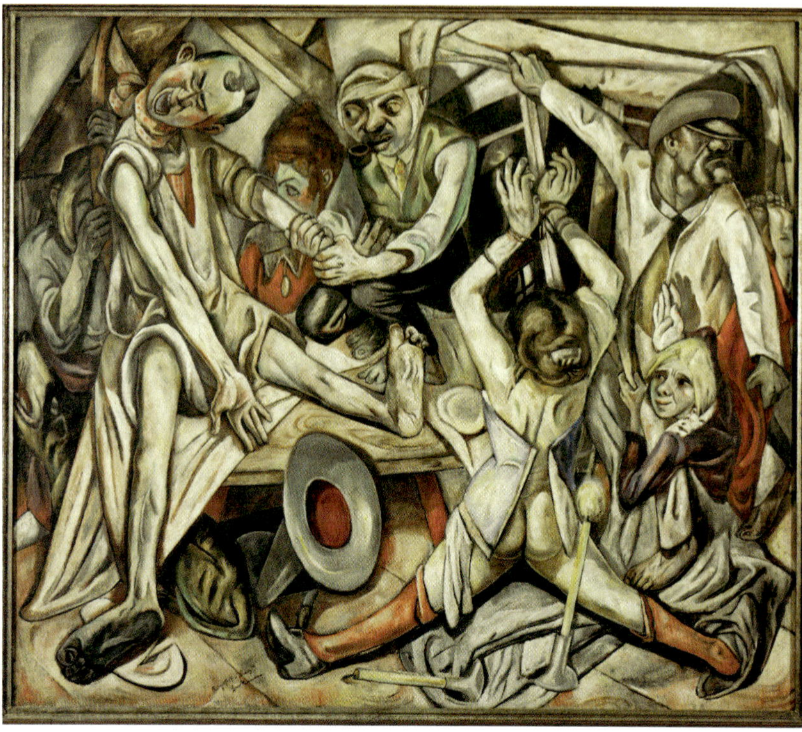

Figure 2.5 Max Beckmann (1884–1950). *The Night* (1919). Oil on canvas.

Collection of Kunstsammlung Nordrhein-Westfalen, Dusseldorf, Germany. Reproduction provided by Erich Lessing / Art Resource, New York.

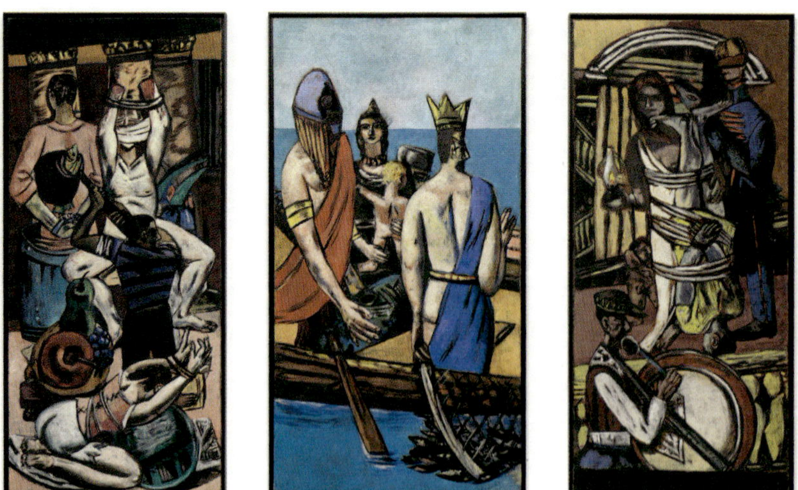

Figure 2.6 Max Beckmann (1884–1950). *Departure* (1932–1935). Oil on canvas, three panels.

Collection of The Museum of Modern Art New York, New York. Reproduction provided by The Museum of Modern Art/Licensed by SCALA / Art Resource, New York.

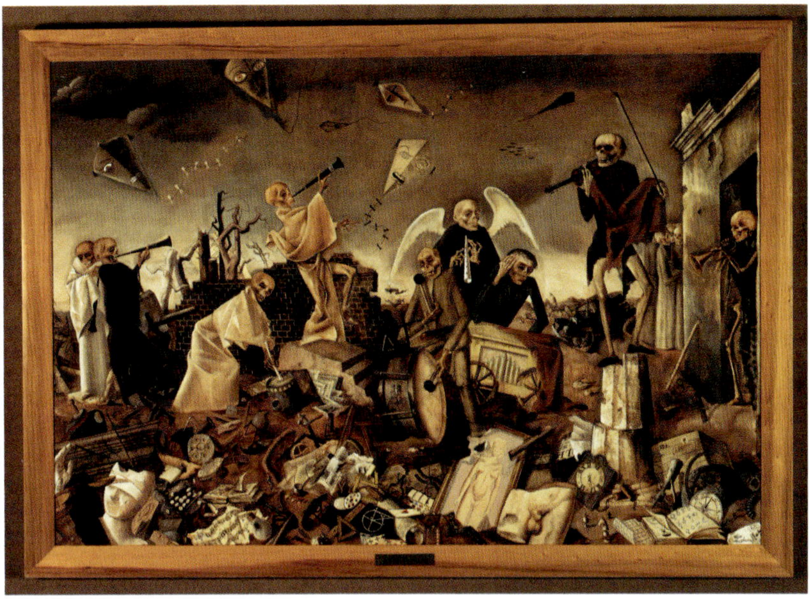

Figure 2.9 Felix Nussbaum (1904–1945). *Death Triumphant (The Skeletons Playing for the Dance)* (1944). Oil on canvas.

Collection of Lower Saxony Sparkasse Foundation, Germany. Reproduction provided by bpk Bildagentur / Lower Saxony Sparkasse Foundation / Art Resource, New York.

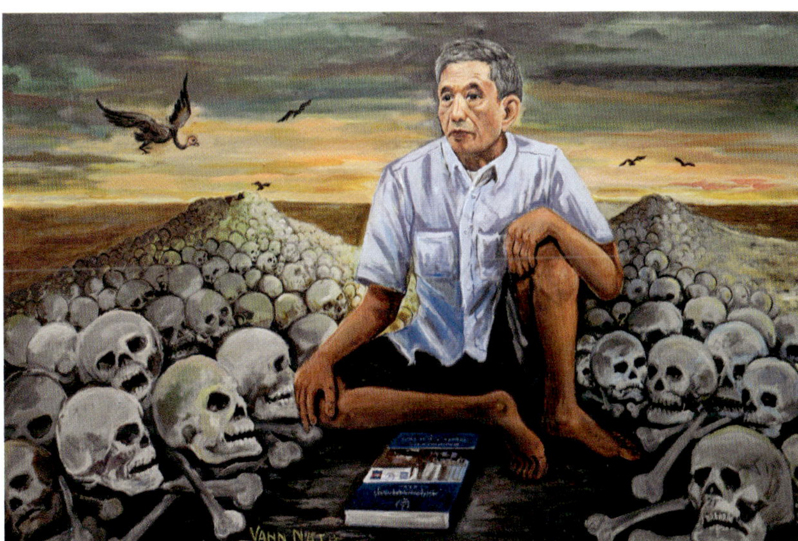

Figure 2.12 Vann Nath (1946–2011). *Duch's Verdict.* Oil on canvas.

Permission provided by Channarong Vann. Reproduction provided by Bophana Center.

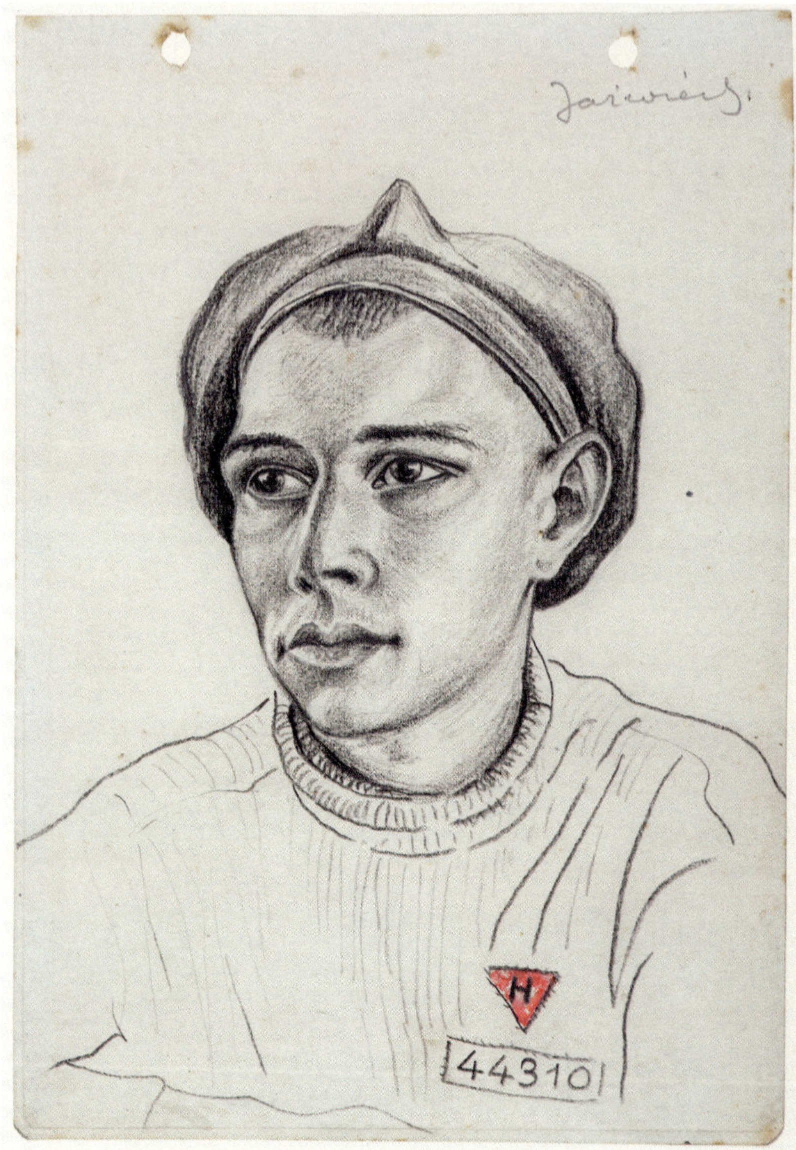

Figure 3.7 Franciszek Jazwiecki (died 1946). *Portrait of Landendum* (Date unknown). Pencil and crayon on cardboard.

Collection of Auschwitz-Birkenau Memorial and Museum. Permission and reproduction provided by Auschwitz-Birkenau Memorial and Museum.

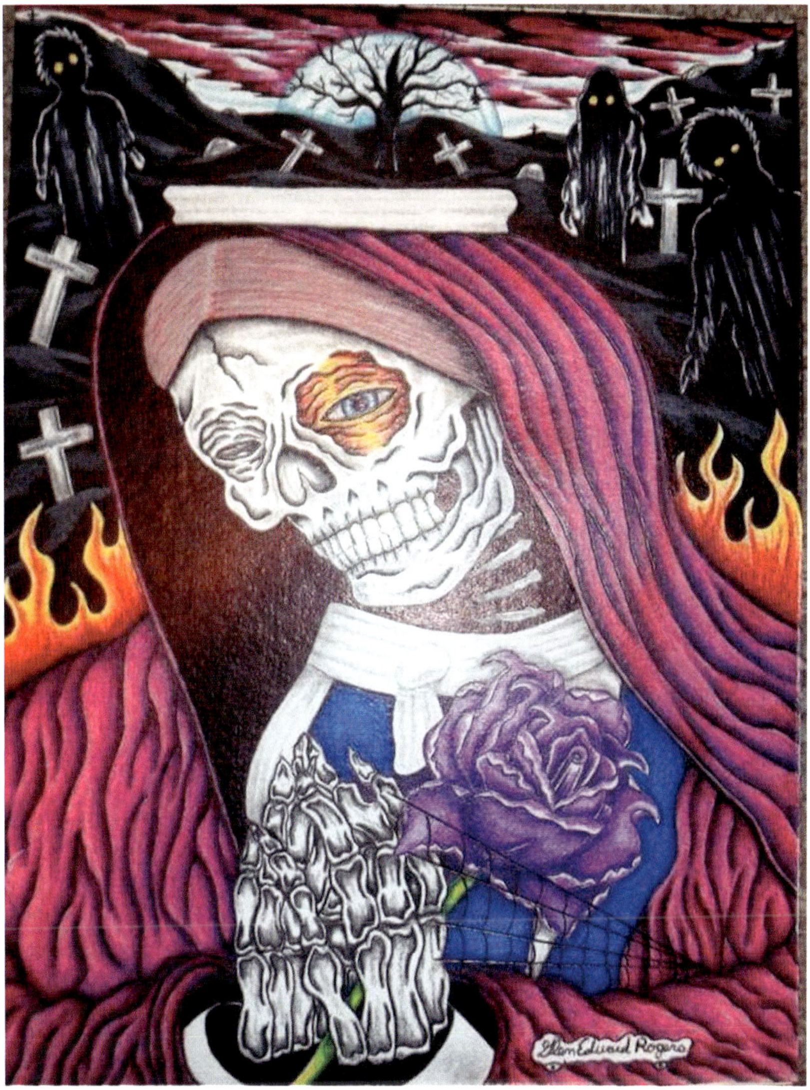

Figure 4.6 Glen Edward Rogers (b. 1962; remains on Death Row). *Untitled* (Date unknown). Colored pencil on paper.

Collection of Mirko K. Permission and reproduction provided by from Mirko K.

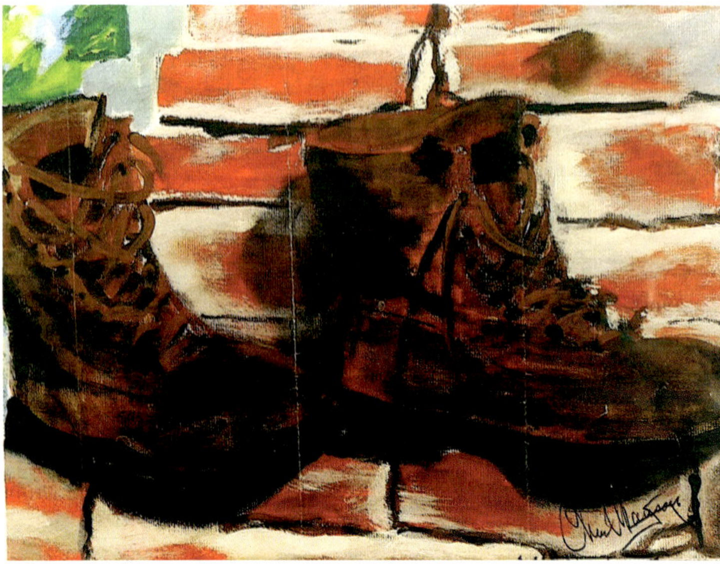

Figure 5.3 Charles Manson (b. 1934; died 2017 of natural causes in prison). *Shoes* (Date unknown). Oil on canvas board.
Collection of Ken Dickerson. Permission and reproduction provided by Ken Dickerson.

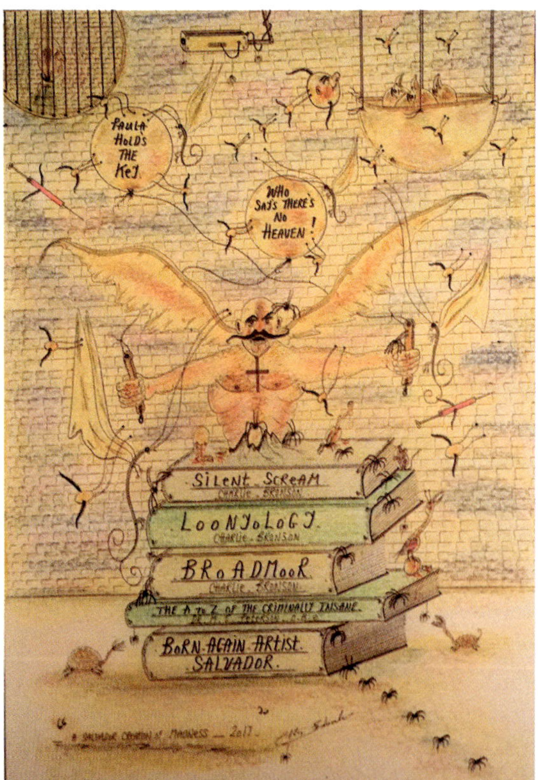

Figure 6.7 Charles Salvador (b. 1952). *Creation of Madness* (2017). Pencils, colored pencils, and ink on paper.
Permission provided by the artist.

While psychopathy often has been associated with criminality, Ronson (2011) underscored that not all are violent criminals—many of them are respected members of society. One may live right next door. Some publications laud the skills associated with psychopathy, believing that such characteristics can be most valuable in heading a Fortune 500 company, running for political office, or successfully trying a court case. Such a person remains charming yet ruthless; they simply have the skills necessary to *get ahead* regardless of who gets in the way. Yet, as Cooper and Penn (2010) warned their readers "[c]areful study . . . will quickly persuade even the most unbiased that psychopaths, of whatever stripe, congenitally violent or otherwise, constitute by their nature an extremely dangerous category" (p. 17).

The following two chapters include members of this extremely dangerous category who are not those who have used psychopathic traits to get ahead, but rather have tortured and killed others simply for their own ghastly motivations. Through their long history of criminal behavior and their congenital violence they demonstrated a marked indifference to the detrimental effects that their violent behavior had on others. These were the ones who hurt others as a result of feeling slighted, because others had it "coming to them," or merely out of morbid curiosity. They may have a long history of criminal behavior and are indifferent to the suffering of others.

And yet, despite these proclivities, or perhaps because of them, some of them have picked up the pencil and brush and created.

4

Wielding a New Weapon

Perpetuating the Multiple Murderer's Psychopathic Cycle Through Art

Many years ago, in a public lecture about working with violent offenders, I flippantly remarked about the crimes of Ted Bundy. One of the presentation attendees waited to meet with me after and reminded me of something I should have considered. She indicated, not unkindly, "please remember who might be in your audience—my next door neighbor lost her daughter to Bundy. These are very real crimes with very real victims. Please don't treat their offenses lightly and don't raise the offender above their status."

This was on my mind when, in 2011, I was asked to provide a series of lectures on the artwork of John Wayne Gacy. He was a serial killer responsible for 33 deaths in his suburban town near Chicago (see Chapter 5). While presenting his paintings, I made it a point to recognize the heinous crimes Gacy had committed. I also stressed that by acknowledging his art we were not negating his crimes; that, instead, perhaps we could learn from his work. While doing so, I acknowledged his victims with solemn regard.

Once again, a woman waited to speak with me after, but with a different message. She told me that her brother was one of Gacy's victims and that she had intended to come to the lecture to protest its focus on the murderer's artistic endeavors. We spoke for about 30 minutes; we discussed the rationale for the presentation: why, in my humble opinion, such an exhibition was necessary and what we could learn from such discussions. At the same time, I listened to her talk about her initial resistance to the show. She admitted that she was reluctant to agree on the exhibition's importance. However, toward the end of our conversation, she recognized that Gacy's persona was not enhanced because of his creative endeavors. She left the lecture seemingly accepting that despite a desire to bury Gacy, to forget him, we could learn from the products he left behind.

In 2013, a discussion ensued with a former editor about these lectures. She became fascinated with the notion that such a heinous individual made art. When I mentioned the work created by many other serial killers and multiple murderers, she became enthralled and believed that this might be a potential book topic.

I have to admit that, while intrigued, there was a part of me that was intensely uncomfortable with this idea. While I saw the educational opportunities in exploring such work, I also recognized that writing this book could potentially perpetuate these individuals' notoriety and in some way minimize or nullify their acts by validating and championing their creative endeavors. She and I continued to have several conversations about this. While I eventually decided I would not nor could not write an entire book about this topic, we recognized that it could be part of a larger conversation about the relationship between art and violence. By making it a subset of a larger discussion, it would minimize the impression of serial killers as misunderstood artists while providing opportunities to learn from their work.

In full disclosure, this chapter remained one of the most difficult ones to write as I continued to balance what I learned from those two attendees—to respect what we could learn while not glorifying these perpetrators. I had to examine my own desire to write a chapter that I knew might still excite a certain subset of readers. Simultaneously, as I became more embedded in the research on these people, I found I was oscillating between desensitizing myself to their horrors and becoming overwhelmed, depressed, and anxious. It was also a confusing chapter; unlike many of my clients and the artists presented earlier, it seems that these men would not nor could not benefit from the art making: in fact, the work they produced and what it represented for them shattered my previously held biases and beliefs on the benefits of art making for those who are violent and aggressive. It forced me to re-examine and reconstruct my understanding. What eventually allowed this chapter to emerge was my own strongly held belief that a book that focused on the interrelationship between art and violence required this examination.

Multiple Homicides: Typologies, Definitions, and Generalizations

For centuries, multiple murders were all included under the same criminal classification. In fact, despite the apparent differences in approach, motive, and victims, such as with the multiple murderers Jack the Ripper, Thomas Griffiths Wainewright, and Billy the Kid, it was not until the 1980s that separate typologies were developed to better understand these crimes and those who committed them. Eventually, the Federal Bureau of Investigation (FBI) determined that there are three separate categories of multiple murders: mass, spree, and serial (Fox & Levin, 2012).

Specifically, a *mass murder* involves killing or massacring "four or more victims within a single episode" (p. 19). A murderous *spree* constitutes a series of killings that involve two or more people, sometimes in two or more locations, but as a one-time event. This is somewhat misleading, however, for the one-time event may take place over several days. However, what differentiates this from serial murder is that there is also no "cooling off" period between the murderous binges.

While there is some discrepancy in the number of murders committed, usually a *serial killer* murders three or more people over more than 30 days. In addition, there is usually a "significant cooling-off period between the killings" (Holmes & Holmes, 2010, p. 5), sometimes weeks, months, or, in some extreme cases, years.

These categories are not nearly so neat, and there is often a blurring of distinctions; what may appear to be one type may in fact fit better under a different category. Some have argued that such classifications might not even be necessary; the category in which a series of murders falls is perhaps less important than understanding the patterns that emerge and the psychological characteristics that may comprise such a killer.

The professional literature almost seems bottomless in examining the psychological characteristics of multiple murderers (Dietrich & Fox Hall, 2010; Fox & Levin, 1998, 2012; Haycock, 2014; Kocsis, 2008; Levin & Fox, 2008; Ramsland, 2006), while serial killer profiling has become the sensationalized subject of television (i.e., *Mindhunters*), movies (*Copycat*), and literature (i.e., Jo Nesbo's *The Snowman* and *The Leopard*). They all seem to underscore the same schema: that while there are certainly exceptions to the now established rules, there are some common, general understandings of the characteristics that many of these perpetrators share.

The majority of these killers have experienced extremely difficult childhoods, littered with neglect, abandonment, and abuse from those they should have been able to trust (Levin & Fox, 2008). "Sociopathic serial killers are likely to have internalized shame and humiliation during childhood that are later transferred into anger and rage . . . malevolent behavior is derived from the experience of shame, the growth of negative self-image, the acceptance of the 'bad' self, and finally a lack of feeling for others" (Fox & Levin, 2012, p. 55).

This does not excuse their crimes. To be abundantly clear: the majority of those who have suffered from such deprivation early in life do not typically nor predictably engage in such horrendous and nefarious actions. In addition, not all people who have developed compensatory psychopathy will murder, let alone conduct multiple killings. However, it is obvious that many of those who engage in mass homicides have difficulty adjusting to these incredible deficits and challenges and turn to these psychopathic reactions to counter their sense of vulnerability and powerlessness.

Often, such murderous actions do not happen until years after their degrading experiences; some multiple murderers do not even begin their murderous acts until they are well into middle age (Levin, 2008). Certainly, many of them had engaged in illicit behaviors early in life and perpetrated sadistic actions, such as torturing and killing small animals or starting destructive fires. However, it is not until their trying and challenging transitions into adulthood that they progress into more lethal actions—sometimes impulsively and explosively, other times intentionally well-planned and methodical. Paradoxically, some of them have committed murders that were simultaneously planned out and impulsive (Haycock, 2014).

It was originally believed that serial murder was committed for "no apparent motive" (Ressler, Burgess, & Douglas, 1988), However, some have come to understand that often motives and rationale do exist; albeit, such drives appear irrational, are often difficult to comprehend, and are impossible to accept (Fox & Levin, 2012). Regardless of whether it appears lucid, it seems that indeed the majority of multiple murderers have developed entrenched justifications and validations for their killings. In 1988, Holmes and DeBurger theorized that there were four motivational classifications for serial murders, including visionary, mission-oriented, hedonistic, and power/control. Porter and Woodworth (2006) believed that those who engage in such specific psychopathic actions "may be more likely than other offenders to derive pleasure from the suffering of others [reflecting] a generalized tendency toward callousness and thrill seeking" (Porter & Woodworth, 2006 p. 487). Others have voiced specific rationales that are related to delusional paranoia or fundamentalist beliefs. Still others "incorporating many elements of earlier classification schemes, a unified typology of multiple murder can be constructed using five categories of motivation applicable to serial and mass killing: power, revenge, loyalty, profit and terror" (Fox & Levin, 2012, p. 22).

Adopting compensatory, pathologically narcissistic characteristics has afforded them the ability to compartmentalize, justify, and separate themselves from their acts. By doing so, they in turn are able to objectify their victims, allowing them to kill without remorse or empathy (Levin & Fox, 2008). In addition, serial killers see themselves as above the law, creating their own moral standards: "the murderous methods of serial killers become their way of asserting their identity and their ability to exert some kind of control over their environment" (Vidal, 2017, p. 122). Serial killers, as are most with psychopathic traits, are skilled at being able to present themselves as normal and healthy, managing expectations and "the impression that we wish to convey others is" a normal healthy characteristic (Levin & Fox, 2008, p. 6). It's what they do with these skills, luring victims into a false sense of security and safety before callously torturing and murdering them, that sets them widely apart.

Some have even developed "alternative truths," lies they tell others or self-delusions to justify their sprees. For example, serial killer Gary Ray Bowles attempted to morally justify his crimes by stressing that he only killed child molesters (Redstall, 2011). While an inaccurate assertion, it points to two seemingly asynchronistic possibilities. One was that he was deliberately lying to justify his actions. The other is that a pronounced cognitive dissonance allowed him to believe such a fabrication was indeed true. If so, he then believed that such a morally outrageous crime deserved punishment and that he was well within his rights to implement and apply his own morally absolute sentence by killing those he claimed were pedophiles.

Whether falsehoods or self-delusions, all perpetrators exhibit a level of callousness and cold-bloodedness, an "instrumental violence," that is incomparable (Haycock, 2014, p. 136).

Societal Repulsion, Collective Fascination

Society seems paradoxically disgusted and captivated by serial killers. Dietrich and Fox Hall (2010) believed that there exists a dichotomous attraction/repulsion for the act of murder and that the serial killer can serve as an avatar that can facilitate and represent this action. Such an icon embodies symbolically what most repels and allures us, allowing us to engage in *coactivation*— a state that allows the simultaneous experience of intensely negative and positive feelings toward an aversive action or item (Andrade & Cohen, 2007). This is similar to the concurrent fear yet excitement and titillation associated with watching a gory horror movie or witnessing the aftermath of a particularly horrendous accident. While we may feel self-loathing and shame for finding such things alluring, an avatar allows us to explore and reflect on such feelings of morbid curiosity without self-incrimination—we can examine the negative and positive sides of ourselves and embrace the shadow.

> For most of us, sitting down with a real serial killer would not be an artistic, philosophical experience, but rather a terrifying, repulsive one. Yet, within a protective frame, safe and secure, we transform the serial killer, already an object of deep curiosity because of his or her fearsomeness, into an icon, an avatar. We revel in this transformation, exploring our darker side that longs to know what it feels like to be the one giving the orders instead of taking them, doing everything we want to, impervious to the consequences. (Dietrich & Fox Hall, 2010, p. 102).

Possessing the artifacts that once belonged to or represent these people simultaneously allows for further distancing while feeding the fascination. It creates yet another protective layer. This includes their paintings and drawings. The irony is that the art simultaneously provides an additional artificial barrier while reinforcing the *realness* of these individuals.

Many serial killers—the notorious and the contemporarily unrenowned—have demonstrated a propensity for creating revealing, profane, or banal imagery. Online auction houses and respectable gallery catalogues reveal a market for not only the works of the infamous but also the works of the "lesser-known" perpetrators, names that may no longer be remembered, but whose actions struck terror and fear in the nation at the time they were committed. These have included Rodney Alcala, Kenneth Bianchi, Ted Bundy, Nicholas Claux, Henry Lee Lucas, Keith Hunter Jesperson, Richard Ramirez, Arthur Shawcross, and Ottis Toole. The market for such artifacts is categorized as "murderabilia" (Hylton, 2007; Junge, 2019).

Art as Murderabilia

"Murderabilia," a word derived by victim rights advocate Andy Kahan (Hylton, 2007), refers to items deemed to be collectible due to their connection with notorious killers; the more infamous the individual, the more valuable the item. Items from serial killers are particularly sought after, and the value of such items—clothing, handwritten letters, Bibles—continues to increase. Art fits within its own rather unique classification.

Interest with this art seems to run counter to research findings. White, Kaufman, and Riggs (2014) examined how the background of various artists influenced perceptions of the art. A fairly large sample of participants were blindly exposed to the art of five different types of what they termed "outsider artists,"[1] including serial killers. The results indicated that overall, art work completed by the group of serial killers was deemed significantly "colder," less creative, and less likable than work created by other groups. Thus, what becomes abundantly clear was that "serial killer art is promoted and sold for reasons beyond any aesthetic merit" (p. 149). An essay introducing the exhibition *Killer Art*, a show that included paintings by serial killers, indicated that

> we wait eagerly for our daily dose of horror to be served with the coffee and croissants. It is hardly surprising then, that a vast and varied body of collectibles, that can quite rightly be described as "Killer Art," has emerged from this caravansary of horror transformed into collective arousal and

[1] Please note that Chapter 2 explored and challenged this term as potentially pejorative and limiting.

> a quick look at the Internet auction sites is enough to give you an idea of its scale. . . . It ranges from the horror appeal of fetishistic objects to banal drawings or watercolors, sketched by the latest serial killer. These drawings or paintings . . . are simply bad, kitsch and at best, astonishingly banal. Nevertheless . . . numerous exhibitions are dedicated to them and the number of collectors . . . is enormous. . . . The appeal . . . is their value of fetishes. (Riva & Vigano, 2001, p. 7)

While this fetishism has been amplified over recent years, it is certainly not new. As already underscored, society is simultaneously frightened and excited by the dark side and "to possess an object, an artifact produced by the imagination of these killer artists, means making contact with them, establishing a bond, moving a step nearer to their dark deeds, perhaps even to exorcise our own fears" (Riva & Vigano, 2001, p. 8). As the previous chapters reflect, established artists who have explored the violent and bloody results of war and violent deaths are valued, such as the paintings of Otto Dix and George. Yet, in some ways, "[m]ore powerful than these . . . are the works of . . . Gacy . . . Ramirez, Schaefer, Henry Lee Lucas, Toole, Bianchi or Claux . . . as these men, besides painting scenes of murder and torture, have also lived and carried them out personally" (Riva & Vigano, 2001, p. 8). These people have simultaneously experienced murder and tried to illustrate it; in so doing, they appeal to society's dark side. Their work has emerged as a stand-alone artistic movement, validated by those that collect them.

Such collections may be more than mere fetishes or avataristic representations of society's desire for coactivation; they may also perhaps be unintentionally valuable in providing an unfiltered and unmasked perspective of the sociopathic persona that would otherwise be unavailable. These artifacts may be appreciated by those who strive to understand. Mirko K. is just such a collector and was kind enough to provide me a small yet open window into this sordid world.

The Collector of the Arcane

Mirko K., a young elementary school teacher from Hamburg, Germany, has been collecting objects owned and created by serial killers since 2013. This has included many paintings and drawings, which are often displayed at his gallery, the Museum of Madness. Speaking from his gallery's office, he was willing to share with me some of the images from his collection while describing the simultaneous repulsion and allure he had for this work.

Mirko K. indicated that his fascination with artifacts that represent and embody destruction began when he was a child, after finding a photograph of his father standing atop New York's World Trade Center. He lived in Germany and would have been quite young when they were destroyed; he never had the chance to see the Towers. He had, of course, heard of the tragedy that occurred on September 11, 2001, but as a historical fable of evil invading the good; the Towers were always somewhat ethereal and abstract to him. Seeing the picture of his father on the top of one of the buildings solidified them, made them—and the tragedy—much more real. It was then "my interests shifted and were surrounded by death or tragic things."

Mirko K. enjoyed the simultaneous allure and repulsion of horror films and had watched them since a child. While watching *Halloween 8*, he became intrigued when one of the movie's characters recited a list of names of well-known murderers. Mirko K. did some online research. He was surprised to discover that the names were of real people, of serial killers. This grounded the horror of the fictional films he enjoyed so much into something real. However, he wasn't satisfied with merely reading about these people; like the photograph of his father, he became driven to find artifacts that made these people less a horror story told to scare others and more tangible, more existent.

He purchased his first piece in 2013, an original courtroom drawing of Ted Bundy's murder trial. He has since accumulated many letters, signatures, articles of clothing, and, of course, art pieces. Mirko K. admitted that such a fascination is unusual and even profane; yet, he was clear:

> I am not glorifying these people. I hate them for what they did. I think these are horrible people. I can understand someone seeing this collection and saying "wow; this is weird. Why do you put stuff on the wall from people who hurt and destroyed so many lives?" But . . . I am just interested.

When Mirko K. purchased John Wayne Gacy's painting of Disney's seven dwarfs from the United States, he had to go to the duty office where it was being held.

> They said to me "please open the package". . . . they looked at me and at the painting and they said "why does someone like you, who has no kids, why do you hang up this stuff? This is a children's painting." And this is the moment where I thought "wow, all the people see the painting but if I told them who made it and what he did to 33 young boys . . . they would say 'wow, this piece is dark as f&^%"' You know what I mean? I compare it to a car accident. When

> you drive by, you don't want to look, you don't want to see, but you will look. Even if you don't want to.

Mirko K. believed that such art allowed others to realize that those identified as monsters in the popular media are in fact real people. "[You hear about them from the movies and TV] but this is the real stuff right in front of you . . . you can touch it. . . . I think people really need to see it so they know it's true." For example, Mirko K. found the drawing he obtained from Lee Boyd Malvo to be a significant and perhaps even a true reflection of the murderer's state at the time he completed it. Seventeen-year-old Lee Boyd Malvo was one of a duo of spree killers known collectively as the DC or Beltway Snipers. In October 2002, he and 41-year-old John Allen Muhammad [Williams] terrorized Washington, DC, for a few weeks (Albarus & Mack, 2012; Holmes & Holmes, 2010). Shooting indiscriminately from a distance, the pair killed 10 people and critically injured three others "with no apparent motive or discrimination of victims" (Holmes & Holmes, 2010, p. 35).

Muhammad was sentenced to death for the murder of all but one of the victims. Malvo's attorneys relied on an insanity defense, stressing that he had been brainwashed by the older man. It didn't work, and the jury found him guilty of terrorism, capital murder, and the use of a firearm in the commission of a murder; he was given a life sentence without the possibility of parole. Mirko K. had one of his drawings.

The sketch Mirko K. possessed, *The Prison Well Made by Mind* (Figure 4.1), was completed after he was sentenced and imprisoned. It is of a singular composition, drawn with deliberate, strong lines that seems to offer a clear albeit contrived message. For Mirko K., it was a powerful reflection of the human behind the monster: "this drawing really shows how lonely he is and . . . how he hates himself for what he did . . . he destroyed his life and many others and he will never get out . . . it really shows the mind of the DC sniper."

For these reasons, Mirko K. provided permission to reproduce images from his collection for this chapter. Recognizably, there is a danger in going too deeply or too broadly with this topic. As online sources and exhibition catalogues revealed, there are many multiple murderers who have created art. There was a danger of this chapter becoming a compendium of many killers. Parameters needed to be established. Mirko K. had an unusual collection of a wide assortment of imagery that provided the structures and illustrations that guided this next section. What emerged was a range of illustrations and personalities that, while not absolute or inclusive, represent a wide continuum of violent perpetrators and the varied expanse of art pieces they created. For this chapter, seven multiple murderers were chosen to represent this horrific collective.

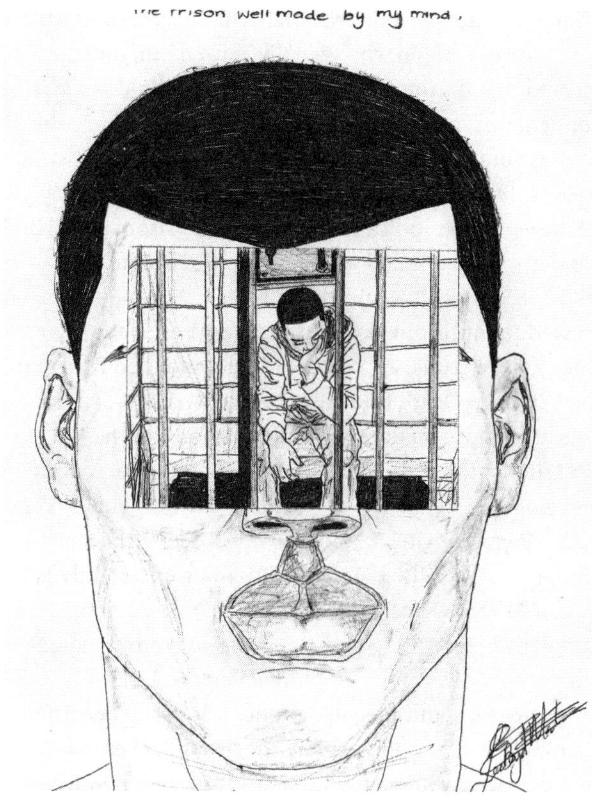

Figure 4.1 Lee Boyd Malvo (b. 1985; remains incarcerated). *The Prison Well Made by Mind* (Date unknown). Pencil, ink on paper.
Collection of Mirko K. Permission and reproduction provided by from Mirko K.

Exploring the Art of Multiple Murderers Through Seven Horrific Profiles

The Coast-to-Coast Killer: Tommy Lynn Sells

Some of Mirko K.'s drawings and paintings seemed contradictorily serene in comparison to the crimes the artists committed. The painting completed by Tommy Lynn Sells, an admitted serial killer with the self-given moniker "Coast-to-Coast," serves as an example of this type of work. Sells went on a three-decade murdering spree that spanned the country (Harrington, 2017).

After the death of a twin sister when they were 18 months old, Sells was sent to live with his aunt. When he was around 7 or 8 years old, he moved back in with his mother; however, she was indiscriminate with his care and would often leave him in the company of a friend who sexually abused him until he was around 14. These acts scarred him for life; he admitted that he would often relive these acts of molestation while executing his own crimes (Malcovich, 2010). He left home when he was still young and hitchhiked back and forth across the country for the next 21 years. In between his sporadic employment history of short-term manual labor, he would periodically spend time in prison; this included a 5-year sentence for rape and assault and a 16-month stint for stealing a truck. During this time, from 1985 to 1999, he murdered at least 22 people across the country; he later confessed to murdering upward of 70 people. He was convicted for the murder of one of his victims, a 13-year-old girl, and died by lethal injection in Texas in 2014. While on Death Row, Sells began to paint and draw.

Sells's works have occasionally appeared in various online venues. Many seem primitive, featuring crude hand tracings, some of them surrounded by blatantly aggressive and violent symbols. These included bleeding skulls, Vendetta masks, a copy of Gacy's Pogo the clown, and the words Helter Skelter (*sic*) painted in crimson red to appear like the bloody letters Manson's Family left on the wall. The painting that Mirko K. possessed seems much more complete and carefully rendered than many of his others; still, it is somewhat ominous, given the subject matter of a murder of crows in the moonlight (Figure 4.2).

Despite its portentous and menacing tone, it is eerily beautiful, perhaps because of its simplicity. The composition consists of seven black birds circling above an unseen ground, silhouetted by a large full moon. It has a limited color palette, mostly black and blues, contrary to the bright, almost garish, puerile compositions in his other works. While his other drawings suggest a desire to deliberately elicit strong, fearful reactions from his viewers, underscoring and potentially reconfessing his murderous ways, this painting seems more spontaneous and less self-conscious. While this work may still elicit dread, it displays, perhaps accidentally, maturity and aesthetic awareness.

Drawings of some of the other perpetrators in this chapter reveal a much more impulsive, primitive, and darker quality.

The Night Stalker: Richard Ramirez

In the mid-1980s, California was terrorized for a little more than a year by a series of brutal rapes and murders. Fourteen months after the killings began, Richard Ramirez, called the "Night Stalker" by the press, was dramatically caught.

Ramirez was raised in Texas by a violently abusive father, from whom he sustained two serious head injuries. To escape from this unpredictable and unstable household, Ramirez often hung around his cousin, Miguel, a former Vietnam

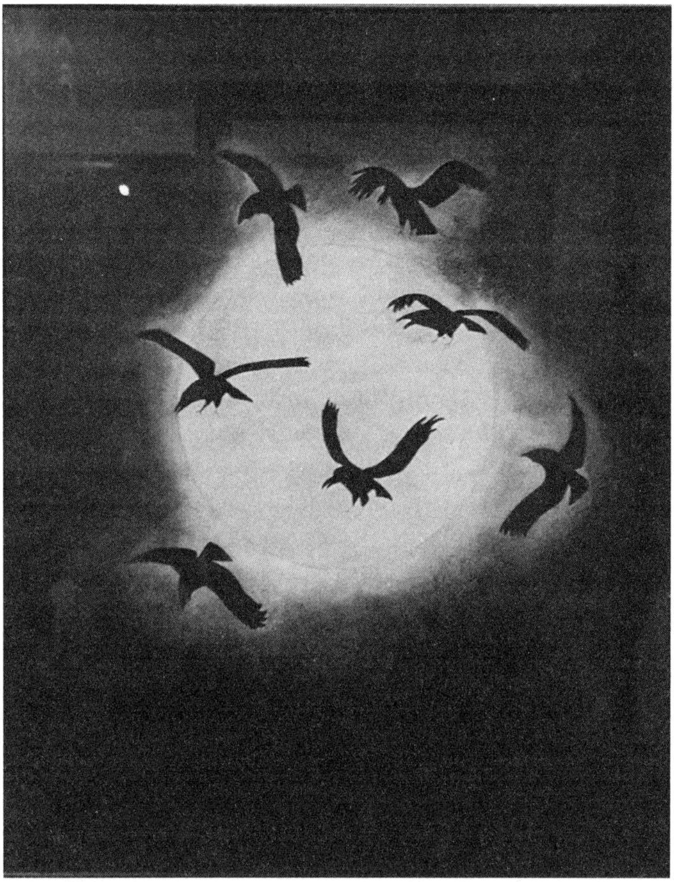

Figure 4.2 Tommy Lynn Sells (b. 1964; executed 2014). *Crows* (Date unknown). Pencil, ink on paper.
Collection of Mirko K. Permission and reproduction provided by from Mirko K.

veteran. Miguel had a penchant for torturing women while in Southeast Asia and would often tell his younger relative about his horrific deeds, showing the young boy photographs of some of the more gruesome acts. Eventually Miguel shot and killed his wife in front of Ramirez; Miguel was found not guilty for the crime by reason of insanity.

During these years, Ramirez was arrested several times for drug-related charges, burglary, and theft. He dropped out of school when he was 17 years old after failing to pass the ninth grade. He eventually relocated to California, where he developed his own proclivity for violence. He was once arrested for attempted rape; however, he was not convicted because the woman refused to testify against him out of fear. His behavior became more erratic; during this time, Ramirez swore fealty to Satan, carving a pentagram into his hand with a knife (Frasier, 1996).

Ramirez became more obsessed with violence, and his aggressive actions escalated, culminating in a killing spree that lasted 14 months. It began in 1984, with the brutal rape and near decapitation of a 79-year-old woman. Throughout the remainder of that year, Ramirez left a trail of victims all over California. He would often break into darkened yet occupied homes, immediately kill any men he encountered before he assaulted, raped, and murdered the women, usually by slashing their throats (Levin & Fox, 2008). His victims ranged from 22 to 80 years old.

Sometimes Ramirez left spray-painted pentagrams on the walls: "one woman related that her attacker forced her to swear allegiance to Satan while she was being raped" (Frasier, 1996, p. 376). By the time he was caught, he had violently attacked and killed 13 people, attempted to kill 5 more, and assaulted countless others.

Ramirez was identified as the assailant after a set of his fingerprints was found on a recovered stolen vehicle (Fox & Levin, 2012). His mug shot was broadcast on television, revealing a tall, lanky man with long and greasy black hair. After someone recognized him from the telecast, Ramirez was chased by frightened and angry citizens; when they caught up to him, one of his pursuers beat him thoroughly with a metal pipe until the police showed up. Sixteen months later, Ramirez was convicted of 13 first-degree murders and 30 other felony charges (Frasier, 1996), and he was subsequently sentenced to death. After 23 years on Death Row, Ramirez died of lymphoma in 2013.

Some of Ramirez's images were primitive, simple line drawings on scraps of notebook or blank white paper. Some had color, many were black and white, perhaps limited by the materials he had access to. While at times Ramirez drew with an assured, confident pencil or pen stroke, several were drawn with sketchy, broken, and inconsistent lines. There was one particularly horrific image found on only one obscure website that I found particularly disturbing. While unavailable for reproduction, it bears describing.

Ramirez separated the page into two halves by a drawn line along the horizontal axis. On the top half there appears to be a butchered human figure on a hastily drawn bed. The figure seems to be outlined with a suggestion in a pool of blood, with more dripping from her arm. There is little to determine if the figure is wearing clothes except that the drawn toes on the feet and the figure's groin are emphasized, leading to the conclusion that the figure is indeed unclothed. The figure's face has few details except two black dots for the eyes and a line depicting a frown; the hair is sketchily unkempt. There is a pot of wilting flowers on a nightstand next to the bed. On the bottom half there are jagged lines coming from a drawn baseline, as if to represent flames. On the bed's headboard over the dead girl's head Ramirez scrawled "rest in agony."

While it is particularly gruesome, certainly reflective of some of the scenes he had enacted, the drawing appears child-like, with little emotional investment. The composition is arranged as if it is a stage setting, showcasing what he had either done or wanted to do. The words on the headboard make light of a very seriously disturbed display with a cruel and callous pun.

The drawing Mirko K. possesses and the one included in this chapter seems more stylized, less expressive (Figure 4.3). A comic-book villain, Venom, is

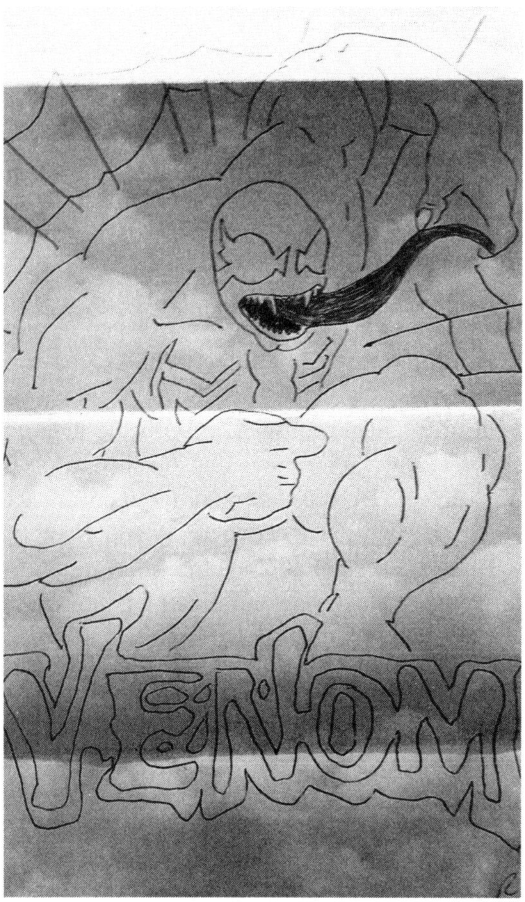

Figure 4.3 Richard Ramirez (b. 1960; died natural causes on Death Row 2013). *Venom* (Date unknown).

Pencil, ink on paper.

Collection of Mirko K. Permission and reproduction provided by from Mirko K.

drawn with a strong clean pencil outline that fills the entire page. There is very little shading or color, except for the mouth and tongue, black and red, respectively. It seems to be traced from another source; there is very little personal or emotional connection to what Ramirez drew. It seems more reminiscent of a middle-school student doodling in class than something drawn by a notorious killer. The stark contrast between Ramirez's drawings and the works created by the others in this chapter would likely lead one to question why these works were included.

While they could easily be disregarded as mere talentless doodles, there seems to be a deliberate attempt toward composition and narration, particularly with the sketch labeled "rest in agony." They are certainly elementary; yet while some would argue that they do not fully represent the extent of what it means to be *art*, his images serve a deliberate purpose. Frankly, these sketches serve as reminders that while some scratches on a piece of paper may be discounted detritus and substandard, they can still offer a valuable window into an otherwise masked persona.

The Gainesville Ripper: Danny Rolling

Danny Rolling's father was a police officer in Louisiana who abused Danny, his mother, and his younger brother. According to one source, Rolling was even beaten when he was 1 year old for not yet crawling. He performed poorly in school and had what his school counselors described as inferiority complexes, poor impulse control, and aggressive acting out behavior (DeLong, 2018). Rolling turned to drugs and alcohol at a young age and was once caught spying on a neighbor's daughter through her window as an adolescent (Hunter, 2019).

Once he was old enough, Rolling joined the Air Force, but was discharged after too much drug use. He married, but his wife left him soon after due to his abusive nature and threats to kill her. Later, in 1977, he raped a woman who resembled his former wife.

Rolling had difficulty maintaining employment, and, from the late 1970s until the early 1990s, he was in and out of the penal systems of Alabama, Florida, Mississippi, and Louisiana for various petty crimes, thefts, and armed robberies. He was able to escape from several of the institutions (DeLong, 2018; Hunter, 2019).

Rolling shot his father in 1990, with the intent to kill. While he wasn't successful, he did wound him badly. After the attempt on his father's life, he obtained stolen false identity papers and fled through Louisiana and Florida, where he began his rampage of rape and murder. He killed five students from the

University of Florida in Gainesville in their home; four women and one of their boyfriends.

Rolling was not arrested for these murders because he was careful about not leaving evidence. Over the next 2 weeks, he continued to burglarize homes and rob gas stations. Eventually he was arrested for these crimes.

Due to similarities in execution, the authorities in Florida suspected there was a relationship between the five victims in Gainesville and three unsolved murders in Shreveport, Louisiana. They collected DNA samples from any inmate who had spent time in Shreveport. Rolling fit this description. While detained for the robberies, samples of his DNA were taken; they matched those found at the home of the murdered students. Eventually, he confessed to being the Gainesville Ripper. Rolling was convicted of murder in Florida and was executed in 2006 by lethal injection (Hunter, 2019).

Once in prison, he began to draw and paint. Many of his images are contrived and common renderings associated with the hardcore biker culture and white supremacy. These include satanic figures, horned skulls, hardcore bikers, sexualized women, glib angelic forms, various carnivorous beasts, and even a portrait of Hitler. They are highly, almost painstakingly detailed, crowded and dense; some of his compositions seem well-planned while others appear haphazard, with teeming and congested arrangements.

Despite the complicated composition and detail, his drawing style seems coarse and unsophisticated, with an almost slapdash approach to proportions and shadowing. There is little subtlety in value. His sketches evoke a high school student doodling in his notebook during algebra class. His drawings suggest a *jailhouse style*, similar to many of the works by inmates who learn draw in prison —stylized, detailed imagery that could translate well to a tattoo, envelopes, or handkerchiefs to be sent home to loved ones (Gussak, 2019; Kornfeld, 1997). His work reflected the unfeeling, glib, and slick persona that terrorized a community. It feels as if he was deliberately trying to elicit a strong reaction, completing the drawings expected of a hardcore murderer.

The painting that Mirko K. has was comparatively simple and restrained (Figure 4.4). In the center of an expanse of royal blue sits a carefully rendered dagger with a jeweled hilt. Around the handle was an entwined hissing serpent carrying a rose in its mouth. Such a symbol is reminiscent of a caduceus, a symbol of healing. However, it belies this potential symbol because the open-mouthed snake seems a bit too dangerous. Below and to the right is a delicate, pale crescent moon and a four-pointed beacon, perhaps a star.

Despite the obvious differences in themes in comparison to his other works, this painting is similar in that while it demonstrates technical skills it lacks sentiment and connection. This composition could just as easily be a sketch for a

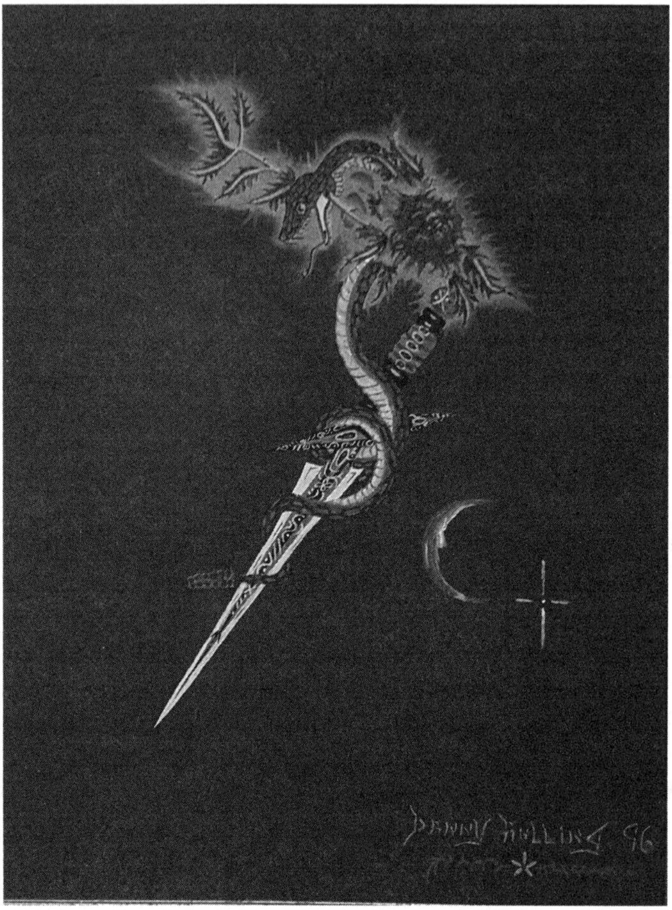

Figure 4.4 Danny Rolling (b. 1954; executed 2006). *Untitled* (Date unknown). Oil on canvas board.

Collection of Mirko K. Permission and reproduction provided by from Mirko K.

tattoo; it is rather derived and impersonal, with the exception of the bold, carefully rendered signature underscored with a flowery design. The dagger and snake float in the center of the blue field without grounding or connection; it is a solitary form with no relationship to anything around it, much like Rolling's inability to relate to others on a human level. It emits and evokes little passion; the painting feels like it was created by someone mimicking feelings but falling far short. Much like the painting, his attempts to imitate emotion and evoke connections do not work; there is a disconnect. There remains an impenetrable facade. The painting feels fake, and so does he.

The I-95 Killer: Gary Ray Bowles

Gary Ray Bowles left his home in West Virginia at a relatively young age after violently assaulting his abusive stepfather. His biological father, a coal-miner, died 6 months before his birth from black lung disease. His mother remarried several times. Her second husband abused Bowles, his mother, and older brother. He fought back when he was 13, severely injuring the man, and he left home shortly after when his mother refused to leave (Redstall, 2011). He lived on the streets for several years, earning money by prostituting himself to men. In the early 1980s, Bowles received a 6-year sentence after sexually assaulting his girlfriend. Shortly after his release, he served 2 more years for unarmed robbery.

In 1994, Bowles began a 6-month spree that resulted in the barbaric murder of six people. He met his victims in "seedy bars, usually gay bars" (Redstall, 2011, p. 136), befriended them, and allowed them to take him to their home where he would often have sex with them. Afterward, he beat and strangled them to death. He stayed in the home of two of his victims for some time. Once he killed them, he often stole their money, credit cards, even their cars.

He was suspected of the murder of the first victim, a middle-aged man who offered him a place to live, after his fingerprints and probation records were found at the crime scene. He murdered four more men over the next 6 months. As the majority of the murders happened close to Interstate 95, a major corridor along the East Coast, he was dubbed the "I-95 Killer."

He soon became identified as one of the FBI's 10 most wanted fugitives. Unfortunately, the police did not catch up to him until after he bludgeoned and suffocated his sixth victim. He was arrested in 1994. Confessing to all six murders, he received the death penalty, and, despite several setbacks and appeals, he was put to death by lethal injection in 2019 by the state of Florida.

Mirko K. owned a drawing by Bowles that depicts a hockey-masked man walking down a deserted road holding a chainsaw in one hand, dragging a scantily clad woman by the hair with the other (Figure 4.5). The murderous figure, dragging his hapless victim, appears relaxed and unaffected by his actions; if it wasn't for the mask, the woman in distress, and the instruments of torture, the figure would appear to be an unassuming man walking down the street in his flip-flops. The sole streetlight shining along a patch of the field and road barely penetrates the dark of the night. The two figures are caught in the spotlight of the street lamp, creating a sharp contrast with their surroundings. The details are striking, from the silhouetted house in the background to the sandals on the unidentified killer's feet.

Yet, despite the technical skill and its intricate, well-organized composition, the image is unoriginal. It is as if Bowles simply captured his perception of what a

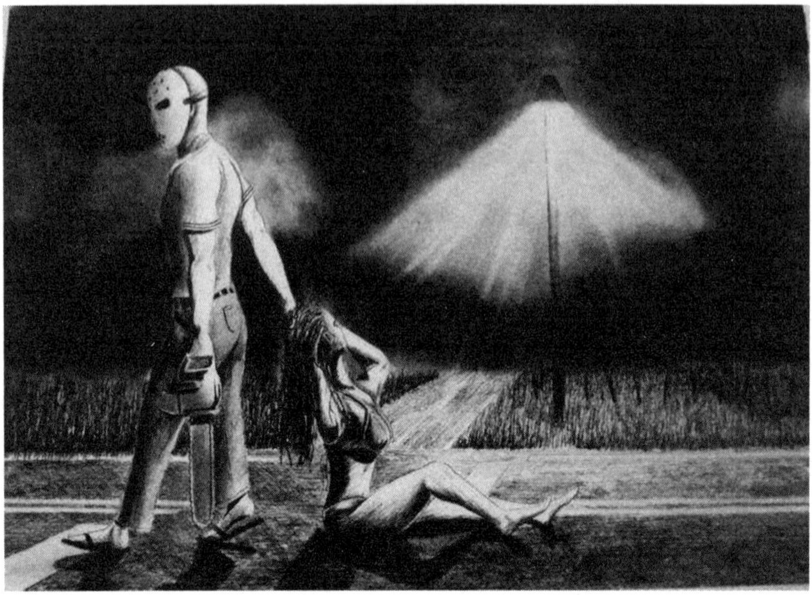

Figure 4.5 Gary Ray Bowles (b. 1962; executed 2019). *Untitled* (Date unknown). Pencil on paper.

Collection of Mirko K. Permission and reproduction provided by from Mirko K.

serial killer is supposed to do, almost like a still from a movie set. The work seems to be a staged cinematic rendition of actors merely going through the motions. Despite the mood it sets in tone and shadow, it remains mechanical and unemotional; any potential expression of fear by the woman is impossible to read; her face is turned away. The perpetrator wears an unexpressive mask, making it impossible to get a sense of what he is experiencing. Together the figures fail to relay any tension or struggle, denying the viewer any real emotional investment in the narrative. It is horrific, to be sure, but technically so; it appears more like a director blocking a scene before actually filming it. The artist is clearly attempting to display and elicit strong feelings, but does not know how to do so. The trite and prosaic composition remains ineffectual.

The Cross Country Killer: Glen Rogers

One of seven children, Glen Rogers, born in Hamilton, Ohio, was expelled from school at 16 years. Shortly after leaving school, he married his 14-year-old girlfriend after she got pregnant by another man. They had a child together as well, but divorced several years later, his wife citing brutal physical abuse. Considered a charming and good-looking man, Rogers generally stayed in Ohio, employed as a construction worker. He had some difficulty with the police; once, when authorities visited him at his home for a domestic violence call, he stuck a flaming blowtorch through the peephole of his front door.

Rogers was arrested in the suspected killing of at least five people, four of whom were women that he met in bars and whom he then raped and brutally murdered in impulsive fits of rage. After murdering one woman in California, he went on a murderous spree that spanned Louisiana, Mississippi, and Florida, thus earning him the "Cross Country Killer" moniker; alternatively, he was known as the "Casanova Killer" for his good looks and his propensity to pick up blonde and red-haired women from bars by asking them for a ride home (Linedecker, 1997; Spizer & Rogers, 2001).

After being listed as one of the FBI's 10 most wanted fugitives, Rogers was arrested following a high-speed pursuit in the stolen car of one of his victims in Waco, Kentucky. In 1997, Rogers was sentenced to death in a Florida court for the murder of one of his victims. Two years later, Rogers was sentenced to death by a California court for murdering a young woman he raped and strangled; she was discovered in her burning pickup truck.

Shortly before his arrest in 1995, Rogers told his sister that he was responsible for more than 70 deaths; however, he later recanted that admission, claiming he was joking. While awaiting his penalty of death to be carried out in Florida, Rogers also claimed that it was he, not O. J. Simpson, who was responsible for the deaths of Nicole Brown Simpson and Ron Goldman. He indicated that he was hired by Simpson to break into the home, retrieve a pair of earrings, and, if need be, murder Simpson's ex-wife (Combs & Eckberg, 2018). Needless to say, this admission created a media sensation; however, following a thorough investigation, there seems to be no evidence that he did indeed carry out these murders.

Rogers remains on Florida's Death Row awaiting the results of his appeals.

Mirko K.'s art piece by Glen Edward Rogers is reminiscent of Mexican *calaveras* paintings (Figure 4.6/see also color plate 10). Rogers's composition depicts a large, central figure seemingly in prayer wearing a magenta cloak or habit. Her hands are fully skeletal whereas the face seems to be decomposing, revealing most of her skull. The colorfully garbed form stands in what appears to be a cemetery, with rising black ghouls, white crosses, and a large rising moon behind a centrally placed dead tree. Directly behind the woman's shoulders are stylized flames, perhaps depicting a hellish landscape. Cobwebs hang between her hands and sleeves, perhaps indicating some time has passed since the figure's death. Everything in this painting is dead except for a large, purple rose she holds by the stem.

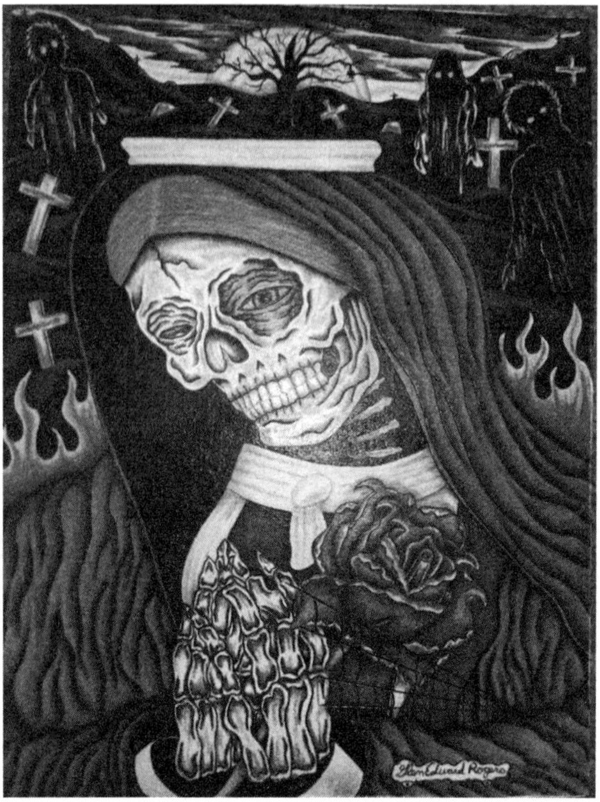

Figure 4.6 Glen Edward Rogers (b. 1962; remains on Death Row). *Untitled* (Date unknown). Colored pencil on paper.

Collection of Mirko K. Permission and reproduction provided by from Mirko K.

Consistent in style to many of his paintings and drawings, it is simultaneously horrific and oddly attractive. Through his colors and compositions, he demonstrates remarkable technical skills. He seems invested in his work. The painting contains a well-defined and clear composition, clean texture, and balance. Much more complicated in execution than others seen in this chapter, nonetheless his painting seems to attempt to portray or elicit horror. It remains superficial, with kitsch and crass representations, almost as if he was completing a school art project about Halloween. It does not seem to be a true reflection of who he is; rather, it is a copy or artificial depiction of what he believes to be evocative and profound. However, make no mistake—he establishes ownership through the ostentatiously emphasized signature at the bottom of the canvas; it is clearly important to him that it be seen.

Torture in the Sierra Nevada: Charles Ng

Charles Ng was born in British Hong Kong. His father, a wealthy executive, believed in harsh discipline and was quite abusive toward his son. As he grew, Ng became more of a loner; he was expelled from several schools for troubling behavior. Ng was sent to a boarding school in England when he was 15 years old after he was caught shoplifting; however, he was soon sent back to Hong Kong after he was caught stealing from other students (Lasseter, 2000).

When he was 18 years old, Ng moved to the United States on a student visa to study biology in a university in California. However, he dropped out after a single semester. Following a hit-and-run accident, Ng joined the Marines to avoid prosecution. He was soon arrested by the military police for stealing weapons. Escaping custody, he made his way back to California. It was there that he reunited with his long-time acquaintance, Leonard Lake, who himself had a long history of unchecked mental illness and sociopathic and sadistic behavior. They lived together in a mobile home in Mendocino County; in 1982, federal authorities raided their home and discovered a stash of illegal weapons. After jumping bail, he was eventually caught, returned to the custody of the US Marines, and, after pleading guilty to desertion and the weapons thefts, he was given a reduced sentence in the Fort Leavenworth disciplinary barracks.

After his release in 1984, Ng moved into a remote cabin in the foothills of California's Sierra Nevada mountains with Leonard Lake. Together, they undertook a spree of kidnapping, rape, and murder, including men, women, and children; the men and children were killed outright while the women were kept in a structure near the cabin called the "dudgeon," where they were slowly tortured, methodically raped, and killed.

After Ng stole a vise from a San Francisco hardware store, Lake went back to pay for the tool. By this time, the police had already been called. When Lake was questioned, the police realized that he was using a false identification that belonged to a man reported missing. They searched his truck and discovered a weapon with a silencer. While awaiting arraignment, Lake swallowed a cyanide pill and killed himself.

While the car Lake was driving was stolen, the license plate was registered to him at the cabin's address. When the police arrived at the cabin, they found a truck and car registered to two other missing men. Upon further exploration, they soon found the dudgeon and a burial site where the remains of 11 men, women, and children were buried. They also discovered a cache of weapons and a couple of videotapes of their incredibly gruesome and sadistic acts. It was later believed that the duo was possibly responsible for the torture, rape, and death of up to 25 people.

Ng escaped to Calgary, Alberta, and hid in a lean-to in a local park; however, he was arrested a month later after shooting at a security guard when he was stopped while trying to shoplift yet again. He served several years in a Canadian prison. After he was extradited to California in 1991 for the murders, he was tried and found guilty for killing 11 people. He is currently on Death Row in San Quentin, awaiting his death sentence (Lasseter, 2000).

His nondescript, bland countenance and calm manner hide a cold-hearted and brutal man, one whose sole aim is to intimidate and dominate others. The drawings and paintings made in prison seem to capture this. While some of them are glibly rendered, depicting fantastical compositions such as the one of a mermaid petting a shark, others are deliberately more brutal and gory. For example, in one colorful drawing, two mermaids have obviously been captured by a skeletal pirate. They are both tied up by their tails, one hanging helplessly while the other is fighting back, its hands around the skeleton's neck. This technically adept piece is highly stylized and garishly colored, yet there is little to no emotion reflected in these pieces—they appear bland and unexpressive.

The colorfully garish art piece that Mirko K. owns seems to uncover Ng's true identity more than any façade he puts forward. The center of the composition holds a large, screaming, mask-like face created with bright, almost gaudy colors. Its skull is split open, lying bare the figure's brains. Difficult to see, there is a small figure standing atop his head holding a chainsaw, obviously the one responsible for the bloodshed. The head floats amid a background of bright flames surrounded by shadow (Figure 4.7).

Although well drawn, it reveals a seemingly deliberate attempt to intimidate and frighten the viewer through this grotesque and monstrous mask. While the main character is obviously a victim, the viewer feels no empathy, given its rendition. Yet, I would argue, this portrait is an accurate reflection of Ng's true self. However, despite its revelation as a potential mirror for Ng's feelings and true personality, the image repels, rather than connects with, the viewer.

The variations in all of his drawings demonstrate no consistency; no singular style arises—it's as if he's experimenting with his art and, by extension, experimenting with his identity, seemingly unable to commit to one in particular. Like the paper he draws on, he is a blank page. Yet Figure 4.7 comes closest to catching a glimpse of the monster within.

There are some drawings so horrendous, so pornographically assaultive, that I have chosen not to include them in this chapter. For example, the work of Gerard Shaefer is a violent affront, a blatant continuation and perpetuation of his sadistic acts.

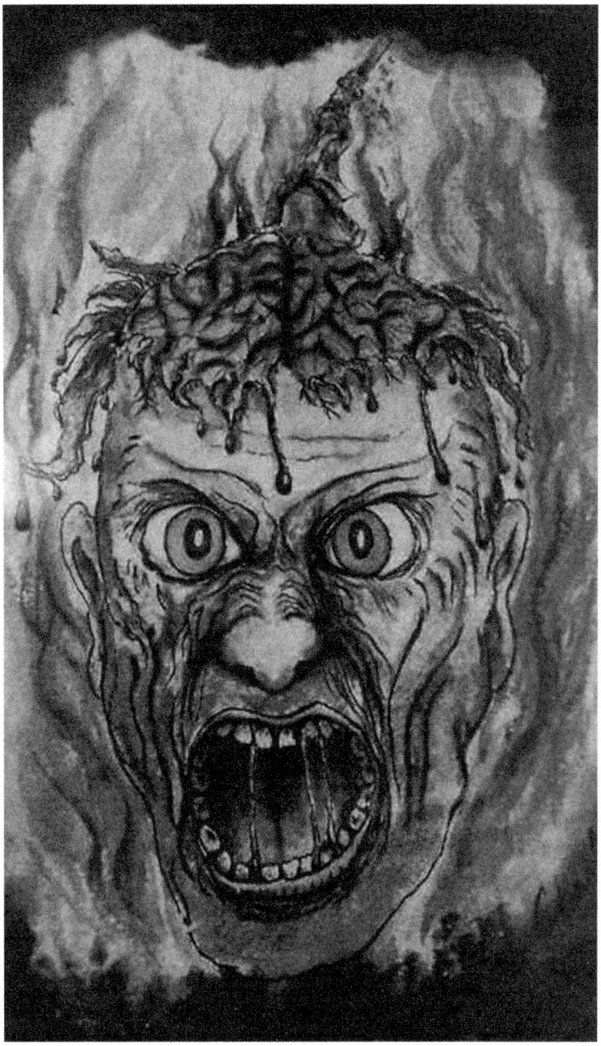

Figure 4.7 Charles Ng (b. 1960; remains on Death Row). *Untitled* (Date unknown). Colored pencil on paper.
Collection of Mirko K. Permission and reproduction provided by from Mirko K.

Killer Fiction: Gerard John Shaefer

Gerard Shaefer, a Deputy Sheriff in Martin County, Florida, was convicted and imprisoned for murdering two women (Kendrick, 2020). Schaefer was born in 1946, the first of three children, in Wisconsin; his family later moved to Atlanta, Georgia. As a child he became obsessed with women's undergarments; he later avoided the military draft by wearing them. He admitted to torturing and killing small animals as a child. He also confessed to spying on a neighbor through her window as a child, a woman it is believed he later killed. He married and became a teacher, but was soon let go by the principal for "inappropriate behavior"; it was unclear what this meant. Shaefer attempted to become a priest, but was rejected. Instead, when he was 25 years old, he became a police officer (Kendrick, 2020).

One year later, Shaefer kidnapped two hitchhikers, tied them to a tree, and threatened to kill them. They were able to escape when he was called away on the radio, and they reported him when they arrived at the station. While Shaefer claimed that he did so to scare the girls from hitchhiking again, his immediate supervisor did not believe him. He was relieved of his badge and charged with the crime. Two months after posting bail, he murdered two teenage girls and buried them in the woods. Shortly thereafter, as the result of a plea bargain for the original charge of kidnapping the two hitchhikers, Shaefer was sentenced to serve a 1-year sentence in prison for aggravated assault (Kendrick, 2020).

Six months after he murdered the two girls, their remains were discovered in the woods where they had been tied to a tree. Given the similarity of their circumstances to the two girls who had escaped, the police were able to obtain a search warrant for the home where Shaefer had lived with his wife and mother. They discovered a great deal of incriminating evidence. Along with some weapons, the police found lurid stories he had written detailing rape, torture, and murder fantasies; items that belonged to the victims; a case containing the teeth of eight separate women and girls who had been reported missing; and jewelry of the neighbor girl whom he had been spying on as a teenager; this girl's bullet-ridden skull had been found at a construction site many years before. While it is likely Shaefer had murdered upward of 30 different women, he was subsequently convicted of and sentenced to two life sentences for the two teenage girls.

Throughout his time in prison, he continued to proclaim his innocence, even after his appeals were denied. However, his jailhouse writings and drawings, later collected for publications called *Killer Fiction*, seemed to reveal a propensity of violence toward women and boast of his killings. In 1995, Shaefer was stabbed to death by another inmate.

Shaefer's mug shot reveals a clean-cut, smiling, and relaxed man; his overall manner was generally cool and composed. Those who interviewed him described him as charming, and the arresting sheriff described his initial impression of Shaefer as "apple-cheeked and wholesome" (see an excerpt from the online video, "Gerald Shaefer: Serial Killer Documentary, part I," https://www.youtube.com/watch?v=FBXFYVA7mjE). Yet his artwork and writings contradicted this innocent image.

Some of his drawings were hastily sketched, some rendered with assurance and confidence. Many of his images are in black and white; when Shaefer did apply color, it was generally muted, with subtle tones. The majority of his sketches portray naked, curvaceous women being tortured, dismembered, and mutilated; some of the women were hanging from a noose or crucifix and others were sexually debased. Sometimes Shaefer drew the entire figure, at other times he focused just on mutilated torsos, and still others displayed grotesque decapitations. All were intensely horrific objectifications of women that sensationalized carnal violence and physical humiliation.

Pictorially Replicating Dangerously Narcissistic Self-Glorification

This chapter sits in the middle of a volume that has argued that one benefit of art making is that it can turn aside violent impulses and can provide a safe container for aggression. I do not make that claim here. I recognize that this is an unlikely and quite dangerous proclamation for this chapter; the notion that engaging in art making could have prevented such atrocities is grandiose at best, irresponsible at worst. What their art does provide, however, is perhaps a clearer vision of who these people were.

In just seven profiles, the works provided by Mirko K. reveal that while these perpetrators and their artistic products are seemingly unique, they are much more alike than different. The first part of this chapter offered various perspectives on the identifying features of the multiple murderer, including pathological narcissism. The artwork provided in this chapter seems to corroborate this.

Explained in the Introduction and Chapter 1, narcissistic grandiosity emerges from a cycle of rejection, reaction, and further rejection, ultimately resulting in potentially unchecked rage and resultant violence. Rejection and abuse by those charged with keeping one safe instigates the development of an idealized and self-aggrandized "false" self; despite this veneer of superiority, the person remains quite vulnerable. Turned off by this "false self," others further reject the person, causing additional betrayal and abandonment, leading to even deeper, unresolved anger. This may be expressed through hostility and violence. (Horney, 1945/1992; Winnicott, 1951, 1965, 1971). As well, given the developed narcissistic self-image, violence and aggression could emerge from a neurotic need for power, social recognition, personal admiration, and achievement—all attributes that a pathologically grandiose person would crave. What emerges is the self-inflating tendency to rely on the objectification of others to reinforce their own superiority. In other words, others are only useful insofar as they serve, and the function of people is merely to feed the hungry needs of the narcissist.

Undoubtedly and emphatically, the narcissistic characteristics, expressions, and resultant consequences of these killers stand far apart from those of the artists reviewed in Chapter 1. Artists like Caravaggio, Cellini, and Dali were indeed, in some ways, equally as narcissistic and violently grandiose; they, too, maintained a neurotic need for power, social recognition, and personal admiration. Yet they sought those out—and received them—through different means. They focused their narcissistic self-aggrandizement into productive expressions that were able to resonate with people and transcend their destructive tendencies. They also had the talent to succeed, for which they were celebrated—*despite* their aggressive and violent personas. Their art provided a container and a form of expression that earned for them the recognition they sought and the admiration they craved. In turn, as I argued, their sense of superiority, aggressive tenacity, and self-glorification allowed some of them to change the course of the aesthetic trajectory of their times. They succeeded despite and *because* of their narcissistic drives.

Still, as their sense of supremacy and entitlement allowed them to feel mastery over others, their lack of respect and objectification of others sometimes resulted in acts of violence. Yet, while the artists from Chapter 1 maintained some level of psychopathy, it was not nearly as extensive as it was for the multiple murderers that comprise this chapter.

Associated with psychopathy is the utter disregard for the welfare of others and an ability to emotionally "shut down" so as not to impede, deter, or interfere with one's own self-preservation. Such ability to emotionally disconnect may provide an impetus for this utter disregard of others; taken to an extreme, this removes the additional safeguard that can help prevent people from indiscriminate killing. In other words, it's easier to kill someone if the killer doesn't see his victims as anything more than an object.

These cases are almost formulaic; each person in this chapter suffered rejection, abandonment, and abuse from his caregivers. To compensate for—or in reaction to—such abhorrent experiences, these victims became homicidal offenders, developing a false self that continued to be further rejected. This ultimately resulted in horrible acts for power, dominance, and profane recognition. Each of these killers was described as being inhumanly unemotional, holding an objective detachment for their victims. Their emotional disconnection and narcissistic hunger was mirrored in their imagery.

Rather than help arrest their narcissistic cycles, creating their works fed their needs and desires. Many of the art pieces demonstrated technical skills but failed to engage emotionally. They appeared mechanical in execution, with very little humanity in the product. "Serial killer art makes visible the peculiarities of someone thought to be barely human at all. It is usually strangely lacking in the natural proclivities of human beings" (Junge, 2019, p. 57). Inasmuch as the art still remains an extension of the person, their products reflected their own lack of connectedness, inhumanity, and banality.

When people were included, they either appeared emotionally blank, monstrously frightening, or horrendously tortured. Instead of drawing the viewers in, they deliberately repelled them. It seemed that the artists were unable or unwilling to relate to the viewer, mirroring their own inabilities to develop healthy relationships. By copying or tracing the super villain Venom from a source that was clearly not his own, Ramirez reflected his own arrested developmental level and further reinforced his alienation from those around him—not even in the act of this drawing was there an attempt made to reflect himself.

Ramirez's drawing labeled "rest in agony," while less composed and which may again be disregarded as a more amateurish, careless doodle than many of the other images presented in this chapter, seems to capture a deliberate composition, a staged scene meant to project and reinforce his lack of empathy for his victims. Despite its attempt to portray a real person, the figure comes across as incomplete, almost cartoonish. In addition, while the drawing seems to be a page out of his own experiences, he is not in it—there is no personal relatedness within the image. While Ramirez's tracing of the super villain Venom seems far removed from "rest in agony," copying or tracing another's work reinforced his lack of personal investment and alienation. Both drawings are cold and impersonal in their own way, unlike Ng's mask-like drawing, which seems to be the closest we get to a genuine self-portrait. However, even in this image, given its horrific and disgusting rendition, Ng is unable to evoke empathy or sympathy for himself—rather, it guarantees the fear and disdain that he has rightly earned *from* others. The image pushes people away, reinforcing his rejection *by* others.

Some of the images do not have to be nearly as profane as Ng's, Shaefer's, or Rogers's to accomplish this. Sell's murder of crows demonstrates skill and ability while still revealing a deliberate distancing and lack of humanity. Rolling's dagger and serpent, while attractively astute, demonstrates an emotional disconnect. Even Malvo's image, *The Prison Made by Mind,* is intended to communicate deep-seated feelings of loss and abandonment but seems fairly cold, calculated, and juvenile; overly technical, it remains an unemotional rendering.

What is underscored in their art is the offenders' inability to connect with others, to create real and healthy relationships. Through their blankness, loss of emotional design, and deliberate attempts at depicting disconnected horrors, they repulse and deter their viewers. This can't help but result in an inability to form healthy connections with others. Unlike real artists who strive to create a bridge, a relationship with their audience (Becker, 1982), these pieces serve to further reinforce the walls that were built around them.

Given that these confined murderers no longer had an opportunity to direct and release their pent-up aggressive drives, they turned to art making as a means of release. However, unlike some who learn to sublimate their aggressive energy into productive and transformative imagery, many of the expressions discussed in this chapter are merely cathartic; an attempt to relive their dominating and murderous actions. These people were unable to develop ego-driven transformation, and their art served merely as an extension of their perverse, primitive drives. It is akin to an unsatisfying, perseverative, masturbatory release.

Finally, many of these works strived to emphasize their creators' monstrous power over the viewer through fear, intimidation, and shock. In essence, even after their imprisonment, they are reinforcing their barbarous identities. While their acts of self-validation, superiority, and power were halted through arrest and confinement, some continued to relive these self-inflating inclinations by replicating their audacious crimes—literally or metaphorically—through violently attacking the viewer with their imagery. In some ways, with no other tools at their disposal to continue their campaign of fear, dominance, and destruction, they wielded their art as a weapon.

5

Extremes on the Same Continuum

Comparing the Art of Gacy and Manson

In the previous chapter, I speculated on how the art of multiple murderers may have been used to try to fortify a narcissistically grandiose identity and continue potential predatory dominance over their victims. To do so, I relied on the work—ranging from the mundane to the profane—of seven multiple murderers. However, Charles Manson and John Wayne Gacy were not included.

Manson and Gacy are arguably two of the most infamous multiple murderers of the twentieth century in the United States. Both were known to a certain extent for their attempts at creative outputs. One was a West Coast, laid back, cult figure; the other a Midwestern, middle-aged, conservative businessman. One was a societal outcast who reveled in his identity as a rebel; the other an established member of his community. Both would arguably have hated being associated with the other.

Even their art was different. Manson's drawings and paintings demonstrate a flair for spontaneity, with a frenetic, almost uncontrollable energy. Gacy's paintings are rigid, constrained, unoriginal, and sophomoric. Well before Manson committed and was arrested for the murders for which he would become infamous, he fancied himself an artist—a musician, a poet, and a painter. Gacy did not begin to paint and draw until after he found himself on Death Row, ostensibly to sell to those attracted to murderabilia to fund his appeal.

They clearly represent extremely divergent points on a very wide continuum. Yet, I would argue, despite these disparities, their art emerged from the same self-aggrandizement and grandiosity as those in the previous chapters, and no amount of creating would curb their monstrous impulses; on the contrary, in some ways, it reinforced them.

Charles Manson

In 1991, I assumed my first position as an art therapist, working in a prison in Northern California. It had also once been the home of Charles Manson. Transferred to another prison before I began work there, much of his artwork remained behind. Stored in the office of one of the artist facilitators of the institution, his drawings were kept locked in a separate file cabinet. They had once been displayed along with many other pieces in the art rooms, but many of his drawings disappeared, pilfered by staff who wanted to own a piece of murderabilia. However, upon request, I was able to leaf through several of his drawings. This was the first time I had been directly exposed to the creative endeavors of a notorious murderer.

Manson, seen as "a definitional oddity" (Fox & Levin, 2012, p. 19), defied categorization. He was not necessarily a mass murderer because the killings for which he was deemed responsible did not occur at the same time, in the same location. Yet he could not be considered a serial killer because while the number of victims exceeded three, the murderous acts occurred over 2 days. While Manson was held responsible for the murders, he in fact did not actually commit them himself; instead, he persuaded his easily impressionable followers to commit the atrocities. Despite all of this, he has been labeled with both designations since the crimes were committed in 1969. Still, it could be argued, it does not matter what he is labeled. Regardless if the murders could be classified or defied categorization, his acts were atrocious, and, ultimately, he would be held accountable for all of them.

By all considerations, Manson had a challenging childhood. He was the son of an unknown father and a 16-year-old prostitute who was repeatedly jailed. As a result, he was taken in by a strict aunt and abusive uncle at a young age; from the time he was 12, Manson was held in a variety of state institutions (Guinn, 2013). He was sent to the Gibault School for Boys, in Terre Haute, Indiana; Indiana Boys' School in Plainfield; and Father Flanagan's Boys Town in Omaha, Nebraska, all for petty theft and robbery. He was later sent to many other detention facilities for a variety of crimes, institutions where he was sexually and physically abused (Manson & Emmons, 1986). By the time he emerged from Treasure Island in San Pedro, California, after a lengthy stint for car theft and pimping, he had spent, all told, 19 years behind bars. He was 32 years old (Frasier, 1996).

Despite his lack of education and disheveled appearance, Manson was considered eloquent and mesmerizing by potential followers. He took advantage of these disillusioned youth by spewing anti-establishment rhetoric and living a carefree lifestyle. He offered them the opportunity to shun restrictions and rules enforced by what he deemed an unrelenting and unfair society. As a result, Manson soon developed cult leader status, becoming the titular head of what was soon known as the "Manson Family" (Bugliosi, 1974).

Manson lived with his followers on Spahn Ranch in Simi Valley, an old film set owned by 81-year-old George Spahn, whom he and his female followers endeared themselves to in order to squat rent free. Well off the beaten path, the Family, which numbered more than 30, sustained their existence by selling drugs and stealing cars. They were encouraged by Manson to take recreational drugs and engage in large group orgies to dispel any inhibitions and reservations they carried with them from their previous existence (Guinn, 2013).

Manson thought highly of his own position and soon began referring to himself as "God" and "Jesus Christ." Relying on such widely diverse sources as the New Testament's book of Revelations and the Beatles *White Album*, he preached evidence of the coming Apocalypse (Bugliosi, 1974). Included among these was one consistent harangue that involved "a race war between the black and whites" (Frasier, 1996, p. 315). According to Manson, the Black race would win, but they would be unable to maintain their position as rulers; Manson and his followers would then emerge from their hiding place in Death Valley where they took shelter during the war, and they would subsequently take over the world (Bugliosi, 1974; Frasier, 1996; Guinn, 2013).

Impatient with waiting for this to naturally develop, Manson convinced his followers that they could hasten the process by "killing prominent members of the white Establishment, then plant evidence implicating black revolutionaries" (Frasier, 1996, p. 315). Manson sent four of his trusted devotees—Charles "Tex" Watson, Susan Atkins, Patricia Krenwinkel, and Linda Kasabian—on August 8, 1969, to a home on Cielo Drive in West Los Angeles to implement his reprehensible plan. According to several sources, this was not an arbitrary decision: the intended victim was record producer Terry Melcher, who had refused Manson a recording contract the year before (Guinn, 2013).

Unknown to Manson, Melcher was out of town and had subleased his home to movie director Roman Polanski and his pregnant wife, Sharon Tate. Polanski left his wife home alone because he had to travel to Europe to work on a film; Tate was unable to accompany him due to her advanced pregnancy. By August 8, she was eight and a half months pregnant. Several friends were visiting her that evening: aspiring screenwriter and Polanski's friend Wojiciech Frykowski; his lover and heiress to the Folger's coffee fortune, Abigail Folger; and Jay Sebring, a well-respected, high-end hair stylist and Tate's former lover. In addition, unknown to the party inside, Steven Parent was visiting the home's caretaker in his small cottage on the grounds (Bugliosi, 1974).

Watson climbed a telephone pole and cut the phone lines to the house. He, Atkins, Krenwinkel, and Kasabian climbed over the fence and walked up the driveway where they came across Parent walking toward his car. To make sure there were no witnesses, Watson stabbed him to death. After instructing Kasabian to stay at Parent's car to provide look-out, he cut open a screen window, climbed in, and let the other two in by the front door. They corralled all of the occupants in the living room, where they tied them up. Throughout the evening and into the early hours of the next morning, the four tortured and butchered Tate, her unborn child, and her three friends. One of the murderers used blood from the victims to scrawl the word "Pig" on the door.

Manson was dissatisfied with how they conducted themselves during the murders. He believed they handled the situation poorly and were sloppy in its execution. From Manson's perspective, the victims should not have realized their fate until it was too late. He was also cognizant that, in the chaos and confusion, they could have been discovered or someone could have escaped. As a result, Manson decided that they would do it again, but this time he would accompany them to show them how it should be done.

The following evening, August 10, Manson and fellow Family member Leslie Sue Van Houton accompanied Tex Watson and Patricia Krenwinkel on a nighttime raid of the Los Feliz home of Leno and Rosemary LaBianca. Unlike those killed the day before, the LaBiancas were relatively unknown. Parents of four children, two each from previous marriages, they were typical, upper middle-class Americans. Both came from modest, immigrant families, and, after years of working hard, Leno became a supermarket executive, Rosemary the co-owner of a high-end dress shop. Three of their children were already grown and living on their own; Frank was 16 years old and still lived at home with his parents. Frank had asked to stay at a friend's house that night, a fortuitous happenstance.

It was unclear why Manson targeted the LaBiancas; although they had attended a party at a nearby home some time prior to the event, it seemed a random decision. Even Manson wasn't entirely sure they would be the next victims; they had been considering other potential targets, including a priest at a nearby church (Guinn, 2013). However, it seemed that ultimately Manson returned to a neighborhood with which he was familiar (Krajicek, 2019).

When they pulled up to the house, Watson and Manson went inside, leaving the girls in the car. They woke the couple at gunpoint, convinced them that they were only going to rob them, tied them up, and placed them in two separate rooms. After they were trussed tightly to Manson's satisfaction, he left, sent the women inside, and ordered the three of them to kill the couple. After butchering them in the most horrendous fashion, the Family members used the victims' blood to write "Death to Pigs," "Rise," and "Helter [*sic*] Skelter" on the walls. They believed that this, along with leaving one of the victims' wallets in a predominantly Black neighborhood, would convince investigators that these deaths heralded a "Black uprising."

Although subsequently arrested for different charges 3 months later, Manson and his followers were ultimately identified as those responsible for these murderous acts. After a 9-month trial, Manson, along with Watson, Atkins, Krenwinkel, and Van Houton, were sentenced to death (Bugliosi, 1974; Guinn, 2013). While awaiting his time on Death Row, in 1972, California invalidated capital punishment; Manson's sentence was commuted to "indeterminate life." He remained in the California correctional system until his death of natural causes in 2017.

Manson, among many of his grandiose self-proclamations, fancied himself a gifted artist, writer, and poet; in particular, he considered himself a musician. Unlike many of the multiple murderers who did not begin creating art until they had been imprisoned, Manson began his artistic explorations long before he went to prison for the murders (Junge, 2019). Early on, he befriended Dennis Wilson of the Beach Boys, hoping that Wilson would help get his music recorded. In fact, in 1968, the Beach Boys recorded "Never Learn Not to Love," a reworked version of a song Manson entitled "Cease to Exist." Manson became quite angry that they changed his song and even threatened to kill Wilson.

Eventually, Manson recorded an album of 14 original songs prior to his final arrest. It was these recordings that Melcher ignored, an act that it was believed served as a catalyst for the deadly events. The album was released a year after the murders by Awareness Records, as *Lie: The Love and Terror Cult* (Aes-Nihil et al., 2011; Guinn, 2013).

While the album was popular among those who collected murderabilia, the general contention was that it was mixed at best. Some supported it. Neil Young recognized him as a poet:

> He had this kind of music that nobody else was doing. He would sit down with a guitar and start playing and making up stuff, different every time, it just kept coming out, comin' out, comin' out. . . . Musically, I thought he was very unique. I thought he really had something crazy, something great. He was like a living poet. (Aes-Nihil et al., 2011, p. 70)

Others contended that he wasn't necessarily a strong musician; one critic indicated that his first album "was not very good, filled with drug-addled, period-piece rants about loss of ego, the comfort of home . . . and eating food from trash cans" (Roberts, 2017, para. 28).

Even still, bands like Guns 'N' Roses and the Lemonheads covered his music. Whether or not Manson was a talented musician, he was tenacious and continued to record his music long after he was imprisoned. This included *Commemoration*, recorded in the chapel of Vacaville, California, Correctional Medical Facility in the mid-1980s. It was later released by White Devil Records in 1994.

Manson continued to have many followers, and quite often they were attracted to him through his music (Aes-Nihil et al., 2011). This included Ken Dickerson.

I read about Dickerson in a newspaper article about his long-running communications with Manson. I reached out to him, and he agreed to speak with me for this chapter.

Thirty three-year-old Dickerson was an artist and musician from the Midwest. He had written to Charles Manson when he was only 19 years old. "What attracted me to talking with the guy was the mystique . . . there were so many different stories out there about what kind of guy he was and I've read so many of the books and I've seen so many of the movies, and [I thought] 'this guy can't really be this nuts.'" In fact, he found Manson to be quite charismatic.

Manson maintained a correspondence with Dickerson, who he nicknamed Soul Soldier (Wiechert, 2018) for many years through letters and phone calls that ended shortly before Manson died. Much of what they discussed revolved around

> a lot of art, a lot of music because . . . I guess he put me under his wing in a way to try to teach me how to play the guitar better. . . . So he would send me music notes and song lyrics and we would go back and forth like that. I would send him song lyrics and my best interpretation of music notation. And then we would talk about art and about how I make my sculptures and masks and stuff and he would tell me that he did the same thing; but he did it obviously in a different way.

Like many of those inside compelled to create, Manson used what was available, crafting many tiny soft sculptures of dolls, spiders, and scorpions out of the thread of his socks (Aes-Nihil et al., 2011). As Dickerson recalled,

> He would pull away the strings on his socks and kind of tie them in certain knots and use [them] to braid and make the legs and head [for insects and dolls] and things like that. . . . He would sculpt things out of . . . rolling papers, that's the best to use. He would use rolling papers to make beads. He made an ankh. . . . He's made faces before . . . he takes them and he wets them down and he takes a spoon and he taps and taps and taps them. . . . And . . . it turns pretty much back into wood. It's amazing I've got a [a lot] of beads. It's just very time consuming.

When paint wasn't available, Manson would make his own pigments. "He would use ketchup and mustard . . . he would water it down or do whatever he did with it to create paints for his beads." Many of Manson's letters, poems, and song lyrics were covered with doodles of spiders and scorpions. The small collection of drawings remaining in the prison where I worked was resonant of many of the images he sketched: cartoon-like forms with word balloons, webs, and heavy-handed symbols.

Along with sheets of his music and lyrics, Manson sent several of his drawings and paintings to Dickerson. Although Dickerson recognized the potential cathartic effect of making art he indicated that Manson "told me, when you do these projects you're putting your soul into it. So every project you do is a part of you."

Manson was essentially self-taught, with little formal art training. His sketches and drawings were inconsistent, with no clear individual style or focus. Some of his drawings seemed to embody the persona he was deliberately trying to portray: unpredictable, erratic, and uncontrolled. Several were perseverative, composed of erratically sketched lines. Some of the images were recognizable, whereas others were abstract; some combine the two, littering a page with abstract and haphazard lines, shapes, and colors, sprinkling in clearly rendered scorpions or spiders. Some were somewhat minimalist, as seen in two of his self-portraits, sketched and painted with only a few lines and shapes. Others were quite complex in composition, filling the page with disconnected and fragmented forms, almost disregarding the constraints of a single composition and directional orientation. However, it seems that, even still, these forms were contrived to reinforce the image he enjoyed presenting to the world: an enigmatic, vaguely incoherent, misunderstood genius.

Two of his images display an interesting range of tone, focus, and control. One of his most recognized drawings was a floating head of the Devil, sketched during his murder trial (Figure 5.1). Despite its friendly countenance, the scribbled, uncontained lines seemed to capture a level of nervous, anxious energy. Figure 5.2 is much brighter, with colorful abstract imagery and layers of shapes and lines hiding any recognizable form it may have contained. It seems there was little planning in this erratic composition.

There was one particular painting that I had never seen before, a work that reinforced my perspective that many of Manson's other pieces were contrivances. Given to Dickerson, this composition is painted on a single sheet of paper that was creased from being folded and mailed. It reveals a pair of worn work boots against a red brick background, with a glimpse of what appears to be a landscape in the upper left corner. It carries his characteristic signature in the bottom right corner. It is distinctive yet minimal in its design, reminiscent of Van Gogh's *Shoes*. The work is fascinating for its paradoxically unique and modest banality and gentle, aesthetic, painterly approach (Figure 5.3/see also color plate 11). In style, theme, and palette, the work is completely different from many of Manson's other works.

Manson's narcissistic self-aggrandizement led him to crave discovery and greatness; if he didn't achieve recognition through his artistic endeavors, then he would do so by leading a violent movement. From Manson's perspective, he deserved prominence and to be taken seriously—whether through his music, art, or violence—he strove to be known: it did not matter how.

The difference between his creations and those of the serial killers' in the previous chapter are that these demonstrate an energy and aesthetic style that was much more pure, nascent, and expressive. Manson did not necessarily pander to his audience; he simply attempted to control the message while encouraging and

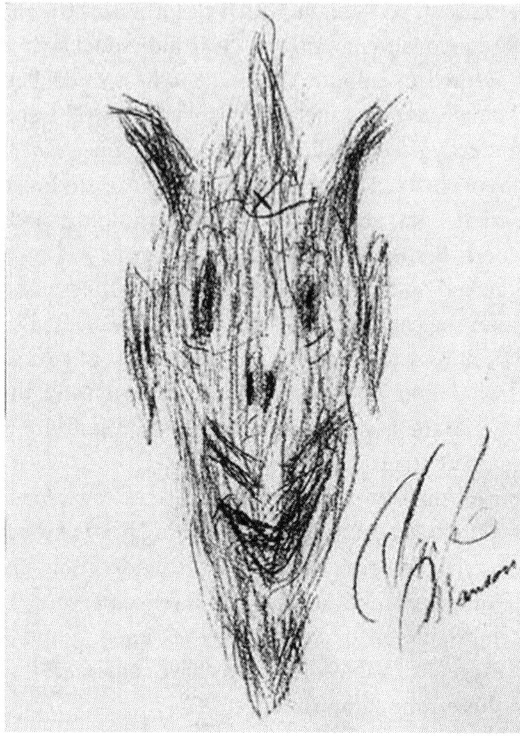

Figure 5.1 Charles Manson (b. 1934; died 2017 of natural causes in prison). *Sketch of Devil's Head* (Date unknown). Pencil on paper.
Reproduction provided by Museum Syndicate.

manipulating others to join him. His narcissism never gave him room to doubt that he wouldn't be recognized for his value. Manson invited the audience to see in him what they needed or wanted to see. Dickerson indicated that he was a "chameleon," never establishing his own identity. Yet his painting of the boots seemed to reveal that he was capable of showing truthfully who he really was; it seems so much more genuine, vulnerable, and reflective.

In his 1970 trial testimony, Manson insisted "You projected fear. You made me a monster and I have to live with that the rest of my life" (Aes-Nihil et al., 2011, p. 61). For a person who was insignificant until the development of the Manson Family, I dare say this was an identity he embraced rather than scorned, reinforcing it for the remainder of his life. In a way, the painting of the shoes perhaps reveals the person he could have potentially been before he put on his mask, the one he wore to portray to the world the monster he thought they wanted to see. On the last page of the book, *The Manson File*, there is a single line crudely

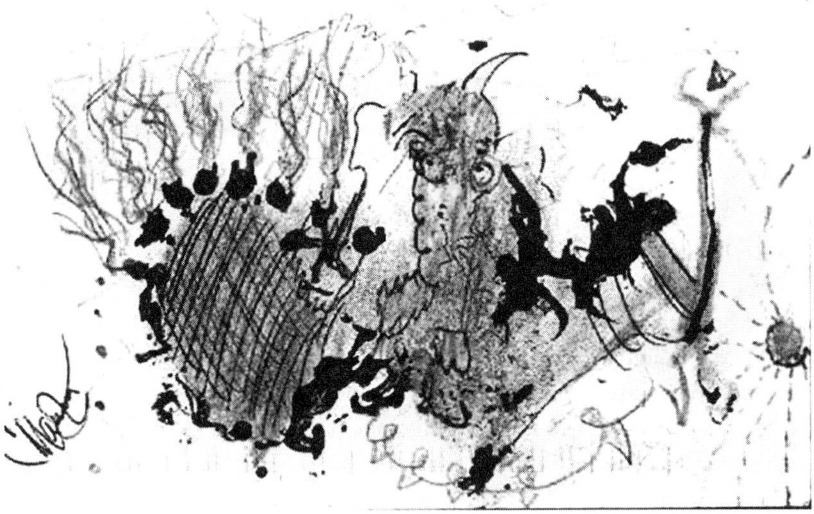

Figure 5.2 Charles Manson (b. 1934; died 2017 of natural causes in prison). *Untitled* (Date unknown). Mixed media on paper.
Reproduction provided by Museum Syndicate.

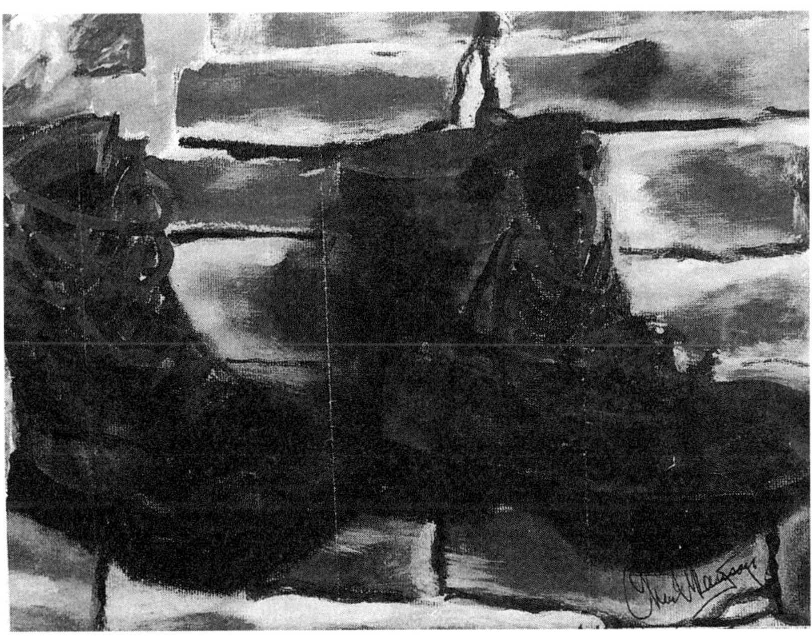

Figure 5.3 Charles Manson (b. 1934; died 2017 of natural causes in prison). *Shoes* (Date unknown). Oil on canvas board.
Collection of Ken Dickerson. Permission and reproduction provided by Ken Dickerson.

written on a blank piece of paper that reflects his own self-aggrandizing and destructive narcissism: "Each night as you sleep, I destroy the world."

John Wayne Gacy

In 2011, I was contacted by Dr. Laura Henkel, then the chief curator of the Sin City Art Gallery in Las Vegas, Nevada. She informed me that her gallery had recently come into the possession of a collection of rather unusual art pieces—the jailhouse paintings of John Wayne Gacy.

She had acquired the rights to show and sell several works of his and wanted to provide an opportunity to explore the sociological and psychological impact of these works through lectures and discussions. The art was provided by a former friend of Gacy and executor to his portfolio, Jim Taranto. The intention was that the art would be sold and the money be donated to victims advocacy groups for restitution.

The proposed show met with some considerable controversy due to the notorious and abhorrent reputation of the featured artist. Regardless, Dr. Henkel was determined to locate people known in their respective fields who were willing to present their perspectives. As a result, I had the honor of providing two lectures with very respected and honorable professionals: noted criminologist, Jack Levin who specializes in serial killers, and the Honorable Sam Amirante, the federal judge who once served as Gacy's defense attorney. Laura Henkel sent me files of Gacy's paintings so I could prepare.

Although I agreed to do it, I have to admit I was not that familiar with Gacy's work—I certainly knew who he was and that he painted, but I was not fully aware of the extent of his portfolio. I soon immersed myself in his life and work.

Gacy became a pinnacle of his community through his business acumen and philanthropic ways. "Gacy, a successful building contractor in Chicago, was politically connected, active in the community and generally well-liked by those that knew him" (Frasier, 1996, p. 161). He made it a point to hire men and boys as unskilled workers for his business to provide them an opportunity to gain experience that would help them later on in life. He would also dress as "Pogo the Clown" to entertain children in the hospital. All this seems to run counter to the fact that he was one of the cruelest multiple murderers in the twentieth century.

Born in Chicago in 1942, John Wayne Gacy was one of three children; he had an abusive father and a mother unable to protect him from his father's belittling and sadistic ways. Gacy was "a sickly overweight child" (Frasier, 1996, p. 161), who suffered from psychomotor epilepsy at a young age. He was considered a sluggish, tragic figure, seen by some as awkward and "doughy." He was often rejected by the girls he approached and would often ingratiate himself awkwardly to others, usually to their discomfort. Still, as a student, Gacy became actively engaged in the community, logging many volunteer hours. He even formed a civil defense squad in which he was the self-appointed captain (Berry-Dee, 2007) and volunteered to work for the political campaign of a candidate for the local Alderman position.

Gacy eventually dropped out of high school in 1961, after which he left for Las Vegas where he worked for a funeral home, first as a member of the ambulance crew and then later in the mortuary cleaning bodies. He eventually returned to Chicago, where he completed a business course after which he obtained a variety of jobs to which he applied himself with overachieving fervor.

Gacy married in 1964 and had two children. He continued to distinguish himself, being recognized in 1967 as the outstanding member of the local Jaycees (Junior Chamber of Commerce), managed several Kentucky Fried Chicken franchises given to him by his father-in-law, and served as a local chaplain.

This all changed in 1968, when, at age 26, he was charged, pleaded guilty, and was sentenced to 10 years for sodomizing the 15-year-old son of a colleague. During the investigation, many young men came forward to claim that Gacy had manipulated and threatened them into engaging in aberrant acts. It also came to light during the trial that Gacy had chained down another boy, a 16-year-old employee, strangled him into unconsciousness and, when he awoke, tried to force him to perform fellatio at knife point. His wife divorced him the day he was sentenced.

Prior to his sentencing, Gacy was evaluated by a psychiatrist. He was found to be of average intellect and that he "enjoyed a total denial of responsibility for anything that went wrong in his life . . . twist[ing] the truth about every wayward move to deflect blame . . . and mak[ing] himself look good" (Berry-Dee, 2007, p. 307). In his trial report, the psychiatrist indicated that Gacy had an antisocial personality disorder. Days prior to his trial where justice would certainly be served, Gacy pleaded guilty to the single charge of sodomy, anticipating that this would result in supervised probation, but no jail time.

He was sentenced to 10 years at the Iowa State Reformatory for Men.

Gacy threw himself into his work in the prison with the same fervor he demonstrated in the business community, completing his high school equivalency diploma, taking college courses, and joining the prison's Jaycee chapter. As a result, he only completed 18 months of his 10-year sentence, being paroled as a model prisoner.

Upon release, Gacy went to live with his recently widowed mother. While there, he did a short stint as a cook in a local restaurant. In 1971, he began his new business venture, PDM (Painting, Decorating, Maintenance) Construction (Amirante & Broderick, 2011; Linedecker, 1980). Around this time Gacy began the string of murders that he would become known for.

Gacy always insisted that the murder of 16-year-old boy he picked up for a sexual tryst was committed in self-defense. He claimed that the boy pulled a knife on him the next morning, that he fought back, and that he did not realize until after the murder that the boy was using the knife to prepare breakfast. He buried his remains in the crawl space of his house; a space that became a tomb for 27 other victims.

Several months later, Gacy was arrested after assaulting a young man; he had lured him into the bathroom of a restaurant, handcuffed him, and attempted to force him to perform fellatio. The boy escaped and went to the police. Gacy was only issued a warning, most likely due to his developing standing in the community.

Shortly after this event, Gacy remarried, this time to a former high school friend who had two small girls of her own. This relationship slowly degenerated as he spent more time pursuing extramarital relationships with young men than with his wife and family. He and his second wife divorced in 1976.

As his family life deteriorated, however, his standing in the community strengthened. Along with supporting and initiating many civic engagements, he invented two clown characters, Patches and Pogo, to entertain at parties and the local children's hospital. He even coordinated the 1978 Polish Constitution Day Parade in Chicago where he met then First Lady Rosalynn Carter (Rumore, 2018).

From 1972 to 1978, Gacy killed 33 young boys. His ritual was fairly consistent: he would lure them home through guile or force, handcuff or chemically immobilize them, and molest and torture them, after which he would invariably strangle or stab them to death. Along with the 27 boys he buried in his crawl space, he buried one beneath the floor in his garage, covering the makeshift grave with concrete. He left the remaining victims in the nearby Des Plaines River. He kept souvenirs from each of his victims hidden in his home.

After almost 10 years, a final kidnapping, and murder, tenacious police officers, careful detective work, and missteps from Gacy finally brought it all to an end. As Detective Kozenczak closed in and invariably strengthened his case, Gacy became erratic and unpredictable. Sometimes Gacy was overly solicitous; other times he became belligerent and volatile. Long an abuser of prescription drugs and alcohol, Gacy was "on a rollercoaster ride of liquor and drugs" (Berry-Dee, 2007, p. 339) during the week prior to his arrest. Gacy continued to unravel as he was placed under constant surveillance and brought in several times to be questioned by police.

The evening before he was arrested, Gacy spent the night at the office of Sam Amirante, his attorney (Amirante & Broderick, 2011). Later the next morning, "Amirante came out of his office visibly shaken. He walked down the hall to the two surveillance officers, and said 'Whatever you do, don't let this guy get away' "

(Berry-Dee, 2007, p. 340). Gacy soon left and drove erratically from the "effects of stress, fatigue and pills[; he] seemed to be making the rounds of his friends' homes, bidding them goodbye" (p. 340). One of his friends told the police that Gacy intended to go to the cemetery where his father was buried, that he had a knife and was talking about suicide. One of the detectives asked if he said anything else. "Sure . . . he says he's killed more than 30 people."

The police had enough cause to arrest him. They caught up to him downtown as he sped through a highly congested area. They forced him to pull over, blocked his vehicle with their cars, pulled their guns, and arrested Gacy. Armed with a warrant, the detectives searched Gacy's home and the premises, venturing into the crawl space. No amount of lime spread over the earth could disguise the smell that assaulted them. They began digging into the dirt floor and their discovery exceeded the worst and most horrifying expectations they might have held. With exhaustive digging and careful exhumation over the next several days the police uncovered the bodies of 27 victims.

Agreeing to cooperate with the police, Gacy was taken back to the house, where he was encouraged to mark the location under the garage floor where he had buried his victims. He also confessed to abandoning some of his victims' bodies in the Des Plaines River. After an extensive search, the remains of the last five victims were eventually recovered from the water.

The nightmare of the murders was over, but his extensive trial, eventual conviction, and his sentence to Death Row was just beginning. Although there was a mountain of evidence against him, he later recanted his confessions and proclaimed his innocence throughout his trial.

Regardless of his proclamations, the defense of a potential mental illness, his abusive and neglected upbringing, and subsequent status in the community, Gacy was found guilty in 1980 of the 33 charges of murder brought against him; he was also found guilty of sexual assault and taking indecent liberties with a child. He was sentenced to 21 consecutive life sentences without parole and was convicted of an additional 12 counts of first-degree murder, which brought with it a penalty of death. Fourteen years later, with all appeals exhausted, the state fulfilled its court-ordered obligation and put Gacy to death. He was 52 years old.

Like the efforts he went to in his businesses and community engagement prior to his arrest, Gacy was determined to change his image—for him, how he was perceived was everything. Similar to the last time he spent in prison, he threw himself into all of his endeavors with ferocity and zeal. One of these was a tireless effort to prove his innocence. It was during this time that he wrote a lengthy transcript entitled *A Question of Doubt: Commentary on the Arrest and Trial of John Wayne Gacy* (Gacy, n.d., unpublished manuscript). He corresponded with anyone who wrote to him and spoke with anyone who traveled to see him, providing information that he felt would dispel his guilt.

One of the other things he did while awaiting his death was to paint.

Unlike Manson, Gacy demonstrated no propensity to paint or draw prior to his incarceration. It seems his intention was to reinvent his image and present himself as a humane person, unable or unwilling to kill. Yet, in my opinion, not only do these paintings fail to polish his damaged reputation, they reinforced his dark, hidden sociopathy.

Jim Taranto was the executor of Gacy's prodigious artistic estate and provided the paintings for the gallery shows and lectures held in Las Vegas. Eager to contribute Gacy's work for educational purposes, he agreed to speak with me about him and allowed me to reproduce the work.

Taranto eventually became a trusted confidant and was one of the last people with whom Gacy communicated. He received many letters as Gacy's May 10 execution day neared. The letters outlined how he was passing on "his legacy" to him; "he knew [just] who to give them to." Unlike others who were selling the paintings for their own personal gain and "using him," Gacy trusted Taranto to take care of the works and use them for positive undertakings.

Taranto understood why Gacy painted—to take advantage of the attraction that the public holds for such notorious work.

> We're dealing with a guy who basically needed to pay for his appeals. For his attorneys. And [he had to figure out] how to do that. Well the guy was probably one of the best con artists around, or however you want to [describe him] . . . but he had to use his head somehow to get revenue together to do things. . . . So . . . he created a new persona. The artist.

Gacy knew he would find an audience for these. And some people have indeed

> been fascinated with the fact that a serial killer did these paintings. They wanted artwork that this man put his hand to the canvas with. . . . I think that's what that was all about. It is a piece of history; there's never been a more prolific serial killer since then and there probably never will be.

Taranto also recognized that Gacy painted to escape, even if momentarily. "Don't forget we're talking about a man incarcerated in an eight by ten cage . . . he emanated his energy from his brain onto the paintings."

Subjects of his pieces included his alter ego Pogo the Clown, well-known celebrities, familiar animated characters such as Mickey Mouse, and several self-portraits, such as Figure 5.4.

He also painted well-known criminals like Al Capone and Charles Manson (Figure 5.5). Some images were more intentionally macabre. For example, he

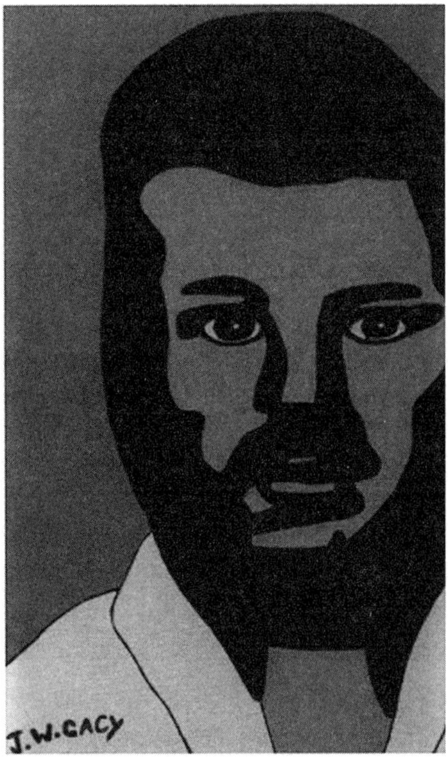

Figure 5.4 John Wayne Gacy (b. 1942; executed 1994). *Self-Portrait* (Date unknown). Oil on canvas board.
Permission provided by Jim Taranto.

did a painting where he superimposed red, bloody handprints over a skull and clown head.

As I presented the work during the lectures, I contended that, despite his own beliefs, Gacy demonstrated little talent; he did not seem particularly adept. While his artistic endeavors seem to portray a confident arrogance reinforced by his expansive use of compositional space and the thick application of bright, garish colors, his portfolio is overall mundane, sophomoric, and unsophisticated. Much of his work involved copying or tracing photographs or other drawings; there was very little originality. The paintings are superficial with very little emotional investment or engagement. And still, all of this is beside the point: Gacy knew how to market himself and titillate potential collectors.

Taranto believed that the paintings of the outlaws, criminals, skulls, and bloody hand prints revealed a "seriously tortured mind"; I argue that Gacy knew

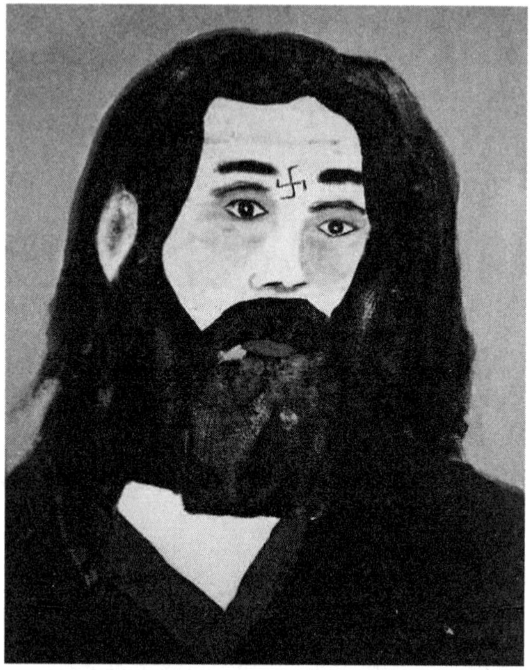

Figure 5.5 John Wayne Gacy (b. 1942; executed 1994). *Charles Manson* (Date unknown). Oil on canvas board.
Permission provided by Jim Taranto.

what was expected from a serial killer and what would sell. Unlike Manson, Gacy was pandering to his audience. He was a shrewd businessman giving the consumer what he wanted (Figure 5.6).

His defense attorney Sam Amirante argued that Gacy clearly had a mental illness (Amirante & Broderick, 2011). During the second lecture, Amirante insisted that the art supported this contention. I argued otherwise.

I do not doubt that there was something psychologically wrong with Gacy. Clearly it would have to take a dangerous, violent, and tortured mind to do what he had done. As reflected through various accounts, particularly as he became more of a focus of the authorities, he began to exhibit persecutory and paranoid tendencies (Amirante & Broderick, 2011; Berry-Dee, 2007; Linedecker, 1980). Even so, it requires a remarkable level of psychopathy to insist on his own innocence with such tenacity, ersatz righteousness, and self-pity for years after his conviction, even in the face of such overwhelming evidence.

Yet, contrary to Amirante, I believe Gacy's artwork did not support his perspective. One way to consider if an artist's works reflect the potential presence of

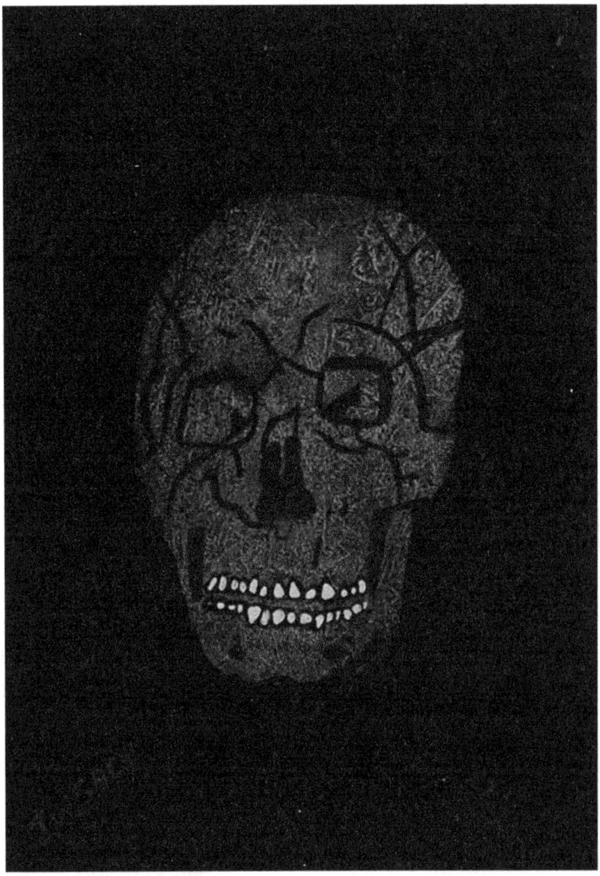

Figure 5.6 John Wayne Gacy (b. 1942; executed 1994). *Skull Painting* (Date unknown). Oil on canvas board.
Permission provided by Jim Taranto.

a serious mental illness is through the formal elements of the work—that is, *how* a drawing or painting is done, not what it is about.

Research has indicated that there are certain characteristics that may determine if a drawing reveals various mental health issues; this may include line quality, space on the page, implied level of energy, the logic and integration of the composition, and the number of colors used and how they are applied (Bucciarelli, 2011; Gantt, 2004, 2016; Gantt & Tabone, 1998; Groth-Marnat, 2003). For example, a person with schizophrenia may complete a drawing that is fragmented, in which the composition is poorly integrated, with erratic and inconsistent line quality; illogical, in which there is no clear relationship between the forms on the page, with objects and shapes included that seem out of place to the intended content; and bizarre and inconsistent color use. On the other hand, a person with a bipolar disorder with mania may complete a drawing that maintains abundant and crowded detail, swirling or looping, inconsistent, almost never-ending lines, an extremely high level of implied energy, and an expansive use of space (Gantt & Tabone, 1997).[1] To be clear, while a single drawing

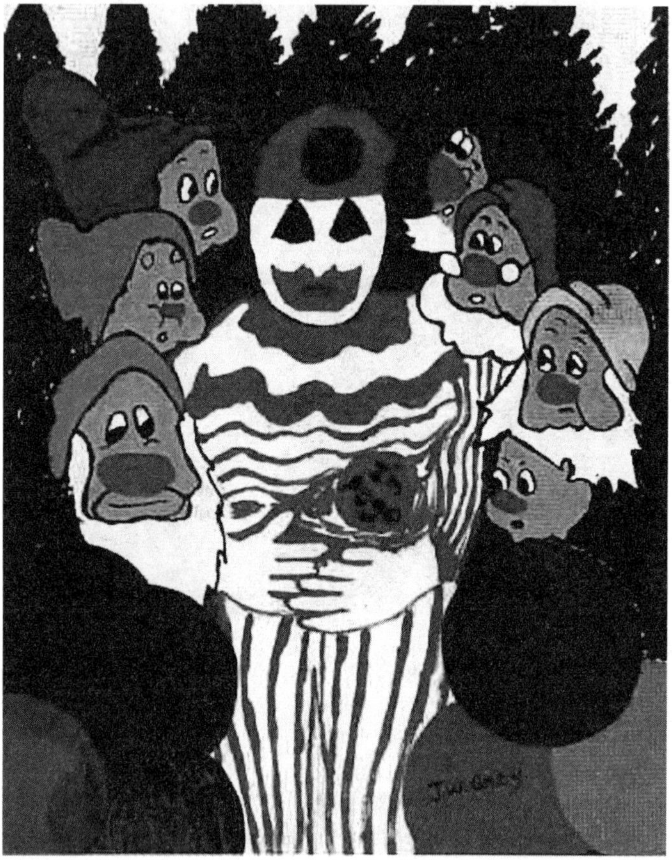

Figure 5.7 John Wayne Gacy (b. 1942; executed 1994). *Death of Pogo* (Date unknown). Oil on canvas board.
Permission provided by Jim Taranto.

[1] This technique was applied to the numerous art pieces of a man on trial for murder to determine the presence of a mental illness at the time of the crime. I testified, based on the drawings' formal elements, that the defendant had suffered from schizoaffective tendencies; this conclusion was independently and blindly corroborated by the other expert witnesses and was determined a reliable method by the courts (Gussak, 2013).

or painting may reveal such a state in the particular moment it was completed, it is more accurate if applied to a series of works to reveal potentially consistent patterns, particularly if given the opportunity to watch the artist complete them. With this in mind, none of Gacy's drawings and paintings seemed to exhibit the acute mental illness Amirante was claiming.

It remains possible that he did indeed suffer from a psychiatric disorder at the time of the murders. However, it is also likely that his developing erratic and paranoid behavior was a result of his increasing abuse of prescription drugs, self-admitted lack of sleep (Gacy, n.d.), and ever increasing pressure from the authorities as they were closing in (Amirante & Broderick, 2011).

The paintings reflected otherwise. His sure hand, strong lines, vivid but appropriate palette, expansive yet controlled compositions, and singular focus for each seem to contradict the presence of a diagnosable psychiatric disorder. Rather, these elements, along with lack of emotional attachment and superficiality, support that he most likely had a psychopathic personality as defined in the Interlogue.

Gacy's arrogance and narcissistic and self-aggrandizing tendencies are clearly represented in Figure 5.7. In it, Disney's beloved seven dwarves, representing innocence and trust, sadly mourn the passing of Gacy's alter ego, Pogo.

Final Words

This chapter removed Manson and Gacy from the collection of serial killers in the previous chapter and set them apart. By separating them, it perhaps elevated them. There might be something to this; in the mythos of American crime, these two have become, in some respects, the epitome of multiple murderers. People of a certain age certainly know who Manson and Gacy were. Much has been written and explored about both, sensationalizing and mythologizing them in the news and popular media. Gacy understood this and at times provided his own best marketing. Both personified the true fear and vulnerability of their times. They were also known for their drawings and paintings.

While they were both multiple murderers, this chapter has made clear just how different they were. Manson's persona embraced anti-establishment rebellion and societal marginalization, whereas Gacy's projected a conservative, business conformity. Manson never attempted to hide who he was and reveled in his insubordinate and uncontrollable reputation. Gacy was careful to prevent people from getting a glimpse behind his mask. Their murderous proclivities, choice of victims, and methods used set these two very far apart from each other. As already indicated, neither would have respected the other.

Their artworks were also considerably different from one another and contradicted their true selves. In broadly simple terms, Manson's crimes were calculated, and he was likely drug-addled as he delusionally justified his actions to instigate societal change and begin a race war; yet his art appeared spontaneous, energetic, frenetic, and without boundaries. Gacy's crimes, on the other hand, were impulsive, self-gratifying, and primitively driven, implemented to satisfy his own desires; yet his drawings and paintings were rigidly planned, emotionally flat, and completely soulless. Still, despite these marked differences, their drive to create art may be quite similar.

Unlike artists who may be driven to create to contain their libidinal and violent drives or to escape and control their violent surroundings, these two, similar to the murderers in the previous chapter, wielded their art as a weapon to feed their own self-grandiosity, self-validation, and hierarchical control. While Gacy made art strictly for business purposes and Manson created images underscoring and reinforcing his embraced monstrously messianic persona, their art seemed to mask who they really were. In their own ways, Manson and Gacy tried to give what they thought the world wanted from their art, but the only way their work connected with people was through the fascination for murderabilia.

PART III

ART FOR CHANGE

6
Charles Bronson Becomes Charlie Salvador
"The Most Violent Inmate" Liberated Through Art

In late spring 1981, Charles Bronson, an inmate of Broadmoor Hospital, a high-security psychiatric institution in Berkshire, England, was walking through the rain to the canteen; he was among 6 residents being escorted by 10 guards. He had been placed in the institution after several years of incorrigibly violent and uncontrollable behavior. He was deemed insane by the system.

Once they were outside, the man broke free and ran. The guards chased him. He jumped for an iron bar, pulled himself up, kicking one of the guards in the face. He quickly clambered up a drainpipe, grabbed onto the gutter, and swung himself onto the roof. This was the beginning of the first of several rooftop sieges.

> This had been planned for months and it had to be the exact week I did it. . . . After twenty-four years as boss of Broadmoor, this week was [Superintendent] McRath's retirement. I crushed him before he left. A mad Broadmite [resident of Broadmoor] brought him to his knees. I'd crippled him. Don't get me wrong. I didn't dislike Dr. McRath. But he had to take responsibility for the brutality in his prized refractory block and the whole godforsaken place he ran. . . . It was run on fear, an iron fist, and his staff were f--king bullies . . . years of misery, beatings, and abuse by the very people who had a duty of care to mentally ill people. (Bronson, 2016, pp. 89–90)

He spent several days on the roof, in the cold and wet. He became hungry, thirsty, and exhausted; he vacillated between seeing the beauty of his surroundings and destroying the rooftop structure to the tune of thousands of British pounds sterling. His health deteriorated, but still he stayed. Through the pain-filled delirium of the third day, he heard his father and brothers, brought in by the facility, calling out to him. He eventually came down the way he went up, on his terms, clambering down the drainpipe.

Since being arrested in 1974 for a petty crime, Bronson has earned the infamous reputation as one of the most ruthless and unpredictably violent inmates to ever carry a prison sentence in England (Bronson, 2016). He has spent considerable time in solitary confinement and acute mental health facilities.

He is currently serving a life sentence.

So what does the most violent inmate do? Naturally, he turns to art.

Almost 20 years ago, an officer approached him while he was sitting in his solitary cell and suggested that perhaps he try drawing—he had heard that it helped people "calm down."

Bronson never had formal training in art. However, he soon became quite adept with his materials. Over time, Bronson created hundreds of drawings. Several years ago, Bronson changed his name yet again, to Charlie Salvador, to reflect his new, more peace-focused and passive personality, crediting his art for the change.

Through a focus on this most notorious inmate, this chapter illustrates the power of art making to redirect aggressive energy and relabel violent identity. It draws from various published accounts of Bronson's crimes and subsequent imprisonment, his autobiographical memoirs, several conversations with someone who was once a close confidant, and my own communications with him. Ultimately, this chapter emphasizes the value that art making can have with even the most ferocious.

Becoming Bronson

Bronson/Salvador was born Michael Gordon Peterson in December 1952, in Luton, England.[1] From a loving, well-respected family, he was described by his aunt as "lovely . . . bright . . . gentle, and mild-mannered." However, he began to get into trouble as a young teenager shortly after his family moved to a new town.

He became part of a small gang of boys who engaged in low-level crimes—petty theft, truancy and fighting. He was often given fines and probation for these offenses. Although he married young and had a son, his behavior eventually caught up with him. When he was 22 years old, he was arrested and received a 7-year sentence for petty thievery.

Shortly after he was imprisoned he began to suddenly display incorrigible and violent tendencies without preamble; he had no hesitation to attack those around him—guards and prison inmates alike. He was transported through a number of different institutions, forced to take psychotropic medications, and eventually placed in isolation. To combat the boredom he felt in isolation, Bronson

[1] All biographical information was obtained through Bronson's own autobiographies (including Bronson 2004, 2007, 2009, and 2016 listed in References at the end of this book) unless otherwise noted.

began a fitness regime. He even published books on the subject (see *Solitary Fitness*, Bronson, 2007). This regimen continued throughout his subsequent imprisonments.

He attempted suicide after he attacked another prison officer and was placed in seclusion; as a result he was given a psychiatric diagnosis and moved to Broadmoor Hospital for the Criminally Insane, then later to Rampton Security Hospital. During this time he unsuccessfully attempted to kill two different inmates. It was then, while in Broadmoor, that he climbed to the roof to protest his imprisonment and treatment. This was the first of several similar episodes (Bronson, 2016).

As a result of his unorthodox protests, excessive property damage, and violent impulses, years were added to his sentence. After serving much of his time in isolation, he was released in 1987—14 years after his original 7-year sentence was imposed. During his short stint outside the prison walls, he became a bare-knuckle boxer—illegal but not unheard of. It was his fight promoter who suggested he change his name from Michael Peterson to Charles Bronson to reflect a more aggressive persona. After 69 days outside, he was once again arrested for robbing a jewelry store. He returned to prison in 1988.

He was given another 7-year sentence.

Bronson continued to demonstrate excessively violent and unpredictable behavior during his second sentence, attacking officers and inmates; he even began a one-person riot and assaulted someone with a spear he fashioned out of a broom handle and broken glass. Once again he was moved through various institutions for security purposes. He was stabbed numerous times in the back by at least two other prisoners toward the end of this stint. He was hospitalized for the rest of his sentence, thus avoiding further trouble that could have prolonged his imprisonment. He was released in late 1992, but was arrested again shortly after.

He was returned to prison for possessing a sawed-off shotgun and conspiracy to rob. While he pled guilty for the possession charge, he stressed that he was not going to use it on someone else but rather was going to use it to shoot himself. While in jail awaiting trial he took the librarian hostage. During negotiations, he made a series of unusual demands—an inflatable doll, a helicopter, and a cup of tea. He released his hostage in disgust when the librarian passed gas. This inauspicious start did not bode well for his third and final stint in prison.

Over the next several years, he continued to—in his own words—"lose it badly," demonstrating erratic and unusual behavior. He began a pattern of violence that included attacking and holding people hostage. His victims included the deputy governor of one facility, the governor of another, and three inmates, including two Iraqi hijackers. During this latter episode, he felt guilty after hitting one of his captives over the head with a metal tray, so he slashed himself with a razor before he released them. He walked to the isolation unit under his own volition. One of his escapades resulted in him being placed in a "Hannibal cage"— a full face mask featured in the film *Silence of the Lambs*, consisting of small holes for the eyes and bars over the mouth to prevent biting.

In 1999, Bronson took a teacher hostage and destroyed much of the prison. The entire siege lasted for 44 hours, for which he received a "discretionary" life sentence. Ironically, Bronson took the teacher hostage after the man criticized some of his drawings.

Finding Art

It was around the mid-1990s when an officer gave Bronson basic art materials and encouraged him to draw. Using the relatively simple and safe materials—lead pencils, colored pencils, and ink on stock paper—Bronson's imagery developed from cartoon-like figures to fairly complex, intricate social and political commentaries. My initial reactions to his work were that his sometimes whimsical, other times biting imagery was controlled, carefully executed, and well-organized. His stylistic flourish is easy to recognize, and although his compositions and messages changed over time, his style has not.

Relying on caricatures, he drew with a steady, firm hand with clear, deliberate yet varied lines. While some of his compositions may first appear erratic, crowded, and fragmented, upon closer examination the pages are actually quite deft and well-organized. Despite the limited, restrictive materials, his drawings appear almost fluid, painterly, with an atmospheric quality achieved through near masterly tinting and shading.

Bronson eventually became known for his work; in 2010, one of his drawings *Triptophenia* was displayed in a Tube station of the London Underground organized by Art Below. Unfortunately, displaying the art of a notorious inmate was deemed too controversial.

> National Victims' Association (NVA), which supports victims and families affected by crime, had criticised display of the artwork. "I would say that the overwhelming majority of victims of crime will be astonished and thoroughly depressed that one of the most violent criminals in the prison system is allowed to engage with the British public in this way," a spokesman said. (BBC News, 2010)

Shortly after, it was taken down by an anonymous party. However, many have celebrated his work; Koestler Trust, the United Kingdom's well-known prison arts charity, bestowed 11 awards on Bronson and his work (see https://www.

koestlertrust.org.uk/koestler-awards/). He has subsequently sold and auctioned off his work to raise money for charities, including for one child who suffered from cerebral palsy.

In homage to his favorite artist, Salvador Dali, Bronson changed his name to Salvador in 2014, to reflect a new peaceful persona (Alexander, 2014). "The old me dried up. Bronson came alive in 1987. He died in 2014 . . . its non-violent all the way. It's a peaceful journey from here on . . . my heart is at peace and my mind is set on art" (para. 3–13).

I felt it necessary to reach out to Salvador directly to find out more.

"Meeting" Bronson/Salvador

In 2016, I spoke with someone whom I had previously contacted for permission to reproduce Bronson's art for an online blogpost I wrote.[2] She indicated that she no longer worked for him and his website, but suggested I contact him directly; she provided me the site online where I could email him. Several days after doing so, I received an international phone call from Salvador's then girlfriend. She told me that he was excited to receive my email for the opportunity to "speak" with me about his work. However, there were obvious complications; given his security level, Bronson would be unable to receive visitors or international phone calls, and it would be extremely difficult for him to mail his responses. However, she would be happy to assist as the "go-between."

We agreed on a system of communication: After I emailed him questions, he would write out his responses. She photographed these letters and emailed them back to me. In this manner, I would hear from him directly, with the photographs of the letters verifying that the responses were indeed from him.

Shortly after, I received an email with Salvador's first letter, where he addressed my inquiry on a possible visit. In his very distinguishable, stylistic script, he wrote,

> Dave my friend; You have more chance of visiting Prince Charles than me. I am a category "A" Prisoner. Have been for 43 yrs. All my visitors have to be checked by cops and prison security so forget it.

After verifying our agreed upon process of future communication, he signed with his recognizable scrawl, a spider dangling underneath.

[2] https://www.psychologytoday.com/blog/art-trial/201410/most-violent-inmate-very-prolific-artist-charles-bronson

Ongoing Communication

Over the next several months, I received several lengthy letters from Salvador and was sent two recordings that Salvador made during a phone conversation, with his permission.

Escape Through Drawing

Salvador attributed art with providing him the impetus to change. Salvador remembered,

> [the ability to make art] was always with me but it took me forever to find it. Actually, it was a prison guard who helped me find it. I was in a cage, in a very dark place, but the guard gave me a lot of trust, art materials, advice. A reason to behave. And I kept at it . . . even though he was a screw, an officer, he trusted me. He gave me stuff that wasn't really allowed at the time. Like pens, and paper and things. And he just comes to me cage one day and he says "Charlie, if you carry on grabbing people hostage and wrapping them up, you're never gonna get out, you know. So, why don't you do something positive and creative? You got all the time in the world . . . You should do art, write, blah, blah, blah" . . . and from that day . . . I am a prolific artist, thanks to him! I tell you what, three cheers for [him]!

He found that while some of his art is appreciated by many on the outside, he often had difficulty inside: "My work is not accepted by many jails. Some refuse me pens, some deny me to post it out. Some say it's offensive." As a result, he self-censured, to "stop me from creating all I wish. My subconscious is always telling me to 'be careful, Charlie. Some psychologist will analyze that one!' So I really don't create all my visions I get in my sleep."

> The truth is, a lot of my work I hold back on. Cuz [*sic*] psychiatrists [and] psychologists would have a party; they seem to enjoy analyzing it, getting involved. Which I despise. It's like tearing into my dreams! Prodding. So I don't always create all I feel [It probably wouldn't leave the jail]. Sadly, art can have bad reactions just like crime. I once remembered Ronnie Kray[3] painted a picture. And a national newspaper got a hold of it and got it analyzed by a criminologist professor. In the report it went on about the color purple and how Ron

[3] One of the notorious Kray brothers, a legendary crime boss in London who was in prison for murder. Bronson was quite close to both of the brothers as they spent many years together inside

> must have felt anger and anxiety, etc., . . . Ron answered 'Stop talking bulls---. Purple was the only colour I had' [so] it shows how art can often be labeled and judged by complete idiots.

Every one of his drawings were created while he was in isolation, and, although he recognized that his pieces were similar in style, they remain vastly different in intent, as he sees each as an emotional and thoughtful response to his current mood or situation. While some are intended to be whimsical and comical, some were derived from strong, overwhelming feelings: "Some days I feel hopeless—no focus! No real desire. So my art becomes gloomy, desperate—probably unbalanced. I never like that state. Makes me sad. Coz [*sic*] I'm so much better than that, [so] a lot I destroy." He rarely reflects on the particular pieces once he creates them: "I create a piece, and I move on—I never look back. To look back is too painful. Plus, art develops in new styles, new forms, new focus! If I ever [do] see a photo of one of my old art [pieces] I always feel 'wow—look how far I've traveled.' "

As Salvador recounted,

> I taught myself from within the Bowels of Hell! And it is the one thing that made me a better man. I now live for art. It's my life. My world. My dreams. I get visions in my sleep. I awake excited to start a new art. My masterpiece probably won't happen until I'm *freed* (if ever). That art would be painted with the sun on my back and the breeze on my face *on grass flowers close by, a dog, birds singing*—a butterfly. My heart will feel like a rainbow as I create it.

As a result of this newfound talent, he has redefined himself: "it's me today; the man, the myth, the artist born again. . . . Proud. Hopeful. Chilled. New me. Give me a f---king break if only a little bit of credit and some trust."

In addition, his art allows him to escape and focus on what and who he loves.

> I continue to create! . . . My dreams of creating a garden—grass—flowers—birds—nice smells. A breeze. The sun on my back. Pure freedom.
>
> I am creating colours, lots of colour—a rainbow dream No eyes on me. No CCTV. No walls, fences, barbed wire.
>
> Only nature's beauty, and nature's sounds.
>
> I then awake inside a concrete coffin in a straitjacket laughing. My eyes are sewn up. But I still see a rainbow. And [his girlfriend's] eyes.
>
> That keeps me going (All I need).

Ultimately, he found that "when I'm creating I feel sane."

To inform this chapter, I asked Salvador and his girlfriend to choose images that they felt represented who he was and aspects of his life. The following images, in no particular order, show a selection of the choices to represent a larger body of his work. Please note, this chapter presents only a very small sample because he has completed hundreds of drawings.

The Art

While Salvador remained decidedly evasive about the significance of his individual pieces, many of his drawings clearly seem to serve as autobiographical illustrations and indictments of his surroundings. At the risk of conducting what Salvador indicated as overanalysis, exploring the drawings for potential meaning is imperative to understanding him and the importance of his work.

"The Poet from Hell," seen in Figure 6.1, is relatively small, around 3 by 5 inches. He completed this piece with ink and colored pencils circa 2000, when he was still Bronson. At first glance it appears to be a sweet, delicate, and simple image. Yet, despite the whimsy of the style, the message is quite provocative.

It is a simple composition; in the center of the small piece of paper is what appears to be the back of a devil's head, identifiable only through its blood red horns. Perched on one of the horns is a bird. The background consists of a pinkish wash with simple line drawings of flying birds in the distance. There is as much emphasis placed on the title of the piece as on the image itself. Given that he recognized himself as a poet as well as an artist, this is clearly self-referential.

Such images seem a surprise, emerging from someone described as a ball of uncontrolled energy. Painted when he was still Bronson, considered an unredeemable and recalcitrant aggressor, the form is carefully rendered, the lines are controlled and precise, and the shading is meticulous and almost delicate. As an autobiographical piece, it is rather profound—a prolific and creative being found within the depths of hell; the only redeeming hope is the bird perched on the horn.

Still, while several of his pieces revealed a playful side (see Figure 6.2), many of his pieces are quite pointed. Figures 6.3 through 6.5 represent drawings that are simultaneously humorous and disquieting; they are just a few of the many drawings that illustrate Bronson's view of his own "madness" and subsequent treatment. Each one is deceptively simple, with a singular focus similar to a comic strip panel, yet each represents quite blatantly the helplessness and pain he experienced.

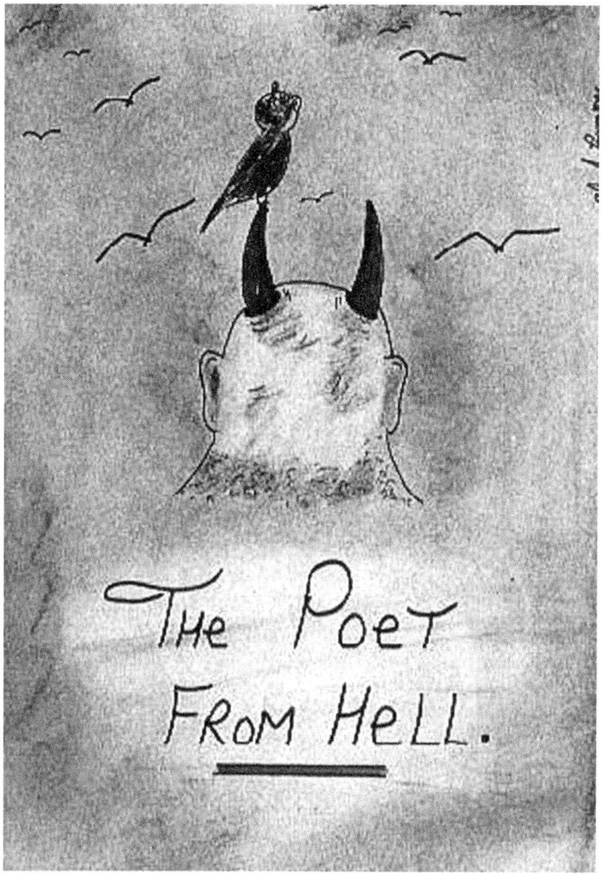

Figure 6.1 Charles Salvador (b. 1952). *The Poet from Hell* (Date unknown). Pencils, colored pencils, and ink on paper.
Permission provided by the artist.

Figure 6.3, entitled *A Day in the Life of Madness*, features a caricature of Bronson speaking to someone with a horse's head, wearing similar garb. Bronson asks the other figure "Look Ned . . . why can't I ride you around the exercise yard? Come on Mate. It is an Asylum!"

The same character appears in *Bronson-1314-LIFE* (Figure 6.4), bound and hung from the ceiling in a cocoon, with only his head sticking out. The character is saying "Oh well . . . time for a kip . . . good night mouse."

Figure 6.5, a two-color drawing completed with pen and pencil, depicts a bound man inside a bricked enclosure, hanging from his ankles. The unidentified

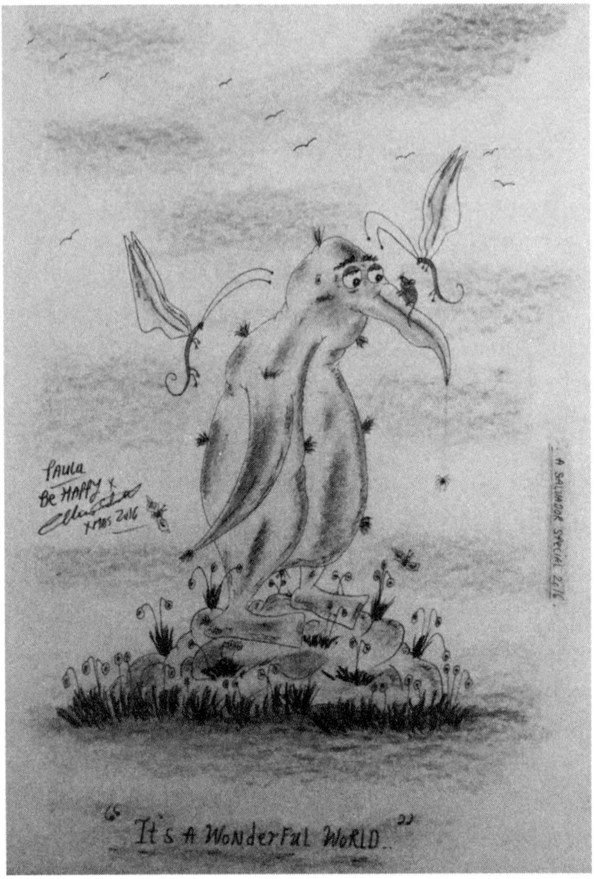

Figure 6.2 Charles Salvador (b. 1952). *It's a Wonderful World* (2016). Pencils, colored pencils, and ink on paper.
Permission provided by the artist.

figure is pierced in the abdomen and back of his head with large, blood-ridden stakes. To the left another cocoon hangs from the ceiling, presumably with a body inside. Blood pours from the figure's head and guts. There is a security camera peering from the right-hand side of the page. A large book sits in the foreground of the page, with the title *Insanity* inscribed on its binding. A small mouse sits on top of the book.

While these images depict the destruction of self, break down of identity, and loss of dignity and control, some of his other images seem to celebrate his new self-perception. Yet, even while they celebrate his new identity, some of the drawings concurrently reflect his disdain for others by directly challenging the

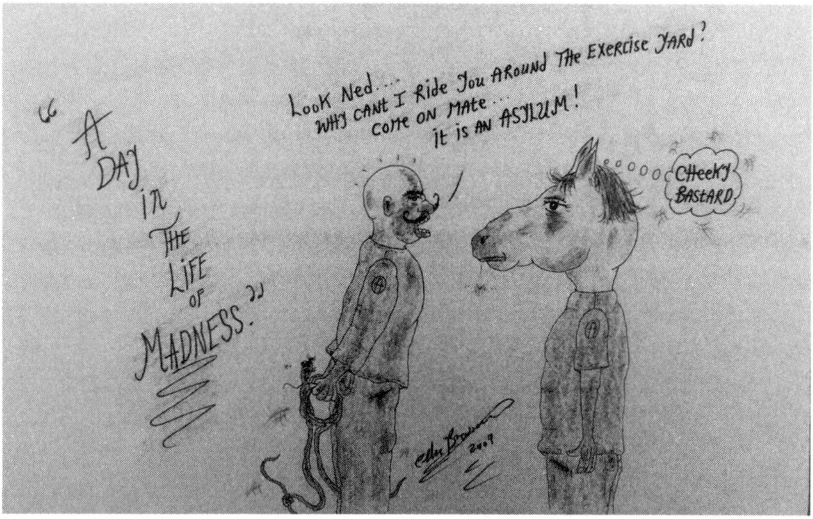

Figure 6.3 Charles Salvador (b. 1952). *A Day in the Life of Madness* (2009). Pencils, colored pencils, and ink on paper.

Permission provided by the artist.

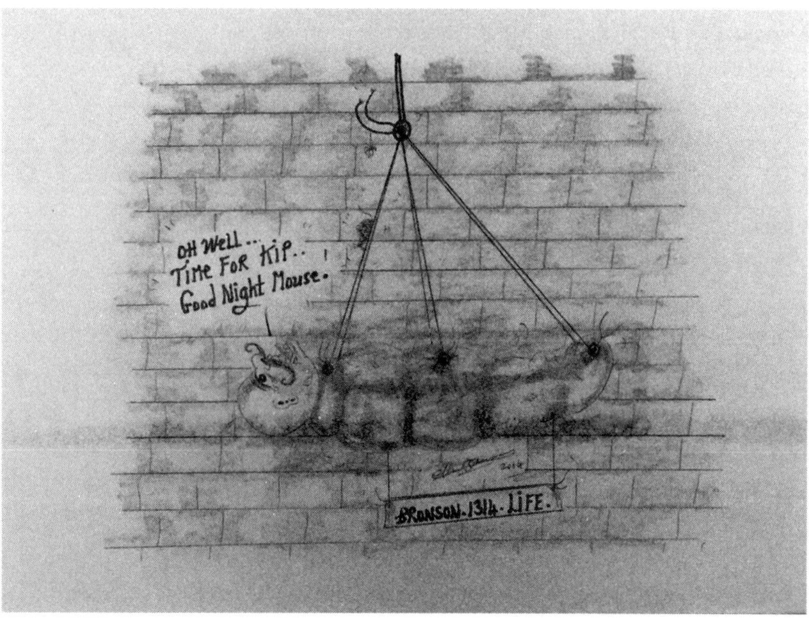

Figure 6.4 Charles Salvador (b. 1952). *Bronson-1314-LIFE* (2004). Pencils, colored pencils, and ink on paper.

Permission provided by the artist.

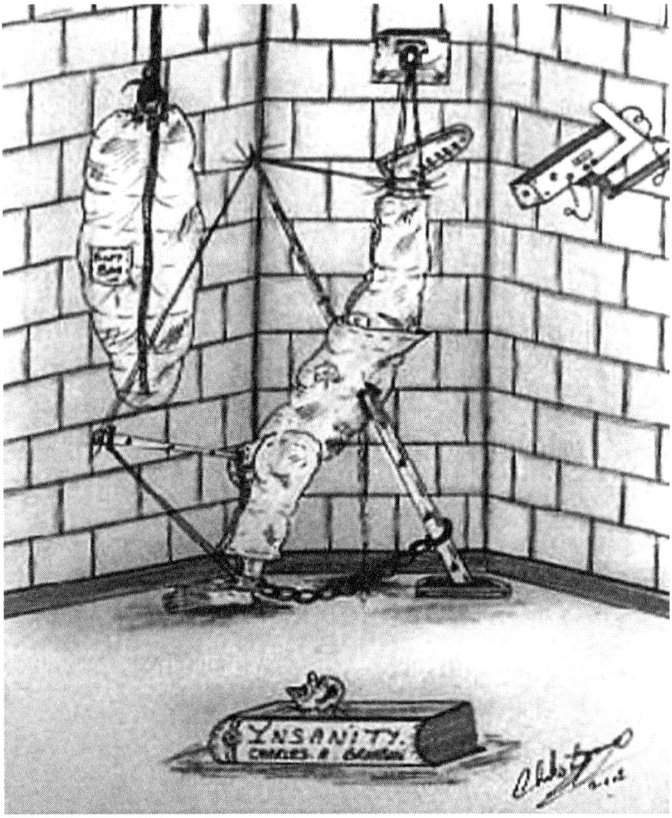

Figure 6.5 Charles Salvador (b. 1952). *Insanity* (2002). Pencils, colored pencils, and ink on paper.
Permission provided by the artist.

viewers to question their own sense of self. Figure 6.6 is a small, colorful self-caricature; however, rather than suffering the indignities of humiliation and pain seen in the previous images, this one depicts the self-figure emerging from the sewn-up cocoon, wearing a beret, holding a painter's palette and paintbrush, standing on a large book entitled *Con-Artist.* Replete with his ubiquitous symbols, the figure has spiders dangling from him, a bizarre bird perched on his shoulder, and a figure hatching from an egg sitting atop the book. The figure is proudly proclaiming "I swopped my sawn-off for a brush. . . . Now!! I'm a born-again artist. . . . A true creator! Who are you?"

Figure 6.7/see also color plate 12, completed after his relationship began with his girlfriend, is even more self-empowering and proud; combining elements

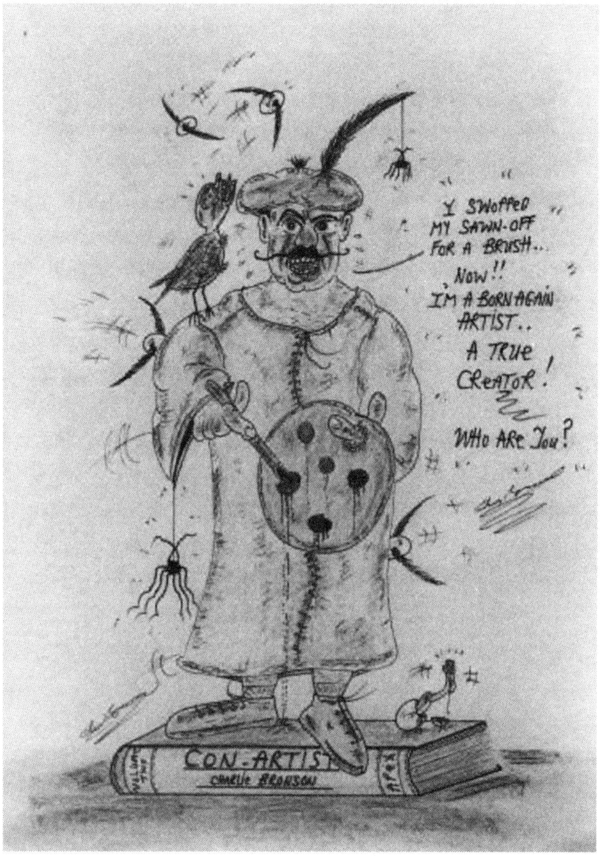

Figure 6.6 Charles Salvador (b. 1952). *Con-Artist* (Date unknown). Pencils, colored pencils, and ink on paper.
Permission provided by the artist.

from his insanity series, such as the pervasive spiders, the brick enclosure, barred windows, and the ever-seeing security cameras, this figure seems even mightier, breaking free despite the ongoing restraint. It celebrates the emerging and developing identity as Bronson transitions into Salvador. The self-caricature is depicted as a winged figure breaking through the top book of a pile of five large editions, three of which are books he authored as Bronson: *Silent Scream, Loonyology,* and *Broadmoor.* The fourth book is a fictional tome entitled *The A to Z of the Criminally Insane*, authored by Dr. M. G. Peterson, an obvious reference to himself as Michael Peterson. The bottom book that supports all of the others has *Born Again Artist, Salvador* scripted on its spine.

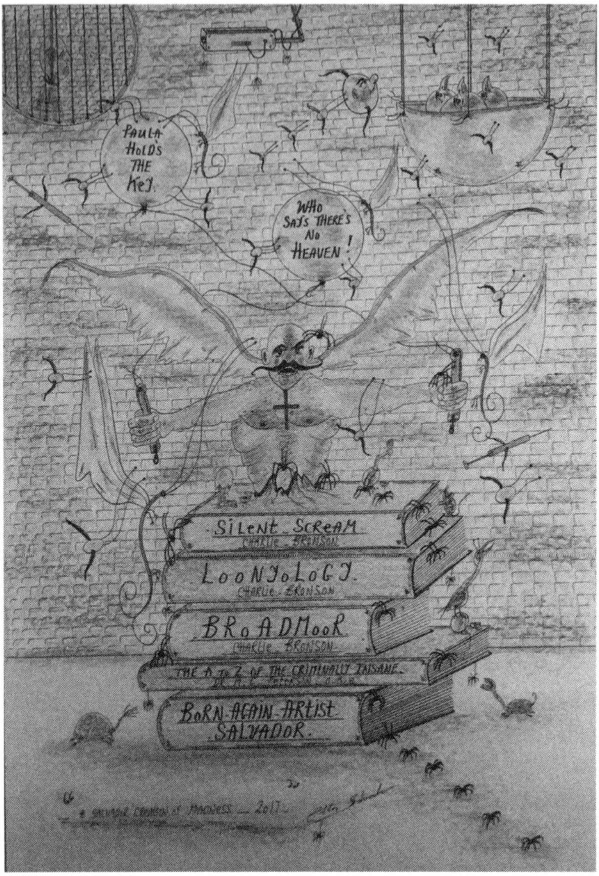

Figure 6.7 Charles Salvador (b. 1952). *Creation of Madness* (2017). Pencils, colored pencils, and ink on paper.
Permission provided by the artist.

Two balloons are attached by wire to the wood clutched in each hand; one has "[girlfriend's name] holds the Key" written on it, while the other one reads "Who Says There's No Heaven." A decidedly optimistic and celebratory piece, but as the muscular figure emerges victoriously, he is still bombarded by the hallucinatory symbols representing his repressive and oppressive environment. In both of these images the figure is looking directly at the viewer, confronting, challenging. They evoke strength even in their cartoon-like depictions.

The busy, crowded imagery of *Subconcious Flow* [*sic*](Figure 6.8), is an example of the many compositions he created later.

This piece, though considerably larger, is still only about 8.5 by 11 inches. This composition screams of frenetic energy, a container of repressed and

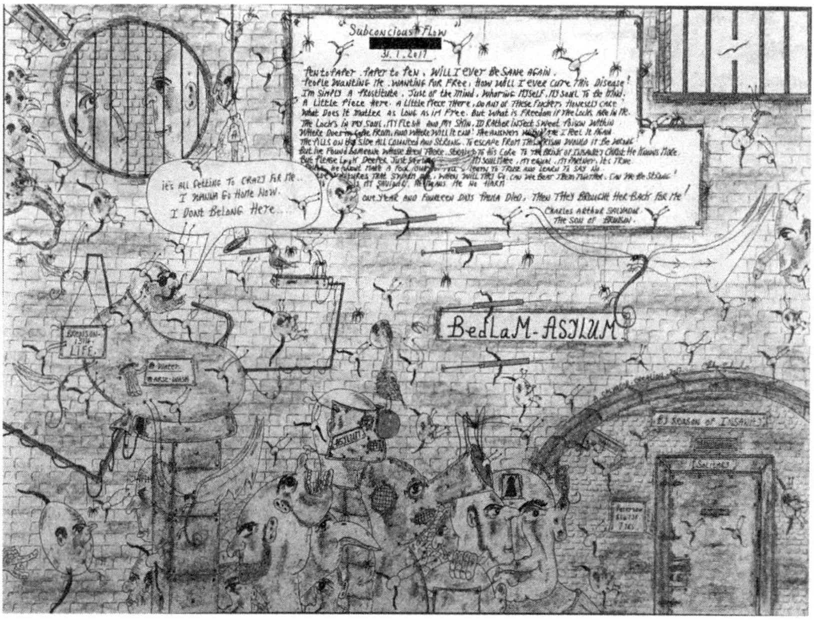

Figure 6.8 Charles Salvador (b. 1952). *Subconcious Flow* (2017). Pencils, colored pencils, and ink on paper.
Permission provided by the artist.

unexpressed frenzy. Completed with ink and colored pencils on cardstock, every square millimeter is covered in well-rendered symbols, floating images, and words. Dominating the page is a neatly rendered poem, "Subconcious Flow," written by his then girlfriend. This last detail is especially significant: by acknowledging his then girlfriend by name [blocked out to protect her identity] and integrating her poem into his drawing, he demonstrates his ability to move beyond his own self and collaborate on a personal level with someone else—it's no longer just about him.

An indictment of the psychiatric institutions that Salvador experienced, this piece in particular captures the nonsensical pandemonium and chaos found inside. In large script, just below the margin, is a sign that reads "Bedlam-Asylum." Throughout the image, the same symbolic *leitmotifs* seen in his previous drawings all seem to congregate en masse in this one piece—so many that the amount of space it would take to categorize and describe each image on this page is mind-boggling.

It includes, among other things, hypodermic needles, winged-insects, and birds against a complex, detailed brick wall with steel, impenetrable doors, and security cameras. And, of course, his spiders and mouse. (While he remains somewhat evasive about his iconography, he did indicate " . . . [the spiders] are happy souls! So are white sharks if you leave them alone. Nature can look after itself . . . humans have to f--k it up.")

On the left part of the page is a clearly identifiable, scared looking self-caricature bound inside a womb-like cocoon connected by wires and pipes to various electronic gadgets. The words, "it's all getting to [*sic*] crazy for me. . . . I wanna go home now. I don't belong here" emit from its mouth in comic book fashion.

Every fresh review of this page reveals something new, and each small section could stand alone as its own art piece. Reminiscent of Hieronymus Bosch's work, *Garden of Earthly Delights* (c. 1485–1505), it would be easy to see how one could get lost among this frenzy. Yet how indicative is his work to a mental illness?

The previous chapter briefly touched on how the formal elements of the drawings and paintings of serial killer John Wayne Gacy could potentially determine the presence or lack of a psychiatric illness. To recap, certain mental health issues might be suggested through *how* a work of art was completed rather than what it may be about. This may include such indicators as how the lines were drawn, how color was used, how much of the page or canvas was covered, how integrated or fragmented the composition appeared, and if there seemed to be some logic in its layout, to name just a few (Bucciarelli, 2011; Eytan & Elkis-Abuhoff, 2013; Gantt, 2004, 2016; Gantt & Tabone, 1998; Groth-Marnat, 2003).

During a Death Row murder trial in 2009, I relied on the formal elements of more than 100 drawings completed by the defendant to determine if he had a mental illness at the time of his crimes (Gussak, 2013). I concluded—and then testified—that, as reflected through their fragmented imagery, chaotic compositions, floating figures, disconnected body parts, varying and inconsistent line qualities, and the inclusion of bizarre and unrelated words and numbers, he likely suffered from schizoaffective tendencies.

Such elements seem pervasive in Salvador's compositions as well. His images appear disjointed, with heads floating without bodies, fantastical figures drawn with inconsistent and varying line qualities, with words and phrases sprinkled throughout.

Yet, I am not completely convinced that this page was completed by someone with a floridly active mental illness, despite its title and manifested meaning. It's too controlled, too deliberate. While the drawing does indeed seem chaotic and fragmented at first, each figurative icon was deliberately considered and carefully placed. Clear and lucid thought had to go into completing this piece.

The exaggerations are quite pronounced, considered, and thoughtful, with humorous surrealistic imagery scattered throughout: a figure on the right edge that has a penis for a nose; one figure has a Hannibal mask covering its features, but with a clown nose in its center; the bird perched on a security camera in the center of the page has a hypodermic needle for a beak. While the horrors remain, as the man hanging from a noose to the left of the poem reminds us, there may be some hope—in the upper right, a stylized bird breaks the continuity of one of the prison bars in the window. The perseverative, detailed, meticulously patterned and modeled brick wall reveals an intense attention to detail and an almost perverse concentration and presence of mind.

The words that are included do not distract from this piece—nor do they in any of his drawings, for that matter. They in fact seem to clarify the image's intent and meaning. By incorporating the loaded titles and irreverent yet poetic dictums, there is no confusion in what Salvador is trying to communicate. His meaning is deliberate and clear.

It's quite possible that he has indeed suffered from severe psychiatric instability, and, by the standards and criteria established by the society to which he belongs, it could be argued that Salvador and his drawings indeed exhibited a mental illness. However, from my perspective, the art seems to belie any actively florid psychosis. On the contrary: his art, despite its otherworldly and ethereal nature, seems to ground him. There is indeed a singularly clear message shouting through the chaos: "I don't belong here."

Identity Redefined

> I never liked myself. I think maybe I was battling with who I had become, what this hellhole had made me.
>
> —Bronson, 2016, p. 91

One of the benefits of engaging in art making is that, essentially, Bronson had an opportunity to redefine his identity, to take on a new, humane label. As indicated in the Introduction, aggression and violent tendencies may emerge and be maintained through ongoing social interactions. Such behavior becomes tied into the identity that a person is given by members of a chosen society. Once a person is called an "aggressor" or seen as "violent," it is perpetuated through social interactions. Unless this characterization is lifted and this identity changed, such aggression may continue. Thus, meaning and identity emerge through social interactions. So do labels.

Regardless of what caused his violent tendencies—and as already underscored, there are many theories to draw from—Bronson's label emerged from how he responded to his frustrations, his difficulties in adjusting to his new surroundings, his own desire to survive and maintain some control in an uncontrollable environment. He was identified as Great Britain's most violent and notorious inmate. Such an identity was perpetuated by the systems into which he was thrown and by the public media. His deviant behaviors were reinforced, and, before long, his whole persona changed to embrace this moniker. As his girlfriend admitted "It was a caricature he took on . . . I think he [reveled in this image] because it gave him an identity . . . that *was* his identity."

As stipulated earlier, one of the benefits that art making offers inside prison walls is an opportunity for inmates to relabel themselves and rise above their state-given identity (Gussak, 2019). Correctional institutions, by their very nature and need for control, dehumanize and objectify the inmates inside. However, engaging in art making provides an opportunity to rehumanize the dehumanized (Cardinal, 1972; Gussak, 2016a; Maizels, 1996; Petullo, 2001; Prinzhorn, 1972/1995).

An inmate becomes recognized as more than a two-dimensional identity. Salvador actively changed to become the "born-again artist," to become "Salvador." By taking on, and broadcasting, this new persona, he is now reinforcing this new label, making it less likely that his social interactions will result in and perpetuate his violent acts.

This begs the question: Is he still aggressive? Perhaps. However, while he no longer is a two-dimensional caricature of an inhumane monster, his aggression is internalized and redirected to become integrated into a more complex persona.

Still Aggressive? Yes, But . . .

Salvador credits art as his redeemer, liberating him from his violent ways. Before his art, he was "dangerous; unpredictable; confused . . . now I can switch off, go into my art world, create, I don't give a f--k what's going on outside the door, it's not my business." Has he changed? While the imagery is striking and humorous at times, and he has indicated that he has embraced a more peaceful and passive persona, my contention is that the aggression is still present. He is not necessarily less belligerent, he has just created a new, safer way to express it.

Catharsis to Sublimation

Salvador progressed from cathartic release of his aggressive and violent impulses to sublimating the drive into a more creative and socially productive form. Kramer (1971/1992) differentiated between catharsis and sublimation. Catharsis is a primitive release, almost a purging of undesirable emotions, including anger. This may result in an outburst of explosive expression, leaving the expresser spent and empty. The danger is that catharsis is temporary, and the emotions that caused the cathartic expression return without resolution. Punching a wall, a bag, or a person may be examples of cathartic expression. Bronson's bare-knuckle boxing, and later his intense workout regime, were all means of cathartically releasing his pent-up frustration and fear.

Sublimation, on the other hand, is a more mature, secondary process. It transforms primitive urges into more complex acts that do not serve direct, instant gratification. Such a complex process requires a displacement of the energy onto a new task and a way to symbolize this energy into a new expressive form. In doing so, it identifies, and, in turn, neutralizes the energy that is driving him—the aggression—integrating it into an act that is socially productive. A threefold change occurs: a new object is identified on which the person's interest now centers, a new social and productive goal is recognized, and a different kind of energy is used through which this goal is attained (Henley, 1986; Kramer, 1971/1992; Waller, 2006).

Salvador's new means of expressing himself required the displacement of aggressive drives into very focused and detailed imagery. The very act of art making neutralized his restless, explosive impulses, integrating them into creating social, seemingly benign, works. His original goal, to release his frustration, fear, and anger by causing harm and damage, has now been supplanted by a new goal: express his frustration, fear, and anger through an accepted art piece—and creating these pieces require *all* of this energy.

As has been made clear in previous chapters, not all sublimated expressions are socially acceptable; they simply have to be socially productive. One simple example may be seen through the clear differences between vandalism and graffiti. Both may be conducted by the restless, bored, aggressive, misunderstood, and frustrated adolescent. Yet, if the cathartic energy that drives someone to destruction through vandalism can be rechanneled, displaced, and integrated, the results may be arguably a less destructive, more creative and colorful manifestation. Granted, graffiti is not considered socially acceptable—quite frankly, it is illegal. Yet it can still be considered as more socially *productive*. And so is Salvador's work. As he admitted, not everyone accepted his work, but creating the pieces is certainly a more productive—and safer—means of expressing and rechanneling his aggressive drives. Thus, his creative expressions feed off his aggression while they simultaneously displace, integrate, and diffuse it.

Humor as Aggression

The humorous elements of the art also bear this out. DiCioccio (2012) recognized that humor could be—for ill or for good—a form of aggressive communication. Freud (1960/1989) recognized humor as disguised aggression. Whereas violence and rage are a primitive and impulsive reaction, an attack through humor requires a refined and more sophisticated response. It doesn't make the attack any less potent, as some of the artists from the Holocaust demonstrated in Chapter 4. Humor can be just as attacking as blatant aggression, but it does so through a more productive and acceptable, even disguised manner. Such expression redirects and sublimates the hostility rather than catharting it—it provided Salvador an opportunity to regain control even when it's been wrested away. Kotthoff (2006) recognized that using humor allows a person to regain a sense of control, wresting it from those seen by society as hierarchically superior. Recognizing that humor is a "double-edged sword," Meyer (2000) argued that while humor can be both a uniter and divider, it serves as an effective means of communication, providing an opportunity to regain power and a potent way of getting the message across. Through humor "[c]ommunicators imply that others' actions . . . are . . . unacceptable, and hence worthy of opposition in the form of discipline by laughter. . . . [V]iolation is stressed over normality" (p. 326). By finding the humor in a serious situation power is regained and the powerful made impotent. This is no less applicable here.

Salvador's work became a more productive and effective means of attack and control through his humor. The very nature of his caricatures was an aggressive confrontation and criticism of the systems in which he found himself. Protesting and taking rooftop stands was unproductive, dangerous, and self-defeating. Instead, Salvador was able to express his frustration with, fear of, and disgust at the prisons and asylums that bound him through a much more constructive and effective manner. In turn, by creating images that are humorous, by creating a way to laugh at the powers that be, he has regained a sense of control over that which controlled him. And this resulted in less bloodshed.

A Caveat

Overall, this chapter argued that Salvador (Bronson, neé Peterson) embodies the essential benefits of art making on the quintessential archetype of the violent offender. While Salvador is not any less aggressive, he has certainly become less violent: simply through the act of sublimating and redirecting his aggressive impulses into humorous and pointed creative expressions, he has relabeled himself.

However, I am not naïve. I recognize that there were many instances during the time that he was creating his art that he displayed some acting-out against the system. Art making is not a panacea. Engaging in art, while valuable, did not magically turn aside his deviant behaviors. However, the ongoing pursuit of creating art over time provided awareness, redirection, restructuring, and an acceptable voice where one was not available before.

Salvador recognized what art making meant for him, and he saw how important it would be for him to continue to create in order to find solace. But it's also important to recognize the reality of his situation. During the time of this writing, his girlfriend became his fiancée, then his wife, and then they divorced; it had not been easy. Salvador will continue to experience many frustrations and undesirable situations that could very well result in a less than stellar reaction. He seemed clear on this possibility and saw the battles he would likely continue to face. On the other hand, to the cynical, his recent peace-loving tendencies may have been a way to manipulate the system into believing he has redeemed his ways and is worthy of release. However, even this may be beside the point. Whether it is truly a redemption or merely an act, as long as Salvador continues his peaceful mantra and makes art, successfully channels his energy into his productions, and finds the proper audience and acceptance for his work, then he could very well be liberated—figuratively and literally.

7
Guernica
Painted from Violence, a Palette for Peace

Perhaps one of the most well-known works in the twentieth century was born from the anger and frustration—and I dare say impotence—that Pablo Picasso felt when the peaceful Basque town of Guernica was completely obliterated by aerial bombings during the Spanish Civil War. The resultant painting, *Guernica*, epitomizes one man's rage and fury in response to turbulent and violent political events. It emerged from violence and is a container for violence. It is also a weapon in the face of sheer aggression. As such, this painting became the template from which an art education program, The Guernica Children's Peace Mural Project, emerged.

Picasso's Evolving Palette

One of the most renowned and celebrated Western artists, Pablo Diego José Francisco de Paula Juan Nepomuceno María de los Remedios Cipriano de la Santísima Trinidad Ruiz y Picasso, or simply Pablo Picasso, created more than 50,000 paintings, sculptures, and prints. Picasso was born in 1881, the first child of a middle-class family in the Andalusian region of Spain. It was from his father whom he received his talented gifts; Ruiz Picasso was an artist, specializing in naturalistic representations. He taught for various fine arts colleges throughout Spain for much of his adult life.

Picasso started showing an early affinity for painting and drawing; as such, his father began training him before he was 10. When he was just 13, Picasso, a precocious yet undisciplined student, began attending the School of Fine Arts where Ruiz taught; he was later sent to study in Madrid. However, not enjoying the structure of school, Picasso stopped attending classes shortly after, but he continued to paint with alacrity. He visited Paris for the first time in 1900; for the next 4 years, Picasso would move back and forth between Spain and France until he ultimately settled in Paris, living there until he died in 1973.

Long synonymous with Cubist paintings, with whom he shared credit in conceiving with Georges Braque, Picasso was known for many creative movements and periods. Early in his career, Picasso focused on Realism in what some labeled his Modernist period. This was followed by the Blue Period, the Rose Period, and an exploration of African art, then known as Primitivism. This was followed by almost 20 years of Cubism and Neoclassicism. Ultimately, Picasso borrowed elements from all of these movements to complete one of his most famous paintings.

Although a volatile and often mercurial man who displayed his passions freely, nothing prior prepared the world for Picasso's visceral and creative reactions to the politically driven strife that surrounded him.

Burgeoning Unrest Turns into a Civil War

There was considerable turmoil after military dictatorship ended in Spain and the Republic was created in 1931. It was marked by a replacement of the moderate Republican government by a "coalition of Monarchists and right-wing Republicans" (Warncke & Walther, 2002, p. 387). By reversing many of the reforms that had been instituted, they prompted civil unrest which led to a massive revolt, including a subsequent strike by miners. This strike was bloodily suppressed by the military under the command of General Francisco Franco who was receiving support from Italy's fascist government. As a result the *Falange*, Spain's version of the International Fascist movement, was created in late 1934.

The Popular Front won the national election and came to power in 1936. Members of the Falange were not pleased. They attempted to destroy the workers' movement through various violent and incendiary methods. Open revolt began following the assassination of the Monarchists' leader. A civil war began in July 1936, with Franco leading the rebellious army. Beginning in Morocco, it quickly spread to Spain. On one side was the Republican government, supported by the Soviet Union and various smaller countries; the other side consisted of the Nationalists, Falangists, and anti-Republicans who were supported by Italy and Nazi Germany. At the forefront of this rebellion was Franco's growing army. This bloody conflict lasted for 3 years and claimed the lives of more than 1.5 million people.

Picasso's Response to Guernica's Destruction

Although living in France, Picasso strongly identified with his Spanish heritage. Decidedly apolitical up until this point, Picasso nevertheless sympathized with the legitimate Republican government.

At the beginning of 1937, Picasso was commissioned by the government to paint a mural for the Spanish Pavilion at the World's Fair, to be held that year in

Paris. His initial theme for the work was to be on the freedom of art. This was to change.

In April 1937, Falangist, Spanish, Italian, and German troops, led by the Nazis, destroyed the quiet, spiritually sacrosanct Basque town of Guernica, in less than 4 hours. There was no reason for it. The town provided no military value. They simply wanted to destroy it.

Picasso was enraged at this senseless destruction and its hundreds of casualties. His visceral anger needed a container. As a response he abandoned the original theme of the Pavilion's mural, and set out

> to work immediately on an immense picture, covering nearly 300 square feet of canvas. [H]e straightaway transformed the pictorial experience of a lifetime into a monumental protest against darkness and brutality. Picasso spent nearly two . . . months on Guernica. . . . [giving] his anger a free hand." (Raynal, 1953, p. 99)

Overwhelming yet not oppressive, the 11.5 by 25.4-foot *Guernica* covers an entire wall (van Hensbergen, 2004). Starkly painted in blacks, whites, and grays, it captured the emotional response and intensity of the slaughter (Figure 7.1). To further its starkness, Picasso used house paint with minimal gloss.

There is no narrative or explanation given about the story being told; there is no caricature or propaganda. He did rely on two of his signature images, his Minotaur and the Harlequin. Picasso often used the Minotaur to symbolize irrational power. The clown figure, partially hidden in the composition, cries

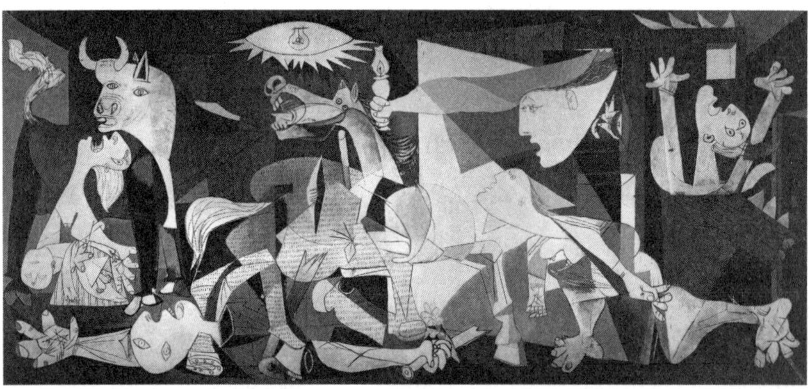

Figure 7.1 Pablo Picasso (1881–1973). *Guernica* (1951). Oil on canvas.

Collection of Museo Reina Sofía, Madrid, Spain. Permission provided by Estate of Pablo Picasso / Artists Rights Society (ARS), New York. Reproduction provided by Succession Picasso / DACS, London 2021 / Bridgeman Images.

a diamond-shaped tear. Traditionally symbolizing duality, Picasso relies on Harlequin to capture potential power over life and death, depicting an additional ambiguity and countermeasure (retrieved from www.pablopicasso.org/guernica.jsp). Yet, even still, the symbolic imagery is so generalized that it can be a depiction of any horrific wartime scene. "Any direct evocation of an identifiable contemporary reality or even a political grouping has been carefully avoided. . . . The meaning of the painting. . . lies in its representation of the destruction of human civilization of war" (Warncke & Walther, 2002, p. 398).

The composition relies on a synthesis of earlier Picasso styles. The monochromatic palette "echo[es] the old use of grisaille . . . the simultaneity of perspective and figures, the juxtaposition of linear and volumed representation, and varying frontal and profiled angle of vision, are all stylistic devices Picasso had already developed in earlier work" (Warncke & Walther, 2002, p. 398). Yet, along with the stylistic combination of surrealistic Symbolism, Primitivism, and Cubism, there seems to be a new element added—a childlike technique. "[T]he foundation on which the combination was established was the basic idiom of children's drawings. Children's principles determined his contouring, the use of detail motifs, and the perspective" (p. 400).

Drawing child-like imagery was likely unusual for Picasso; he did not do so even when a child himself. He began drawing and painting sophisticated compositions at a young age, possibly never progressing through a typical infantile development. Yet why did he choose such a style for this piece? Perhaps therein lies its emotional impact. This painting is composed of nothing but victims—beasts and people alike—caught in the helpless barrage that rained down on them. The vivid monochromatic contrast is an emotional assault on the eyes that is simultaneously felt viscerally in the soul. Yet it is the child-like innocence that communicates the gut-wrenching helplessness of these victims and, in turn, Picasso's impotence. It seems as if we are looking through the eyes of an innocent waif.

This painting emerged from one of Spain's most horrific and violent episodes of the mid-twentieth century, and it captures the hopelessness and helplessness that the people experienced. In that regard, it is art that emerged from a violent environment. But it also gave vent to Picasso's aggressive and visceral reactions to what he could not control. Begun as an exercise in explosive catharsis, it ultimately provided sublimation of all that was roiling inside him. His aggressive and angry energy needed to be dispersed elsewhere, and this painting provided its containment.

In 1995, almost 60 years after this painting's completion and 50 years after the bombing of Hiroshima, two art educators—one from the United States and one from Japan—decided to use the painting as a template with which to address and confront violence and destruction around the world.

The Guernica Children's Peace Mural Project

Art education professor Dr. Toshifumi Abe, from the Osaka Women's College in Japan, visited Dr. Tom Anderson, Professor of Art Education at Florida State University, in the early 1990s. Dr. Anderson knew no Japanese and Dr. Abe knew very little American English. However, with determination, enthusiasm, and help from a bottle of sake, a series of discussions ensued about the value of community murals to reflect, embrace, and champion local values, morals, and sensibilities.

Abe returned to Japan shortly after. However, their conversations stayed with him, germinating until June 1995. He called Anderson with an idea. Building off Anderson's community mural programs, he wanted to develop a children's mural project between their two respective countries to memorialize the 50th anniversary of the bombing of Hiroshima. It was to be held in 2 months time. "In partnership with Tadashi Yasuda of Art Japan, an arts and culture network, Abe initiated the project, and asked [Anderson] to collaborate on the Project Statement. . . . [It] articulated its hopes that through remembering the horrific results of the atomic bomb, such devastating warfare can be avoided now and forever more" (Anderson, 2002, p. 142).

In several conversations I had with Dr. Tom Anderson, I learned about the development and success of and the philosophy behind what became known as the Guernica Children's Peace Mural Project. The only parameters established for the mural were that it had to be the size of Picasso's painting. Abe believed that the symbolic impact of Picasso's anti-war statement would be considerably powerful; as Anderson indicated, "if you're going to do a peace mural project with an anti-war, paradigm," *Guernica* would provide the best template. It turns out that the similarities between Picasso's paintings and the children's murals were more than that of size.

The first mural was developed by children in Tallahassee, Florida, home of the university where Dr. Anderson taught (Figure 7.2). Its overarching theme focused on making the world a more peaceful place. A workshop was held during a local after-school program to encourage disadvantaged and troubled youth to "be productive and do meaningful things rather than get in trouble." These students had already created several murals around town; it was natural to invite them to participate in this new project. These 10 to 12 children, with the help and guidance of adult volunteers, "got a chance to express 'What peace means to me.' . . . [E]verybody got respected, everybody's opinion was heard."

Several people from Hiroshima, Japan, happened to be in Tallahassee at the time and agreed to speak with the students. As descendants of those who had experienced the dropping of the atom bomb on their city, they talked about how

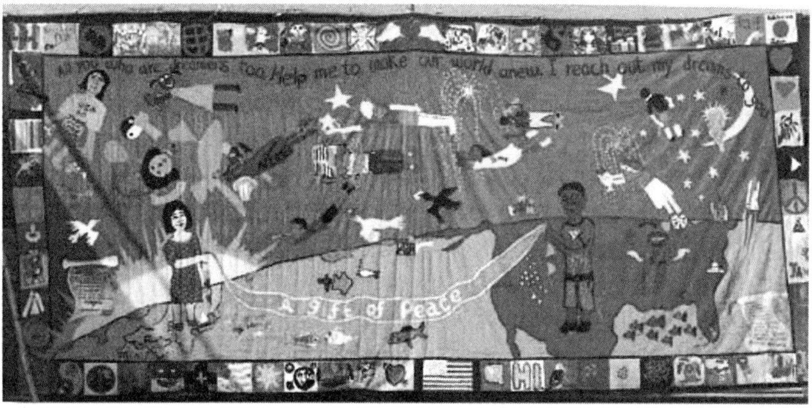

Figure 7.2 Guernica Children's Peace Mural Project. *Children of Tallahassee*. Paint on canvas.
Permission and Reproduction provided by Dr. Tom Anderson.

the tragic event affected their culture. One taught the students how to make paper cranes, an origami shape long associated with peace (Coerr, 1977). Over time, the students began to feel a connection with these people. As a result, they decided that, in the mural,

> they would send presents to Japanese children symbolically . . . we asked them "how are they going to get these presents?" Some of them had read a book called *Tar Beach* in which kids fly over the Brooklyn bridge. . . . And so they said "well, we'll just fly like they did in *Tar Beach*."

Together, the children mapped out the composition, with adults offering their support and suggestions. The children included themselves in their composition, holding the gifts they wanted to give to the children in Japan. "They're flying off from Florida over to Japan . . . all up in the sky [with] things like a chocolate milkshake, a chicken leg, a rap CD or cassette."

During the process, adults and teenagers alike learned about the importance of relationships—not only between the United States and Japan, but also with each other. To accomplish the final piece, they learned how to cooperate and compromise "on content, on size, on placement, on theme, just who's going to paint what. You have to agree, disagree, negotiate . . . and so within the group as well as extra-group . . .you have to develop these relationships." Furthermore, they came to understand "that other kids . . . are . . . like they are, and have the same hurt, the same joy, the same love, the same fear. But it's not only relationships [between] the kids, but with adults too."

After the painting was completed, a ceremony was held honoring it. Anderson next took the mural with him to Japan to visit Abe. Japanese children in their local schools were given an opportunity to view it, reflect on what peace meant from their cultural perspective, and create their own mural in response. Both murals were displayed in Donari-cho and Tokushima, Japan, with much fanfare and many dignitaries in attendance.

Given its success, Anderson and Abe approached colleagues around the world and set up a group that would expand their idea into a global project. What began as one mural sent to Japan became two murals that went to another country where its children responded; then those three murals went elsewhere; "so the two murals went on to Korea, I believe, the three murals went on to Papua New Guinea, the four murals went on to Australia, the five murals went on to Texas." At each location, the children were encouraged to think about what peace meant for them in relation to their own local issues and concerns. Or, as Anderson indicated, "One of our principles was to think globally and act locally." By doing so, each country would understand the issues of the previous country's people, *from their perspective.* As a result, each mural differed greatly from one another, each with a very different focus. Yet, while "the murals rose out of different conditions [it was] always with the overarching purpose of creating peace."

Similar to Picasso's *Guernica*, the murals addressed social and environmental violence. While Anderson had no love for Picasso, recognizing what a difficult—at times hateful—person he could be, the artist's painting embodied how valuable art making was to turn aside violence. "While Picasso was an a----, he created a wonderful painting that embodied the concept of peace; a lot of people in a lot of different cultures in a lot of different times have seen this representation." His painting reflected a local event that occurred in a small provincial town that few knew of and brought it to global attention.

At times, the context of the murals changed, and thus the responses from the artists. While the original mural was created to address a historical tragedy that occurred 50 years prior, other issues of conflict and violence were much more immediate. For example, "we had kids from Palestine and Israel painting a mural together in spite of the fact that they couldn't get across the border . . . [the facilitators] figured out a way to get kids from Palestine into Israel to paint and then back into Palestine." Some paintings were completed in Gaza and Afghanistan during their crises. Even in the heat of the violence, many of the murals focused on "making the world a better place in spite of the negative initiation. . . . We did a mural in India with blind children and they did their composition with yarn on the surface. And so you know, that's a kid that's coming from a difficult circumstance and working it out through art." For Anderson, that was the value of art. "It gives us the ability to express our feelings about life, about what is and what may be, and our values in relation to those considerations, and as such it allows us to deal with violence in a way that is not violent; in a socially sanctioned way."

But this was not always the case.

For example, one of the murals was painted in Kuwait by children who experienced the Iraqi invasion in the early 1990s (Figure 7.3). Unlike some of the murals that contained more hopeful or even innocuous messages, this one contained symbols of violence and war.

> They couldn't or chose not to take the tanks and the guns out of the imagery . . . there was a lot of violence. . . . You know, I never learned if they didn't understand the assignment or if [the uncontained violence] just bubbled up. They couldn't help it. . . . [S]o there was a lot of violence in that mural . . . but even when they were dealing with current problems, the point was to try and deal with them constructively and in a way that would contribute to peaceful coexistence. Because it's all about the relationships.

For some, the art provided an opportunity for reflective distance that allowed the recognition of relationships to emerge, to see the hopeful and the optimistic. On the other hand, some were so embedded in their violent context that they didn't have the objective opportunity to gain the space necessary to reflect and change.

Still, for Anderson, the nuanced differences between and among the participants melted away. The members of the different cultures recognized the local issues of each mural. While the violence the French experienced was very different from that of the Chinese or Japanese, there developed a universal

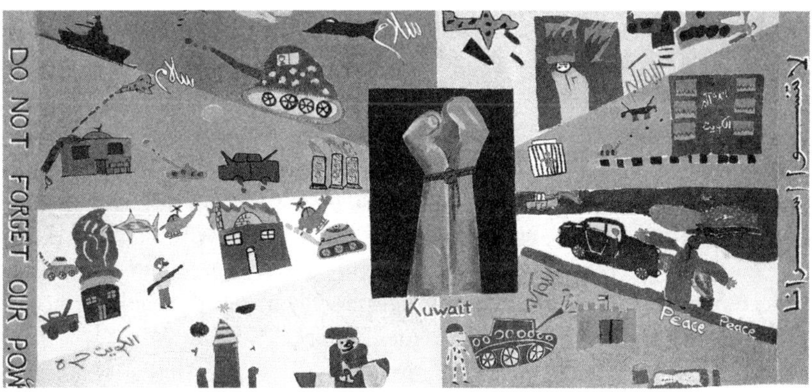

Figure 7.3 Guernica Children's Peace Mural Project. *Children of Kuwait.* Paint on canvas.

Permission and Reproduction provided by Dr. Tom Anderson.

understanding that "violence is violence . . . when you betray somebody, when you hurt somebody, when to try and gain power over someone . . . we all bleed." And giving the children that global awareness and understanding removes political influence: "it takes it away from objectifying," and it rehumanizes the other. As Anderson stressed, "stereotypes are not good for peace on earth. And so you know, what can we do to break down stereotypes that cause people to be afraid of and violent to each other?" For Anderson, the art was the "tool that we used to establish the relationships" that helped break down these divides. As artists, they used the tools they had available; the art provided them with avenues of expression to break through limitations, more so than those relying solely on words.

Anderson, reflecting on Susan Langer's (1941) ideas, recalled "that art brings to consciousness and holds for observation the subjective life of human beings in a way that's not didactic. . . and didactic speech and didactic actions are not philosophically value based. It gives instruction." By relying on language and words to attempt to explain something so inherently subjective, the concept can be minimized or may result in a lack of understanding or even acceptance.

Even still, when all was said and done, it wasn't about the art for Anderson. "The art was the medium and the product was the process itself." Harkening back to his initial discussions with Dr. Abe, Anderson underscored that it was the art that provided the connection between two people who couldn't understand each other, or, as he put it, "the art was the horse we rode."

Perhaps not entirely unexpected, working with art educators from all around the world did pose its challenges. Anderson remembered there were tensions at times. He ruefully acknowledged "there were times during this when I thought, 'I can see why the world can't get along because we in this peace project are having trouble negotiating with each other.'" Yet, while Anderson recognized that the tension was detrimental at times to the art making process, the art persevered and succeeded in spite of the difficulties; in essence, it simply could not die.

Despite its struggles, the project has persevered, revealing new ways for art making to create connections. For its 10th anniversary, a mural project was completed and subsequently an exhibition was held on the Indonesian island of Bali. As Anderson recounted wistfully, "Indonesia was occupied by the Japanese and the Japanese did bad things to the Indonesian people. And the 10th anniversary was held on the date that Indonesia declared independence from Japan. And a huge contingent of Japanese people were there—it was goosebumps city." While Anderson has since retired and is only peripherally involved with the project, it carries on with former students, colleagues, and friends.

Yet, even still, while the title of the project came from the similarity in size of the murals to their namesake, there seems to be several other parallels between Picasso's *Guernica* and the children's paintings. In my opinion, it is these similarities that likely resulted in their impact and success.

The Children's Palette Parallels Picasso's Painting

Although there are obvious differences between Picasso's landmark canvas and the output from children around the world, there are several striking similarities. The original *Guernica* painting depicted an event that occurred in a provincial town, destroyed despite its lack of any real military or economic importance. By painting his mural, Picasso raised awareness of the event worldwide. Picasso painted it for the Spanish Pavilion at the Exposition Internationale des Arts et Techniques dans la Vie Moderne, which boasted pavilions sponsored by countries from around the world, including Italy, Germany, the Soviet Union, and Canada. His painting had a decidedly multi- and transcultural audience, and his message overcame all national and cultural constraints.

The Children's Guernica Mural Project, as Anderson indicated so aptly, focused on amplifying the local to reflect global conditions; the children considered topics that addressed "a local theme, like the village garbage dump." However, once that mural went to another country, its message would be viewed and understood through the lens of *those* children, who then responded with their own design. In this manner, their messages became generalized and universal. This provided an opportunity to validate the artists, to give them a sense that they were seen and heard, and it turned their impotence into constructive communication. This, in turn, facilitated cross- and transcultural acceptance and understanding.

Picasso's painting successfully channeled his impotent rage through a composition that was simultaneously ambiguous yet powerfully resonant. The ambiguity and generalizable symbolic content allowed it to be internalized by all viewers. The specific event of Guernica was the catalyst from which emerged an anti-war, anti-violence message that resonates across countries and across time. Similarly, the children's murals resonated across all cultural strictures by communicating their message through generalizable symbolic imagery rather than didactical or lexiconic language.

Part of what amplified the universal messages of these works was the childlike quality in which they were painted. While Picasso's painting was an amalgamation of many of his previous aesthetic styles, some have argued that what gave it the greatest impact was its childlike, unsophisticated nature (Warncke & Walther, 2002). It was through this device that the helplessness and destroyed innocence resonated and could, in turn, be repaired.

With the children's mural, it is the fact that they *are* children that make the message so potent. It is obvious that not all of the children were at the same developmental level. Yet, rather than being detrimental to the process, the different developmental levels reinforced the images' authenticity and validated the children's processes and messages (Anderson, 1997). Their messages were more visceral, intuitive, instinctual, and primitive, which, in turn, made them most impactful. The children were able to reflect on their notions of peace and respond in voices purer than those of adults: innocence and naïvety led the charge. While adults facilitated and organized the project, they allowed the process to unfold naturally. The message was the children's, with no filter. Through this, the viewer is reminded constantly of the real victims of societal violence and aggression.

Ultimately, Picasso and these children relied on art as a tool to strike back. Through their respective processes, they regained control, facilitated connections and community, and helped make sense of the senseless. This helped mitigate the helplessness, fear, frustration, and anxiety that emerged from overwhelming circumstances. To traverse all of this, they used art: "It was [t]he vehicle—not the end, but the vehicle" (Anderson, 2002, p. 150).

8

Continuing the Dance

How Art Therapy Both Reveals and Mitigates Violence and Aggression

"Eric" was an 11-year-old boy seen in private practice. He was referred to art therapy because he needed a therapist who could address his anger. He was White, slight in stature, and dressed in baggy slacks and oversized shirts. His parents were divorced. He lived with his mother and saw his father inconsistently once every several weeks. He was on medication for attention-deficit disorder.*

He talked about his admiration for rappers and hip-hop musicians, and he would often recite some of their more aggressive lyrics. Eric's presenting concerns were difficulty following directions at school and "acting out" behaviors toward his mother at home, problems that were perpetuated by further inappropriate outbursts. Difficulty at school resulted in additional belligerence, causing Eric to get into trouble with his mother—the cycle was continuous.

Eric's affect was flat and blunted when he arrived for the first session. He was controlled in both his behavioral presentation and in his drawing style. When he spoke, he told fantastical and exaggerated stories and required constant redirection. As the sessions continued, he began to exhibit more aggressive and resistive tendencies. During one early session Eric expressed his displeasure through loud outbursts of anger and resentment, ripping up the paper in front of him. In another, he spent the entire time sullenly sitting with his face turned toward the wall saying very little.

When Eric was in a good mood, he exhibited a wicked sense of humor. He once came to a session with yellow "caution" tape taken from a construction site wrapped around his forehead and arms. Still, he had difficulty focusing and needed several prompts to stay on task.

Eric was consistently reminded of expectations and was responded to with patient but firm redirection. Eventually he was able to begin each session with

* The first part of this chapter is adapted from two of the author's previous publications: Gussak, D. (2006). Symbolic Interactionism, aggression and art therapy. In F. Kaplan (Ed.), *Art Therapy and Social Action* (pp. 142–156). London: Jessica Kingsley; and Gussak, D. (2016). Aggression and art therapy: A social interactionist perspective. In D. Gussak & M. Rosal M. (Eds.), *The Wiley handbook of art therapy* (pp. 329–336). Oxford: Wiley-Blackwell.

a description of what happened during the week followed by a quick check-in drawing. After a few rapid, energetic drawings, which were generally superficial and schematic, he was able to sit and address the tasks at hand.

He enjoyed creating three-dimensional forms. During one session, Eric was asked to create a sculpture with polystyrene blocks that were used for packing material, large Popsicle sticks, and paint. He worked diligently on the project. At first it was difficult to ascertain what he was creating, but eventually he indicated that it was a torture chamber (see Figure 8.1) and that he got the idea from a program he watched with his father on television the night before. The image is quite graphic.

The poorly developed human form lies on top of what appears to be a torture platform. Jutting out and through the form are sticks, painted in red, which highlight the places where they emerged from the figure. Eric knew the sculpture was graphic, and he was surprised when it was placed carefully on a shelf, accepted, and undisturbed throughout his remaining sessions.

After this pivotal creation, Eric talked more in sessions. Although he would have periodic episodes of aggressive outbursts, he disclosed more about the incidents that made him angry at school and at home. He spoke about the way he responded to his mother and various ways he could handle difficult situations with his parents.

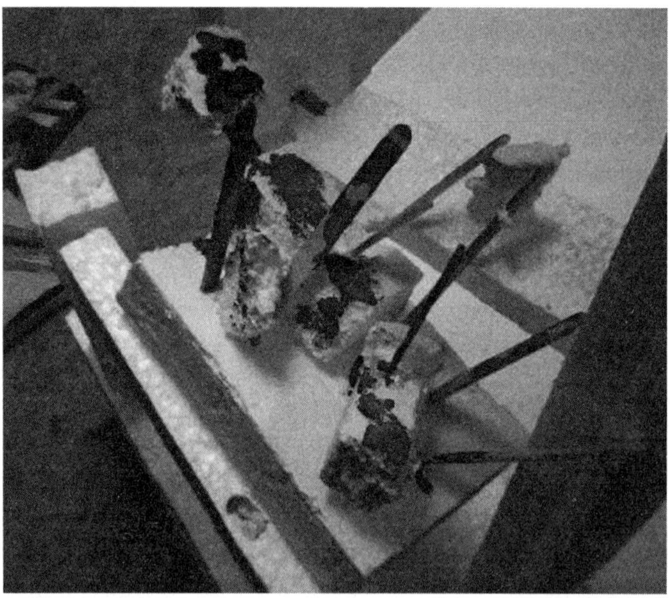

Figure 8.1 "Eric." *Torture Chamber.* Polystyrene blocks (packing material), popsicle sticks, and paint.

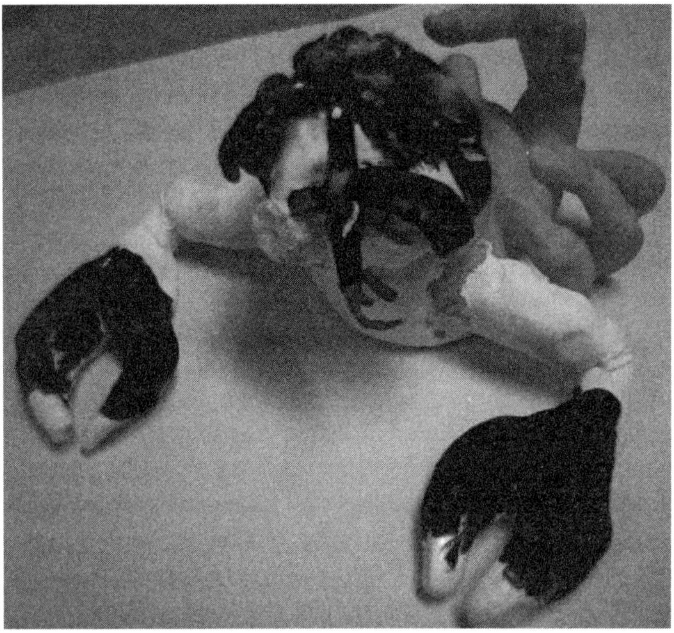

Figure 8.2 "Eric." *Anger Beast.* Model magic and paint.

In one session, he described his anger as a separate animal. He was asked to sculpt what his anger beast would look like. Using sculpting compound and paint, he created the *Rastafarian-Scorpion Anger Beast* (see Figure 8.2).

This sculpture was completed with a large E on his chest (his own initial). Unlike the torture chamber, he took his time with this piece; it was meticulously constructed and painted over several sessions. He immediately started working on the piece upon arrival at each session. After the sculpture was finished, he proudly showed it to his mother and explained to her what it was. He used the piece to verbalize his frustrated and aggressive feelings. Essentially, this final art piece reflected the "self" presented in an acceptable fashion. It was a side of him that he took pride in, albeit still a reflection of his aggressive nature. Over time, Eric found he was able to speak more about what was upsetting him. While by no means perfect, he eventually developed stronger coping skills and a much more authentic self-identity.

It Needs an Art Therapist

During a presentation in 2014, I emphasized that although the book *Art on Trial* relied on the drawings of a man on trial for murder as evidence of a mental illness, it was not about art therapy. However, a colleague with whom I was presenting argued that "while it is not about art therapy, it needed an art therapist to write it." He explained that although it was not about a therapeutic intervention, nor did it present a clinical trajectory, it required an art therapist to recognize the insights and nuances of what the art revealed.

Like that book, this book was not intended to be about art therapy, but I drew from my identity as an art therapist when writing it. The previous chapters introduced and illustrated the relationship of art and art making by violent and aggressive people and the creations of those within violent environments. Until this chapter, art therapy has only been addressed peripherally in the Introduction to provide a context for understanding the relationships between the psychological and sociological aspects of violence and art making.

Yet I realized that although not an art historian or a criminologist, I could draw on my experiences as an art therapist, particularly one who works with violent and aggressive clients, to examine the sociological contexts, psychological dynamics, and aesthetic results of violent artists and artists in violent environments. Conversely, it is these understandings of the natural relationship between art and violence that allowed me to examine the value of art therapy to address the cycle of violence.

Therefore, as the book progressed, I believed there was a need to provide a chapter on how art therapy has been used to address aggressive and violent people. In order to inform a wide audience—the non–art therapist, the neophyte, and the advanced clinician—this chapter provides a brief and simple introduction of art therapy followed by an overview of an early debate that framed the field, how this dichotomous perspective has evolved into various psychodynamic perspectives and approaches, and the evolution and adoption of the theoretical orientation that guides my own work. Experiences of art therapy with violent clients illustrate how this adopted epistemology has been applied, followed by a brief summary of the overall benefits of art therapy with violent and aggressive people. The chapter concludes with a section examining the various ways that art therapy has been effective for those within violent environments.

Art Therapy: A Working Understanding

The American Art Therapy Association's website defined art therapy as

> a mental health profession that uses the creative process of art making to improve and enhance the physical, mental and emotional well-being of individuals of all ages. It is based on the belief that the creative process involved in artistic self-expression helps people to resolve conflicts and problems, develop

interpersonal skills, manage behavior, reduce stress, increase self-esteem and self-awareness, and achieve insight. (http://www.arttherapy.org)

Early understanding of art as a therapeutic intervention spanned a long continuum between two rather diverse theoretical applications: art as therapy, focusing on the process of art making, and art psychotherapy, focusing on the finished created product (Gussak & Rosal, 2016; Kramer, 1971/1993; Naumburg, 1966; Ulman, 1992). While some may use the final product to explore therapeutic issues, mental wellness, and defenses and as a catalyst for communication, others may rely on the properties of the materials and art making process to develop a therapeutic trajectory. Early debates raged over these two divergent viewpoints.

Ulman (1992) proposed a synthesis of these two perspectives; rather than relying merely on one end or the other, art therapists can instead traverse the continuum as needs arise. As this conciliation was accepted, an understanding slowly emerged that art and art making can be simultaneously therapeutic and informative: *how* the art therapy is practiced depends on the setting and the clinician's theoretical orientation.

Recognizing the various characteristics of art materials available and the degree of structure within an art directive (Lusebrink, 1990), an art therapist can facilitate expression, catharsis, and sublimation of aggressive and libidinal impulses (Kramer, 1971/1993). Adjusting the materials and directives can also potentially increase problem-solving and self-awareness, improve mood, and increase internal locus of control (Gussak, 2006, 2009b). Eventually, it can validate an individual's sense of self-worth (Garai, 2001) or can alleviate anxiety through centering or grounding (Fincher, 1991; Rhyne, 1973/1996). And all of this can occur without verbal interaction or even tacit understanding (Gussak, 1997b, 2019).

At the same time, with varying degrees of effectiveness, the completed piece can provide a catalyst for uncovering subconscious or unconscious thoughts and beliefs for the one who created it (Naumburg, 1966). The final product can also serve as a burgeoning self-object or transitional object to enable a healthy individuation process (Robbins, 2000), expedite communication, increase self-worth, and support the development of self-awareness and identity (Gussak, 2019). In the long run, the collected products resulting from several sessions can provide a permanent record of the therapeutic trajectory that can be used as a map of progress.

While initially art therapy arose from a psychodynamic genesis, a variety of theoretical orientations have been developed that help frame the various ways that art therapy can be applied and provide vocabulary on its effectiveness. Along with various psychodynamic perspectives, this book's Introduction drew on the theoretical orientations of cognitive-behavioral therapy and neurological and neurobiological considerations, both of which have provided the scaffolding for particular art therapy approaches. In addition, over time, art therapy has been viewed through the lens of Jungian/archetypal analysis (Abbenante & Wix, 2016; Swan-Foster, 2017), humanistic and phenomenological perspectives (Betensky, 1995), transpersonal and mindfulness approaches (Franklin, 2016; Isis, 2016), person-centered approaches, and social justice and advocacy movements (Talwar, 2016, 2018), to name just a few.

Object Relations to Social Interactionism: A Personal Transition

Mirroring the theoretical orientation of my own art therapy education, my initial epistemology relied on an *object relations* perspective to potentially explain dynamic and volatile interchanges and how art therapy can help alleviate these concerns. Some theorists recognized the natural marriage between object relations and art therapy. Klein had already underscored how art making can help repair a poor object relationship in order to facilitate a healthy individuation (Waller & Dalley, 1992). "The artist's aim is to recreate a new reality . . . [and] is therefore able to re-create the phantasy and to give it life in the external world. This process mirrors the small child's acknowledgment that the mother has an independent life of her own. The basis of the urge to paint, in Klein's view, lies in this desire to make reparation for the destructive infantile feelings toward mother" (p. 14).

Similar to how Klein used toys in her therapeutic interactions with children, Dalley (1990) argued that the art process provides a safer means of expressing rejection and aggression that emerges from a poor object relationship. In turn, the art, as a securely protected and safely accepted container for what the child is communicating, can become the catalytic object from which trust, security, and eventual rapprochement can emerge.

Adapting and applying Winnicott's transitional phenomena (1951, 1971), Waller (2006) further recognized how a child's created art piece can serve as a viable transitional object between the therapist and the child. This promotes the child's *transition* from their usual insecure attachments to developing more secure ones. Reflecting on Winnicott's "squiggle game," in which the therapist and child engage in a joint drawing (alternating who will take the lead in scribbling a line on the page for the other to follow), Waller emphasized that "the child is able to express and share emotions and to learn new patterns of relating . . . leading to becoming more confident and reactive" (p. 277). Eventually, the child internalizes a new sense of control, thus mitigating his or her anxiety, fear, and aggressive responses to uncertainty.

Others have successfully explored how art therapists can mitigate narcissistic injuries that are aggressively and violently expressed through the object relations lens (Waller, 2006). Lachman-Chapin (1979) was an early proponent of applying Kohut's theories of narcissistic development and injury to interactions in the art therapy studio. She believed that the art therapist could serve as an empathic nurturer who could facilitate the development and acceptance of art pieces as self-objects. These could, in turn, become containers for individuals' initially rejected grandiosity and exhibitionism. Eventually these objects would become catalysts for cohesion of the self.

One art therapist, Ferrara (1992), applied this lens when working with adolescents in a residential treatment facility. These children had narcissistic and regressive tendencies that manifested in emotional and behavioral problems. The artwork of one of her clients served as self-objects "that helped nourish his inner self and emotional needs and promote personal growth" (p. 49). In another example, Sholt and Gavron (2006) applied an object relations model to explore how clay work facilitated catharsis, revealed unconscious dynamics, and induced regression for the sake of ego development—steps necessary to begin healing the object relationship between the child and the mother *imago* to facilitate individuation.

I initially relied on object relations to examine how art therapy can help explore object relationships to facilitate a productive separation-individuation process for healthy identity formation (Blos, 1962; Fox, 1997; Gussak, 1991, 1997a; Waller & Dalley, 1992). However, over time and through exposure to new and various viewpoints, my epistemology began to evolve and take on new dimensions. I have come to transition from the psychodynamically oriented object relations approach to a sociological perspective, embracing the *social/symbolic interactionism* and *labeling theories* to explain the value of art making and art therapy with violent and aggressive clients. For me, this orientation has provided a more satisfactory framework by which to understand how a social context can perpetuate an aggressive and violent identity, and, in turn, how art making can provide long-standing change and facilitate acceptance and relabeling. For that matter, from my perspective, this epistemology became the ideal lens through which to examine and understand the relationship between violence and art within and between social, cultural, and political contexts.

Revisiting Social Interactionism as an Art Therapy Epistemology

The Introduction further delineated how social and symbolic interactionism, as a theoretical orientation, can help provide a framework for understanding the propagation and maintenance of aggressive and violent tendencies. Furthermore, it explored how art making may help alleviate or redirect violent and aggressive energy. Such perspectives have guided my own understanding of how art therapy becomes instrumental in working with violent and aggressive clients.

To recap, through new interactions, new meanings emerge, and, in turn, if accepted and shared, a new label can be created. Violent and aggressive tendencies can be halted and perhaps even reversed by redefining and reinforcing new actions. This can, in turn, lead to the emergence and securing of new identities. Art and art making have been found to initiate and support this process (Gussak, 2019).

Mead (1964) argued that interactions do not have to be just between two people, but rather also can occur between a person and an object. Blumer's assertion bears repeating: meaning that arises from such interactions is "not intrinsic to the object but arises from how the person is initially prepared to act toward it . . . objects—all objects—are social products in that they are formed and transformed by the defining process that takes place in social interaction" (1969, pp. 68–69). It is through using, sharing, and interpreting the use of objects that action and interaction are defined. Such objects include art—art made by others and art made by oneself (Becker, 1982; Gilmore, 1990). By interacting with materials in the making of an artwork, interacting with the piece, and relating with another through the shared meaning of a completed art product, a person may initiate a process of redefining him- or herself.

Once again, the art therapist can use this to help facilitate therapeutic change. The art—the process and the final product—can be used to develop appropriate interactions and decrease aggressive tendencies. As the sessions continue, the art that is made is accepted by another—the therapist. Eventually the person comes to recognize that, by extension, he or she is accepted. Once a client feels validated, the work may begin to evolve into more complex imagery and investment in the process, potentially deepening the interaction and relationship between the therapist and the client. This, in turn, can further alter the violent identity.

Often, simply teaching a client how to use art materials for self-expression creates a new mode of interaction. "Mastery of art materials promotes a new sense of self-worth apart from previously established deviant and negative identities" (Gussak, 2019, p. 54). This process helps create a scenario whereby new interactional patterns begin to occur.

It is worth reinforcing that art can provide the means to interrupt the cycle of aggression by (1) strengthening a sense of self; (2) providing an avenue to express negative emotions such as distress and sadness, which when unchecked can result in anger and aggression; (3) creating new meanings; and (4) tapping into empathic responses (Gussak, 1997a, 2004a; Gussak, Chapman, Rosal, & Van

Duinan, 2003). Developing empathy becomes crucial in mitigating hostile and violent aggression against another; once another's perspective is recognized, understood, and accepted, in turn recognizing the other as an autonomous being, it would be difficult to intentionally cause harm. Initiating and maintaining interaction through the shared meaning of art and the art making process promotes empathic relationships. In making art, the artist will anticipate "how other people will respond, emotionally and cognitively, to what they do" (Becker, 1982, p. 200) further reinforcing empathy and perspective.

Accepting the potency of social interaction in facilitating change does not have to operate in a theoretical vacuum. Regardless of what psychological orientation a therapist emerges from—cognitive, humanistic, psychodynamic, or social justice—it can still be accepted that the *interaction* and meaning derived from this can facilitate relabeling and identity formation, eventually creating therapeutic change.

The case of Eric reveals how the art therapy process, and its relationship with the final product, helped facilitate a new identity and therefore a change in behavior. Certainly, other theoretical orientations could be applied to inform the development of Eric's aggressive and violent tendencies. Specifically, neurobiological influences seemed evident through his potential diagnosis of attention deficit disorder; such difficulty resulted in frustration and loss of focus and control, emerging through poor impulse control and angry responses. Those subscribing to self-psychology and object relations perspectives would recognize that developing a false self in response to his familial difficulties simultaneously helped create an armor to keep people at bay while reinforcing a narcissistic force that he could not or should not be (conceivably) harmed (Horney, 1945/1992): this emerged literally through the caution tape and metaphorically, through his behavior. In turn his art processes allowed him to express his own grandiosity without fear of judgment thereby potentially mitigating any anger and tension resulting from nonacceptance (Lachman-Chapin, 1979). Various cognitive and behavioral interventions were attempted to help formulate new problem-solving skills and strengthen an internal locus of control. Yet I would argue that it was through social interaction that his cycle of aggression was interrupted and fundamentally transformed.

His interaction with the materials and with me began to formulate new concepts of self and helped him develop new definitions, new labels. Ultimately, it was this interaction with the materials and his products and my acceptance and validation of his finished pieces that allowed Eric to interrupt the cycles of aggressive identity by strengthening his awareness of self, thus creating new interactions and eventually relabeling himself. These new labels were further reinforced, first by his parents, and then eventually by others, perpetuating and maintaining a more productive and healthier identity.

Jason: Supremacy Transformed

Jason[1] attended the art therapy sessions as part of a study conducted on the efficacies of art therapy in correctional settings. He primarily worked with art therapist Lariza Fenner-Lux, under my supervision. He was 23 years old at the time and in prison for first-degree murder.

A prior member of the US Marine Corps, he shot someone after a drunken altercation in a bar. Self-identified as a "Nazi skinhead," he was a tall, lanky man covered with tattoos, including swastikas, SS lightning bolts, and eagles, culminating in a 4-inch cockroach on his head. He rarely smiled and would often spew profanities. He believed in "Aryan superiority" and was aggressive toward those from different cultures, often getting into altercations with African American inmates.

His aggressive identity was maintained through interactions with the staff and other detainees; he was labeled by the system as an incorrigible and hostile inmate, an identity that he seemed to revel in. Thus, his identity was firmly established by the time he was referred to the art therapy group to address socialization, anger management, and impulse control—three traits that the correctional staff did not feel he could possibly accomplish successfully.

While he enjoyed the activities, the other group members avoided him. He remained hostile to the African American inmates who made up the majority of his group.

Jason quickly exposed his aggressive nature. He grabbed a pen during the first group meeting and, acting out a stabbing motion, announced that he "could easily use it to puncture someone in the neck." It took several minutes to convince Jason to give the pen back—just short of having to call in reinforcements. He indicated afterward that he was only "playing."

It was only because of his enthusiasm for making art and his promises that he would follow the established parameters that Jason was allowed to stay in the group. As the group progressed, he became increasingly enthusiastic and more verbal. He interacted well with the others and even said, "I made friends with the oil pastels." At the end of the 8-week period allotted for his particular group he indicated that he was disappointed because he did not want the art therapy sessions to end.

Initially, Jason's primary visual vocabulary reflected his original identity as that of a white supremacist. One of the first projects involved completing an inside-outside origami box. The group members were asked to consider what facade

[1] This case is adapted from one first presented in Gussak, D. E. (2006). Symbolic interactionism, aggression and art therapy. In Frances Kaplan (Ed.), *Art therapy and social action* (pp. 142–156). London: Jessica Kingsley; and later for Gussak, D. E. (2019). *Art and art therapy with the imprisoned: Re-creating Identity*. New York: Routledge.

they showed others within the prison and what they were reluctant to reveal. The outside of Jason's box was covered with the Nazi SS symbol and a swastika.

Inside the box was a smaller one he made from scraps, with a lock drawn on it (Figure 8.3).

He said, "What you see on the inside, no one sees; if someone were to ever get in, they would see this." He turned over the inside locked box and on its surface were swirls of blues, greens, and black. He described these designs as "my true core of a whirlwind of emotions." He made it clear that he was inaccessible and that he hid behind his carefully honed identity. Even if someone managed to break through, there would still be a cyclone of emotions to contend with.

Over time, Jason was recognized for his exceptional creativity. This, in turn, provided an opportunity for him to be accepted by and connect more with others in the group. The lightning bolts he created were ultimately adopted by the group as symbols of unity and group cohesion rather than as SS iconography, as originally intended.

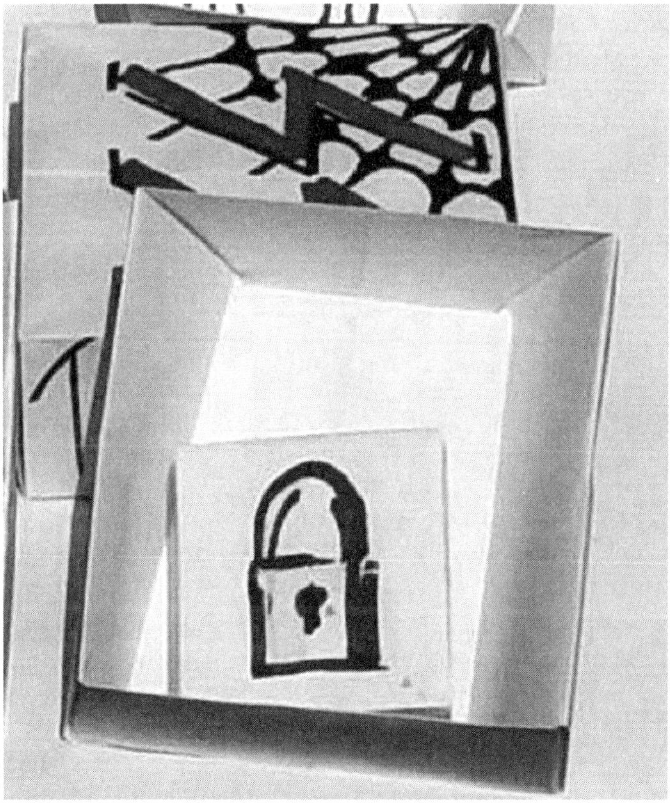

Figure 8.3 "Jason." *Inside Box.* Markers on paper.

During the second to last session he participated in a group mural on which the six members of the group drew their "self-symbols" (Figure 8.4). At the bottom corner of the mural, Jason drew two figures holding up the lightning bolts surrounded by two strands of barbed wire with a ring of fire in between. This image essentially separated Jason from the rest of the group and reflected his isolative and hostile identity. However, the rest of the men in the group used lightning bolts to reach out from their sections and penetrate the boundaries of his image. At this point, Jason responded by drawing lightning bolts coming from his image and permeating the space around him. Thus, he interacted openly with the others through a new, shared symbol. Although he remained isolated, the mural reflected his need for camaraderie; barriers were slowly being breached.

The group members were asked to draw a mandala during their final session. Each person was provided a round piece of paper and asked to simply draw within the circle. During previous sessions, Jason had sketched disembodied or free-floating eyes, some with tears dripping from their corners. On this final piece, Jason started with the same stylized eye. However, this time, he used the eye to begin drawing a face. Although the image was incomplete, he had begun to create a more cohesive self-image. Essentially, this final project illustrated what Mead (1964) described as the self, developing through appropriate social experiences and activities. Through positive interactions and acceptance that Jason found within the art therapy group sessions, his prior self-identity had slowly been replaced with one more accepted by the group members, and

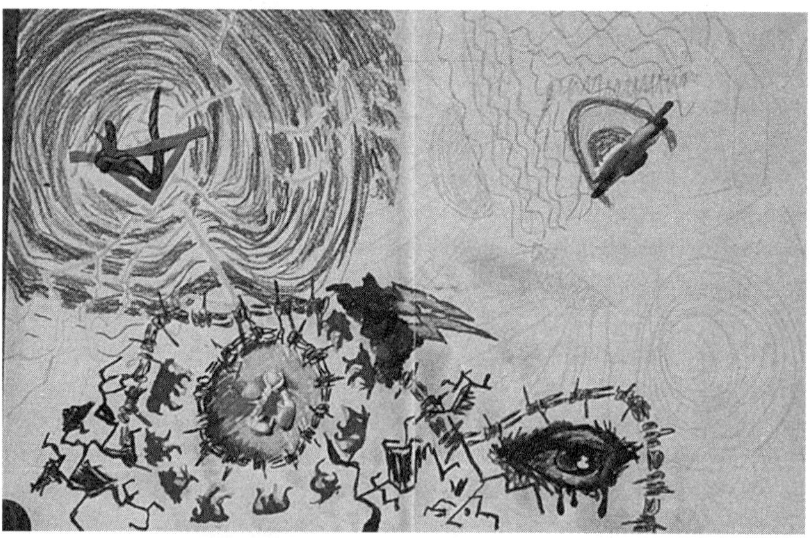

Figure 8.4 Prison group project. *Self-Symbol Mural.* Crayons, pastels, colored pencils, and markers on paper.

eventually by those outside the group. These images were shown to the correctional and mental health staff, and he seemed to relish the compliments he received. As time progressed, Jason became known for his art, drawing images that were quite different from his original sketches. While he maintained his *skinhead* persona—and changing that would entail more than shedding his tattoo-covered skin—his identity became so much more, and he was seen as greater than what his skin revealed. His interactions with his peers of other races and identities improved as he—in turn—saw them as more than skin-deep. The art provided a bridge to and between them.

Much of this book can inform the art therapist, particularly as it underscores the natural drive and value of art making for those who experience violence or act violently themselves. However, previous chapters also provided perspectives on art made by those described as incorrigible psychopaths, in particular serial killers. These chapters underscored that the art making did not offer any transformation in their violent tendencies; on the contrary, their art was used as a weapon against other potential and hapless victims. However, these seem to be more an exception than the rule. Some people, knowing what I do, question the value of using art with hardened criminals. When this arises, I retell the story of "Vince."

Vince: Art Therapy with a "Recalcitrant Sociopath"

Vince was first introduced in *Drawing Time: Art Therapy in Prisons and other Correctional Settings* (Gussak, 1997a). He has since appeared in many presentations and publications as an example of a person who seems so irredeemable that he does not earn the benefits such services offer. Vince, a middle-aged White man (who looked much older) was in a Northern California prison serving a life sentence for armed robbery and murder. He was clean-cut and neat, always making sure that his prison blues were well pressed. He was considered dangerous even by the correctional staff, and he seemed to embrace the identity given him: the *recalcitrant sociopath*. He walked with a swagger and was often confrontational and threatening. He expressed disdain for others, claiming intellectual superiority. He had a substantial record of assaulting other inmates and occasionally staff.

He had been arrested and imprisoned several years before I saw him. Vince had planned a bank robbery with a small gang for which he was the self-designated leader. Despite a fairly detailed scheme, he did not account for the bank's silent alarm. After one of the tellers triggered it, the police arrived in force. A gunfight ensued, resulting in one officer getting shot in the leg. Recognizing the hopelessness of his situation, Vince grabbed a bank employee hostage and fled the scene in his car. As the police closed in, Vince recognized the futility of his situation, but, rather than let the hostage go, he shot him in the head, killing him instantly. When asked later why he did this, his chilling response was simple: "If he was stupid enough to get caught as a hostage, he deserved to die." His callousness and lack of remorse was cited throughout his file. Vince was sentenced to "life without."

While in the prison's "general population" Vince attempted to kill himself by slitting his wrists, resulting in severe blood loss and a short-term coma. After he regained consciousness and was deemed healthy enough, he was transferred to the psychiatric unit where I worked. While it was not completely clear if it was indeed an intentional attempt, he claimed he tried to kill himself to demonstrate how "stupid the staff were" and that he was smarter than them. According to him, he was always in control; as a result, the staff would be unable to stop him from doing whatever he wanted to do, including killing himself. Throughout his stay on the unit he held contempt for the services offered, deeming them a waste of his time.

Because of Vince's obstinate rejection of some of the other services offered, the treatment team decided that he might benefit from art therapy services. It was thought that in this nonverbal group, Vince could do less damage.

Surprisingly, despite his feelings that such groups were a waste of time, he not only participated, he also strove to show that he excelled. This corresponded to his narcissistic beliefs that he could excel in anything he did.

Supplies were limited due to security risks; while three-dimensional art directives are often valuable as an intervention, clay could not be used. To overcome these limitations, other, safer materials and processes were offered. Papermaking was used in one of the groups that Vince took part in. The paper pulp could be molded and shaped, eventually drying into a three-dimensional form of the artist's creation. Although verbose and self-aggrandizing throughout, Vince willingly participated. Notwithstanding his well-established defenses, Vince's paper-making piece revealed his sociopathic dynamics.

Vince taped a wrinkled piece of handmade paper onto the second piece at the corner. On the top piece Vince wrote "Do Not Lift" (Figure 8.5). Of course, when the viewer does (for who wouldn't be compelled to do so?) they are faced with the message "Bite Me" (Figure 8.6). It was funny. I laughed. The officers laughed. The other group members laughed. On the surface, it appeared to be a simple practical joke. However, his aggressive dynamics were clearly reflected in this piece, albeit in visual form; whoever failed to heed the warning—whoever was "stupid" enough to disregard the sign—deserved the assault.

Vince's aggressive and violent tendencies emerged as a humorous attack against others'. Similar to Bronson and a couple of the artists presented in the chapter on the Holocaust, Vince was wielding humor to subtly attack others. In

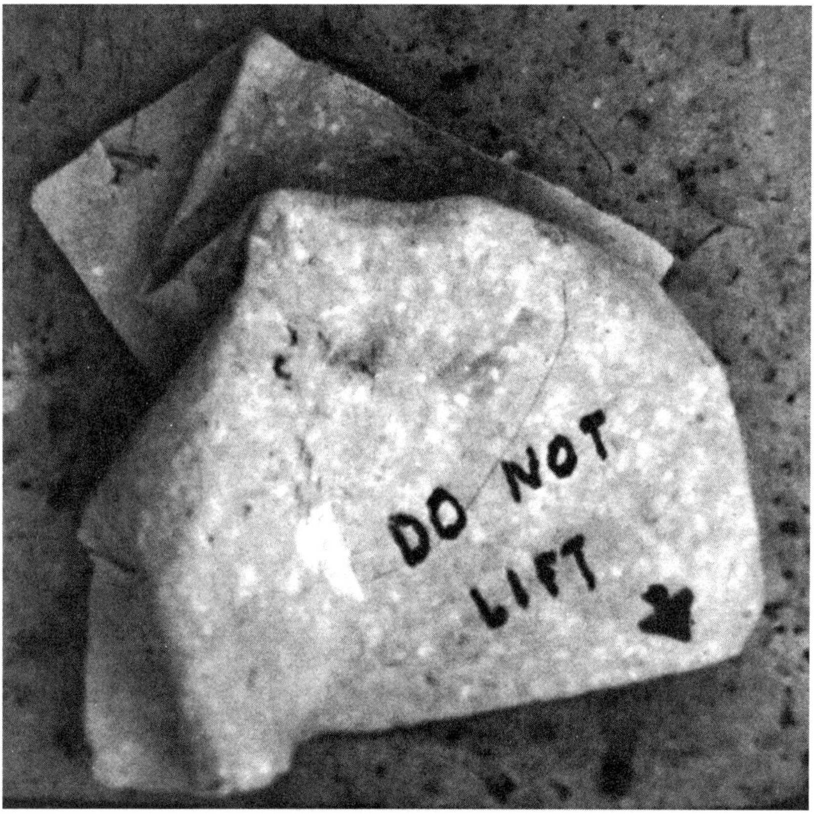

Figure 8.5 "Vince." *Do Not Lift.* Handmade paper and markers.

this manner, similar to many of the other people throughout this book, Vince used the art as a weapon. Vince did not change, nor would he—however, his violent attacks on others were rechanneled into a much safer expression. As I have continuously proclaimed since, "I have been attacked with a chair, and I have been attacked by someone's art—I would much rather be attacked through their art."

Several weeks later, Vince attended a session in which the art process involved making masks. This is a valuable directive that addresses identity and often reveals what is hidden from others (Gussak, 1997a, 2019). Again, given the limitations of the materials that could be used inside, the participants had to rely on paper plates to make these face coverings. Vince completed Figure 8.7, which portrayed the face of a demon, under which he wrote "Trust me."

A well-rendered image created in markers, the piece revealed Vince's increased investment in the process as he continued art therapy. This product

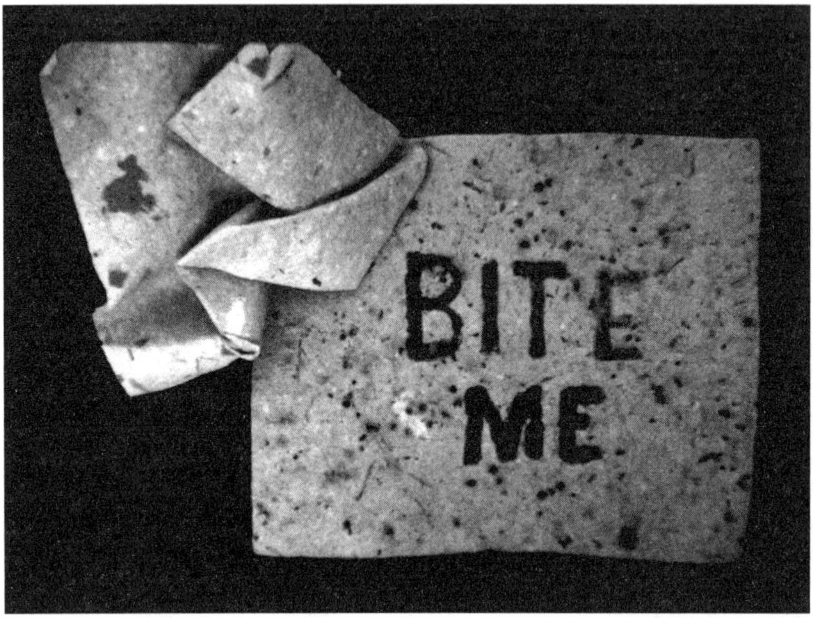

Figure 8.6 “Vince.” *Bite Me.* Handmade paper and markers.

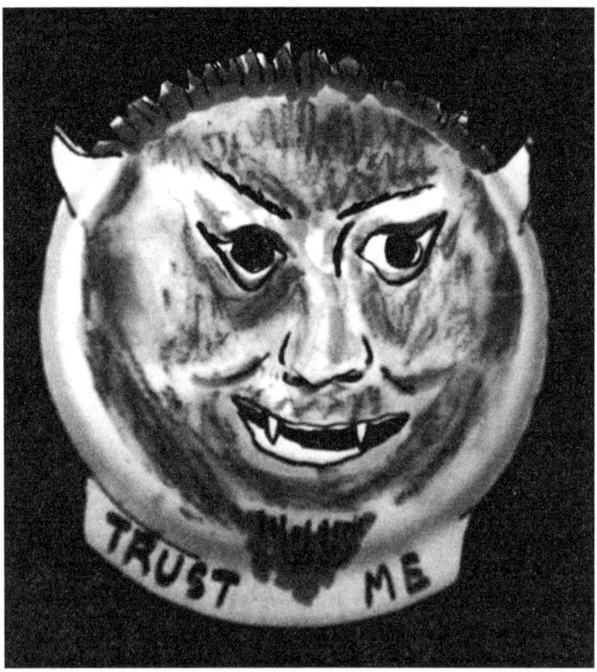

Figure 8.7 “Vince.” *Trust Me.* Markers on a paper plate.

certainly earned the accolades of others who saw it. However, once again, his dynamics were revealed—if you trust the devil, you deserve what happens. The difference between this piece and the papermaking product was that this message was much more patently transparent: while the derogatory insult in the previous piece was hidden under another sheet, this piece was clear right on the surface. While it continued to serve as an aggressive warning, it also demonstrated how much more open Vince was. He would likely never change, but art therapy helped by simultaneously revealing his dynamics and redirecting his violent tendencies.

Specific Advantages Delineated

What seems to have emerged over the years are several clear advantages of using art therapy in working with aggressive and violent clients.

- *Art therapists take advantage of the relationship between aggression and creativity.* As Dissanayake indicated, "the impulse that drives some people to violence are the same impulses that drive the artist to create" (1988, p. 139). Aggression may be considered a positive force by many psychological and sociological theorists but only if the impulse is properly channeled or contained. This brings us to the next point.
- *Art therapists can facilitate the catharsis and eventual sublimation of violent impulses.* While initially the violent energy may emerge through cathartic expression, if such energy is redirected, focused, displaced, and contained, the energy can be sublimated into a socially productive manifestation (Henley, 1986; Kramer, 1971/1993; Waller, 2006). Simply put, "imagination and artwork can help transform destructive aggression into constructive strength" (alavineshad, Mousavi, & Sohrabi, 2014, p. 115).
- *Art therapists can provide a means to express vulnerabilities, frustrations, and irritations even while not compelling clients to talk about them.* Often, frustration may arise when a person is unable or unwilling to explain what he may be frustrated by, or perhaps he does not wish to disclose his vulnerabilities to avoid appearing weak. Art making allows the disclosure and release of these feelings without requiring the ability or desire to put it into words. Banks (2012) recounted a case with a resident in a low-security unit for offenders. In "seeking security and containment [of his anger and aggression] . . . [she used] the art making process to help [him] develop the foundations of a therapeutic relationship . . . [the] freedom to express his feelings . . . and to experience not being judged by anyone" (p. 23).
- *Art therapists can offer mechanisms to help establish new labels.* People are defined by their labels; negative ones may perpetuate violent identities

(Bartusch & Matsueda, 1996). Eventually, people own these identities. It is through relabeling or reversing detrimental labels, validating new behaviors, and redefining the actions of those seen as aggressive that such tendencies can be halted and perhaps reversed. Art making may aid in developing appropriate interactions and create new self-labels, in turn decreasing aggressive tendencies (Gussak, 2007, 2019). If an artwork is accepted, by extension its artist is accepted. Thus, the final points.

- *Art therapists can help slow down the cycle of narcissistic rage.* The art therapy process can strengthen one's sense of self; provide an avenue to express negative emotions such as distress, which may result in anger and aggression; create new meanings; and tap into empathic responses (De Bethune & Linhardt, 2020; Gussak, 2004a; Gussak et al., 2003; Major, 2020). In addition, "art allows [the expression of] undeniable urges of the grandiose self and exhibitionistic desires without shame, thereby releasing tensions and nurturing creativity for future outlets" (Lachman-Chapin, 1979, p. 3). This, in turn, can reverse the narcissistic injury often associated with violent acts.
- *Art therapists take advantage of the bridge created between the individual and society through art, reinforcing a more productive identity.* Once a person is relabeled, a more productive, humanized identity is accepted; empathy is realized; and narcissistic rage is controlled. Their new identity is reinforced by the society at large through ongoing interactions. As a result, the person is not as compelled to express his frustrations through rage or devolve into aggressive tendencies.

And One More Thing . . .

While art and art therapy have been demonstrative in addressing aggressive and violent people, this book has also underscored that art is valuable in garnering self-expression in those who find themselves in violent environments. Art educators, facilitators, and therapists have found themselves working with people in the throes of communal and societal violence, becoming bridge builders and peacemakers (Gussak, 2002).

Thus, one other advantage emerged.

- *Art therapy can help bring order out of chaos.* Art therapists who work with those experiencing violent events understand that art has the power to induce a sense of peace (Chapman, Appleton, Anderson, Kapitan, & Gussak, 1997; Kapitan, 1997), allow a safe and healthy expression of anxiety and helplessness (Malchiodi, 1990), provide a means to communicate when

> words are just not available (Riley, 1992), and safely channel frustration and aggression (Kramer, 1971/1993). Art therapists recognize that art making can provide a secure way to interact and can allow participants to address anxiety and conflict in a safe way. It can provide a sense of mastery and control for people during a time when such feelings elude them. Art therapists can facilitate a sense of communal unity and belonging. "Well known in art therapy is that art transforms chaos into order. . . . Peacemaking can be learned in this relationship . . . especially in the art therapy setting" (Kapitan, 1997, p. 255).

In addition, art making has been used to instill a sense of peace by providing a holding environment for those who have experienced traumatic environmental upheavals. In 1992, Los Angeles erupted in violent riots, looting, and wanton destruction after the acquittal of the officers who beat Rodney King. Art therapists, recognizing that "words cannot express the impact of the images evoked by this crisis: the fires, the mobs, the beatings" (Riley, 1992, p. 139), volunteered to provide an opportunity for adults and children to express their feelings through workshops and expressive arts groups. As one of the art therapists indicated, "Art was helpful in this circumstance in externalizing their fears" (Riley, 1992, p. 143). The art allowed members of this community to communicate their experiences in ways that they were not able to do verbally.

In 1996, art therapists worked with survivors and traumatized victims of the Oklahoma City bombing that killed 168 men, women, and children. Art interventions were used to promote feelings of "sharing, caring, togetherness, security, and safety that had been so shattered" (Jones, 1997, p. 94). Art and art therapy provided a mutual language, a bridge, for those to feel that once again they could belong to a community, that they were not alone in their suffering.

Art therapists have relied on art in violent environments to overcome cultural barriers and provide a common voice within which healing can begin. Byers (1996, 1998) offered art therapy services for children, families, and mental health workers who experienced the violence of the West Bank and Gaza, in Israel, to establish "emphatic bridges among children of different backgrounds 'so that they may come to see that despite variations in living conditions, children everywhere have common fears, hopes and aspirations' "(1996, p. 240). The art therapy training and crisis intervention sessions offered a semblance of control and promoted empathy from which the cycle of violence could be diminished, with art furnishing a common language.

Stone (1998) successfully used art to address posttraumatic stress disorder (PTSD) in Spanish-speaking, South American women in Australia who were victims of torture. All of her clients indicated a profound impact on their sense of security. The art provided her clients a means to communicate their feelings of disempowerment, trauma, and victimization in a safe way and provided a means to overcome their own vulnerability.

For several years, the art therapy program at Florida State University, in conjunction with the University's Center for the Advancement of Human Rights, sent art therapy students to Thailand to work with victims of the sex trade. These women were part of a socially corrupt and violent environment that perpetuated the victim identity and reinforced the sense of helplessness and hopelessness that such crimes against nature fomented. These girls and women experienced art as a way to connect with their therapists and provide a means for them to regain a semblance of control and create a new identity—one of humanity and healing—within a structure bent on marginalizing and objectifying them. The art at least initiated the opportunity for them to become anew.

Following the bombing of the World Trade Center on September 11, 2001, art therapists mobilized to bring their services to those who suffered trauma to address their grief, loss, and fear (DiSunno, Linton, & Bowes, 2011; Gonzalez-Dolginko, 2002). Wise (2005), an art therapist specializing in trauma work, established the Saturday Project, a group art therapy program to work with children who witnessed the destruction in their nearby neighborhoods. Believing that "integrating the search for meaning with art therapy [is] helpful in lowering levels of anxiety" (p. 144), she found that, as the project continued, the attendees began to develop a connection with one another, a growing sense of support and openness that was lost following the tragedy. This resulted in a reduction of their anxiety and a "soften[ing of] their sense of isolation" (p. 153). Because of the quick and valuable response of art therapists following this violent act of aggression, Senator Hillary Clinton (NY-D) issued the following statement that has subsequently been entered into the Congressional Record:

> [S]ince the terrible tragedies of September 11, many Americans, both adults and children, have been forced to deal with a level of pain and anxiety that most people have never had to endure before. . . . [M]any of us have witnessed [art therapy's] enormous benefits in helping both children and adults alike express their emotions in a very personal, touching way. While nearly every person in our country has been irrevocably changed by that day's events, we know that children are particularly vulnerable to the long-term emotional consequences that often accompany exposure to trauma. One of the ways in which children have coped with the aftermath of September 11 is by reaching for their crayons, pencils, and paintbrushes to express some of what they are feeling. . . . These simple, yet heartfelt, drawings, which do such a wonderful job of expressing the complex emotional terrain that these children are navigating, have moved us all. Adults, too, have used creativity to help cope with the difficult emotions that so many are experiencing. I heard the story of a woman who was one of the last

people to be rescued from the World Trade Center rubble after being trapped for more than a day. She drew a picture while in intensive care of herself under the rubble with angels and God hovering above her. Another victim of the disaster drew pictures of flowers and spoke about how grateful she was to be alive. Although sometimes the healing qualities of art may be less tangible or obvious than its aesthetic qualities, they may be even more important. . . . [T]here are almost 5,000 trained and credentialed art therapists . . . among the army of mental health professionals who support those suffering from psychological trauma from the attacks, and undoubtedly will continue to serve the needs of individuals coping with subsequent stress disorders. (Art Therapy Recognition, 107th Congress, 2001)

Epilogue

Bringing the Dance to a Close

The intent of this book was to present the interrelationship between art and violence. Initially, the objective was to support an argument that art emerges from libidinal impulses such as aggression, and, in turn, art can help mitigate, control, or turn aside aggression and violence. Hence, as indicated in the Introduction, the intended title for this book was "The Frenzied Tango of Art and Violence."

I have to be honest: while many colleagues liked the title, a colleague from the Florida State University School of Dance clarified that perhaps my concept of the Tango was somewhat misunderstood. The premise of the title was built on my belief that there were only *two* partners—violence and art—engaged in a frenetic dance. In my vision, they were equally dominant and submissive with one another: sometimes one would lead, sometimes the other, sometimes they would change in the middle of a set routine, and, at still other times, both simultaneously fought to dominate the entire dance. To me, in my philistine ignorance, nothing captured a two-partner dance better than the Tango. So, while my colleague made it clear that the dance I imagined wasn't necessarily a Tango, I held onto the title because I still found it to be poetic. It stayed. Well, for a little while. The title was, in fact, undone in an unanticipated way.

It gradually became clear that the visual of the two-partner dance did not exactly hold up during the 7 years it took to research and write this book: what emerged was something much more complicated.

After the Introduction provided a brief summary of various theories on the genesis of aggression and violence and potential perspectives on its interrelationship with art, Chapter 1 provided examples of six violent and aggressive artists. In many of these cases, particularly those whose violent impulses arose out of narcissistic injuries—Caravaggio, Cellini, and Dali—the artistic drive arose from the same impulses that drove their violence. It could be argued that, in such cases, art making may have, in some ways, satisfied their grandiose attention-seeking and allowed them to circumvent these injuries that would have led to even further violence. Of course, it was not always successful because their violent and aggressive tendencies continued. Still, it seems the creative impulses arose from the same narcissistic genesis as their violence. And quite frankly, their art was *good*.

The remaining three artists demonstrated impulsive acts through the repression of self-control and restraint because of substance use or neurological/

mental health issues. In such cases, art became a means by which to perhaps mitigate and redirect the impulsive discharge of energy exposed by the reduction of effective resistance and defenses. In such cases, art making became a means to sublimate their aggressive tendencies, finding a way to redirect the energy into a socially productive form of expression. Here, too, art may not have always been successful, with the demons far too strong for their container; however, it could be argued that, without their art, circumstances could have been worse, and their creative drives benefitted from this aggressive, impetuous energy.

Messy as it was, and not always successful, the narratives still seemed to support patterns in which art emerged from the sublimation of libidinal impulses and narcissistic energy and was somewhat effective in containing the urges and compulsions.

Chapter 2 introduced six more artists—Goya, Beckmann, Nussbaum, Vann Nath, Traylor, and Rockwell—whose work emerged from their violent surroundings. More aligned with theoretical perspectives on how art and art therapy benefit those who experience trauma, this chapter explored how art arose from the need to escape and regain control in uncontrollable and helpless surroundings. Their art was their only weapon in time of war or civil unrest. In many ways, they, too, demonstrated aggressive propensities, reacting strongly and sometimes violently to their volatile surroundings. They were angry and reactive but ineffectual and at times impotent. It wasn't until they picked up a brush and creatively redirected the libidinal energy that emerged from their situations that they found a weapon by which they fought back.

So far so good: the title remained, in my view, an apt metaphor.

It was when developing Chapter 3 that the original allegory of a two-partner, binary relationship began to unravel. This chapter juxtaposed the art of an extremely violent and narcissistic man—Adolf Hitler—with the art of those who were the targets of his irrational hatred. The second part of this chapter held firm; the artists who emerged from the Holocaust, like those in Chapter 2, used their art to simultaneously strike back and maintain a humanizing identity while providing some solace and escape. Creating their works effectively undercut their predators' determination to eradicate any evidence of their existence and humanity. They fought back with the only tools and weapons at their disposal.

However, presaging the artists with sociopathic and psychopathic tendencies in the following section, Hitler's work brought into stark contradiction the presumed positive benefits of art making through his use of art to reinforce his own grandiose and domineering needs. Granted, as others have argued, if he was artistically adroit, he may have been satisfied with his art containing his self-aggrandizing narcissism, similar to several of the artists featured in Chapter 1. However, he wasn't and it didn't. The art was unable to redirect and contain his aggressive and violent predilections. Its rejection fueled his narcissistic injury.

Then, as I argued in Chapter 3, he *redirected* his artistic and creative predilections to build the dictatorial pedestal from which he wreaked political devastation.

> He portrayed what he thought an artist was supposed to be but without the emotional essence and connection. His desire to create was no longer to feed his own self-aggrandizing persona; it was to gain power and recognition in an environment where creating art was akin to superiority. However, as he could not succeed, it resulted in a narcissistic injury that has rivaled no other.

He then, in turn, used art as just one of many instruments to further his own debilitating and devastating objectives.

This section on Hitler provided a glimpse of what was to emerge in the next couple of chapters on the art of multiple murderers. In examining their endeavors in Chapters 4 and 5—admittedly two of the most difficult and disturbing chapters to write—I realized the original metaphor was no longer suitable for these people; it was incomplete. This became obvious through the glaring realization that while the drive for making art emerged from the same narcissistic genesis as their vile actions, art making did not dissipate, mitigate, or redirect their violence. It failed in ending their cycle of psychopathy. I argued that quite the reverse occurred—it reinforced it.

Unlike art makers who sublimate their aggressive energy into productive and transformative imagery, at a minimum, art making was merely cathartic for these murderers; at its extreme, they used their drawings and paintings as a monstrous attempt to resume their dominating, psychopathic actions.

Unable or unwilling to undergo an ego-driven transformation, their art emerged as an extension rather than a redirection of their perverse, primitive drives. In doing so, they tried to use their works to retain power over the viewer through fear, intimidation, and shock. Rather than reforming, they were reinforcing their barbarous identities. While their acts of self-validation, superiority, and power were halted through arrest and confinement, some continued to relive these self-inflating experiences by replicating their audacious crimes—literally or metaphorically—and violently attacking the viewer with their imagery. With no other tools at their disposal, they wielded their art to continue their campaign of fear, dominance, and destruction. There was a reason that these chapters were so difficult for me to write, why they took so long and pervaded my dreams. Long after they are gone, their art continues to linger. In almost a bastardized mirroring of the witnesses to—and victims of—violence in Chapters 2 and 3, the art of the multiple murderers lived on past their horrendous deeds.

To reconcile the damage this realization wreaked on my original metaphor, another participant in the dance had to be considered: art as a dangerous weapon. No longer a beneficial panacea, safe container, or catalyst for sublimation, the power of art was used to inflict, not repair.

Once I realized the existence of this more complicated interrelationship, the trajectory of Charles Bronson's transformation presented in Chapter 6 became clearer. His story revealed a much more complex process than originally understood. His art began as a means to confront and express his anger, frustration, and hostility through its literal narrations and humorous caricatures. As he began to embrace a new identity, no longer as Great Britain's most violent inmate but now as a "con" artist, his drawings became an expressive outlet. His art—emerging from the same libidinal drives as his aggression and predilection toward violent impulses—was transformed from a weapon of attack into an instrument of containment, mitigation, and sublimation. Furthermore, as his new art was accepted, so was he, thus facilitating this change in his identity from one of violence to one of acceptance and peace.

As Chapter 7 revealed, art educators Tom Anderson and Toshifumi Abe recognized this complex interplay when they used Picasso's pictorial dance of destruction and creation as a template to develop an arts program from which children could transform their own worlds. In response and reaction to violence against an innocent village, Picasso relied on his art as a weapon wielded against the perpetrators and, sublimating his own aggressive reactions, as a container for his own impotence and anger. From this emerged a method of facilitating change by guiding children who are experiencing societal and cultural strife to redirect their helpless and hopeless frustrations into a transformative message of peace. As an art therapist working with violent individuals, the ways in which art is fed by aggression and used to redirect violence constantly informs my work. As I explained in the final chapter, I came to learn when and how the relationship between art and aggression reveals itself through these complex interplays—as containment, expression, sublimation, humanization, and resistance or as a weapon. Through this, I learned when and how to facilitate the art process to either amplify or diminish these interrelationships. In essence, I learned when and how to help speed up or slow down the dance depending on the needs of the artist.

Thus, no longer could the image of a simple dance made up of two partners capture the complexity of this interrelationship between art and violence. It is much messier, frenzied, feverish, and chaotic. Perhaps a Tarantella?

Final Thoughts: Adjusting My Perspectives

During the process of researching for, reflecting on, and writing this book, two seemingly antithetical and counterintuitive notions emerged.

- Aggressive and violent impulses are not always bad
- Art making is not always good.

Many societal rules and therapeutic interventions seem to be built off the premise that aggression and violence are to be avoided or eradicated. This is easy to understand. My primary work has been built on working with violent offenders whose very actions have been crimes against people and property, often expressed through unchecked impulses. Inherent in these systems is the tendency to place negative and long-lasting labels on those who engage in such tendencies. What has naturally emerged is the common belief that violent expression and aggressive impulses are destructive and counterproductive.

Some examples illustrated in several of these chapters provided scenarios in which violence was indeed detrimental to the artists themselves and others, as, for example, the actions of the multiple murderers and even those of some of the established artists like Caravaggio, Cellini, and Dali. They demonstrated how unchecked actions emerging from narcissistic cycles can be harmful and dangerous.

People such as Pollock and Dadd demonstrated the destruction that emerges from impulsive reactions to situations that arose from diminished control due to substance abuse or neurological impairment. However, as the opening chapters revealed, aggressive energy may also be a valuable and beneficial force from which change can occur and creative expression arise. Such forces can and will contribute to actions that may overcome adversity and resolutely resist limitations. Societal protest against injustice—such as the French Revolution, the Civil Rights and Suffragist movements, or today's Black Lives Matter—while not always destructive, rely on aggressive pushback and violent demonstrations.

Artists such as Goya, Picasso, and Nussbaum relied on their aggressive and retaliatory impulses against the injustice they witnessed and experienced to create monumental works of expression. While not always socially acceptable, they have been socially productive. Aggressive energy, sometimes revealed either through impulsive or calculated violent expression, becomes a drive and, when sublimated properly, can be instrumental for change, development, and creativity.

On the other hand, art making is not always good. Recognizably, this runs counter to beliefs that I have embraced and relied on since becoming an art therapist. Sometimes art making may not always be the balm that we would like it to be. It doesn't magically transform everything into good. Make no mistake. Art is never benign, innocuous, or insignificant. It is a powerful, potent, and sometimes dangerous tool that can be used—to alleviate or magnify—violence and aggression. Who uses this tool determines whether it is constructive or destructive. Art is and remains an extension of its creator. For some, "art becomes the great equalizer, humanizing those that have been previously dehumanized. Only when someone creates are they recognized as being alive" (Gussak, 2019, p. 171). Contrarily, for those who wish it to be, art is a dangerous and malicious weapon.

As I bring this dance to a close, I reflect back on that car-ride discussion I had with my friend more than 20 years ago, with which I opened this book, and all that has emerged during the completion of this project. Recognizably, this examination is far from complete, and there are many more explorations of and reflections on the interrelationship between violence and the arts that can and need to happen—and not just visual art, but music, dance, writing, and drama as well. Yet I believe that, as preliminary conversation starters, these chapters have satisfied, informed, and solidified my own realization of the relationship between art and violence and that while art making does not seem to induce aggressive and violent impulses where none existed before, there seems to exist a distinct and clear interdependence and co-reliance between art and violence. Indeed, the messy, complex, frenzied dance continues unabated.

References

Abbenante, J., & Wix, L. (2016). Archetypal art therapy. In D. E. Gussak & M. L. Rosal (Eds.), *The Wiley Handbook of Art Therapy* (pp. 37–46). West Sussex, UK: Wiley.

Adams, K. L., & Winter, A. (1997). Gang graffiti as a discourse genre. *Journal of Sociolinguistics, 1*(3), 337–360. doi:10.1111/1467-9481.00020

Adler, A., Ansbacher, R. R., & Ansbacher, H. L. (1964). *Individual psychology of Alfred Adler*. New York: Harper Collins.

Adorno, T. (1982). *Prisms*. Cambridge, MA: MIT Press.

Aes-Nihil, J. Bouga, N., Parfrey, A., Rice, B., Rocket, J., Schreck, N., & Stevenson, J. (2011). *The Manson file: Charles Manson as revealed in letters, photos, stories, songs, art, testimony and documents*. Port Townsend, WA: Feral House.

Akinola, M., & Mendes, W. B. (2008). The dark side of creativity: Biological vulnerability and negative emotions lead to greater artistic creativity. *Personality and Social Psychology Bulletin, 34*(12), 1677–1686. doi:10.1177/0146167208323933

Alarco, P. (2008). Dream Caused by the Flight of a Bee Around a Pomegranate a Second Before Waking Up. Museo de Arte Thyssen-Bornemisza. Archived from the original on 2008-02-29. Retrieved 2008-01-07. web.archive.org/web/20080915052714/http: // www.museothyssen.org/thyssen_ing/coleccion/obras_ficha_texto_print388.html

alavineshad, R., Mousavi, M., & Sohrabi, N. (2014). Effects of art therapy on anger and self-esteem in aggressive children. *Social and Behavioral Sciences, 113*, 111–117.

Albarus, C., & Mack, J. H. (2012). *The making of Lee Boyd Malvo: The D. C. Sniper*. New York: Columbia University Press.

Alexander, E. (2014, August). Charles Bronson changes name to Charles Salvador: "The old me dried up." *Independent*. http://www.independent.co.uk/us.

Alfers, S. (2010). Poetry from the Theresienstadt Transit Camp, 1941–1945. *Rocky Mountain Review, 64*(1), 47–70.

American Psychiatric Association. (2013). *Diagnostic and statistical manual of mental disorders* (5th ed.). Washington, DC: American Psychiatric Association.

Amirante, S. L., & Broderick, D. (2011). *John Wayne Gacy: Defending a monster*. New York: Skyhorse.

Anderson, C. A., & Bushman, B. J. (2002). Human aggression. *Annual Reviews of Psychology, 53*, 27–51.

Anderson, T. (1997). Art, education, and the bomb: Reflections on an international children's peace mural project; *Journal of Social Theory in Art Education, 17*, 71–97.

Anderson, T. (2002). The Guernica Children's Peace Mural Project. *Journal of Art & Design Education, 19*(2), 141–152.

Andrade, E., & Cohen, J. (2007). On the consumption of negative feelings. *Journal of Consumer Research*, · February 2007. doi:10.1086/519498

Archer, J. (2009). Does sexual selection explain human sex differences in aggression? *Behavioral and Brain Sciences, 32*, 249–311.

Arn, J. (2019). How Goya's "Third of May" forever changed the way we look at war. *Artsy.net*. https://www.artsy.net/series/stories-10-art-historys-iconic-works/artsy-editorial-goyas-third-may-forever-changed-way-war

Art Therapy Recognition, S12154, 107th Congress (2001). https:// https://www.govinfo.gov/content/pkg/CREC-2001-11-29/pdf/CREC-2001-11-29-pt1-PgS12154-2.pdf

Arts in Exile. (n.d.). Felix Nussbaum: Triumph Des Todes (Triumph of Death), painting (1944). *Arts in Exile*. https://kuenste-im-exil.de/KIE/Content/EN/Objects/nussbaum-felix-triumph-des-todes-en.html

Ayres, B. D. (1994, March 13). In a city of graffiti, gangs turn to violence to protect their art. *The New York Times Magazine*. http://www.nytimes.com/1994/03/13/us/in-a-city-of-graffiti-gangs-turn-to-violence-to-protect-their-art.html

Bacciagaluppi, M. (1989). The role of aggressiveness in the work of John Bowlby. *Free Associations, London, 16*, 123–134.

Bagnall, R. W. (1929). The present South. *Crisis, 36*(9), 303.

Baker, L. A., Jacobson, K. C., Raine, A., Lozano, D. I., & Bezdjian, S. (2007). Genetic and environmental bases of childhood antisocial behavior: A multi-informant twin study. *Journal of Abnormal Psychology, 116*(2), 219–235. doi.org/10.1037/0021-843X.116.2.219

Bandura, A., & Huston, A. C. (1961). Identification as a process of incidental learning. *Journal of Abnormal Social Psychology 63*, 311–318. doi:10.1037/h0040351

Bandura, A., Ross, D., & Ross, S. A. (1961). Transmission of aggression through imitation of aggressive models. *Journal of Abnormal and Social Psychology, 63*(3), 575–582. doi.org/10.1037/h0045925

Banks, L. (2012). Free to talk about violence: A description of art therapy with a male service user in a low security unit. *International Journal of Art Therapy, 17*(1), 13–24. doi:10.11080/17454832.2012.658578

Bartusch, D. J., & Matsueda, R. L. (1996). Gender, reflected appraisals and labeling: A cross-group test of an interactionist theory of delinquency. *Social Forces, 75*(1), 145–176.

Bayse, D. J., Allgood, S. M., & Van Wyk, P. C. (1992). Locus of control, narcissism, and family life education in correctional rehabilitation. *Journal of Offender Rehabilitation, 17*(314), 47–64. doi:10.1300/J076v17n03_03

BBC News. (2010). Charles Bronson artwork removed from London Underground. *BBC News Channel*. http://news.bbc.co.uk/2/hi/uk_news/england/london/8650364.stm.

Beck, A. T. (1999). *Prisoners of hate: The cognitive basis of anger, hostility, and violence*. New York: Harper Collins.

Becker, H. S. (1963/1991). *Outsiders: Studies in the sociology of deviance*. New York: The Free Press.

Becker, H. S. (1982). *Art worlds*. Berkeley: University of California Press.

Belkofer, C. M., & Konopka, L. M. (2008). Conducting art therapy research using quantitative EEG measures. *Art Therapy: Journal of the American Art Therapy Association, 25*(2), 56–63. doi:10.1080/07421656.2008.10129412

Belkofer, C. M., Van Hecke, A. V., & Konopka, L. M. (2014). Effects of drawing on alpha activity: A quantitative EEG study with implications for art therapy. *Art Therapy: Journal of the American Art Therapy Association, 31*(2), 61–68. doi:10.1080/07421656.2014.903821

Benson, S. (1998). Review: Victorian fairy paintings, *Marvels & Tales, 12*(2), 401–403.

Berkowitz, L. (1990). On the formation and regulation of anger and aggression: A cognitive-neoassociationistic analysis. *American Psychologist, 45*(4), 494–503.

Berry-Dee, C. (2007). *Serial killers: Up close and personal.* Berkeley, CA: Ulysses Press.

Betensky, M. G. (1995). *What do you see?: Phenomenology of therapeutic art expression.* London: Jessica Kingsley.

Bhattacharya. J., & Petsche, H. (2002). Shadows of artistry: Cortical synchrony during perception and imagery of visual art. *Cognitive Brain Research, 13*(2), 179–186. doi:10.1016/S0926-6410(01)00110-0

Bhattacharya, J., & Petsche, H. (2002). Drawing on mind's canvas: Differences in cortical integration patterns between artists and non-artists. *Human Brain Mapping, 26*(1), 1–14. doi:10.1002/hbm.20104

Bieber, S. (2003). Chronology (of Max Beckmann). In S. Rainbird (Ed.), *Max Beckmann* (pp. 261–283). New York, The Museum of Modern Art.

Blatter, J., & Milton, S. (1981). *Art of the Holocaust.* New York: Rutledge Press.

Blos, P. (1962). *On adolescence: A psychoanalytic interpretation.* New York: Macmillan.

Blumer, H. (1969). *Symbolic interactionism: Perspective and method.* Berkeley: University of California Press.

Bonn, S. A. (2014). How to tell a sociopath from a psychopath: The important distinctions between criminal psychopaths and sociopaths. Blogpost. *Psychology Today.* https://www.psychologytoday.com/us/blog/wicked-deeds/201401/how-tell-sociopath-psychopath

Bouchard, T., & McGue, M. (2002). Genetic and environmental influences on human psychological differences. *Journal of Neurobiology, 54*(1),4–45. doi:10.1002/neu.10160

Bowditch, L. (2008). Unpacking Pollock's "male and female": Art persona, hermaphrodite, anima and individuation. *Notes in the History of Art, 27*(2/3), 65–69.

Bowlby, J. (1977). The making and breaking of affectional bonds. *British Journal of Psychiatry, 130,* 201–210.

Boyett, C. (2015, January). Auschwitz' forbidden art. https://www.cnn.com/2015/01/23/world/art-auschwitz/index.html

Boyle, D. (2009). Shattering silence: Traumatic memory and reenactment in Rithy Panh's S-21: The Khmer Rouge Killing Machine *Framework: The Journal of Cinema and Media, 50*(1/2), 95–106.

Bray, X., & Payne, E. (2018). *Ribera: Art of violence.* London: Giles.

Breet, L., Myburgh, C., & Poggenpoel, M. (2010). The relationship between the perception of own locus of control and aggression of adolescent boys. *South African Journal of Education, 30,* 511–526.

Breiner, M., Tuomisto, L., Beuyea, E., Gussak, D., & Aufderheide, D. (2011). Creating an art therapy anger management (ATAM) protocol for male inmates through a collaborative relationship. *International Journal of Offender Therapy and Comparative Criminology. 56*(7), 1124–1143.

Britannica. (2002). Max Beckmann: German painter. *Britannica.* https://www.britannica.com/biography/Max-Beckmann

Bronson, C. (2004). *Insanity: My mad life.* London: John Blake.

Bronson, C. (2007). *Solitary fitness.* London: John Blake.

Bronson, C. (2009). *Bronson.* London: John Blake.

Bronson, C. (2016). *Broadmoor: My journey into hell.* London: John Blake.

Brower, M., & Price, B. (2001). Neuropsychiatry of frontal lobe dysfunction in violent and criminal behaviour: A critical review. *Journal of Neurology, Neurosurgery, and Psychiatry, 71*(6), 720–726.

Brown, J. (2011). Conversation: Andrew Graham-Dixon, author of "Caravaggio: A life sacred and profane." https://www.pbs.org/newshour/arts/caravaggio.

Bucciarelli, A. (2011). A normative study of the Person Picking an Apple from a Tree (PPAT) assessment. *Art Therapy, 28*(1), 31–36. doi:10.1080/07421656.2011.557349

Bugliosi, V. (1974). *Helter skelter: The true story of the Manson murders*. New York: W. W. Norton.

Buk, A. (2009). The mirror neuron system and embodied simulation: Clinical implications for art therapists working with trauma survivors. *The Arts in Psychotherapy, 36*(2), 61–74.

Buruma, I. (2014). *Theater of cruelty: Art, film, and the shadows of war*. New York: New York Review Books.

Bush, D. M., & Lipari, R. N. (2005). Substance use and substance use disorder by industry: Short report. https://www.samhsa.gov/data/sites/default/files/report_1959/ShortReport-1959.html

Bushman, B. J., Baumeister, R. F., & Stack, A. D. (1999). Catharsis, aggression, and persuasive influence: Self-fulfilling or self-defeating processes? *Journal of Personality and Social Psychology, 76*(3), 367–376.

Buss, D. N., & Dedden, L. A. (1990). Derogation of competitors. *Journal of Personality and Social Relationships, 7*, 395–422.

Byers, J. G. (1996). Children of the stones: Art therapy interventions in the West Bank. *Art Therapy: Journal of the American Art Therapy Association, 13*(4), 238–243.

Byers, J. G. (1998). Hidden borders, open borders: A therapist's journey in a foreign land. In A. R. Hiscox & A. C. Calisch (Eds.), *Tapestry of cultural issues in art therapy* (pp. 309–326). London: Jessica Kingsley.

Cardinal, R. (1972). *Outsider art*. Westport, CT: Praeger.

Carpenter, W. (2010). Laughter in a time of tragedy: Examining humor during the Holocaust. *The Denison Journal of Religion, 9*(3), 1–14.

Carr, R. (2008). Neurotransmitters, neuromodulators and hormones: Putting it all together. In N. Hass-Cohen & R. Carr (Eds.), *Art therapy and clinical neuroscience* (pp. 76–91). London: Jessica Kingsley.

Carrier, D. (1987). The transfiguration of the commonplace: Caravaggio and his interpreters. *Word Image: A Journal of Verbal/Visual Enquiry, 3*(1), 41–73 doi:10.1080/02666286.1987.10435366

Caspi, A., McClay, J., Moffitt, T., Mill, J., Martin, J., Craig, I. W., Taylor, A., & Poulton, R. (2002). Role of genotype in the cycle of violence in maltreated children. *Science. 297*(5582), 851–854. doi:10.1126/science.1072290. PMID: 12161658.

Cela-Conde, C. J., Marty, G., Maestú, F., Ortiz, T., Munar, E., Fernández, A., Roca, M., Rosselló, J., & Quesney, F. (2004). Activation of the prefrontal cortex in the human visual aesthetic perception. *Proceedings of the National Academy of Sciences of the United States of America, 101*(16), 6321–6325. doi:10.1073/pnas.0401427101

Cellini, B. (2009). J. C. Bondanella & P. Bondanella (Trans.), *My life*. New York: Oxford University Press.

Chametsky, P. (2010). Objects in history in 20th century German art: Beckmann to Beuys. Berkeley: University of California Press.

Chapin, M. (2016). The therapist as artist. In J. Rubin (Ed.), *Approaches to art therapy* (3rd ed., pp. 33–49). New York: Routledge.

Chapman, L., Appleton, V., Kapitan, L., Anderson, C., & Gussak, D. (1997, November). *Violence and vulnerability: A developmental perspective*. Panel presented at the American Art Therapy Association 28th Annual Conference, Milwaukee, WI.

Claridge, L. (2001). *Norman Rockwell: A life*. New York: Random House.
Classical Arts Universe. (n.d.). Salvador Dali: The burning giraffe: An analysis. *Classical Arts Universe*. https://classicalartsuniverse.com/dali-the-burning-giraffe-analysis/
Clayton, T. (1998). Building the New Cambodia: Educational destruction and construction under the Khmer Rouge, 1975–1979. *History of Education Quarterly*, *38*(1), 1–16.
Coerr, E. (1977). *Sadako and the thousand paper cranes*. New York: Puffin Books.
Cole, R. (1999). Ruby Bridges and a painting. In M. H. Hennessey & A. Knutson (Eds.), *Norman Rockwell: Pictures for the American people* (pp. 105–114). New York: Harry N. Abrams.
Cole, T. B. (2009). Moon landscape. *JAMA*, *302*(22), 2403. doi:10.1001/jama.2009.1625
Collinson, M. (2010). Italy's treasures: Benvenuto Cellini. *Italy Magazine*. https://www.italymagazine.com/featured-story/italys-treasures-benvenuto-cellini
Combs, S., & Eckberg, J. (2018). *O. J. Simpson and Glen Rogers: The Juice, Road Dog & murder on Bundy Drive*. Bloomington, IN: Barnes and Bauer.
Cooley, C. H. (1964). *Human nature and the social order*. New York: Schocken Books.
Cooper, H. A. A., & Penn, B. (2010). Negotiating with psychopaths: Coping with a medical-legal conundrum. *Journal of Applied Security Research*, *6*(1), 1–31. doi:10.1080/19361610.2011.529544
Court, A. (Feb. 25, 1990). The legend of Jack the Dripper. *The LA Times*. https://www.latimes.com/archives/la-xpm-1990-02-25-bk-2003-story.html.
Dali, S. (1942/1993). *The secret life of Salvador Dali*. Garden City, NY: Dover.
Dalley, T. (1990). Images and integration: Art therapy in a multicultural school. In C. Case & T. Dalley (Eds.), *Working with children in art therapy* (pp. 161–198). New York: Routledge.
Dawkins, R. (2006). *The selfish gene* (30th anniv. edition). New York: Oxford University Press.
De Bethune, M., & Linhardt, K. (2020). Cultivating resilience through creative altruism with institutionalized youth in foster care In M. Berberian & B. Davis (Eds.), *Art therapy practices for resilient youth*. (pp. 227–251). New York: Routledge.
De Francisco, J. (1983). Implosive art therapy: A learning-theory based, psychodynamic approach. In L. Gantt & S. Whitman (Eds.), *Proceedings of the eleventh annual conference of the American Art Therapy Association* (pp. 74–79). Baltimore: American Art Therapy Association.
DeLong, W. (2018, October 24). The true story of Danny Rolling, The Gainesville Ripper who inspired "Scream." All That's Interesting. https://allthatsinteresting.com/danny-rolling-gainesville-ripper
DiCioccio, R. L. (2012). Humor as aggressive communication. In R. L. DiCioccio (Ed.), *Humor communication: Theory, Impact and Outcomes*. (pp. 93–106).
Dietrich, A., & Kanso, R. (2010). A review of EEG, ERP, and neuroimaging studies of creativity and insight. *Psychological Bulletin, 136*(5), 822–848. doi:10.1037/a0019749
Dietrich, E., & Fox Hall, T. (2010). The allure of the serial killer. In S. Waller (Ed.), *Serial killers-philosophy for everyone: Being in killing* (pp. 93–102). Sussex, UK: Blackwell.
Dine, T. (2016). Oneiric hidden symbolism of Dali. *European Journal of Research and Reflection in Arts and Humanities, 4*(2), 57–63.
Dissanayake, E. (1988). *What is art for?* Seattle: University of Washington Press.
Dissanayake, E. (1992). *Homoaestheticus: Where art comes from and why*. New York: Free Press.

DiSunno, R., Linton, K., & Bowes, E. (2011). World Trade Center tragedy: Concomitant healing in traumatic grief through art therapy with children, *Traumatology, 17*(3) 47–52.

Dollard, J., Miller, N. E., Doob, L. W., Mowrer, O. H., & Sears, R. R. (1939). *Frustration and aggression*. New Haven, CT: Yale University Press. https://doi.org/10.1037/10022-000

Dominiczak, M. H. (2017). Art at the time of turmoil: Max Beckmann. *Clinical Chemistry, 63*(9), 1552–1554, doi.org/10.1373/clinchem.2016.266833

Drummond, K. (2006). The migration of art from museum to market: Consuming Caravaggio. *Marketing Theory, 6*(1), 85–105.

Duke, A. A., Smith, K. M. Z., Oberleitner, L. M. S., Westphal, A., & McKee, S. A. (2018). Alcohol, drugs, and violence: A meta-meta-analysis. *Psychology of Violence, 8*(2), 238–249. https://doi.org/10.1037/vio0000106

Dunlop, N. (2005). *The lost executioner: A story of the Khmer Rouge* London: Bloomsbury.

Dutlinger, A. D. (2002). Art and artists in Theresienstadt. In A. D. Dutlinger (Ed.), *Art, music and education as strategies for survival: Theresienstadt 1941–1945* (pp. 10–50). New York: Herodias.

Eburne, J. P. (2008). *Surrealism and the art of crime*. New York: Cornell University Press.

Eco, U. (2007). *On ugliness*. New York: Rizzoli.

Elliott, F. A. (1983). Biological roots of violence *Proceedings of the American Philosophical Society, 127*(2), 84–94.

Elsby, L. (n.d.). Felix Nussbaum: Self portraits of a Jew in turmoil. Yad Vashem: The World Holocaust Remembrance Center. https://www.yadvashem.org/articles/general/felix-nussbaum.html

Eng, E. (1956). Cellini's two childhood memories. *American Imago, 13*(2), 189–203.

Eytan, E., & Elkis-Abuhoff, D. L. (2013). Indicators of depression and self-efficacy in the PPAT drawings of normative adults. *Arts in Psychotherapy,40*(3), 291–297.

Feist, G. J. (1998). A meta-analysis of personality in scientific and artistic creativity. *Personality and Social Psychology Review, 2*(4) 290–309.

Feldmann, T. B. (1989). Creativity and narcissism: A self-psychology examination of the life and work of Jackson Pollock. *Arts in Psychotherapy, 16*(3), 201–209.

Felstiner, J. (2000). Felix Nussbaum: Art defamed, art in exile, art in resistance, edited by Karl Georg Kaster (Book Review). *Judaism, 49*(4), 495.

Ferguson, E. (2018). The face behind the masks—Review: 'Modigliani: Unmasked' at The Jewish Museum. *Washington Free Beacon*. https://freebeacon.com/culture/review-modigliani-unmasked-at-the-jewish-museum/

Ferrara, N. (1992). Adolescent narcissism and ego regression: An art therapy case illustration. *Journal of Child & Youth Care, 7*(1), 49–56.

Fincher, S. F. (1991). *Creating mandalas for insight, healing and self-expression*. Boulder, CO: Shambala.

Finklestein, H. (1975). Dali's paranoia-criticism or the exercise of freedom. *Twentieth Century Literature, 21*(1), 59–71.

Fisher, K. (2010). Expressing the age: How the painting of Jackson Pollock displayed the political culture of Abstract Expressionism. *Philologia*, 2(1). doi:http://doi.org/10.21061/ph.v2i1.113

Fleming, W. (1970). *Arts & ideas*. New York: Holt Rinehart Winston.

Fox, A. F., & Levin, J. (2012). *Extreme killing: Understanding serial and mass murder*. Thousand Oaks, CA: Sage.

Fox, J. A., & Levin, J. (1998). Multiple homicide: Patterns of serial and mass murder. *Crime and Justice, 23*, 407–455. doi:10.1086/449274

Fox, W. M. (1997). The hidden weapon: Psychodynamics of forensic institutions. In D. Gussak & E. Virshup (Eds.), *Drawing time: Art therapy in prisons and other correctional settings* (pp. 43–55). Chicago, IL: Magnolia Street Publishers.

Frankl, V. (1959/2006). *Man's search for meaning*. Boston, MA: Beacon Press.

Franklin, M. (2010). Affect regulation, mirror neurons, and the third hand: Formulating mindful empathetic art interventions. *Art Therapy: Journal of the American Art Therapy Association, 27*(4), 160–167. doi:10.1080/07421656.2010.10129385

Franklin, M. A. (2016). Essence, art and therapy: A transpersonal view. In D. E. Gussak & M. L. Rosal (Eds.), *The Wiley handbook of art therapy* (pp. 99–111). West Sussex, UK.: Wiley.

Frasier, D. K. (1996). *Murder cases of the 20th century*. Jefferson, NC: McFarland.

Freud, S. (1960/1989). *Jokes and their relationship to the unconscious*. New York: W. W. Norton.

Freud, S. (1990). *Beyond the pleasure principle (The standard edition)*. New York: W. W. Norton.

Frey, J. G. (1936). From Dada to Surrealism, *Parnassus*, 8(7), 12–15, doi:10.1080/15436314.1936.11466615

Fried, M. (1997). Thoughts on Caravaggio. *Critical Inquiry, 24*, 13–56.

Friedlander, H. (1995). *The origins of Nazi genocide: From euthanasia to the final solution*. Chapel Hill: University of North Carolina Press.

Fromm, E. (1972, February 27). The Erich Fromm theory of aggression. *The New York Times*. SM14.

Fromm, E. (1973/1992). *The anatomy of human destructiveness*. New York: Picador.

Gablik, S. (1993). *The reenchantment of art*. London: Thames and Hudson.

Gacy, J. W. (n.d.). *A question of doubt: Commentary on the arrest and trial of John Wayne Gacy* (unpublished manuscript).

Gantt, L. (2004). The case for formal art therapy assessments. *Art therapy: Journal of the American Art Therapy Association, 21*(1), 18–29.

Gantt, L. (2016). The Formal Elements Art Therapy Scale (FEATS). In D. Gussak & M. Rosal (Eds.), *The Wiley handbook of art therapy* (pp. 569–578). West Sussex, UK: Wiley.

Gantt, L., & Tabone, C. (1998). *The formal elements art therapy scale: The rating manual*. Morgantown, WV: Gargoyle Press.

Gantt, L., & Tripp, T. (2016). The image comes first. In J. King (Ed.), *Art therapy, trauma and neuroscience: Theoretical and practical perspectives* (pp. 67–99). New York: Routledge.

Garai, J. (2001). Humanistic art therapy. In J. A. Rubin (Ed.), *Approaches to art therapy* (pp. 149–162). Philadelphia, PA: Brunner-Routledge.

Gassier, P. (1955). *Goya: Taste of our time (Vol. 13)*. Cleveland, OH: Skira.

Gay, P. (1989). *Freud: A life for our time*. New York: Doubleday.

Georgievska, M. (2016, December 30). Goya's Los Caprichos: The aqua tinted etchings that condemned human behavior in late 18th century Spain. *The Vintage News*. https://www.thevintagenews.com/2016/12/30/goyas-los-capricho s-the-aqua-tinted-etchings-that-condemned-human-behavior-in-late-18th-century-spain/

Gerber, J. (1994). The use of art therapy in juvenile sex offender specific treatment. *The Arts in Psychotherapy, 21*(5), 367–374. doi:10.1016/0197-4556(94)90064-7

Gibson, I. (1998). *The shameful life of Salvador Dali*. New York: W. W. Norton.

Gilbert, M. (2012). *The Holocaust*. London: Folio Society.

Gilmore, S. (1990). Art worlds: Developing the interactionist approach to social organization. In H. S. Becker & M. M. McCall (Eds.), *Symbolic interaction and cultural studies* (pp. 148–178). Chicago: University of Chicago Press.

Goldenberg, N. R. (1986). Anger in the body: Feminism, religion and Kleinian psychoanalytic theory. *Journal of Feminist Studies in Religion*, *2*(2), 39–49. http://www.jstor.org/stable/25002040

Goldman-Rubin, S. (2000). *Fireflies in the dark: The story of Friedl Dicker-Brandeis and the children of Terezín*. New York: Holiday House.

Golub, L. (1955). A critique of Abstract Expressionism. *College Art Journal*, *14*(2), 142–147. doi:10.1080/15436322.1955.10795673

Gonzalez-Dolginko, B. (2002). In the shadows of terror: A community neighboring the World Trade Center disaster uses art therapy to process trauma. *Art Therapy, Journal of the American Art Therapy Association*, *19*(3), 120–122. doi:10.1080/07421656.2002.10129408

Govier, T. (2008). Violence, nonviolence, and definitions: A dilemma for peace studies. *Peace Research*, *40*(2), 61–83.

Graham-Dixon, A. (2010). *Caravaggio: A life sacred and profane*. New York: W. W. Norton.

Green, G. (1978). *The artists of Terezín*. New York: Hawthorn Books.

Greenberg, C. (1961/1989). *Art and culture: Critical essays*. Boston: Beacon Press.

Greysmith, D. (1973). *Richard Dadd: The rock and castle of seclusion*. New York: Macmillan.

Griffith, J. E., Pennington-Averett, A., & Bryan, I. (1981). Women prisoners' multidimensional locus of control. *Criminal Justice and Behavior*, *8*(3), 375–389.

Groth-Marnat, G. (2003). *Handbook of psychological assessment* (4th ed.). New York: Wiley.

Guinn, J. (2013). *Manson: The life and times of Charles Manson*. New York: Simon and Schuster.

Gussak, D. (1991). *A case study of art therapy with a selectively mute, withdrawn man with schizophrenia: Exploring a relationship on a page*. Unpublished Master's Thesis: Vermont College, Montpelier University.

Gussak, D. E. (1997a). The ultimate hidden weapon: Art therapy and the compromise option. In D. Gussak & E. Virshup (Eds.), *Drawing time: Art therapy in prisons and other correctional settings* (pp. 59–74). Chicago: Magnolia Street Publishers.

Gussak, D. E. (1997b). Breaking through barriers: Art therapy in prisons. In D. Gussak & E. Virshup (Eds.), *Drawing time: Art therapy in prisons and other correctional settings* (pp. 1–11). Chicago: Magnolia Street Publishers.

Gussak, D. E. (2002). Art therapists as bridge builders for peace. *Journal of Multicultural and Cross-cultural Research in Art Education*, *19/20*, 94–102.

Gussak, D. E. (2004a). Art therapy with prison inmates: A pilot study. *Arts in Psychotherapy*, *31*(4), 245–259.

Gussak, D. E. (2004b). Art made it real: My Terezín musings. *Journal of Multicultural and Cross-cultural Research in Art Education*, *22*,155–161.

Gussak, D. E. (2006). Symbolic Interactionism, aggression and art therapy. In F. Kaplan (Ed.), *Art therapy and social action* (pp. 142–156). London: Jessica Kingsley.

Gussak, D. E. (2007). The deviant adolescent: Creating healthy interactions and re-labeling through art therapy. In D. B. Arrington (Ed.), *Art, angst and trauma: Right brain interventions with developmental issues* (pp. 132–149). Springfield, IL: Charles C. Thomas.

Gussak, D. E. (2009a). The effects of art therapy on male and female inmates: Advancing the research base. *Arts in Psychotherapy*, *36*(1), 5–12. doi:10.1016/j.aip.2008.10.002

Gussak, D. E. (2009b). The benefits of art and art therapy with prison inmates. In H. O. Thomashoff & E. Sukhanova (Eds.), *The person in art: Conceptual and pictorial frames on art and mental health* (pp. 117–125). New York: Nova Science.

Gussak, D. E. (2009c). A brief essay on the art of the Holocaust. In: *Florida State University's museum catalogue for the Holocaust Institute for Educators and Museum of Fine Arts Exhibition* (pp. 2–4). Tallahassee: FSU Museum of Fine Arts.

Gussak, D. E. (2013). *Art on trial: Art therapy in capital murder cases*. New York: Columbia University Press.

Gussak, D. E. (2016a). Art therapy in the correctional milieu. In D. E. Gussak & M. L. Rosal's (Eds.), *The Wiley handbook of art therapy* (pp. 478–486). West Sussex, UK: Wiley.

Gussak, D. E. (2016b). Aggression and art therapy: A social interactionist perspective. In D. Gussak & M. Rosal (Eds.), *The Wiley handbook of art therapy* (pp. 329–336). West Sussex, UK: Wiley.

Gussak, D. E. (2019). *Art and art therapy with the imprisoned: Re-creating identity*. New York: Routledge.

Gussak, D. E., Chapman, L., Rosal, M., & Van Duinan, T. (2003, Nov.) *Witnessing aggression and violence–Responding creatively*. Plenary presentation at the American Art Therapy Association Annual Conference, Chicago, IL.

Gussak, D. E., & Rosal, M. L. (2016). An introduction. In D. Gussak & M. Rosal (Eds.), *The Wiley handbook of art therapy* (pp. 1–4). West Sussex, UK: Wiley.

Gussak, D. E., & Virshup, E. (Eds.). (1997). *Drawing time: Art therapy in prisons and other correctional settings*, Chicago: Magnolia Street Publishers.

Haas-Cohen, N., & Findlay, J. C. (2015). Art therapy and the neuroscience of relationships, creativity, and resiliency: Skills and practices. New York: W. W. Horton.

Halpern, R. (2006). *Norman Rockwell: The underside of innocence*. Chicago: University of Chicago Press.

Hamann, B. (1999). *Hitler's Vienna: A dictator's apprenticeship*. New York: Oxford University Press.

Hare, R. D. (1993). *Without conscience: The disturbing world of the psychopaths among us*. New York: Guilford.

Harpending, H., & Draper, P. (1988). Antisocial behavior and the other side of cultural evolution. In T. E. Moffitt & S. A. Mednick (Eds.), *Biological contributions to crime causation* (pp. 293–307). Dordecht, NL: Martinus Nijhoff.

Harrington, R. (2017). *The brutal Texan: The shocking true story of serial killer Tommy Lynn Sells*. Columbia, SC: Self-published.

Harris-Frankfurt, E. (2014/2020). Francisco Goya: Spanish artist. *Britannica*. https://www.britannica.com/biography/Francisco-Goyaref129726

Haxthausen, C. W. (1984). Beckmann and the First World War. In C. Schulz-Hoffmann & J. C. Weiss (Ed.), *Max Beckmann: Retrospective* (pp. 69–80). New York: W. W. Norton.

Haycock, D. A. (2014). *Murderous minds: Exploring the criminal psychopathic brain: Neurological imagining and the manifestation of evil*. New York: Pegasus Books.

Hazut, T. (2005). From dark black to bright pink: The power of art expression and creation in coping with life under threat, Israel 2001–2002. In D. Kalmanowitz & B. Lloyd (Eds.), *Art therapy and political violence: With art, without illusion* (pp. 91–105). New York: Routledge.

Helfenstein, J. (1999). Bill Traylor and Charles Shannon: A historic encounter in Montgomery. In J. Helfenstein & R. Kurzmeyer (Eds.), *Bill Traylor 1854–1949: Deep Blues* (pp. 96–108). New Haven, CT: Yale University Press.

Henley, D. R. (1986). Approaching artistic sublimation in low-functioning individuals, *Art Therapy*, *3*(2), 67–73, doi:10.1080/07421656.1986.10758826

Hennessey, M. H. (1999). The four freedoms. In M. H. Hennessey & A. Knutson (Eds.), *Norman Rockwell: Pictures for the American People* (pp. 95–104). New York: Harry N. Abrams.

Hewitson, M. (2017). Introduction: Visualizing violence. *Cultural History*, *6*(1), 1–20. doi:10.3366/cult.2017.0132

Hibbard, H. (1983). *Caravaggio*. New York: Harper & Row.

Hiemer, E. (1938). *Der giftpilz* (*The poisonous mushroom*). Germany: Julius Streicher.

Higgins, C. (2018). Master of gore: The violent, shocking genius of Jusepe de Ribera. *The Guardian*. https://www.theguardian.com/artanddesign/2018/sep/19/jusepe-de-ribera-art-of-violence-master-of-gore-dulwich

Hinton, A. L. (2014). Justice and time at the Khmer Rouge tribunal: In memory of Vann Nath, painter and S-21 survivor. *Genocide Studies and Prevention: An International Journal*, *8*(2) 7–17. doi:http://dx.doi.org/10.5038/1911-9933.8.2.3

Hinton, A. L. (2018). *The justice facade: Trials of transition in Cambodia*. New York: Oxford University Press.

Hlavek, E. (in press). *Meaning making through art making: From the Holocaust to contemporary practices*. NY: Routledge.

Hobbs, R. C. (1985). Early abstract expressionism and surrealism. *Art Journal*, *45*(2), 299–302 doi:10.1080/00043249.1985.10792314

Hoffman, F. J. (1948). From Surrealism to "The Apocalypse": A development in twentieth century Irrationalism. *Journal of English Literary History*, *15*(2), 147–165.

Holmes, R. (1971). Violence and nonviolence. In J. A. Schaffer (Ed.), *Violence: Award winning essays in the Council for Philosophical Studies competition* (pp. 101–135). New York: David McKay.

Holmes, R., & DeBurger, J. (1988). *Serial murder*. Beverly Hills: Sage.

Holmes, R. M., & Holmes, S. T. (2010). *Serial murder* (3rd ed.). Thousand Oaks, CA: Sage.

Horney, K. (1939). *New ways in psychoanalysis*. New York: W. W. Norton.

Horney, K. (1945/1992). *Our inner conflicts: A constructive theory of neurosis* (Reissue edition). New York: W. W. Norton.

Hoving, T. (1999). The great art communicator. In M. H. Hennessey & A. Knutson (Eds.), *Norman Rockwell: Pictures for the American people* (pp. 29–31). New York: Harry N. Abrams.

Huesmann, L. R. (1988). An information processing model for the development of aggression. *Aggressive Behavior*, *14*, 13–24.

Huesmann, L. R., Moise-Titus, J., Podolski, C. L., & Eron, L. D. (2003). Longitudinal relations between children's exposure to TV violence and their aggressive and violent behavior in young adulthood: 1977–1992. *Developmental Psychology*, *39*(2), 201–221.

Hunter, G. C. (1994). Who's really in charge of my life, anyway? Locus of control and cognitive substance abuse treatment in a federal prison. *Journal of Rational-Emotive & Cognitive Behavior Therapy*, *12*(4), 219–224.

Hunter, J. T. (2019). *A monster of all time: The true story of Danny Rolling—The Gainesville Ripper*. Columbia, SC: RJ Publishing.

Hylton, H. (2007, June 5). Cracking down on "Murderabilia". *Time Magazine*. http://content.time.com/time/nation/article/0,8599,1629655,00.html.

Ineedartsandcoffee.com. (2014). Jackson Pollock: An explosive life. (Blog post). http://ineedartandcoffee.blogspot.com/2014/05/jackson-pollock-explosive-life.html.

Ishizu, T., & Zeki, S. (2011). Toward a brain-based theory of beauty. *Plos One*, *6*(7), e21852. doi:10.1371/journal.pone.0021852

Isis, P. D. (2016). *Positive art therapy*. In D. E. Gussak & M. L. Rosal (Eds.), *The Wiley Handbook of Art Therapy* (pp. 90–98). West Sussex, UK: Wiley.

James, W. (1890/1918). *The principles of psychology. Vol.1 and Vol.2*. New York: Henry Holt.

Jones, J. (1997). Art therapy with a community of survivors. *Art Therapy: Journal of the American Art Therapy Association*,*14*(2) 89–94.

Jones, J. (2015). Jackson Pollock review: This is art as nervous breakdown . . . and it's majestic. *The Guardian*. https://www.theguardian.com/artanddesign/2015/jun/29/jackson-pollock-blind-spots-tate-liverpool-review-art-as-nervous-breakdown.

Junge, M. (2019). *An art therapist's view of mass murders, violence and mental illness*. Springfield, IL: Charles C. Thomas.

Kaimal, G., Ray, K., & Muniz, J. (2016). Reduction of cortisol levels and participants' responses following art making. *Art Therapy: Journal of the American Art Therapy Association*, *33*(2), 74–80. doi:10.1080/07421656.2016.1166832

Kalmanowitz, D., & Lloyd, B. (2005a). Introduction. In D. Kalmanowitz & B. Lloyd (Eds.), *Art therapy and political violence: With art, without illusion* (pp. 4–13). New York: Routledge.

Kalmanowitz, D., & Lloyd, B. (2005b). Art therapy and political violence. In D. Kalmanowitz & B. Lloyd (Eds.), *Art therapy and political violence: With art, without illusion* (pp. 14–33). New York: Routledge.

Kapitan, L. (1997). Making or breaking: Art therapy in the shifting tides of a violent culture. *Art Therapy: Journal of the American Art Therapy Association*, *14*(4) 255–260.

Kaster, K. G. (1997). *Felix Nussbaum: Art defamed, art in exile, art in resistance: A biography*. New York: Overlook Press.

Kempf, N. S. (2002). What's in a name? Folk art defined. *Western Pennsylvania History*, 32–39.

Kendrick, P. (2020). *American Ripper: The enigma of America's serial killer cop*. New Smyrna Beach, FL: Bluewater Press.

Kiehl, K. (2006). A cognitive neuroscience perspective on psychopathy: Evidence for paralimbic system dysfunction. *Psychiatry Research, 142*(2–3), 107–128.

King, J. L. (2016a). Art therapy: A brain-based profession. In D. Gussak & M. Rosal (Eds.), *The Wiley handbook of art therapy* (77–89). West Sussex, UK: Wiley.

King, J. L. (2016b). *Art therapy, trauma and neuroscience: Theoretical and practical perspectives*. New York: Routledge.

King, J. L., Knapp, K. E., Shaikh, A., Li, F., Sabau, D., Pascuzzi, R. M., & Osburn, L. L. (2017). Cortical activity changes after art making and rote motor movement as measured by EEG: A preliminary study. *Biomedical Journal of Scientific & Technical Research*, *1*(4), 1062–1075. doi:10.26717/BJSTR.2017.01.000366

Klein, M. (1946). Notes on some schizoid mechanisms. *International Journal of Psychoanalysis, 27*, 99–110.

Klein, M. (1964). Love, guilt and reparation. In M. Klein & J. Riviere (Eds.), *Love, hate and reparation* (pp. 57–109). New York: W. W. Norton.

Klein, M. (2017). *Modigliani unmasked*. New Haven, CT: Yale University Press.

Kleiner, F. S., Mamiya, C. J., & Tansey, R. G. (2001). *Gardner's art through the ages* (11th ed.). New York: Harcourt College Publishers.

Knafo, D. (2003). What does a man want? Reflections on "Surrealism desire unbound." *Studies in Gender and Sexuality*, *4*(23), 287–307. doi:10.1080/15240650409349229

Kocsis, R. N. (2008). *Serial murder and the psychology of violent crimes.* Totowa, NJ: Humana.

Kohut, H. (1971). *The analysis of self: A systematic approach to the psychoanalytic treatment of narcissistic personality disorders.* New York: International Universities Press.

Kornfeld, P. (1997). *Cellblock visions: Prison art in America.* Princeton, NJ: Princeton University Press.

Kotthoff, H. (2006). Gender and humor: The state of the art. *Journal of Pragmatics,38*(1), 4–25. doi.org/10.1016/j.pragma.2005.06.003

Krajicek, D. J. (2019). *Charles Manson: The man who murdered the Sixties.* London: Arcturus.

Kramer, E. (1971/1993). *Art as therapy with children.* Chicago: Magnolia Street Publishing.

Krause, K. (2009). Beyond definition: Violence in a global perspective. *Global Crime, 10*(4), 337–355.

Krug, D. H., & Parker, A. (2009). A journal of critical inquiry and professional learning: Telling tales of community. *Art, Aesthetics, and Cultures, Art Education, 62*(4), 33–40. doi:10.1080/00043125.2009.11519027

Kruszynski, A. (2003). Beckmann and the triptych: A sacred form in the context of modernism. In S. Rainbird (Ed.), *Max Beckmann* (pp. 95–128). New York: Museum of Modern Art.

Kurzmeyer, R. (1999). The life and times of Bill Traylor [1854–1949]. In J. Helfenstein & R. Kurzmeyer (Eds.), *Bill Traylor 1854–1949: Deep Blues* (pp. 169–177). New Haven, CT: Yale University Press.

Lachman-Chapin, M. (1979). Kohut's theories on narcissism: Implications for art therapy. *American Journal of Art Therapy, 19*(1), 3–9.

Lackner, S. (1977). *Beckmann. (from the Library of Great Painters).* New York: Harry N. Abrams.

Lackner, S. (1984). Exile in Amsterdam and Paris 1937–1947. In C. Schulz-Hoffmann & J. C. Weiss (Eds.), *Max Beckmann: Retrospective* (pp. 145–158). New York: W. W. Norton.

Lambert, G. (2000). *Caravaggio.* Koln: Taschen.

Langer, S. (1941). *Philosophy in a new key. A study in the symbolism of reason, rite and art.* Cambridge, MA: Harvard University Press.

Lasseter, D. (2000). *Die for me: The terrifying true story of the Charles Ng/Leonard lake torture murders.* New York: Pinnacle Books.

Lawson, M. (2007, May 31). Most sacred monsters. *The Guardian.* https://www.theguardian.com/commentisfree/2007/jun/01/film.comment

Lee, A. (2006). *The ugly Renaissance: Sex, greed, violence and depravity in an age of beauty.* New York: Doubleday.

Levin, J., & Fox, J. A. (2008). Normalcy in behavioral characteristics of the sadistic serial killer. In R. N. Kocsis (Ed.), *Serial murder and the psychology of violent crimes* (pp. 3–14). Totowa, NJ: Humana.

Levy, T. M., & Orlans, M. (2000). Attachment disorder as an antecedent to violence and antisocial patterns in children. In T. M. Levy (Ed.), *Handbook of attachment interventions* (pp. 1–26). San Diego, CA: Academic Press.

Linedecker, C. L. (1980). *The man who killed boys: A true story of mass murder in a Chicago suburb.* New York: St. Martin's Press.

Linedecker, C. L. (1997). *Smooth operator: The true story of seductive serial killer Glen Rogers.* New York: St. Martin's Paperbacks.

Lippard, L. (1994). Crossing into uncommon grounds. In M. D. Hall & E. W. Metcalf (Eds.), *The artist outsider: Creativity and the boundaries of culture* (pp. 2–18). Washington, DC: Smithsonian Institution Press.

Lippincott, L. (1988). Murder and the fine arts: Or, a reassessment of Richard Dadd. *J. Paul Getty Museum Journal, 16*, 75–94.

Lorenz, K. (1967). *On aggression*. New York: Bantam Books.

Loughery, J. (2002). Sexual violence: Baroque to Surrealist. *The Hudson Review, 35*(2), 293–300.

Love, G. D. (1991). Consideration of the inmate student's locus of control for effective instructional leadership. *Journal of Correctional Education, 42*(1), 36–41.

Lubart, T. I., Mouchiroud, C., Zenasni, F., & Averill, J. R. (2004). Relations entre créativité et agression (Links between creativity and aggression). *Revue Internationale de Psychologie Sociale, 17*(2), 145–176.

Lusebrink, V. B. (1990). *Imagery and visual expression in therapy*. New York: Plenum Press.

Lusebrink, V. B. (2004). Art therapy and the brain: An attempt to understand the underlying processes of art expression in therapy. *Art Therapy: Journal of the American Art Therapy Association, 21*(3), 125–135.

MacKinnon, D. W. (1962). The nature and nurture of creative talent. *American Psychologist, 17*(7), 484–495.

Macnab, P. (1888). Benvenuto Cellini. *Magazine of Art (Jan.)*, 172–175.

Mahon, D. (1953). On some aspects of Caravaggio and his times. *Metropolitan Museum of Art Bulletin, 12*(2), 33–45.

Maizels, J. (1996). *Raw creation: Outsider art and beyond*. London: Phaidon.

Major, C. (2020). Strength-based art therapy with adolescent psychiatric patients. In M. Berberian & B. Davis (Eds.), *Art therapy practices for resilient youth*. (pp. 159–174). New York: Routledge.

Malchiodi, C. (1990). *Breaking the silence: Art therapy with children from violent homes*. New York: Brunner/Mazel.

Malcovich, B. (2010, May 16). Interview with a murderer. *The Southern Illinoisan*. Thesouthern.com/news/local/interview-with-a-murderer/article_12b60fc2-60a6-11df-b581-001cc4c002e0.html

Mann, C. (1980). *Modigliani*. New York: Oxford University Press.

Manson, C., & Emmons, N. (1986). *Manson in his own words*. New York: Grove Press.

Matto, H. C. (1997). An integrative approach to the treatment of women with eating disorders. *Arts in Psychotherapy, 24*, 347–354.

May, R. (1972). *Power and innocence: A search for the source of violence*. New York: W. W. Norton.

McNatt, G. (2000, June). Re-examining Rockwell. *The Baltimore Sun*. https://www.baltimoresun.com/news/bs-xpm-2000-06-19-0006190015-story.html

McNiff, S. (2005). Foreword. In D. Kalmanowitz & B. Lloyd (Eds.), *Art therapy and political violence: With art, without illusion* (pp. xii––xvi). New York: Routledge.

Mead, G. H. (1964). *On social psychology*. Chicago: University of Chicago Press.

Meyer, J. C. (2000). Humor as a double-edged sword: Four functions of humor in communication. *Communication Theory, 10*(3) 310–331. doi.org/10.1111/j.1468-2885.2000.tb00194.x

Meyers, J. (2006). *Modigliani: A life*. Orlando, FL: Harcourt.

Meyjes, M. (Director). (2002). *Max*. (film). Pathé Productions.

Mider, D. (2013). The anatomy of violence: A study in literature. *Aggression and Violent Behavior, 18*, 702–708.

Milton, S. (2002). Art in the context of Theresienstadt. In A. D. Dutlinger (Ed.), *Art, music and education as strategies for survival: Theresienstadt 1941–1945* (pp. 10–50). New York: Herodias.

Milton, S. (2003). Art in the context of Auschwitz. In D. Mickenberg, C. Granof & P. Hayes (Eds.), *The last expression: Art and Auschwitz* (pp. 60–67). Evanston, IL: Northwestern University Press.

Morrin, P. (1999). Bill Traylor: Artist-bricoleur. In J. Helfenstein & R. Kurzmeyer (Eds.), *Bill Traylor 1854–1949: Deep Blues* (pp. 31–32). New Haven, Conn: Yale University Press.

Mueller, R. T. (2018). Action painting. The Trauma and Mental Health Report. (Blogpost). https://trauma.blog.yorku.ca/2018/09/action-painting/

Mundy, J. (2001). Letters of desire In J. Mundy (Ed.), *Surrealism: Desire unbound* (pp. 11–53). London: Tate.

Murphy, C. (2009). The link between artistic creativity and psychopathology: Salvador Dalí. *Personality and Individual Differences, 46*(8), 765–774.

Naifeh, S., & Smith, G. (1998). *Jackson Pollock: An American saga*. New York: Clarkson Potter.

Nath, V. (1998). *A Cambodian prison portrait. One year in the Khmer Rouge's S-21*. Chon Buri, Thailand: White Lotus.

National Endowment for the Arts. (2015). *How creativity works in the brain*. Washington DC: National Endowment for the Arts.

Naumburg, M. (1966). *Dynamically oriented art therapy: Its principles and practice*. New York: Grune & Stratton.

Nethersole, S. (2018). *Art and violence: In early Renaissance Florence*. New Haven, CT: Yale University Press.

Norman Rockwell Museum. (2020). Norman Rockwell: Murder in Mississippi—an Exhibition. Norman Rockwell Museum. https://www.nrm.org/2020/06/norman-rockwell-murder-in-mississippi/exhibition

O'Connor, F. V. (n.d.). Jackson Pollock: American Artist. Legacy. https://www.britannica.com/biography/Jackson-Pollock/Legacy

Ochsner, K. N., Beer, J. S., Roberstson, E. R., Cooper, J. C., Gabrieli, J. D. E., Kihsltrom, J. F., & D'Esposito, M. (2005). The neural correlates of direct and reflected self-knowledge. *Neuroimage, 28*, 797–814.

Orwell, G. (1968/2019). Benefit of clergy: Some notes on Salvador Dali. In S. Orwell & I. Angus (Eds.), *As I please (1943–1945), the collected essays, journalism and letters, George Orwell, Vol. 3* (pp. 156–164). Boston: Nonpareil Books/Godine.

Österman, K., Björkqvist, K., Lagerspetz, K. M., Charpentier, S., Caprara, G. V., & Pastorelli, C. (1999). Locus of control and three types of aggression. *Aggressive Behavior, 25*(1), 61–65. doi:10.1002/(SICI)1098-2337(1999)25:1<61::AID-AB6>3.0.CO;2-G

Packard, S. (1977). Learning disabilities: Identification and remediation through creative art activity. In R. H. Shoemaker & S. E. Gonick-Barris (Eds.), *Proceedings of the Seventh Annual Conference of the American Art Therapy Association* (pp. 57–61). Baltimore: American Art Therapy Association.

Parsons, L. (January 18, 2005). Modigliani—an artist between worlds. World Socialist Website. https://www.wsws.org/en/articles/2005/01/modi-j18.html

PDR. (n.d.). The whims (1799) and the follies (1815–23) of Francisco Goya. Public Domain Review. https://publicdomainreview.org/collection/the-whims-1799-and-the-follies-1815-23-of-francisco-goya

Perry, D. G., Perry, L. C., & Rasmussen, P. (1986). Cognitive social learning mediators of aggression. *Child Development, 57*(3), 700–711.

Petropoulos, J. (2000). *The Faustian bargain: The art world in Nazi Germany.* New York: Oxford University Press.

Petullo, A. (2001). *Self-taught and outsider art: The Anthony Petullo collection.* Chicago: University of Illinois Press.

Phillips, R. (2015). Art enhances brain function and well-being. *The healing power of art and artists.* https://www.healing-power-of-art.org/art-and-the-brain

Pike, A. A. (2013). The effect of art therapy on cognitive performance among ethnically diverse older adults. *Art Therapy: Journal of the American Art Therapy Association, 30*(4), 159–168. doi:10.1080/07421656.2014.847049

Pontara, G. (1978). The concept of violence. *Journal of Peace Research, 15*(1), 19–32.

Porter, S., & Woodworth, M. (2006). Psychopathy and aggression. In C. J. Patrick (Ed.), *Handbook of psychopathy* (pp. 481–494). New York: Guilford.

Prinzhorn, H. (1972/1995). *Bildnerei der geisteskranken (Artistry of the mentally ill).* New York: Springer-Verlag.

Pyle, G. J. (1913). Benvenuto Cellini: The man and his art. *Sewanee Review, 21*(2), 235–242.

Rainbird, S. (2003). A gathering storm: Max Beckmann and cultural politics 1925--1938. In S. Rainbird (Ed.), *Max Beckmann* (pp. 157–163). New York: Museum of Modern Art.

Raine, A. (2013). *The anatomy of violence.: The biological roots of crime.* New York: Pantheon Books.

Ramsland, K. (2006). *Inside the minds of serial killers: Why they kill.* Westport, CT: Praeger.

Rangell, L. (1978). The creative thrust: A psychoanalytic theory. *American Imago,35*(1/2), 27–44.

Raynal, M. (1953). *Picasso. Taste of our time (Vol. 4).* Cleveland, OH: Skira.

Redstall, V. (2011). *Serial killers: Up close and very personal.* London: John Blake.

Ressler, R. K., Burgess, A. W., & Douglas, 1. E. (1988). *Sexual homicide: Patterns and motives.* New York: Lexington Macmillan.

Reynolds, R. (1999). Cognitive behavioral counseling of unresolved grief through the therapeutic adjunct of tapestry-making. *Arts in Psychotherapy, 26*, 165–171.

Rhyne, J. (1973). *The gestalt art experience.* Monterey, CA: Brooks & Cole.

Rich, N. (2010). Celebrity memoirs: The one that made all the rules. *The Daily Beast.* https://www.thedailybeast.com/celebrity-memoirs-the-one-that-made-all-the-rules

Riley, S. (1992). Art captures the impact of the Los Angeles crisis. *Art Therapy: Journal of the American Art Therapy Association, 9*(3), 139–144.

Riva & Vigano. (2001). The shadow of the monster (essay). In *Killer art. (Exhibition catalogue)* (pp. 7–8). Bologna, Italy: Mondo Bizarro Press.

Riviere, J. (1964). Hate, greed and aggression. In M. Klein & J. Riviere (Eds.), *Love, hate and reparation* (pp. 3–56). New York: W. W. Norton.

Robbins, A. (2000). *The artist as therapist* (2nd ed.). London: Jessica Kingsley.

Roberts, R. (2017, November 20). Charles Manson's life as a failed musician, Beach Boys hanger-on, and mediocre songwriter. *Los Angeles Times.* https://www.latimes.com/entertainment/music/la-et-ms-charles-manson-music-20171116-story.html

Rockwell, P. (1999). Some comments from the boy in a dining car. In M. H. Hennessey & A. Knutson (Eds.), *Norman Rockwell: Pictures for the American people* (pp. 67–80). New York: Harry N. Abrams.

Rogers, C. (1954). Toward a theory of creativity. *ETC: A Review of General Semantics, 11*(4), 249–260.

Romi, S., & Itzkowitz, R. (1990). The relationship between locus of control and type of aggression in middle-class and culturally deprived children. *Personality and Individual Differences, 11*(4), 327–333.

Ronson, J. (2011). *Psychopath test: A journey through the madness industry.* New York: Riverhead Books.

Rosal, M. L. (1986). The use of art therapy to modify the locus of control and adaptive behavior of behavior disordered children. Unpublished doctoral dissertation, University of Queensland, Brisbane, Australia.

Rosal, M. L. (1993). Comparative group art therapy research to evaluate changes in locus of control. *Arts in Psychotherapy, 20*, 231–241.

Rosal, M. L. (2016a). Cognitive-behavioral art therapy revisited. In D. Gussak & M. Rosal (Eds.), *The Wiley handbook of art therapy* (pp. 68–76). West Sussex, UK: Wiley.

Rosal, M. L. (2016b). Cognitive-behavioral art therapy. In J. Rubin (Ed.), *Approaches to art therapy* (3rd ed., pp. 333–352). New York: Routledge.

Rosal, M. L. (2019). *Cognitive behavioral art therapy: From behaviorism to the third wave.* New York: Routledge.

Rosenberg, P. (2003). Women artists in the camps/Depictions of women. In D. Mickenberg, C. Granof, & P. Hayes (Eds.), *The last expression: Art and Auschwitz.* (pp. 60–67). Evanston, IL: Northwestern University Press.

Roth, E. (1978). Art therapy with emotionally disturbed-mentally retarded children: A technique of reality shaping. In B. K. Mandel, R. H. Shoemaker, & R. E. Hays (Eds.), *The dynamics of creativity* (pp. 168–172). Baltimore: American Art Therapy Association.

Rothenberg, A. (2017, August 22). Jackson Pollock's creation of Abstract Expressionism: Pollock used the creative Janusian process and overcame bipolar. Blog post. https://www.psychologytoday.com/us/blog/creative-explorations/201708/jackson-pollocks-creation-abstract-expressionism.

Rozum, A. (2001). Integrating the language of art into a creative cognitive-behavioral program with behavior-disordered children. In S. Riley (Ed.), *Group process made visible* (pp. 115–138). Philadelphia, PA: Brunner/Routledge.

Rumore, K. (2018, December 17). Timeline: Suburban serial killer John Wayne Gacy and the efforts to recover, name his 33 victims. *Chicago Tribune.* https://www.chicagotribune.com/history/ct-john-wayne-gacy-timeline-htmlstory.html

Sagarin, E. (1975). *Deviants and deviance: An introduction to the study of disvalued people and behavior.* New York: Praeger.

Salamon, J. (2004, Sept.) Keeping creativity alive, even in Hell. *New York Times.* Section E. p. 23. https://www.nytimes.com/2004/09/10/arts/design/keeping-creativity-alive-even-in-hell.html

Sassen, R. (2000). Mirroring a world gone mad: Beckmann and Kentridge. *De Arte, 61*, 35, 24–46. doi:10.1080/00043389.2000.11761303

Savage, J., & Wozniak, K. H. (2016). *Thugs and thieves: The differential etiology of violence.* New York: Oxford University Press.

Schjeldahl, P. (2002, April 12). Hitler as artist: How Vienna inspired the Führer's dreams. *The New Yorker.* https://www.newyorker.com/magazine/2002/08/19/hitler-as-artist

Schulz-Hoffmann, C. (1984). Bars, fetters, and masks: The problem of constraint in the work of Max Beckmann. In C. Schulz-Hoffmann & J. C. Weiss (Eds.), *Max Beckmann: Retrospective* (pp. 15–52). New York: W. W. Norton.

Shannon, E. C. (1999). The Depression in Montgomery, Alabama. In J. Helfenstein & R. Kurzmeyer (Eds.), *Bill Traylor 1854–1949: Deep Blues* (p. 179). New Haven, CT: Yale University Press.

Shoham, S. G. (1999). Caravaggio: The violent enlightenment. *Journal of Criminal Justice and Popular Culture, 6*(3) 67–82.

Sholt, M., & Gavron, T. (2006). Therapeutic qualities of clay-work in art therapy and psychotherapy: A review. *Art Therapy, 23*(2), 66–72. doi:10.1080/07421656.2006.10129647

Sobel, M. (2009). *Painting a hidden life: The art of Bill Traylor.* Baton Rouge: Louisiana State University Press.

Sobel, M. (1996). *Images of things unknown: The work of Bill Traylor.* [Unpublished essay] Retrieved from: https://ir.vanderbilt.edu/bitstream/handle/1803/7247/Q6.C18.Sobel.pdf?sequence=1&isAllowed=y

Soderstrom, H., Hultin, L., Tullberg, M., Wikkelso, C., Ekholm, S., & Forsman, A. (2002). Reduced frontotemporal perfusion in psychopathic personality. *Psychiatry Research Neuroimaging, 114*, 81–94.

Solomon, J. C. (1944). Review of The secret life of Salvador Dali: An autobiography (Review of the book The secret life of Salvador Dali: An autobiography). *American Journal of Orthopsychiatry, 14*(2), 375. https://doi.org/10.1037/h0097458

Sontag, S. (2003). *Regarding the pain of others.* New York: Picador.

Southgate, M. T. (2002). Christ and the woman taken in adultery. *JAMA, 287*(6), 689. doi:10.1001/jama.287.6.689

Spear, R. E. (1985). The critical fortune of a realist painter. In Mina, L. Salermo, & R. E. Spear (Eds.), *The age of Caravaggio* (pp. 22–27). New York-Milan: Met Publications.

Spizer, J., & Rogers, C. Jr. (2001). *The Cross-Country Killer: The Glen Rogers story.* Dallas, TX: Top Publications.

Spotts, F. (2002). *Hitler and the power of aesthetics* (pp. 151–168). New York: Overlook Press.

Stallings, J. (2010). Collage as a therapeutic modality for reminiscence in patients with dementia. *Art Therapy: Journal of the American Art Therapy Association, 27*(3), 136–140.

Stanska, Z. (April 7, 2018). Salvador Dali, the burning giraffe. *Daily Art Magazine.* https://www.dailyartmagazine.com/salvador-dali-the-burning-giraffe

Stevens, A. (1995). Jungian approach to human aggression with special emphasis on war. *Aggressive Behavior, 21*(1), 3–11.

Stewart, D. (March 2005). Modigliani: Misunderstood. A new exhibition positions the bohemian artist's work above even his operatic life story. *Smithsonian Magazine.* https://www.smithsonianmag.com/arts-culture/modigliani-misunderstood-84411676

Stewart, E. G. (2004). Art therapy and neuroscience blend: Working with patients who have dementia. *Art Therapy: Journal of the American Art Therapy Association, 21*(3), 148–155. doi:10.1080/07421656.2004.10129499

Stokes Sims, L. (1999). Bill Traylor: Inside the outsider. In J. Helfenstein & R. Kurzmeyer (Eds.), *Bill Traylor 1854–1949: Deep Blues* (pp. 92–95). New Haven, CT: Yale University Press.

Stone, B. A. (1998). Self-body image and PTSD in Australian Spanish speaking trauma and torture survivors: Empowerment through imagery-art-dialogue. In A. R. Hiscox & A. C. Calisch (Eds.), *Tapestry of cultural issues in art therapy* (pp. 176–198). London: Jessica Kingsley.

Storms, P. L., & Spector, P. E. (1987). Relationships of organizational frustration with reported behavioural reactions: The moderating effect of locus of control. *Journal of Occupational and Organizational Psychology, 60*(3) 227–234. doi:10.1111/j.2044-8325.1987.tb00255.x

Storr, R. (2003). The Beckmann effect. In S. Rainbird (Ed.), *Max Beckmann* (pp. 11–15). New York: Museum of Modern Art.

Stuart, H. (2003). Violence and mental illness: An overview. *World Psychiatry, 2*(2), 121–124.

Sujo, G. (2003). The drawings of Bachrach-Baree: Chronology of a death march. In D. Mickenberg, C. Granof, & P. Hayes (Eds.), *The last expression: Art and Auschwitz*. (pp. 50–59). Evanston, IL: Northwestern University Press.

Swan-Foster, N. (2016). Jungian art therapy. In J. Rubin (Ed.), *Approaches to art therapy* (3rd ed., pp. 165–188). New York: Routledge.

Swan-Foster, N. (2017). *Jungian art therapy. Images, dreams and analytical psychology*. New York: Routledge.

Swanson, G. E. (1975). Reviewed work(s), The anatomy of human destructiveness, by Erich Fromm. *American Journal of Sociology, 80*(5), 1243–1245.

Swartz, M., Swanson, J. W., Hiday, V. A., Borum, R., Wagner, H. R., & Burns, B. J. (1998). Violence and severe mental illness: The effects of substance abuse and nonadherence to medication. *American Journal of Psychiatry, 155*(2), 226–231.

Szajnberg, N. M. (2012). Caravaggio four centuries later: Psychoanalytic portraits of ambivalence and ambiguity, *Journal of the American Psychoanalytic Association,61*(2), 311–331.

Szalay, J. (2016). The Renaissance: The "rebirth" of science & culture. *Live Science*. https://www.livescience.com/55230-renaissance.html

Talwar, S. (2016). Creating alternative public spaces: Community-based art practice, critical consciousness, and social justice. In D. E. Gussak & M. L. Rosal (Eds.), *The Wiley handbook of art therapy* (pp. 840–847). West Sussex, UK: Wiley.

Talwar, S. (Ed.). (2018). *Art therapy for social justice: Radical intersections*. New York: Routledge.

Tate.org.uk. (n.d.). Richard Dadd: The Fairy Feller's Master-Stroke—1855–64. https://www.tate.org.uk/art/artworks/dadd-the-fairy-fellers-master-stroke-t00598

Taylor, R. P. (2002). Order in Pollock's chaos. *Scientific American, 287*(6), 116–121.

Tripp, T. (2016). A body-based bilateral art protocol in preprocessing trauma. In J. King (Ed.), *Art therapy, trauma and neuroscience: Theoretical and practical perspectives* (pp. 173–94). New York: Routledge.

Troller, N. (trans. Cwernyak-Spatz, S. E.) (1991). *Theresienstadt: Hitler's gift to the Jews*. Chapel Hill: University of North Carolina Press.

Tromans, N. (2011). *Richard Dadd: The artist and the asylum*. London: Tate.

Tuomisto, L. (2014). Inmates learn to understand and manage anger through art. In D. Gussak (blog author), *Art on trial: Confessions of a serial art therapist*. Blog with Psychology Today. https://www.psychologytoday.com/blog/art-trial/201408/inmates-learn-understand-and-manage-anger-through-art)

Turl, A. (2019). Outsider art is a lie. *Red Wedge*. http://www.redwedgemagazine.com/online-issue/outsider-lie

Ulman, E. (1992). A new use of art in psychiatric diagnosis. *American Journal of Art Therapy, 30*, 78–88.

Umberger, L. (2018). *Between worlds: The art of Bill Traylor*. Washington DC: Smithsonian African Art Museum.

Ungureanu, D. (2017). *From Paris to Tlön: Surrealism as world literature*. London: Bloomsbury Academic.

Van Hensbergen, G. (2004). *Guernica: The biography of a twentieth-century icon*. New York: Bloomsbury.

Vega, J. (1994). The dating and interpretation of Goya's "Disasters of War." *Print Quarterly, 11*(1), 3–17.

Vidal, R. (2017). The power of negative creation—Why art by serial killers sell. In M. J. Blanca & R. Vidal (Eds.), *The power of death: Contemporary reflections on death in western society* (pp. 115–124). New York: Berghan Books.

Viladegut, A. G. (n.d.). Francisco de Goya- Zaragoza, 1746–1828. *Colleccio Gelonch Viladegut*. http://www.gelonchviladegut.com/en/autor/francisco-de-goya/

Vojtech, B., Kotouc, K. J., Kruzkova, M. R., Kuna, M., Munk, J., Park, A., Sormova, E., & Vaclavek, L. (2002). *Art against death: Permanent exhibitions of the Terezín Memorial in the former Magdeburg barracks*. Terezín, Czech Republic: Helena Osvaldova for the Terezín Museum.

Volavkova, H. (Ed.). (1993). *I never saw another butterfly: Children's drawings and poems from Terezín Concentration Camp, 1942–1944*. New York: Schocken Books.

Walby, S. (2012). Violence and society: Introduction to an emerging field of sociology. *Current Sociology, 6*(2), 95–111.

Wallace, M. T., Barry, C. T., Zeigler-Hill, V., & Green, B. A. (2012). Locus of control as a contributing factor in the relation between self-perception and adolescent aggression. *Aggressive Behavior, 38*(3), 213–221. doi:10.1002/ab.21419

Waller, D. (2006). Art therapy for children: How it leads to change. *Clinical Child Psychology and Psychiatry, 11*(2), 271–282. doi:10.1177/1359104506061419

Waller, D., & Dalley, T. (1992). Art therapy: A theoretical perspective. In D. Waller & A. Gilroy (Eds.), *Art therapy: A handbook* (pp. 3–24). Buckingham, UK: Open University Press.

Walton, D. (1978). *A Rockwell portrait*. Kansas City: Sheed, Andrews, and McMeel.

Warncke, C. P., & Walther, I. F. (2002). *Picasso*. Koln: Taschen.

Waska, R. T. (2000). Hate, projective identification, and the psychotherapist's struggle. *Journal of Psychotherapy Practice and Research, 9*(1), 33–38.

Wegman, C. (1985). *Psychoanalysis and cognitive psychology*. Orlando, FL: Academic Press.

Weissová, H. (1998). *Zeichne, was du siehst: Zeichnungen eines kindes aus Theresienstadt/Terezín: Maluj, co vidíš, kresby jednoho dítěte z Terezína (draw what you . . .)* (German, Czech and English edition). Prague: Wallstein Verlag.

Welles, O., Howard, T., Cotten, J., Reed, C., Krasker, R., Valli, A., & Greene, G. (1949). The third man. London: London Film Productions.

Werckmeister, O. K. (1997). Hitler the artist. *Critical Inquiry, 23*(2), 270–297.

White, A. E., Kaufman, J. C., & Riggs, M. (2014). How "outsider" do we like our art?: Influence of artist background on perceptions of warmth, creativity, and likeability. *Psychology of Aesthetics, Creativity, and the Arts, 8*(2), 144–151. https://doi.org/10.1037/a0036115

Wiechert, H. (2018, January 9). 32-year-old artist remembers Charles Manson as his mentor and friend. *Bellville News-Democrat*. https://www.bnd.com/living/magazine/article193609219.html

Wilkin, K. (2015). Bill Traylor: American artist. *The Hopkins Review, 8*(1), 32–44. doi.org/10.1353/thr.2015.0004

Williams, E. (2011). *Giraffe*. London: Reaktion Books.

Wilson, L. (2003). *Alberto Giacometti: Myth, magic and the man*. New Haven, CT: Yale University Press.

Wilson, L. (2016a). *Louise Nevelson: Art is life*. New York: Thames & Hudson.

Wilson, L. (2016b). Psychoanalytic study of artists and their art: Its relevance for art therapists. In D. Gussak & M. Rosal (Eds.), *The Wiley handbook of art therapy* (pp. 17–25). West Sussex, UK: Wiley.

Winnicott, D. W. (1951). *Collected Papers: Through paediatrics to psycho-analysis*. London: Tavistock.

Winnicott, D. W. (1965). Ego distortion in terms of true and false self. In *The maturational process and the facilitating environment: Studies in the theory of emotional development* (pp. 140–152). New York: International Universities Press.

Winnicott, D. W. (1971). *Playing and reality*. London: Tavistock.

Wise, S. (2005). A time for healing: Art therapy for children, post September 11, New York. In D. Kalmanowitz & B. Lloyd (Eds.), *Art therapy and political violence: With art, without illusion* (pp. 142–153). New York: Routledge.

Wittkower, R., & Wittkower, M. (1963/2007). *Born under Saturn: The character and conduct of artists: A documented history from antiquity to the French Revolution*. New York: New York Review Books.

Wix, L. (2010). *Through a narrow window: Friedl Dicker-Brandeis and her Terezín students*. Albuquerque: University of New Mexico Press.

Wolfgang, M. E. (1961). Pioneers in criminology: Cesare Lombroso (1825–1909). *Journal of Criminal Law & Criminology, 52*(4), 361–391.

Yau, J. (1989). Bill Traylor's life and art. *Columbia: A Journal of Literature and Art, 14*, 136–145.

Zaidel, D. W. (2010). Art and brain: Insights from neuropsychology, biology, and evolution. *Journal of Anatomy, 216*(2), 177–183. doi:10.1111/j.1469-7580.2009.01099.x

Zaidel, D. W. (2014). Creativity, brain, and art: Biological and neurological consideration. *Frontiers in Human Neuroscience, 8*(398), 1–9. doi:10.3389/fnhum.2014.00389

Zimbardo, P. G., Haney, C., Banks, W. C., & Jaffe, D. (1973, April 8). The mind is a formidable jailer: A Pirandellian prison. *New York Times Magazine*, Section 6, 38.

Index